9.95

ROMERO

The word remains. This is the great comfort of one who preaches. My voice will disappear, but my word, which is Christ, will remain in the hearts of those who have willed to receive it.

Oscar Romero
Homily of December 17, 1978

ROMERO

A LIFE

James R. Brockman, S.J.

ORBIS BOOKS

Maryknoll, New York 10545

The Catholic Foreign Mission Society of America (Maryknoll) recruits and trains people for overseas missionary service. Through Orbis Books, Maryknoll aims to foster the international dialogue that is essential to mission. The books published, however, reflect the opinions of their authors and are not meant to represent the official position of the society.

Library of Congress Cataloging-in-Publication Data

Brockman, James R.
　　Romero: a life/James R. Brockman.
　　　p.　cm.
　　Rev. ed. of: The word remains. c1982.
　　Bibliography: p.
　　Includes index.
　　ISBN 0-88344-652-9
　　1. Romero, Oscar A. (Oscar Arnulfo), 1917–1980.　2. Catholic
Church—El Salvador—Bishops—Biography.　I. Brockman, James R.
Word remains.　II. Title.
BX4705.R669B75　1989
282'.092—dc19
[B]　　　　　　　　　　　　　　　　　　　　　89-35577
　　　　　　　　　　　　　　　　　　　　　　　CIP

To
Maura Clarke,
Jean Donovan,
Ita Ford,
Dorothy Kazel,
and all who have given their lives
for the gospel in El Salvador

Contents

Preface

Three decades ago, Pope John XXIII startled the world by announcing that he was calling a general council of the world's bishops, the first such council since the one that had met at the Vatican in Rome more than a century ago. The Second Vatican Council, he said, would have the task of bringing the church up to date. Pope John's reason was simple. The modern world was going its own way, and the Catholic Church was having little influence upon it. The gospel of Jesus Christ should be like yeast in the dough of society, but the twentieth-century church was not getting the yeast into the dough. It would have to reform its own structures and its own attitudes. It would have to try to understand better the world it offered salvation to. And it would have to return to its own roots in the gospel of Jesus Christ.

The world's Catholic bishops met in the four lengthy sessions of Vatican II from 1962 to 1965. They fashioned a book of documents on the church and the world, and then the bishops went home to try to put them into effect. In Latin America, the bishops soon began preparing for an assembly of bishops to meet in 1968 at Medellín, in Colombia, where they would look at their own part of the world and formulate the church's response to its situation in the light of Vatican II.

When the bishops of Latin America looked at their part of the world, they saw an area of 300 million people where most persons were Catholic but were poor and oppressed, where undernourishment and early death were the fate of millions, especially of children, and where modern economic and social development was worsening, rather than bettering, the lives of most inhabitants. The church, they said, could no longer acquiesce in such a situation and it had to raise its voice to proclaim the people's liberation. Injustice was not God's will.

Oscar Romero lived his life amid the poverty and injustice of Latin America. He became a priest before Vatican II and a bishop after Medellín. As archbishop of San Salvador, he became the leader of the church in his native land. But as archbishop he also became a man of the poor, their advocate when they had no other voice to demand justice for them. He suffered and gave his life on their behalf.

Ten years after his death, Romero has attained world renown as a man who preferred to die rather than shirk what his conscience and his heart told him he must do. Every day since his death people have flocked to visit his tomb and draw strength from him. Many have come from afar; one of them was Pope John Paul II. But most have been the ordinary poor people of El Salvador, who hold him in their hearts.

This book tries to tell his story.

Author's Note

This book is a revised edition of an earlier book, *The Word Remains: A Life of Oscar Romero,* published in 1982. For the present book I have been able to take into account various sources that were not available to me earlier. I have also expanded some parts of the earlier work and condensed others where it seemed called for, and I have tried to improve the translation of quotations from the Spanish, besides retouching the style of the book in general and correcting errors found in the earlier edition.

Conditions in El Salvador at the time the first book was published made it advisable to conceal the identity of various persons mentioned in the text and of some that provided information. This need has not entirely disappeared, and certain persons are still left unnamed, some by their own request.

I am grateful to many, too numerous to list, who supplied information, corrections, suggestions, encouragement, and hospitality while I was preparing both books. Readers of the present book who notice mistakes of fact or interpretation will earn my gratitude by pointing them out to me so that I can correct them in future work.

Abbreviations

ANEP   Asociación Nacional de la Empresa Privada—National Private Business Association

BPR   Bloque Popular Revolucionario—Popular Revolutionary Bloc (coalition of popular organizations)

CEDES   Conferencia Episcopal de El Salvador—Bishops' Conference of El Salvador

CELAM   Consejo Episcopal Latinoamericano—Latin American Bishops' Council

ECA   *Estudios Centroamericanos—Central American Studies*

FAPU   Frente de Acción Popular Unificado—United Popular Action Front (coalition of popular organizations)

FARO   Frente de Agricultores de la Región Oriental—Eastern Region Farmers' Front (a national organization by 1976)

FECCAS*   Federación Cristiana de Campesinos Salvadoreños—Christian Federation of Salvadoran Peasants

FPL   Fuerzas Populares de Liberación—Popular Liberation Forces

LP-28   Ligas Populares 28 de Febrero—February 28 Popular Leagues (coalition of popular organizations)

ORDEN   Organización Democrática Nacionalista—Democratic Nationalist Organization (government rural organization used to repress independent organizations)

UTC*   Unión de Trabajadores del Campo—Farm Workers' Union

---

*Federated since 1975, FECCAS and UTC often used the combined form: FECCAS-UTC.

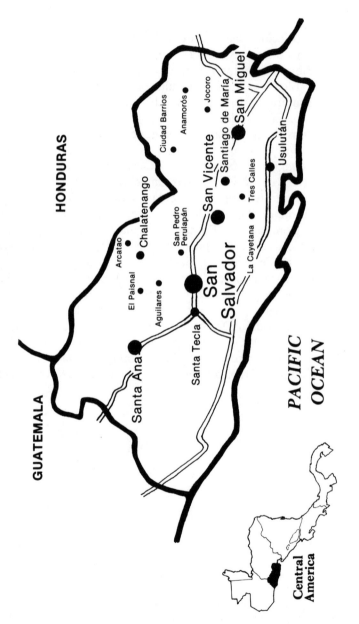

The New Pilot

February–May 1977

On February 22, 1977, two priests from San Salvador sat in jail in Guatemala City, still somewhat shaken by the experiences of the preceding four days. Armed men had captured each of them without warning and expelled them from El Salvador, turning them over to Guatemalan police, who now held them captive.

One was an American, Bernard Survil of the diocese of Greensburg, Pennsylvania, known as Padre Bernardo to his parishioners in the Lourdes barrio of San Salvador. He had been returning to his house about 7:30 P.M. on February 18 when four men seized him. Explaining apologetically that they were only following orders, they took him to the border and on into Guatemala.

On his way to Guatemala City, Survil met another priest, also a captive. He was Willibrord Denaux, a Belgian of the Brugge (Bruges) diocese, who was Padre Guillermo to the people of the barrio of San Antonio Abad in San Salvador, where he had worked for five years. Denaux's captors had been rougher than Survil's, tying him naked to the bare springs of a bed for twenty hours without food, drink, or the chance to use a toilet, talking about shooting him and throwing him into the Lempa River. They took him, bound and blindfolded, to Guatemala, and now he had one eye bandaged from the mistreatment.

Both priests had lost their money and personal papers, and Denaux had lost his watch and his car. The Guatemalans jailed both men as undocumented aliens, along with a former Jesuit priest, Juan José Ramírez, who had been expelled from El Salvador a week before after being beaten and tortured with electric shocks during a ten-day imprisonment.[1] Now the three were about to be expelled from Guatemala.

Survil and Denaux were writing letters to Archbishop Luis Chávez y González, who was retiring as archbishop of San Salvador, and to the clergy. As they recounted their experiences in their letters, they tried to understand what was happening. "It seems to me," wrote Survil, "that there is a

1

strong attempt to change abruptly the unity that Archbishop Chávez created out of the various gifts that are found in the archdiocese."

"It seems that for the church of El Salvador," wrote Denaux, "the moment of trials, of the desert, has come. But it leads one day to paradise, to the Lord's kingdom, which we should all form, the kingdom of love, peace, justice, and mutual understanding. I pray to the Lord to give you strength to achieve this union and cooperation with the new archbishop and with each other."[2]

On the same day that the two priests wrote their letters, the new archbishop of San Salvador, Oscar Arnulfo Romero, was installed in a simple ceremony in the church of San José de la Montaña, next door to the seminary. The times required a swift transition from one archbishop to another; the tension throughout El Salvador, and especially between church and government, discouraged a more solemn act in the cathedral with government officials present.

Romero was coming aboard in the midst of a storm. Not only had Survil, Denaux, and Ramírez been expelled from the country; some six weeks earlier the government had expelled two Jesuit seminarians who had applied for release from the order and were awaiting dispensation from their vows. They had been working with peasant organizations. On January 29 the government had also arrested and expelled a Colombian, Mario Bernal, parish priest of Apopa, a small town near San Salvador.[3] And on January 13 a bomb had destroyed the car and garage of Father Alfonso Navarro and badly damaged the parish house.[4]

The expulsions came after months of agitation and rising tension. The government of Colonel Arturo Armando Molina had passed a mild land-reform law in 1975. The landowning and business class, which had ruled El Salvador for generations, was able to dilute it so that reform would move at a creeping pace. In 1976, when the congress approved the first reform project, distributing to 12,000 peasant families 150,000 acres of land belonging to some 250 owners, the ruling class mounted a campaign against it. Since they owned the major newspapers and most of the radio and all of the television stations, that was easy to do. Even though the owners would receive fair market value for their land and the move would ease some of the rising tension among the peasantry, who existed on inadequate plots or with only day labor during the harvest season, the landed class cried that it was the beginning of communism. In October of that year President Molina yielded to their demands and scuttled the program.[5]

For peasants who had worked for reform it was a disappointing setback. The law in El Salvador did not recognize peasant unions independent of government control, but peasants had formed them anyway. Two of them had Christian origins: the Christian Federation of Salvadoran Peasants (FECCAS) and the Farm Workers' Union (UTC). FECCAS had begun with Christian Democratic sponsorship in the 1960's, but its leadership had drifted to the left. Formed in 1974, UTC had federated with FECCAS in

1975.[6] To most of their peasant members, however, FECCAS and UTC represented not an ideology but simply a hope for a decent piece of land to live on and to farm. To the landowning oligarchy, they were Lenin and Satan in one.

The archdiocese of San Salvador under Archbishop Luis Chávez, who had led it since 1938, backed the peasants' right to organize and exert political pressure. Given the political nature of the organizations, the hierarchy was uneasy about the clergy's participating in them, and some Jesuits were not altogether sorry to see the two seminarians, who had become passionately involved in the peasant cause, leave the order.

That the church would encourage in peasants such ideas as social justice and the right to organize was enough to bring upon its head, and especially on the heads of rural pastors, the wrath of the ruling class. Early in December 1976 Eduardo Orellana, a large landowner in the Aguilares area north of San Salvador, was shot and killed during an argument with a crowd of FECCAS members. According to reports, he was accidentally killed by his brother;[7] and the police who were present did nothing, though ordinarily the police were more than willing to arrest or attack peasants on the complaints of landowners. The organizations of businessmen and landowners, however, took as fact that "a known leader"[8] of FECCAS and UTC had killed Don Eduardo, "a man with a heart of gold."[9] They insisted in newspaper advertisements that the "hordes" of FECCAS and UTC had attacked Orellana's hacienda under the instigation of "third world priests, native and foreign, who . . . continue to push farm workers into violating not only the laws but the fundamental principles of Christianity."[10] (The epithet "third world priests," a favorite with the oligarchy, seems to derive from a priests' group of Argentina, the Priests for the Third World.) These priests, said the newspaper ads, preached hatred, subversion, and class struggle.[11]

The media campaign attacked the weak points of the church and the two organizations by recalling that some of the priests were foreigners (as was half the Salvadoran clergy) and that FECCAS and UTC had no legal standing. While most of the world would blush at this lack of legal protection for workers, to the Salvadoran oligarchy the organizations' lack of legal standing simply bolstered the conviction that they were involved in subversive activities.[12] Moreover, the oligarchs were not embarrassed to remind the public of article 157 of the Salvadoran constitution:

> Clerics and laity shall be forbidden to engage in political advertising in any form by invoking religious motives or making use of the people's religious beliefs. In the churches, on the occasion of acts of worship or religious instruction, criticism shall not be made of the laws of the state, of its government, or of individual public officials.[13]

Amid such tension Luis Chávez y González, about to retire at the age of seventy-five after thirty-eight years as archbishop of San Salvador, was leaving behind a clergy committed to siding with the poor and the oppressed, according to the directions given to the church by Vatican Council II and the 1968 Latin American bishops' assembly at Medellín. That legacy would be important for his successor.

The clergy of the archdiocese favored Arturo Rivera Damas, who had been auxiliary since 1960, to succeed Chávez. Rivera had greatly influenced the direction that pastoral practice had taken in the archdiocese. He was personally popular, soft-spoken but strong and steady. For the wealthy class of El Salvador, however, and the government they controlled, Rivera was undesirable. They did not want anyone who would continue the ways of Archbishop Chávez and might even go further. To some he was another of those communist priests who aroused the peasants and lower classes with talk of justice and liberation. They would be content with one of the known conservatives—that is, practically anyone but Rivera.

Rome's choice was Oscar Arnulfo Romero, former auxiliary bishop of San Salvador and for the past two years bishop of tiny Santiago de María. He occasionally wrote or spoke piously about the church's social teaching, but he had shown his conservatism as auxiliary of San Salvador, and especially as editor of *Orientación,* the diocesan newspaper. The forty-odd businessmen, government and military leaders, and society ladies whom the apostolic nuncio, the Vatican ambassador, consulted on the choice all were favorable to the choice of Romero.[14]

On February 10, 1977, *La Prensa Gráfica* of San Salvador published a brief interview with the archbishop-to-be. "We must keep to the center, watchfully, in the traditional way, but seeking justice," he said. The mission of the priest "is eminently religious and transcendent," but on the other hand, "the government should not consider a priest who takes a stand for social justice as a politician or a subversive element when he is fulfilling his mission in the politics of the common good." The latter words might have given pause to some readers, but the smiling face of the bishop, sitting in a garden and surrounded by well-wishers in Santiago de María, was reassuring.

Most Salvadorans, however, had other things on their minds during February 1977. The presidential campaign was drawing to a close. Election day was set for February 20. General Carlos Humberto Romero (no relation to Archbishop Romero), candidate of the government party, former minister of defense and public security, represented the views of those who held private property to be sacred and wanted dissenters squelched. Colonel Ernesto Claramount, a retired cavalry officer, was the candidate of the opposition coalition. After years of fraudulent elections, Salvadorans wondered if this time things just might be different. They were not to be.

Reports of massive fraud began before the votes were counted. Persons working for the government added names and duplicated names on voter lists; they stuffed ballot boxes; military and civilian personnel intimidated voters at the polling places; opposition observers were threatened, arrested, and assaulted at the polls and were not allowed to watch the count. The government party coordinated its actions by radio, and the opposition recorded six hours of the transmissions, which it later submitted to two United States congressional subcommittees. As reports of fraud piled up in the days after the election, the protests mounted, although the government had not yet announced the results.[15]

On February 21, the day after the election and the day before Oscar Romero was to become archbishop of San Salvador, he sent a letter to the priests of the archdiocese. He was aware that most of the clergy were unhappy with his naming, and the letter was an offer of friendship: "I wish to tell you of the spirit of cooperation that I offer you and that I need from you so that together we can share the honor that Christ gives us of helping him build his church, each one in his own vocation."

As priests working together, Romero continued, they needed to form a friendship "based on our faith in the sacramental reality that identifies us with the one priesthood of Christ and that bears the human warmth of understanding, of mutual respect and forgiveness, of honesty, loyalty and all the human virtues that nourish our supernatural communion on the natural and psychological levels." At the time he became a bishop he had decided always "to offer the best of my modest service to priests and to be always available for dialog as a simple friend." That was the only way to dispel misunderstandings and prejudices, he added, "and to bring together in pastoral unity the richness of legitimate pluralism." Romero ended with two invitations: to join him in taking possession of the cathedral on Saturday, March 5, and to join him at dinner on Monday, March 7. He also offered them hospitality in the seminary whenever they wished to stay there.

The day after he wrote this letter, Romero became archbishop of San Salvador. That afternoon, the bishops in a body visited the outgoing president, Arturo Molina, who did not realize that Romero had just become archbishop. Molina told the bishops, as Bishop Rivera recalled later, that the church had gone astray and that he wanted to speak to them about getting it back on the right path. "I tried to explain to him," said Rivera, "that the church was just being faithful to Vatican II and Medellín, and that what was happening was the result of an increased awareness on the part of the church in this community and in no way was it a departure from the right path."[16]

After the bishops' meeting with the president, Archbishop Romero left for Santiago de María to wind up affairs in his former diocese, which was now without a bishop. In San Salvador, as the extent of the electoral fraud became increasingly evident, the opposition organized various rallies downtown in Plaza Libertad, and on February 24 Claramount announced that he would remain in the square until an honest result was announced. Several thousand people remained with him, and protest strikes in factories, stores, and bus companies began to bring the capital to a standstill. On

February 26 the government declared General Romero the winner by a two to one margin.

The next day was Sunday, and the crowd in the plaza swelled to some 40,000-60,000 people. Father Alfonso Navarro said an evening mass in the square, and most of the crowd then dispersed. After midnight, troops with armored cars cordoned off the square and gave the remaining 6,000 people ten minutes to disperse. Many left, but the troops opened fire on the 1,500 or 2,000 who remained. The crowd fled to El Rosario church on one side of the plaza. There they remained besieged until about 4:00 A.M., when Bishop Rivera, Archbishop Chávez, and the Red Cross arranged a truce.[17]

The weary Rivera was returning to the seminary when he unexpectedly met Archbishop Romero, who explained, "They called me in Santiago at midnight, and here I am."

"I told him," Rivera later recalled, "where we had come from and that he had better not leave the city, because these times required the pastor's presence and decisions would have to be made that only he could make. He told me that from then on he would always be on hand."[18]

Protests continued all that day of February 28, and troops fired on rioters. The government admitted eight deaths; others calculated forty to sixty, still others one hundred to three hundred.[19] It was a day that would be remembered in Salvadoran history.

For that same day priests and religious had scheduled a pastoral meeting to study the phenomenon of Protestantism in El Salvador. Those who showed up at the Domus Mariae retreat house quickly turned their attention to more urgent topics. The government had now arrested and deported three priests, a former priest, and the two former Jesuit scholastics. On February 21 the Guardia Nacional had arrested and tortured the parish priest of Tecoluca in the San Vicente diocese, releasing him with a fractured skull. Government officials were saying that several priests outside the country should not return. The newspaper attacks on the work of the church were continuing; six bombs during the preceding year had damaged the Jesuit university; and the parish house of Opico had been searched in January. And even as the clergy met in Domus Mariae, crowds were rioting over the rigged election and the killings in Plaza Libertad.

Rivera and Chávez told of their experience at El Rosario church early that morning. The bishops and priests agreed that the act of publicly taking possession of the cathedral scheduled for March 5 would have to be postponed. So would the dinner with the clergy scheduled for March 7. The archdiocese would begin publishing an information bulletin to be broadcast on the archdiocesan radio, and an emergency committee of three priests would meet each morning. Anyone with proof of new incidents was invited to notify the archbishop, and the archdiocese thus began to be an important source of information, countering to some extent the misinformation and propaganda supplied by the regular press, radio, and television.[20]

On March 5 the Salvadoran bishops' conference met in special session, its first meeting since its regular semiannual three-day meeting in January. Archbishop Chávez, the president, had retired, and those present agreed that the vice-president, Bishop Pedro Arnoldo Aparicio, of the diocese of San Vicente, should succeed him. Archbishop Romero was elected vice-president. The others present were Bishop Rivera, Bishop Benjamín Barrera, of the diocese of Santa Ana, and Barrera's auxiliary, Bishop Marco René Revelo. The other member, Bishop Eduardo Alvarez, of the diocese of San Miguel, was absent.

The bishops discussed the situation. The day before, troops and civilians had surrounded the church and parish house of San Martín, twenty miles east of San Salvador, in the early morning. They tried to arrest the pastor, Rutilio Sánchez, but someone rang the church bells and so many parishioners gathered that the government forces left him and contented themselves with sacking a house where four seminarians were living.[21] The government had told Father Kevin John Murphy, O.S.B., an American, to leave the country and had refused readmission to seven other priests who had been out of the country. The expulsions, the many cases of persons arrested and not seen again ("disappeared" in the parlance that has become common in Latin America), the large numbers of persons killed, of those tortured, of political figures who had left the country (including the defeated presidential candidate, Colonel Claramount, and the vice-presidential candidate, José Antonio Morales Ehrlich) demanded notice from the bishops. Romero said that the church must make a statement about the outrages that were being committed. Wasn't it hypocritical to continue relations with the government? Bishop Barrera remarked that a break with the government could bring worse evils. Rivera said that it was not a matter of breaking relations but of seeking and speaking the truth, since the church was the only voice able to speak out and the people expected it to. He proposed a public statement and read aloud one that he had brought with him. The conference named Romero and Monsignor Freddy Delgado, the secretary, to tone down a few expressions, and approved the statement as amended.

In it, the bishops expressed their concern for the violence against the peasants, for the deaths and disappearances, for the publicity campaign, threats, and intimidation against the church, and for the expulsion of priests in particular. But the human rights abuses, they said, revealed a greater and deeper evil, the lack of social justice, the state of suffering in which the large majority of the nation's people must live. "This is the basic sin that we as shepherds must call attention to."

The church's mission, the bishops went on, is to proclaim the kingdom of God, the reign "of peace and justice, of truth and love, of grace and holiness," in the words of the liturgy. In El Salvador its task is "to struggle for and to further justice, to know the truth, to achieve a political, social, and economic order conformed to God's plan." This means unmasking the false humanism of profit, social position, power, and privilege and giving dignity and the means of decent existence to those who are forgotten and excluded. "Therefore, even at the risk of being misunderstood or persecuted, the church must lift its voice when injustice possesses society."

Although it excludes no one from its task of proclaiming the gospel and furthering the reign of God, the church must show clearly that it is with those for whom no one else shows concern, that it "cannot remain unmoved before those who have great tracts of land and those who have not even a minimum to farm for subsistence, between those who have access to culture, to recreation, to an opulent life, and those who must struggle day to day in order to survive, who live in habitual unemployment and with a hunger that debases them to the direst levels of undernourishment."

The message concluded with a call for an end to the violations of human rights.[22] The statement was to be read at mass on Sunday, March 13.[23]

Meanwhile, Romero encouraged all his priests to continue their normal "postconciliar pastoral work," or to resume it if events had led them to interrupt it,[24] and called a meeting of the clergy, inviting especially the foreigners, for March 10. Besides the priests, a number of women religious also attended, 154 persons in all. This was Romero's first meeting with his priests in a body, and he was aware that many, perhaps most, were not happy with his naming.[25] He was supposed to be the firm conservative who would rein in those priests of the archdiocese whom, in the eyes of the government and the upper classes, the aged Archbishop Chávez had not been able to control.

Romero quickly disarmed most of the latent hostility. He asked all for their cooperation and told the foreign priests especially that no one should feel like a foreigner, but rather as if he were in his own home. The meeting, in line with Romero's desire for dialog, became a consultation on what to do in the difficult circumstances,[26] and he received two pages of suggestions.[27]

At one point during the meeting, Rutilio Grande, pastor of Aguilares, the rural area north of the capital where Eduardo Orellana had been killed, asked if priests in hiding could "come down to the valley yet." Grande and his team of Jesuits were feeling acutely the tension in their region,[28] and the newspaper attacks had centered on them.

One week after the bishops' letter had been prepared, Bishop Rivera was in a parish meeting when Romero arrived unexpectedly. He had second thoughts about the letter to be read in the masses the following day. It was untimely, it was partial, he didn't know why it had been issued. Rivera replied softly that it was indeed timely and that naturally it seemed partial because in the circumstances it had to defend those whose rights had been outraged, those who were the weakest.

Romero replied, "I'll read it at the eight o'clock mass in the cathedral, but not in San José de la Montaña." The latter church is next to the seminary, and Romero was to say a mass there at noon on Sunday, March

13, as his introduction to the parish in which the seminary and his own offices were located. Many people from the wealthy Colonia Escalón would be present.

"All right, if you read it in the cathedral, it's broadcast by radio, and that's enough," said Rivera.[29]

That same day, Saturday, Rutilio Grande set out from Aguilares, where he had been pastor since 1972, to say an evening mass at El Paisnal, a village a few miles away. An old man and a boy of fifteen rode with him. He himself had lived his first twelve years in El Paisnal before going to the seminary. At that time the Jesuits were in charge of the seminary, and Rutilio decided to become a Jesuit and entered the novitiate at the age of seventeen. Later he himself was prefect of discipline at the seminary, where he became a friend of Oscar Romero, then living there with the Jesuits. When Romero became a bishop in 1970, Rutilio was master of ceremonies at the episcopal ordination. Known to bishops and priests throughout the country, he remained a national figure after leaving the seminary work.

In Aguilares, Rutilio was working with a team of younger Jesuits among the thirty thousand peasants, or campesinos, of the area. Thirty-five haciendas used most of the flat land in the area for sugar cane and left the rocky hillsides to campesinos, many of whom had no land at all and could work only during the cane harvest. The Jesuits began developing "delegates of the word" in the rural settlements, and the sight of peasants having meetings and choosing leaders disturbed the landowners, especially since FECCAS was also organizing in the area. Rutilio, in his sermons, denounced the injustice of a few dominating and exploiting the many for their own profit; and the experience of learning to apply the lessons of the Bible to their own lives was already opening the eyes and lifting the aspirations of the peasants. A life of Rutilio published after his death remarks dryly: "It was not necessary to tell the campesinos that they were oppressed or who their oppressors were. Both were evident."[30] The landowners, however, saw only that a threat to their power had arisen since the Jesuits came to the area, and since 1974 local landowners, police, and military commanders had accused the Jesuits of subversion and communism. Much of the media campaign of the preceding months centered on them.

Midway to El Paisnal, in the midst of flat fields of tall sugar cane, high-powered bullets struck Rutilio and the old man and boy who rode with him. All three died on the spot.[31] It was about 5:30 P.M.

The news soon reached San Salvador, twenty miles away. About 8:00 P.M., President Molina called the archbishop to offer condolences.[32] Romero asked him for a thorough investigation of the murders, and Molina assured him one would be made.[33]

Romero arrived at Aguilares about 10:00 P.M. The three bodies lay on tables in the church, covered with sheets. Jesuits and other priests had been gathering, and townspeople and campesinos filled the church. Romero conferred with the Jesuit provincial superior and agreed to celebrate the mass of the dead with the other priests and the people. Over a dozen priests concelebrated with the archbishop, and Romero and the provincial both preached. The emotional service lasted until near midnight. Before driving back to San Salvador, Romero conferred with the provincial and the other priests about a common funeral at the cathedral for the three dead and pressed upon the provincial all the money he was carrying.[34]

The next morning, Sunday, March 13, Romero offered the usual eight o'clock mass in the cathedral. He read the bishops' statement of March 5 and repeated it at noon in San José de la Montaña, "and he gave such a beautiful commentary that we sat listening to him [on the radio] during dinner and seeing how the wisdom of God was in him," said Bishop Rivera.[35]

The following morning, Monday, the papal nuncio, Archbishop Emanuele Gerada, presided at a funeral mass for the three murder victims in the cathedral. Over a hundred priests concelebrated, and the crowd overflowed into the streets and public square. It was, said a priest present that day,[36] an expression of mourning and protest not only for the three victims who lay before them but for all victims of the violence, including the many who had disappeared and could have no funeral of their own.

From the pulpit Romero addressed the crowd and those listening to the radio. The cathedral, he said, was a sign of the universal church that morning, the presence of the three dead giving it the perspective of a "church beyond history, beyond human life." If it were an ordinary funeral he would speak of his own friendship with Father Grande—"at peak moments of my life he was very close to me, and those gestures are never forgotten"—but this was, rather, the moment "to gather from this death a message for all of us who remain on pilgrimage."

The message that Romero drew was from Pope Paul VI's apostolic exhortation *Evangelii Nuntiandi*. To the struggle of third world peoples for liberation, the pope said, the church offers its own presence and its own message, a message to lift up and dignify human beings. It offers an inspiration that comes from faith, a faith, said Romero, "that speaks to us of an eternal life." Without faith, "all will be feeble, revolutionary, passing, violent." The liberation that Grande preached was a liberation based on faith, "and because it is often misunderstood, even to the point of homicide, Father Rutilio Grande died."

Like Grande, continued Romero, the church in its preaching is inspired by love and rejects hatred. "Who knows if the murderers that have now fallen into excommunication are listening to a radio in their hideout, listening in their conscience to this word. We want to tell you, murderous brothers, that we love you and that we ask of God repentance for your hearts, because the church is not able to hate, it has no enemies. Its only enemies are those who want to declare themselves so. But the church loves them and dies like Christ: 'Father, forgive them, they know not what they do.' "

In the name of the archdiocese Romero thanked Grande and his two companions, "co-workers in Christian liberation," as well as "all those who labor in this way in the church, enlightening with faith, enlivening with love, wise with the church's social teaching."[37]

Romero could write a polished, formal sermon, but he was also a confident speaker who could be even more eloquent when speaking from an outline or a few notes, as he did this day. That he chose to eulogize the work of Rutilio and his co-workers and to speak so specifically of the church's work of liberation carried no comfort for those who wanted a church withdrawn from the concerns of the world, a church that would not disturb the status quo. At the same time, he carefully rejected violence and materialism and tried to unify his listeners around the pope and the bishop of the diocese.

The same day, Romero wrote to President Molina: "Deeply concerned about the murder of Father Rutilio Grande and two campesinos of his parish of Aguilares with him, I write to tell you that a series of comments arise in connection with this event, many of them unfavorable to your government. Since I have not yet received the official report that you promised me Saturday night by phone, I judge it to be most urgent that you order an exhaustive investigation of the facts, since the government has in its hands adequate tools to investigate and administer justice in the land."

The unfavorable comments about the government arose partly from the examination of the bodies made after the Saturday night mass by a doctor with extensive experience in forensic medicine. He had no instruments for an autopsy, but the wounds appeared to him to have been made by a type of gun used by the police.[38]

The church, Romero wrote Molina, had published the excommunication of the authors of the crime "and is not willing to participate in any official act of the government as long as the latter does not put all its effort into making justice manifest in regard to this unprecedented sacrilege, which has horrified the whole church and stirred up in the country a new wave of repudiation of violence."[39]

Molina replied the same day, saying that he was deeply concerned about the matter and had ordered "an exhaustive investigation" as soon as he had heard of the shooting in order to discover the culprits "and apply strictly the rigor of the law." The government did not rule out that "such actions can form part of a series of antisocial acts that for purely political ends seek to disrupt the nation's peace and order, with the deliberate purpose of domestic and international self-justification and implied blame of the government of the republic." He concluded by reaffirming the government's effort to clear up the case, "confident that the Almighty will make justice shine forth."[40]

Molina's suggestion that opponents of the government might have committed the murders could not be directly refuted as long as the real murderers remained unknown. But if he thought that might be true, why did the government not carry out a more serious investigation? Six weeks later, the lawyer chosen by Romero to follow the case reported "an embarrassing and clear indifference toward the investigation on the part of state organizations." A suspect ordered arrested by a judge was living unconcernedly in El Paisnal, and no one had ordered the bodies exhumed and examined.[41] The bullets are still in the graves.

Two meetings were held the day after Grande's funeral. The clergy of the archdiocese held a daylong meeting to discuss what measures to take in the wake of the murders, and the national bishops' conference met privately for an hour and twenty minutes.

The bishops took note that their message had been read in most churches on the preceding Sunday and that no newspaper had published it because of censorship. Some radio stations had carried it, however, when they broadcast Sunday masses in which the letter was read. Romero informed the bishops that the archdiocese was considering what action to take next, and read them the letter President Molina had written him. The murders on the road to El Paisnal had changed the situation radically, and the bishops could not help exchanging rumors and speculations on who might have committed them. FARO (Eastern Region Farmers' Front), a large landowners' organization, and ORDEN (Democratic Nationalist Organization), the government's paramilitary organization for fighting subversion, came easily to mind. The nuncio, who was present with the bishops, wondered if he should go and see the president and the president-elect. Bishop Aparicio said it was important that the military vicar, Bishop Eduardo Alvarez, use his influence; but Alvarez was not at the meeting. They adjourned at 11:30 A.M. without taking any action.[42]

The meeting of the archdiocesan clergy began at 9:30 A.M. with practically all the priests of the archdiocese in attendance, plus several others from the Santa Ana diocese, many men and women religious, and several lay people. Romero read them his letter to the president and the reply. After a period of prayer, they broke up into smaller working groups. Romero asked the groups to consider four matters: basic points in which they must all be united so that the church would present a common front; actions that all could support; what public opinion the church had been able to form with the bishops' message, the radio station, bulletins, and such; further discussion and suggestions. He asked for a clear and frank dialog that would help inform him. The opinions expressed and votes to be taken would have only the force of a consultation; he himself would make the decisions about what to do.[43]

Virtually everyone present agreed that the church was under persecution, along with other groups struggling for justice that were persecuted by the power structure of government, military, FARO, and ANEP (National Private Business Association). The church was persecuted because of its fidelity to Vatican II and Medellín, to the directives arising from the 1976 archdiocesan pastoral week, and especially to its work among the long-neglected campesinos. The church needed to unite around the bishop and his clergy, and priests who were not yet in harmony with the pastoral methods of the archdiocese should study and reflect on them.[44]

A few spoke emotionally against the nuncio's identification with the government and upper classes. Numerous practical suggestions were offered. Some were noncontroversial, such as maintaining close communication with the archbishop and continuing to supply information to the public. Others found little support and were not acted upon, such as celebrating Holy Week only in the cathedral and asking the military vicar and chaplains to resign. Two others took up long discussions and afterward caused great public controversy: closing the Catholic schools for several days and the single mass for the following Sunday.[45]

The day before, Romero and Bishop Aparicio, president of the bishops' conference, had met with the governing board of the federation of Catholic schools. The meeting had first voted thirty-one to twenty-three to close the schools in protest; the two bishops voted against the proposal. Out of respect for their opinion, a second vote was taken, in which the association decided twenty-nine to twenty-four not to close the schools. Asked now in the clergy meeting if his vote of the day before was definitive, Romero said he would like to continue the discussion before making a definitive decision.[46]

Opponents of closing the schools spoke of the risks involved. Proponents spoke of the impact that it would have in showing concern over the persecution, especially on the persons responsible, many of whom had children in the Catholic schools. The closure was not to be regarded as a vacation; rather, the students and their families would be given a questionnaire to fill out and some sort of reading material to think about. The vote was overwhelming: only six voted against the closure; seven abstained. Romero felt he now had enough enlightenment to make his decision.[47]

Those opposed to the single mass argued that it would be misunderstood and many would complain at not being able to get to mass and holy communion; it could also seem like a pure show of power. Those in favor argued that the mass should be linked to the reality of life, that the single mass would show in a pastoral way the exceptional conditions in the country, that it could be a good catechesis on the mass itself, and that the lack of other masses would show what expulsions of priests from the country could lead to.[48]

After an examination of the pros and cons in the morning, a preliminary sounding produced eighty-four votes in favor and eighty-two against. A discussion in the afternoon produced a large majority in favor. That night Romero met again with representatives of the schools and a committee selected to draw up the public report on the meeting. It was then that he announced his decision to close the schools and to have the single mass.[49]

Those present at the meeting had also agreed, with much less discussion, that all that had happened should be publicized, that the church should not seem to support the government or other power groups by attending public functions like the installation of the new president, blessing banks, and such, that a pastoral letter should be prepared for Easter or Pentecost, and that a committee should study how to observe Holy Week in view of all that was happening. A committee of three was named to help Romero write the bulletin that would issue from the long meeting, which finally broke up at 6:30 P.M.[50]

Romero issued the news bulletin that evening. It spoke of the violence and persecution, of the church's difficulty in performing its ministry under such conditions, of its duty to be faithful to Vatican II and Medellín, and of its need to be united. It announced that all Catholic schools would suspend classes for three days of reflection, that the only mass to be held the following Sunday would be in the cathedral, that the church would not participate in official functions until the situation was resolved, and that a permanent committee would keep watch on the situation and remain in touch with the archbishop. It was signed by the archbishop and the chancellor.

In regard to the single Sunday mass, the bulletin clearly said:

[The archbishop has decided] to summon all pastors and chaplains to be present on Sunday, March 20, to celebrate a single eucharist with the bishop in the cathedral church at 10:00 A.M.; hence all parish and chaplaincy masses are canceled, and all the faithful are invited to join the single eucharist by means of radio YSAX.[51]

It would have been clear to at least all the clergy and religious who had been at the meeting on the day after Grande's funeral that no other masses were to be held on Sunday; however, someone not familiar with what had been discussed and decided might think that only masses at the time of the cathedral mass were forbidden. A circular delivered to the pastors the following day called special attention to the section of the bulletin that prohibited all other masses, but it also contained the phrase, "please cancel any other mass scheduled to be celebrated at that hour in your parish or chaplaincy." Apparently, someone in the archdiocesan office had misunderstood what Romero intended.[52]

The confusion was to complicate relations with the nuncio, whom the clergy meeting had noted as one of the few negative notes in the record of the church's performance in recent days. He had missed the previous clergy meeting but the next day had appeared at the president-elect's presentation of credentials. As chief celebrant of Grande's funeral mass the nuncio had seemed out of place.[53]

The next day, Wednesday, Romero met at 5:00 P.M. with the president and two vice-presidents of ANEP, the businessmen's association, perhaps the strongest organized group in the country. With Romero were three diocesan priests who were to become his most frequent advisers. The meeting accomplished little or nothing. ANEP wanted the archdiocesan radio station to stop broadcasting anything but classical music, the schools to stay open, and the single mass scheduled for Sunday to be reconsidered. The ANEP representatives accused the church of stirring up the people and causing unrest in the country. When they were asked, however, what they were prepared to do to help calm the situation, they had nothing to offer. They were there only to change Romero's mind by emphasizing their own strength and were not interested in discussion. The meeting ended as it had begun, in an atmosphere of mutual distrust.[54]

On Thursday morning the nuncio, Archbishop Gerada, called Romero, asking him to come to the nunciature at 10:30. Romero was busy and did not go at 10:30; the nuncio called again saying to hurry because he had to leave for the seashore to rest.

After that inauspicious prelude, Romero arrived at the nunciature at 11:15, accompanied by a priest whom he had taken along as a witness and consultant. To his surprise, his own secretary, a Mexican priest known as Father Evaristo, was there with the nuncio. Romero had accepted Evaristo for a year's trial period to work in Santiago de María and had brought him with him to El Salvador; he returned to Mexico shortly after this incident.

The nuncio invited Romero and Evaristo to speak together in private. Evaristo, it developed, had been giving the nuncio his own version of the clergy meeting and its conclusions. Romero, he had said, was being manipulated by a group of communist priests, who had changed him radically, since Romero was too good in himself, too much a man of prayer and sacrifice, to slip into the errors that were being committed.

After expressing his views, Evaristo took Romero back to the nuncio, who was with the priest whom Romero had brought along. The nuncio began a fifteen-minute scolding of Romero, calling him irresponsible, imprudent, and inconsistent in his actions as bishop. The single mass scheduled for Sunday came in for special disapproval. As the nuncio caught his breath, the priest who accompanied Romero broke in and said that Romero's decisions had come after a long consultation with his priests. They had discussed them together all day Tuesday in a meeting the nuncio had promised to attend but had missed. Gerada replied that his car had broken down on the way to a diplomatic affair and spoiled his plans to go to the clergy meeting. Since San Salvador is a compact city and cabs were available, the explanation was not impressive.

Romero tried to explain the unity among the clergy that had been achieved by the recent events and the discussions, and that the single eucharist of the archdiocese gathered around its pastor was a unique opportunity to bring all the faithful into that unity. To every explanation of the Sunday mass, the nuncio kept saying, "No, that is not done," or simply shook his head. Finally, Romero said quietly but firmly that he would not go back on his decision, which had been amply discussed with his priests.

Romero's companion suggested a possible compromise: have the special mass but allow the individual pastors to have other Sunday masses if they so decided. The nuncio hesitated; he wanted the special mass dropped. Romero was not interested; his decision was made. Gerada then shifted to another argument. The mass could degenerate into a demonstration, with grave consequences for the church. Romero replied that the organizers were taking means to keep that from happening. Gerada mentioned that the state of siege decreed by the government forbade public gatherings. Romero pointed out that the government was permitting soccer games that drew large crowds.

Gerada finally lowered the angry tone he had been using. Romero left the meeting firm, but disillusioned and uneasy. Gerada had used the same arguments made by the ANEP representatives the day before. Romero had felt accused and judged guilty by the nuncio in a matter that was entirely his own concern as archbishop. Gerada had mentioned nothing positive about Romero's actions, had been deaf to dialog, had carped and reprimanded.[55] This was certainly not the way Romero wanted to deal with the pope's representative, with whom he had previously had good relations.

Romero met the next morning with most of the priests from the city, plus a few from rural areas, and a few women religious. He wanted them to discuss the Sunday mass frankly, not because he wanted to reconsider his decision, but to help them understand it better and to find out just how much backing he had in what was proving to be a controversial matter. Some explained that they disagreed with the decision because it would deprive many people of mass on Sunday; a few suggested allowing evening masses or giving holy communion in the parishes. But the immense majority were with him. So were the campesinos and the poor of the city, the pastors assured him. The priests saw the single mass as a needed show of unity and of moral and prophetic force.

After the discussion, Romero asked for a vote on his decision. Seventy-one voted in favor and one against, and one abstained. All sixty-three pastors and chaplains present voted their support, and he and they proceeded to make preparations for the mass.[56]

With the clergy so clearly behind him, Romero returned to the nunciature at 5:00 P.M. together with several priests. Gerada had said that many pastors of the city were complaining to him about the mass, and Romero wanted to explain to him that the pastors were in favor of it. But the nuncio had not returned from Guatemala, which he also served as nuncio and often visited, and Romero consented to talk with the monsignor who was secretary of the nunciature. The secretary chided Romero like a schoolboy. Romero's theological and pastoral arguments for the single mass were valid, he admitted, but according to canon law Romero could not dispense the whole diocese from Sunday mass as he was doing. The priests with Romero replied that Bishop Rivera, who had assisted at the discussions, was a professional canonist of good reputation and he had raised no objections. Their opinion was that the bishop did have such power in his own diocese. The secretary disagreed.

Romero, who had remained quiet, then gave his opinion, after overcoming the secretary's interruptions. He reviewed the theological and pastoral reasons behind his decision and repeated that it had been made after extensive consultation and discussion, in accord with the church's hierarchical structure. He had the support of the clergy and the people, and the opposition only of the upper classes, who generally did not back the church, especially the church of Vatican II and Medellín. He took full responsibility; he felt at peace and thought he had taken the right course.

The discussion continued but did not advance. The meeting ended at six o'clock, and Romero decided not to try to see the nuncio again. That evening, Bishop Rivera, another canonist, and a theology teacher met to consider the canonical aspects of the Sunday mass. They agreed that Romero had the right to dispense the diocese from the Sunday mass obligation.[57]

Later that Friday evening, when Gerada returned from Guatemala, he learned of the preparations for the one mass to be held on Sunday in front of the cathedral. He quickly tried to arrange an interview with Romero for Saturday morning. But on Saturday Romero was saying mass for the patronal feast of St. Joseph in El Paisnal, where the people received him with an ovation.[58] Sometime Saturday the nuncio wrote Romero a letter marked "strictly confidential." The letter expressed all Gerada's objections and fears at the course the archdiocese was taking: it was not right to deprive the faithful of mass; he had understood from their meeting and the circular that only masses at ten o'clock would be canceled; people should have a chance to choose; mass in the plaza would be less profitable for people; the other bishops had not been consulted in a matter that would have national repercussions. Moreover, he was disturbed by the phrase in the clergy's declaration about not taking part in official functions until the situation was cleared up. It seemed "provocative and dangerous."[59]

The mass went ahead as planned. People filled the plaza and side streets, and many more listened on the radio. A hundred thousand strong,[60] it was the largest demonstration of Salvadoran church unity within memory.[61] Pastors present with their parishioners reported that for many it marked a return to the church after a long estrangement.[62]

On Monday Romero answered the nuncio's letter. He had tried to see him on Saturday afternoon, he said, in the only free half-hour he had. Nevertheless, he said, "I affirm categorically that there was no agreement [to permit other Sunday masses] but rather a dialog" in the Thursday meeting. He told him of the pastors' vote in favor of the mass as arranged, that clergy and faithful in general had backed his procedure, and that a hundred thousand people had participated with great devotion in the mass. As for notifying other bishops, he wrote: "It seems to me that an archdiocesan matter is the concern only of the archbishop. Besides, no bishop of any other diocese manifested his disagreement about what we were preparing in this archdiocese. None of them showed any disquiet during the week in regard to the national dimension or repercussion. Furthermore, I myself consulted persons in the government ahead of time and even the future president, General Romero. I came away from these talks with a clear impression of the positive aspects, although I understood the concerns expressed." Concerning the "provocative and dangerous" refusal to participate in government functions, no one in the government had seen it thus. It was, rather, "a firm stand of the church before an avalanche of violations of the human rights of campesinos and of priests, native and foreign."

The stern, almost exasperated tone of Romero's letter suggests that the argument with the nuncio had been wearing. He concluded by suggesting that now that the incident was over they "reflect serenely" on what the archdiocese had done in following Romero's conscience.[63]

Two days later, March 23, Romero went to see President Molina and repeated his demand for an investigation of the three murders and for cooperation with the church's own investigation. He had prepared an agenda of matters to discuss. Besides demanding an investigation of the murders of Grande and his two companions as well as guarantees for the lives of priests and lay workers, he wanted to talk about the priests who had been expelled, about FARO, and about ORDEN; and he wanted to set up a mechanism for dialog between the church and the government and begin discussing such matters as legalized abortion and religion classes in public schools.

Molina was polite and even asked Romero to preside over the meeting, which also involved Molina's secretary, Colonel Eliseo López Abarca, and two of Romero's priests. But Molina was evasive and diffuse, killing time and dodging questions. He mostly ignored Romero's agenda. He had a theory that international communism had killed Grande in order to put church and government at odds and disturb the country. The exiled priests should best wait for the new president before returning. He would try to give some directions to ORDEN. He was providing the investigation of the murders, but could not guarantee the results, given the poor quality of the country's juridical apparatus.

At one point Romero interjected that the church would believe the promises when it sa̅: them accomplished. That would become a refrain during the next three years. He left the meeting convinced that Molina had not the least intention of doing anything.[64]

Romero had been archbishop for a month. A clergy that had at first received him with displeasure and distrust had by now gladly accepted him as its leader. The crowds at the funeral and the single mass had been huge, and Romero felt the common people responding to him, sometimes with applause. On the other hand, he had lost ground with the ruling class, some of whom were obviously complaining to the nuncio and the other bishops, as well as to him. Tension with the government had risen to a new height. And, what was most alarming and painful, he was at loggerheads with the pope's own representative in the country, who seemed incapable of understanding what Romero was doing and why. The nuncio and the nuncio's secretary had berated him, even in the presence of other persons.

Romero decided to go quickly to Rome and explain personally to the pope and to his curia what was happening in the archdiocese and what he as archbishop was doing. The nuncio's behavior left no doubt that unfavorable reports must be going to Rome. Besides, the government had its own ambassador at the Vatican. Like St. Paul, who went to Jerusalem to explain his work among the gentiles to Peter and the other apostles, he would go to Rome to see Paul VI and lay before him his case.

He left for Rome with Monsignor Ricardo Urioste on Saturday, March 26, and arrived on Sunday afternoon. They went to the lodging run by a community of nuns for visiting priests, and as soon as they were settled Romero wanted to visit St. Peter's. He knelt in prayer for a half-hour before the high altar, said to be built over the tomb of St. Peter, while Urioste waited patiently. Then he went to visit the tombs of the popes. He lingered at the tomb of Pius XI, the pope who had stood up to Hitler and Mussolini. He had been pope when Romero first went to Rome as a student, and he had impressed Romero deeply.

From St. Peter's, they went to call on Pedro Arrupe, superior general of the Jesuits and of the martyred Rutilio Grande. Fifty-nine Jesuits, forty-four of them priests, lived and worked or studied in El Salvador, all but one in Romero's diocese. Besides the Aguilares parish, they operated the Central American University, a large high school, and several smaller apostolic works. The university and the high school educated many sons and daughters of the upper class, and both were thorns in the side of the oligarchy. The university published the intellectual magazine *Estudios Centroamericanos,* generally known by the acronym *ECA.* Both the university and *ECA* had suffered vigorous attacks in the press campaign of the preceding months, and six bombs set off on the campus during 1976 had been part of the campaign to intimidate one or both of them. A few Jesuit students studied theology at the university.

Though some would complain about Jesuit influence in the archdiocese and on Romero, the Jesuits and their apostolates were resources at his disposal that he could not neglect. He had studied theology under the Jesuits, and he had become friends with several Jesuits when he lived in the seminary and the Jesuits staffed it; but he had not been particularly close to the group as such. As a bishop he had supported the removal of the Jesuits from the seminary in 1972, and as editor of the diocesan weekly he had published an editorial that accused their high school of instilling Marxism, which touched off a storm of controversy and a judicial investigation of the school. Rutilio's death, however, now brought Romero necessarily closer to them and especially to the provincial, who arrived in Rome on Tuesday, bringing an extensive dossier on conditions in El Salvador, including a detailed account of events before and after the death of Rutilio Grande.

Romero's first act on Monday morning was to ask for an appointment with Cardinal Sebastiano Baggio, prefect of the Congregation for the Bishops, which keeps an eye on the performance of bishops around the world, chooses new ones, and occasionally removes one from office. He received an appointment for noon, and he and Baggio spoke for a half-hour in private.

While waiting for the interview with Baggio, Romero and Urioste went to the Secretariat of State with the bulletins that the archdiocese had published and copies of Romero's exchange of letters with the nuncio and the president. The monsignor in charge asked them to prepare a brief report summarizing the matters in the documents. They prepared five typed pages that evening and left the report at the secretariat on Tuesday morning.

That evening Romero offered mass and had supper in the Latin American College, to which he had belonged for six years when he was a student at the Gregorian University. Four of those years had been war years, and he still remembered the meager rations of food and having to take refuge from air raids.[65] After supper he talked with the students about El Salvador.

The next morning Romero read over the dossier that the provincial had brought. It recounted in a half-inch-thick sheaf of typewritten pages the poverty of the peasantry, the long history of political manipulation and frustrated attempts at reform, the power of ANEP and FARO, the movement to organize the people and its repression by the state, the church's efforts to encourage the struggle for justice recommended by Medellín and the campaign of slander and persecution it had met, the expulsions of priests and some of the tortures and murders of campesinos, the career and death of Rutilio Grande, including Grande's own explanation of the Aguilares pastoral project, the church's reaction to Rutilio's murder, the clergy meetings, and the meetings with the nuncio, the president, and ANEP. It reviewed the reasons for the single mass on Sunday and for the closure of Catholic schools. Finally, it offered a seventeen-page "theological reading of the events" based on Vatican II's Pastoral Constitution on the Church in the Modern World.

The pope's regular Wednesday audience was at 11:00 A.M. For Romero, seeing the pope was the essence of the trip to Rome. Paul VI singled him out among the others present at the audience and introduced him to the group. Then, when the audience was finished, he took Romero to another room for a private talk. Romero presented the pope with a photograph of Rutilio Grande and explained what he was trying to do in his archdiocese, how he was trying to put into practice what Vatican II and Medellín and Paul himself had taught. The pope took both of Romero's hands in his and urged him: "Courage! You are the one in charge!"[66]

Romero took advantage of a free afternoon to write at least two letters. One he sent to Guatemala to Emanuele Gerada, the papal nuncio, explaining that he had wanted to tell him about this "almost improvised" trip to Rome but had not had a chance before Gerada left for Guatemala. He hoped to see the nuncio after his return to El Salvador, he wrote, to talk about the visit to Rome. "I forward from here, the center of the church's unity, and with the deep satisfaction of having taken the hand of the Holy Father, the same feelings of attachment, friendship, and gratitude that I have always professed for you."[67] After the dispute about the mass of March 20 and the exchange of harsh words, it was urgent to resume good relations with the nuncio, with whom Romero had previously gotten on well and who had favored him for archbishop.[68]

The other letter was to Cardinal Baggio, and it accompanied payment of a $5 fee to Baggio's Congregation for the Bishops. The $5 he was happy to pay, he said, but in regard to the $750 that the congregation was asking him to pay the Secretariat of State for his naming as archbishop, "I respectfully ask you to obtain, if possible, an exemption or reduction, since my recent transfer from the diocese of Santiago de Maria, which is very poor, makes payment very difficult for me."[69] The fee was later reduced to $500, and he paid it the following September.[70]

Friday, April 1, was Romero's last day in Rome. He wanted to be sure to be home for Palm Sunday and for all the Holy Week services in the cathedral. He met at 11:30 in the Secretariat of State with Archbishop Agostino Casaroli, secretary of the Council for the Public Affairs of the Church, which handles the church's relations with governments. They spoke in private, and to Urioste Romero seemed contented when he left.

He went to the airport late that afternoon satisfied that he had presented his case before Peter. The pope had strengthened and encouraged him, and that made up for the difficult moments he had experienced. Things had gone fairly well in the Secretariat of State, where Casaroli and the monsignors had backed him in general while urging him to be prudent. Things had gone somewhat less well in the Congregation for the Bishops, where the secretary had lectured him roundly on what he should and should not do. He had found warmth and backing at Vatican Radio, which had interviewed him, and at the Jesuit headquarters. He had dined with the editor of the Spanish edition of *l'Osservatore Romano,* the Vatican newspaper.

Romero arrived home the day before Palm Sunday. A group of priests and lay people met him at the airport and took him to the cathedral, where they offered mass with him. He gave the press pictures of himself handing the Holy Father a photograph of Rutilio Grande. It summed up all he wanted to say.[71]

Before Romero's trip to Rome, the press had begun an attack on the Catholic schools, centering it on the Colegio El Sagrado Corazón, a girls' school run by the Oblates of the Heart of Jesus. A group of parents made angry accusations of Marxist indoctrination of the students, newspapers published banner headlines,[72] a confrontation between the principal and the group of parents took place, but the other schools[73] and the clergy[74] published statements of support for the school, and their unanimity showed once more the unity of the archdiocese. The fuss had grown up around the Sisters' efforts to have the students reflect on the social condition of their country and on the death of Rutilio Grande and his companions. The issue was still simmering when Romero returned. It was not the first time that Catholic schools had been in disputes over the teaching of social doctrine. In 1973 Romero himself had touched off a memorable battle for the Jesuit high school. Now he was on the other side of the battle line.

In their March 15 meeting the clergy had urged Romero to publish a pastoral letter for Easter or Pentecost. He seems to have written it unaided, continuing to work on it during the trip to Rome and even between planes at the New York airport. "The Paschal Church,"[75] as he called it, was published at Easter. It was his first pastoral letter to the archdiocese and his formal introduction to the people, who nevertheless had seen him in action and listened to his voice for a month and a half.

The archdiocese, Romero wrote, was living a "paschal hour" coinciding with the paschal season of the liturgy. That was the meaning he saw in the events surrounding his taking the helm from his predecessor, and so he chose to make it the subject of his letter of introduction and first formal greeting to the archdiocese. At the same time he invited all to "a reflective dialog" with the church, "which is always desirous of dialog with all in order to communicate to them the truth and the grace that God has entrusted it for guiding the world according to his divine plans." The church, he said, does not live for itself, but to bring to the world the truth and the grace of the paschal mystery.

The paschal mystery, wrote Romero, is "the event of Christian salvation through the death and resurrection of our Lord Jesus Christ," which Vatican Council II made "the center of its reflections on the church and its mission in the world." God prepared this event through the wonders he worked in the people of the Old Covenant, especially in the exodus from Egypt, a "rescue from death through the protection of the blood of the lamb." It involved a passage "from slavery through sea and desert to a promised land, to freedom and repose." Each year the rescued people celebrated their passage, not only as a memory of the past, but as a redemption that became present, and they relived the Lord's wonders. The Passover was ever present; God remained Israel's Savior throughout the nation's history.

Jesus' last Passover transformed what was figure and preparation into the Christian paschal reality. Through his own passage through death to resurrection, Christ became the Passover personified. He died on the cross as the paschal lamb, "and at a paschal supper established his eucharistic memorial, which will make the wonder of his redemption present amid all human circumstances." His death destroys the reign of sin, and his resurrection "implants now in history the reign of eternal life and offers us the capacity for the most daring transformations of history and of life." Christ has entered first into a new world, a "rescued universe," and his gift of the Holy Spirit enables human beings to "identify with Jesus in his victory over evil and in the renewal of their own lives." While the kingdom of Heaven will be perfectly fulfilled only after death, the Risen One has inaugurated it in history by his passage from death to resurrection.

When Romero in his letter spoke of a "paschal hour" being lived in the archdiocese, he meant, he said, "all this copious potentiality of faith, hope, and love that the risen Christ—living and working—has stirred up in the various sectors of our local church and even in sectors and persons who do not belong to it or share as yet in our paschal faith." The archdiocese was making real what the Latin American bishops had urged at Medellín: "Let there be seen in Latin America the ever brighter face of a church authentically poor, missionary, and paschal, disentangled from all temporal power, and daringly committed to the freedom of the whole person and of all persons."[76]

The church must be a paschal church. It "is born of the Passover and lives to be sign and instrument of the Passover in the midst of the world." In it, Jesus continues to live his paschal mission. "The church is the body of the risen Christ, and by baptism all the members that make it up live that tension of Passover, that passage from death to life, that passage that never ends called conversion, which is the unceasing demand to kill in oneself all that is sin and make live with ever growing power all that is life, renewal, holiness, and justice." One cannot be part of the church without being faithful to that movement from death to life, "without a sincere movement of conversion and faithfulness to the Lord." The church's very reason for being is to make tangible and operative the power of Christ's death and resurrection, to be Christ's instrument for redeeming all people. And the new archbishop added that he himself wished to be, as far as he could, a shepherd with the sentiments of the Good Shepherd, who "came not to be served but to serve and to give his life" (Matt. 20:28).

The church, said Romero, is a community that is the sign of new life, and its preaching is the truth that saves. Fidelity to its Lord "obliges it, with the urgency of a world in need of salvation, not to adulterate in the least its teaching and its ministry." Its service to God, said the council, is to save the world. The Latin American bishops at Medellín concretized that service when "they realized that the Spirit of the Passover urgently impelled our church to dialog and service towards our peoples. 'We are,' they said, 'on the threshold of a new epoch of history on our continent, an epoch full of a longing for total emancipation, of liberation from every servitude, of personal maturity, and of collective integration.' "[77] Medellín had proclaimed that the church could not be indifferent to the "silent cry from millions of people begging their pastors for a liberation they find nowhere else."[78]

"These legitimate aspirations of our people," wrote Romero, are "an evangelical summons" to the church of San Salvador. The church was acquiring a deeper awareness of its own mission and so must have "the wisdom and the courage to speak the word and take the stance that Christ demands in these complicated circumstances." It was a moment that demanded responsibility, commitment, prayer, and discernment of the signs of the times. The church's mission, he said, quoting Vatican II, is "essentially religious, but for that reason profoundly human."[79] The church, said Pope Paul VI,[80] preaches liberation and associates with those who act and suffer for it, while holding to its spiritual vocation as primary. It refuses to replace its proclaiming of God's kingdom with the proclaiming of human types of liberation. But the gospel teaching of love for the needy and suffering imposes a necessary connection between preaching the gospel and preaching liberation. To fulfill the church's mission, its members must not divorce faith from life and must develop a "Christian sensitivity to people's afflictions" in order to "brighten their hopes" and share in the "positive construction of history."[81] All must convert themselves to the radical demands of Jesus' Sermon on the Mount.

Precisely because the church's service to humanity is not essentially political or socioeconomic, wrote Romero, the church seeks "a sincere dialog and healthy cooperation with those who have political and socioeconomic responsibilities." That such cooperation not compromise the church's freedom and autonomy, "the church is ready to renounce any privilege when it risks blurring the purity of its testimony." The church in El Salvador "has always been ready for such cooperation and dialog with the authorities of the state and the economic and social powers of the country." It suffers when, "to the people's harm and confusion, these relations are clouded by misunderstanding or incomprehension of its difficult responsibility to defend the rights of God and of human beings."

The letter is heavy with quotations, as Romero labored to make clear that he was following the teaching of the universal church. The quotations come principally from Vatican II, but also from Paul VI's "Evangelization in the Modern World,"[82] from Medellín, and from Cardinal Eduardo Pironio, prefect of the Congregation for Religious and formerly president of CELAM, the Latin American bishops' organization. The letter contains the basic ideas that Romero would elaborate in his later pastoral letters and in his preaching. It sets out a vision of the church's mission that challenged deeply held preconceptions and self-interests of the powerful in Salvadoran society.

On April 18, President Molina invited all the bishops and the papal nuncio to meet with him and with some members of his cabinet and with the president-elect and vice-president-elect on April 20 at his offices.[83] But on April 19, another event put the government and the nation into a cruel crisis. One of two small guerrilla groups operating in the country, the Popular Liberation Forces, or FPL, kidnapped the foreign minister, Mauricio Borgonovo, and demanded as his ransom the release of thirty-seven political prisoners. Molina opened the meeting on April 20 by saying that it had nothing to do with the Borgonovo case, which was on everyone's mind. However, part of the press associated the meeting with the Borgonovo kidnapping.[84]

The purpose of the meeting, said Molina, was to discuss "the deterioration of relations between the church and the state." Certain priests, he said, especially foreigners, had participated directly in such events as the recent election and the February 28 occupation of Plaza Libertad, and some had used the Holy Week ceremonies to accuse the government of killing Rutilio Grande and of destroying Christian communities through ORDEN. Catholic schools were confusing parents with their teachings. The church, he suggested, should make its priests, especially the foreigners, think about their actions and follow the law strictly.

Romero began his reply to Molina by noting first his concern for Borgonovo and repeating the church's condemnation of violence from any source. From the moment he became archbishop, he went on, he had been seeking dialog with the government. He had forbidden the clergy to make public accusations against persons or institutions for deeds not clearly established, like Grande's death. But the government itself, he implied, was the cause of the tension. It should not confuse Marxism-Leninism and the church's evangelization as approved by Vatican II and Medellín, and therefore it was unjust to accuse as Marxist or subversive any priest who was simply giving himself wholly to the church's task. As long as a priest followed the church's thought, he would have the firm and total support of the archdiocese, and in this the church could not yield.

Romero suggested that in future dialogs the bishops receive earlier notice and an agenda for the meeting and that after the present meeting both sides publish a joint statement. To remedy the government's misunderstanding of the church's language, he proposed creating a discussion group of government and church representatives. And if some priests had attacked the government in their Holy Week ceremonies, Molina should give specific facts.

Molina accepted the proposal for the joint statement. It was never prepared, however; the government and the archdiocese each issued its own report of the meeting, the archdiocese feeling that the government's was incomplete. As for the Holy Week accusation, Molina could only show the bishops a photograph taken in a parish of the archdiocese that supposedly proved his point that some priests had accused the government of Grande's murder.

Bishop Aparicio, the president of the bishops' conference, backed the archbishop and told Molina that much of the blame for the deterioration of relations was the fault of the Guardia Nacional, which made false accusations against priests. The government often got wrong information from subalterns and should be more careful about believing what they reported, he said. The church had never taken part in party politics, but at times its defense of the rights of peasants was seen in that light. The church could not renounce its duty, especially in a country with so much injustice. He then spoke of the seizures of lands by peasants, a topic that was exciting the landowners at the time. The seizures were reactions to clear injustices committed by landowners, he said. Campesinos had tried to explain this to the Guardia Nacional but had not been allowed to present their views. A mediating commission of landowners and campesinos should try to work out the problems without coercion from the military. Aparicio also complained that the education ministry had refused for two years to talk with representatives of the Catholic schools and that the health ministry was requiring women to take birth-control pills as a condition for receiving medicines. He asked the government to clear up the status of ORDEN, supposedly a civic organization, which actually took orders from the local military commanders, and to put a stop to FARO's propaganda against the church, in which FARO enjoyed full access to the media, while others were denied it.

President-elect Romero asked why it was in the archdiocese especially that the government was having problems with certain priests, and Bishop Rivera replied that problems were generally especially acute in the San Salvador area, the center of the nation's activities, where population from the rest of the country flowed. To meet these needs, he said, the archdiocese had believed it necessary to ask its clergy to become sensitive to the situation and the pastoral response it called for. The result was a pastoral style that was more dynamic and more committed.[85]

The meeting did little or nothing to heal the breach in church-state relations, which events were soon to worsen.

Even as the bishops met with the government, Borgonovo's mother was publishing desperate pleas to her son's kidnappers in the newspapers. He was the scion of a prominent family, a product of Catholic schools, young, married, a father. The kidnapping dramatized, as it was meant to do, the tension already reigning in the country over the deaths and disappearances of arrested persons. If the captivity and threatened murder of a prominent and wealthy citizen was so horrible, was not the disappearance of any person into the secret cells of the security forces also horrible? Borgonovo's mother implied as much a few days later when she issued a statement of solidarity with the mothers of all prisoners.[86]

Romero published appeals to both the FPL and the government to abstain from any act of violence and offered the church's mediation in the crisis.[87] Appeals from all sorts of organizations and from individuals filled the papers for weeks. Some seemed to be part of a campaign organized by the family, others seemed spontaneous. Most appealed to the FPL for compassion. Some also appealed to the government to negotiate with the kidnappers. But the government adamantly refused, and on April 29 Molina made a formal refusal on radio and television. To yield, he said with military logic, would be to set a precedent that would endanger others. Anyway, he added, the prisoners whose release was demanded were not in the government's hands or were being held for trial.[88] The family appealed directly to the FPL through newspaper ads and asked Romero for his help. He offered to do all he could and also published two appeals of his own to the kidnappers.[89] They were silent.

Meanwhile the church found itself in another confrontation with the government. May 1 is Labor Day in El Salvador, as in most of the world. In 1977 it fell on a Sunday. Labor unions planned their traditional demonstrations in spite of warnings from the government. Troops broke up the demonstrations, and at least eight demonstrators died. Romero visited the Red Cross headquarters to offer his help.[90]

That afternoon the government arrested Jorge Sarsanedas, a Panamanian Jesuit, as he returned to the capital from saying mass in the country. He had helped in Aguilares while a seminarian two years before and was now finishing his theology studies in San Salvador. Both Romero and the Jesuit provincial asked to see him and were refused for several days.[91]

Meanwhile, Rubén Zamora, a member of the National Justice and Peace Commission and professor at the Central American University, had also been arrested, and Romero was not allowed to see him either. Tendentious stories in the press kept attacking various priests of the archdiocese.[92] On May 5 a bomb went off in the archdiocesan printing shop, the second since Romero's return from Rome.[93]

Romero and the provincial were finally able to see Sarsanedas early on the morning of May 6, as the government prepared to deport him. The commander of the Guardia Nacional spoke with them at length and asked Romero to sign a statement that Sarsanedas had been arrested at 9:00 A.M. Sunday, at the time of the Labor Day incident, and that he had been treated well. But he had been arrested in the afternoon, and Sarsanedas told them he had been kept blindfolded, had been kicked and insulted, and had been fed only twice in five days. Romero refused to sign.

Romero and the provincial followed the Guardia car carrying Sarsanedas to the airport and were able to see him board the plane for Panama. At the Guardia headquarters, a guard had noted down the license plate number of the provincial's car. Now, as they left the airport, Romero remarked to the provincial that he had better get a new car, as the present one could be a bomb target. The provincial decided to trade it in.[94]

That afternoon Romero wrote to Molina protesting and detailing what had happened, including his refusal to sign the mendacious statement. "I remind you, Mr. President, that there exists between us an agreement that any accusation or complaint against a priest who works in our country will be communicated to and discussed with the bishop responsible before coercive measures are taken. Once again this agreement has not been honored."

And now the government was continuing to propagate the slander. "As I write this letter I hear on the radio and read in the press a statement of the Interior Ministry that basically affirms that Father Sarsanedas was expelled from the country for being found engaged in subversive activities, along with other Central American Jesuits and Salvadoran priests. . . . Mr. President, this report confirms me in the impression that facts are willfully distorted and a campaign of arbitrary persecution is being followed against priests, native and foreign. I greatly lament this tendency toward the progressive 'deterioration' of relations between your government and the church that concerned you in the recent meeting with the bishops."[95]

The archdiocesan radio had become the most popular station in El Salvador, and Romero was its most popular figure. But the government was unhappy about its straight-talking ways. In his Sunday sermon on May 8, Romero spoke of the threat to close the station down and of the bombs that had gone off in the print shop of the archdiocese, a few yards from the seminary building. Obviously, some people were trying to silence the church's voice. "Who knows if this may be the last time that I communicate with you by radio? God grant it is not. . . . If, unhappily, they silence the radio, seek the word of God from your parish priest; don't miss mass on Sunday. The archdiocesan office will keep publishing its information bulletin. Look for it in your parishes. Don't keep isolated from this communication of the word. For while the forces that persecute and defame the church have all the newspapers, all the radio stations, all the television on their side, the struggle is unequal."[96]

As though to underline these words, the minister of the interior called in the directors of the archdiocesan radio station two days later to warn them to stop criticizing the government, threatening them with a heavy fine and even with closure of the station.[97]

All the pleas for Borgonovo's safety were in vain. The government had not budged. The kidnappers were silent. On the evening of May 10, Borgonovo's body was found, and the nation reeled in shock.

Romero said the funeral mass at noon on May 11 in San José de la Montaña church in a charged atmosphere.[98] He offered words of consolation to the family but also reminded the government dignitaries and members of the oligarchy present: "The church is not communist but is the hope of God, the hope of eternal life; it preaches hope, and the joy of what we hope for." The church, he said, rejects violence just as Christ does. "I have said so a thousand times, and none of its ministers preaches violence."[99]

That afternoon at 5:30 four men entered the rectory of Resurrection parish in San Salvador and shot Alfonso Navarro, the young pastor, and a fifteen-year-old boy of the parish. Navarro died after arriving at the hospital and, according to a witness, pardoning his murderers. The boy died the next morning.

President Molina called Romero that evening to offer condolences. Romero asked for a careful investigation of the murders.[100] Little had been done about the murders of March 12, and now, only two months later, the unthinkable had happened again—a priest cut down with an innocent parishioner. It was, if possible, even more senseless than the first killing, for a group calling itself the White Warrior Union said it had killed Navarro in retaliation for Borgonovo's death.[101]

Romero, who had buried the foreign minister on one day, buried another of his priests on the next. Two hundred priests from all over El Salvador concelebrated the funeral mass with him in Navarro's own church. The radio carried the archbishop's sermon, which opened with the words: "They tell how a caravan, guided by a desert Bedouin, was desperate with thirst and sought water in the mirages of the desert. The guide kept saying, 'No, not that way, this way.' This happened several times, until one of the caravan, his patience exhausted, took out a pistol and shot the guide, who, dying, still stretched out his hand to say, 'Not that way—this way.' And so he died, pointing the way. The legend becomes reality: a priest, pierced with bullets, who dies pardoning, who dies praying, gives his message to all of us who at this hour unite for his burial, and we wait to receive it."

Alfonso's message, continued Romero, was "a protest, a rejection of violence: 'They kill me because I point the way to follow.' And we, the church, repeat once more that violence resolves nothing, violence is not Christian, not human." Life is sacred—the life of the boy who lay dying and the life of the priest to be buried that day, just as much as the life of the foreign minister, who had been buried the day before. "Violence is produced by all, not only by those who kill but by those who urge to kill. I would like to address my words from here to the president of the republic— if what he told me yesterday by telephone is sincere, that he would be concerned to investigate this murder, just as he would be concerned and is concerned, I presume, about that of his foreign minister. The life of Mr. Borgonovo was sacred, but so was the life of the priest who is lost to us today, as was the life of Father Grande, who also was shot to death, two months ago. And in spite of the promises of investigation, we are still far from knowing the truth."

Violence, "even in those who merely do not do whatever is possible to uncover its origins, is criminal. In this campaign of slander, they are sinners as much as those who point the weapons to kill. How can they possibly be allowed to say this is only the beginning? How can they possibly be allowed to threaten to take more lives?"

The slanders and threats were continuing. Handbills had even appeared with the slogan, "Be a patriot, kill a priest."

Romero concluded with an appeal for unity. "This is not the hour, brothers and sisters, to be divided between two churches. It is the hour to feel ourselves one church that strives for Christ's resurrection, that brings redemption not only beyond death but here on earth; to strive for a world more just, more human; to strive for a social sensitivity that makes itself felt in every setting; to struggle against violence, against criminality."[102]

On May 13, the day after Navarro's funeral, the bishops' conference held a special meeting, along with the nuncio. The first item they discussed was the disunity they were noticing among themselves, even though in public they still preserved a façade of union.

Bishop Aparicio, the president, said he saw the cause of their disunion in the special mass that Archbishop Romero had held at the cathedral on March 20 after the death of Rutilio Grande. Romero objected that a bishop was the authority in his own diocese and that the mass was a diocesan matter. Aparicio and Bishop Alvarez mentioned the different attitudes that bishops showed toward "pro-Marxist" priests, a question that had been much discussed in the regular three-day meeting in January.

The bishops agreed that at the moment they must present a united front and must back Romero, for he had a difficult task. They were, however, still concerned about relations with the government. Romero reminded them that the president had shown a lack of sincerity by ignoring his own promises. He had promised to investigate seriously the murders and not deport priests without first taking the government's complaints to their bishop.

After this private discussion about themselves, the bishops met with the laymen who composed the church's National Justice and Peace Commission, who urged the bishops to issue a statement supporting the archbishop in the situation of violence and persecution that the church was facing. The bishops, they said, were the only ones who could speak out against the violence and it was important that they speak in unison. Bishop Revelo, auxiliary bishop of Santa Ana, and Monsignor Freddy Delgado, secretary of the bishops' conference, agreed to draw up a statement.[103] The following Tuesday, May 17, the bishops met again and approved the text of their pronouncement, which had been written by Revelo.

"We join with the archbishop of San Salvador and with him we condemn the wave of violence, of hatred, of slander, and of vengeance that overshadows the land," the statement said. "We share the sorrow that burdens his shepherd's heart before the cruel murder of two priests of his presbytery and the innocent victims that fell with them." The bishops condemned communism and capitalism, and went on to reject the Catholic traditionalism that the local press campaign was putting out to harass the church. "We would be false to our mission as shepherds if we were to reduce evangelization to mere practices of individualistic piety and disincarnate sacramentalism." They called for reflection, dialog, and unity. "To cling more and more to one's own advantage, ignoring the cry of the dispossessed, is to create a favorable climate for totalitarian violence."[104]

On the same day that the bishops were approving their statement, the government sent troops into the Aguilares area to evict peasant families that had occupied land on the Hacienda San Francisco at El Paisnal. The campesinos had long rented the land, but now the owner was evicting them and they had nowhere to live or to farm. The troops forced them out at gunpoint, and the next day two thousand soldiers with armored cars surrounded the town of Aguilares.

That night and the following day troops moved through the town, searching and ransacking houses. The government announced that one soldier and six civilians had been killed in an armed encounter. Eyewitnesses reported that at least fifty townspeople were shot dead and hundreds of others taken away. A soldier killed a parishioner who tried to ring the church bell in alarm. The three remaining Jesuits were seized in the early morning hours and quickly expelled from the country.[105] The pastor of Chalatenango, who was visiting Aguilares, was arrested and beaten. Romero was called the next day to come to the headquarters of the Guardia Nacional in the capital to get him.[106]

Romero tried to go to Aguilares himself to see the situation and to remove the Blessed Sacrament from the church, which the soldiers were using as a barracks. The army would not let him pass, and he then sent the chaplain of the Guardia Nacional. The guardsmen arrested the chaplain and kept him prisoner for an hour.[107] Soldiers shot open the tabernacle and strewed the hosts on the floor.[108]

About 4:00 P.M. on May 19 Romero went to meet the interior minister, who told him about the expulsion of the Jesuits. An hour later, he joined a meeting of the bishops with the president. Romero reminded the president once more of his promise not to expel priests without discussing their cases with their bishops. Not only were they expelled without a shadow of due process, but once again the government had published accusations of "subversive activities" to justify its action.

"In none of the now numerous expulsions of priests, for all that we have requested, have we received proof of the supposed subversive acts of these priests," said the archdiocese the next day. "We consider these deeds a clear proof that the government of the republic is bent on depriving the Catholic people of El Salvador of those priests who are committed to the service of the people. Persecution of the church is justified in the name of the struggle against atheistic communism. Some affirm that no such persecution exists. But in light of the facts and of the threats that hang over certain priests, to us and to the immense majority of the Catholic people the persecution is very clear."[109]

On May 23 Romero wrote a weary letter to Molina enumerating the cases of Sarsanedas, Navarro, the three Aguilares Jesuits, the Chalatenango pastor, and the desecration. "I do not understand, Mr. President, how you can declare yourself before the nation Catholic by upbringing and by conviction and yet allow these unspeakable outrages on the part of security forces in a country that we call civilized and Christian." He was also disturbed, he went on, by the slanders that the government was publishing about priests and about the church's pastoral activity. "Finally, I do not understand, Mr. President, the motives of the military authorities in not allowing me to go to the church of Aguilares to see for myself and to guarantee the church property of the Catholic people of Aguilares. Does the person of the archbishop also put in peril the security of the state?"[110]

May 29 was Pentecost Sunday. Romero had become archbishop just before Lent began. The church of San Salvador had lived some three months of hardship and death, of Lent and Holy Week. Nevertheless, Romero could see signs of resurrection and the new life of the Spirit.

In his homily he spoke of Pentecost as the beginning of the church. "What I have wanted to do is to define what the church is. Because in the measure in which the church defines itself, knows itself, in which it lives out what it is, it will be strong. The church has no enemies. Its only enemies are those who willfully declare themselves so." The church's essential mission is religious, to unite human beings to God. And human beings open up to God in prayer. "This is why the church preaches before all else its religious mission—to teach us how to pray."

Because of this religious mission, Romero continued, the church must defend "the signs of its transcendence"—the eucharist, trampled in Aguilares, and its priests, defamed and maltreated. The church also represents the security found in possessing the truth that it teaches. "This Spirit of truth is what gives the church power to preach, to write, to speak on the radio—to speak the Spirit of truth in the face of lies, to undo ambiguities." From its duty to speak the truth arises persecution. "Persecution is something necessary in the church. Do you know why? Because the truth is always persecuted. Jesus Christ said it: 'If they have persecuted me, they will also persecute you' " (John 15:20).[111]

From Carpenter to Bishop

1917–1976

Oscar Arnulfo Romero y Galdámez was born in Ciudad Barrios, in the department of San Miguel, at 3:00 A.M. on August 15, 1917. His parents were Santos Romero and Guadalupe de Jesús Galdámez.[1]

Ciudad Barrios, named for a nineteenth-century political figure, Gerardo Barrios, lies in the eastern part of El Salvador, only ten miles from the Honduran border. No road, however, connects it to Honduras, and until the 1940's it could be reached only on horseback or by foot from the rest of El Salvador. Its primitive name of Cacahuatique still adorns the mountain range that overlooks it and recalls the Indian people whose blood mingled with that of the conquerors to form the present people of El Salvador.

Ciudad Barrios is almost three thousand feet above sea level and noticeably cooler than the plains below. Steep wooded slopes surround it, and its cobblestone streets become torrents during rainstorms. Its tile roofs and adobe walls make it look like thousands of other Latin American towns. In Oscar Romero's childhood, most roofs were of thatch, according to an aged townsman. The Romero home, more solid than most, still stands on one corner of the main plaza, across from the domineering brick church that has replaced the church of Romero's childhood.

The child was almost two years old before he was baptized in the church across the square by Father Cecilio Morales on May 11, 1919. The priest noted in the baptismal register that he was the legitimate son of his parents and that his godparents were Josefa Gavidia and Lázaro Bernal, "to whom I explained what was necessary." Later hands have squeezed in the information that he was ordained a priest and made bishop of Santiago de María and metropolitan archbishop.[2]

Father Nazario Monroy, a townsman who was twelve years older than Oscar Romero, recalled that Santos, father of Oscar, "was not pious" and had to be given religious instruction before marrying,[3] a circumstance that suggests he lacked the rudiments of Christian doctrine, though he did teach his son to pray in early childhood, as a lament written by Oscar at his father's death testifies. He was from Jocoro, a town in the neighboring department of Morazán, and the government had sent him to Ciudad Barrios about 1903 as telegrapher and postmaster. The office was in the Romero home on the plaza, and the Romero children delivered letters and telegrams in the town. Oscar learned to send and receive telegrams, and one of his brothers followed their father's profession as a telegrapher. The work could hardly have been taxing for either father or children, and indeed Santos found time to grow cacao and coffee on twenty acres of hillside that his wife had inherited and that lay about two miles from town. The children early learned to milk the cow and help with chores.[4]

The family's means were modest, however, and one of Oscar's brothers recalled that various children shared one bed. Amenities like electricity were not missed, since no one else in town had them either. Light came from kerosene or carbide lamps, and the town boasted carbide street lights on the central square.

Guadalupe de Jesús, Oscar's mother, was from the town. Her photograph shows a square jaw that was even more pronounced in her son Oscar. Her first child was Gustavo, Oscar Arnulfo her second. Then followed Zaída, Rómulo (who died in 1939, while Oscar was studying in Rome), Mamerto, Arnoldo, and Gaspar. A daughter, Aminta, died at birth. Their father also had at least one illegitimate child, a daughter, who still lived in Ciudad Barrios at the time of Oscar Romero's death.[5]

Elderly townsfolk remembered Oscar as a serious child, studious and pious, though one may wonder if the memories owed something to his later history. A friend of the family recalled going into the woods to find the proper herbs to save the boy's life during a serious illness when he was small. A cousin recalled an illness "from the evil eye" at age seven.[6]

When he was old enough, Oscar entered the local public school, which offered only the first three grades. After that his parents sent him to study under a teacher named Anita Iglesias until he was twelve or thirteen.[7] The boy's father taught him to play the bamboo flute and to read music, and in the seminary he learned the piano and harmonium.[8] At some time in his life he acquired a taste for classical music, and as archbishop he often listened to it on his car radio. Marimba music was also a favorite of his by the time he was archbishop, if not long before.[9]

His father was against Oscar's studying further, and he apprenticed the boy to a carpenter, who after Romero's death still worked in the same shop where the future archbishop learned to make doors, chairs, tables, and coffins. The old man remembered him as the best of his apprentices, a serious boy who would stop to visit one of the town's two churches after work. From the church on the upper limit of the town, near the carpenter shop, he must often have looked out at the mountains of Honduras to the north and the peaks of Santa Ana in the west, almost all the way across El Salvador. At the time of Romero's death, a fellow apprentice still worked in the same shop and recalled that his brother had been a classmate of Oscar's in school. The old master carpenter proudly showed visitors a joiner's gauge that Oscar Romero made of mahogany and that still served in the making of coffins. On visits to Ciudad Barrios as priest and bishop, Romero would always stop in at the shop to say hello and inquire if the gauge was still in use.[10]

When Oscar was thirteen, in 1930, Father Monroy returned to the town from studies in Rome to offer his first mass. The vicar-general of the San Miguel diocese was present for the occasion, and young Oscar had a chance to speak with him about his desire to go to the seminary, a desire that it seems had arisen in him at the suggestion of the town's mayor.[11] Santos Romero was reluctant to let his son go, but soon Oscar did leave Ciudad Barrios for the minor seminary in San Miguel, run by the Claretians.[12] For a boy from a remote village, it was a big step.

San Miguel was seven hours by horseback down a winding trail. In 1930 it had a population of 17,569.[13] It is flat and hot, whereas Ciudad Barrios is mountainous and temperate. In time-honored fashion, Oscar sent his laundry home and the family sent it back clean on one of the mules of Juan Martínez, a merchant, or with their friend Jorge Gutiérrez, who rode his horse to San Miguel on business each Monday.

Oscar returned to the family for vacations. A younger brother remembered seeing him rise from the common bed during the night to pray. Like the town carpenter, others had noticed his visits to the churches even before he went to the seminary. Prayer was to become the force and mainstay of his life. As archbishop, Romero would sometimes quietly leave the intense discussions of his counselors on how the church should act in the continual crises, in order to go to the chapel and pray over his decision. The advisers learned to tell him to go and pray when they could not agree. "He always made the right decision that way," said one.

In later years, Romero remembered his years in the San Miguel seminary with pleasure. In 1962, as a priest in San Miguel, he wrote in the diocesan paper: "Under the shelter of Mary's Immaculate Heart, the Claretian Fathers and the seminarians were one family, with the same spirit as their founder, St. Antonio María Claret."[14] A poem that he wrote in the minor seminary reflects the view of the priesthood that was forming in him:

> Your word is pardon and gentleness for the penitent,
> your word is holy instruction, eternal teaching;
> it is light to brighten, advice to hearten;
> it is voice of hope, fire that burns,
> way, truth, sublime splendor,
> life — eternity.
> But not is the temple alone your battlefield:

> you range the world with your sword upraised,
> the redeeming cross. . . .[15]

In 1937 he went on to the national seminary in San Salvador, run by the Jesuits for the bishops, entering second year of theology studies.[16] A few months later, his father died. Oscar committed his grief to paper in a sort of prose poem that was found among his papers after his death:

> The sun goes slowly to its setting, the afternoon grows languid. My eyelids, drooping sadly, are robbing the day of its splendor, its joy, its light. How sad is the evening! . . .
> Everything, my God, speaks of sadness, of weeping.
> But, oh, within my breast today is an eventide more sorrowful. My gaze, lost beyond the distant peaks of the east, looks for comfort; but the east, my unforgettable east, has become for me a setting sun. . . .
> My father is dead! Dear Father, I who each evening turned my gaze to the distant east, sending you my loving distant thought, would think of you on the porch of the home I remembered, . . . would see you turning your gaze to the west where your son was. . . .
> Only the memories remain, memories of childhood—how you would pace the bedroom floor as my child's understanding memorized the Our Father, the Hail Mary, the Creed, the Hail Holy Queen, the commandments that your fatherly lips taught me. . . . I still see you one night waiting for us to return with Mother from our trip to San Miguel, waiting with a toy for each of us made with your own hands. . . .[17]

At midyear, Romero's bishop sent him to Rome for the rest of his studies. Although he had made a year and a half of theology studies in El Salvador, he would start in first year in the Gregorian University. Awaiting him in Rome was his good friend from the San Miguel seminary, Rafael Valladares, who became an auxiliary bishop of San Salvador in 1956. He and Romero remained close friends until his death in 1961. In 1979, on the anniversary of Valladares's death, Romero noted in his diary,[18] "I still feel him very near."

A Venezuelan seminarian who boarded the ship Romero was on when it stopped at La Guaira recalled their meeting:

> It was the first time I left my country and I was eighteen years old. The separation from everything I considered my own pained me deeply. I boarded the ship, tearing myself away from my family tearfully, and I went to look for the assigned cabin. Right there on the deck of the ship I met a seminarian of my own age, also in cassock and browned like me from the tropical sun, and we had the following dialog.

He asked me, "Are you going to Rome?"

"Yes."

"Me too. To the Gregorian University?"

"Yes."

"Me too. To first year theology?"

"Yes."

"Me too."

A bit annoyed for what in my sorrow seemed a mockery, I said, "My name is Alfonso Alfonzo Vaz."

He laughed with that candor of his and, offering me his hand, said, "I can't say 'Me too' to that. My name is Oscar Romero, and we're going to be great classmates."

The next eleven days on the Italian ship became an adventure for them and other seminarians also going to Rome. They joked with the new Italian words they were learning and let the ship's photographer take a few pictures, expensive for seminarians' pockets, for future memories. Oscar would serve two or three masses each morning for the various priests on board, including the nuncio to El Salvador, who was being replaced. At night, he would invite the others to say the rosary with him on deck instead of going to the movies, which he said were old and insipid.[19] If he disliked movies then, his taste later changed, since he loved to attend them when on vacation trips as a bishop.[20] In El Salvador he apparently felt too self-conscious to go.

Pius XI was pope when Romero arrived in Rome. The pope's opposition to Fascism and Nazism impressed Romero, who remained devoted to him the rest of his life. When the pope died in February 1939, the seminarian approached the catafalque to put his hand on the dead pope's right arm.[21] During Romero's last trip to Rome, in 1980, while visiting Pius XI's tomb he told the priest who accompanied him, "This is the pope I most admire," and he recalled Pius's words: "While I am pope, no one will laugh at the church."[22]

The Latin American seminarians lived at the Latin American College, operated by the Jesuits. Their studies were at the Gregorian University under Jesuit professors. A friend and fellow student of those years, Monsignor Carlos F. Enríquez, of Ciudad Juárez, Mexico, remembered Romero as "of medium height, dark complexion, deliberate bearing, like one who is not hurried to arrive because he knows he will get there. With other persons he was peaceable, calm—like one who knows that life has to be taken as it comes—rather quiet, a bit shy." Oscar's intellectual capacity, he recalls, was above average, and his writing and speaking ability especially notable. "His conduct was irreproachable; I never knew of anything that would lessen this judgment. He was observant of the regulations, pious, concerned for his priestly training in every aspect. With others, he could make friends and was regarded by us who were his friends for his simplicity and desire to help."[23]

The seminarians spent vacations at a villa by the sea or in the mountains. Oscar, who was a good swimmer, became the unofficial instructor for those who could not swim. Father Alfonzo Vaz recalls that once Oscar challenged the rest to swim out to a rock and, arriving first, sat on the rock to await the others. Unfortunately, he sat on a nest of sea urchins, which left him unable to sit anywhere for days. Bravely or self-consciously, he said nothing to the other seminarians, but the infirmarian gave him away.[24]

In September 1939 Italy and Europe were caught up in the conflagration of World War II. Pius XII had succeeded Pius XI a half-year before. About the war years, Romero wrote in 1962:

> Europe and almost the whole world were a conflagration during the Second World War. Fear, uncertainty, news of bloodshed made for an environment of dread. At the Latin American College rations grew smaller by the day. Father Rector would go out looking for something to eat and return with squashes, onions, chestnuts, whatever he could find, under his cloak. Hunger forced several Italian seminaries to close. The Latin American College had to cope with the situation, since all of its students were foreigners away from home; those who could return to their homelands took their chances in doing so. Those who stayed suffered more than ever from the separation. Almost every night sirens warned of enemy planes and one had to run for the shelters; twice they were more than an alarm and Rome's outskirts were scarred by horrible bombings.[25]

Romero received the licentiate degree in theology *cum laude* after the 1940–41 school year.[26] Since he was not yet twenty-four years old, as required by church law, he had to wait to be ordained a priest and was finally ordained on April 4, 1942, in the college chapel.[27] In March 1940 he had published in the house magazine of the Latin American College some reflections on the priesthood as a sharing in the cross and resurrection of Christ. "This is your heritage as a priest: the cross. And this is your mission: to portion out the cross. Bearer of pardon and peace, the priest approaches the bed of the dying, and a cross in his hand is the key that opens the heavens and closes the abyss." And he summed up his thoughts saying that the priesthood means "to be, with Christ, a crucified one who redeems and to be, with Christ, a risen one who apportions resurrection and life."[28]

Romero and Valladares, who had been ordained in 1940, stayed on in Rome to take doctoral degrees in theology. Romero specialized in ascetical theology, planning a dissertation on Christian perfection in different states of life according to the teaching of Luis de la Puente, a sixteenth-century Spanish ascetical writer.[29] While working on it, he noted one day in his diary:[30] "In recent days, after reading some of Father la Puente at the curia, principally the life of Father Alvarez, the Lord has inspired in me a great desire for holiness. I've been thinking of how far a soul can ascend if it lets itself be possessed entirely by God. It is a shame to waste such precious time and such valuable gifts."

Before he could finish the doctorate work, he returned to El Salvador, no doubt summoned by his bishop. He and Valladares left Rome in August 1943, just after Romero's twenty-sixth birthday,[31] stopping in Spain and Cuba. Because they were coming from Italy, the Cuban police arrested them and put them into an internment camp. There the harsh conditions made Valladares ill, but Redemptorist priests in Havana learned of their plight and got them to a hospital. Eventually, the Cubans decided they were not enemy aliens, and they were able to sail to Mexico and then travel by land to El Salvador, arriving at Christmastide to a public reception in the central plaza of San Miguel.[32]

Back home at last, young Father Romero offered solemn mass for his friends and relatives in Ciudad Barrios. After Romero's death a family member of Father Monroy in Ciudad Barrios still treasured a souvenir card with the prayer:

May this sacrifice that we offer please you, O Lord. Govern with constant protection your servant, the Roman Pontiff. — Oscar A. Romero — my first solemn mass, Ciudad Barrios, January 11, 1944.

The bishop quickly sent Romero as parish priest to the town of Anamorós, in the department of La Unión.[33] Young priests in priest-scarce Latin America become pastors quickly. Like Ciudad Barrios, Anamorós is a mountain town. A stained snapshot shows Romero during this time with two campesinos, looking very thin in cassock and round clerical hat.[34]

After a few months the bishop called Romero to San Miguel to be secretary of the diocese, a post he was to hold for the next twenty-three years. Oscar's mother also moved to San Miguel with her youngest child, and lived there with her daughter. Her health was poor, and in her last years her left arm was paralyzed. The family farm had been lost to a mortgage holder after her husband's death, and the other sons had also left Ciudad Barrios. Until her death in 1961 she remained close to Oscar in San Miguel, where she is buried. Her husband is buried in Ciudad Barrios.[35]

As secretary, Romero set to work. Valladares became editor of *Chaparrastique,* the diocesan weekly (from San Miguel's primitive name, which still graces a nearby extinct volcano), and Romero helped him and filled in when Valladares was away. Later he became editor of the paper and continued until he left San Miguel. The two complemented each other, Valladares cheerful and outgoing, Romero more retiring. But both were energetic and dynamic.

In El Salvador, most priests do several jobs, each of which would be considered full-time in many other places, but Romero's activity was prodigious. He soon became pastor of the cathedral parish, living and centering his parish activities at the nearby church of Santo Domingo, and chaplain of the little colonial church of San Francisco, where the venerated image of Our Lady of Peace was housed while the cathedral remained unfinished. Our Lady of Peace is the patroness of El Salvador, after the Divine Savior himself. Romero remained devoted to her and to the image in San Miguel all his life. As pastor of the cathedral, he had the image under his care and directed great activity to promoting devotion to Our Lady of Peace.[36]

Residents of San Miguel long remembered Romero's years there. He completed the cathedral's construction. He grew famous as a preacher, and at one time five radio stations in the small city simultaneously broadcast his Sunday morning mass, according to a co-worker. He visited the countryside and the city jails. He organized catechism classes and first communions. He promoted the Legion of Mary, the Knights of the Holy Sepulcher, Alcoholics Anonymous, Catholic Action, the Cursillos de Cristiandad, the Apostleship of Prayer, the Guardians of the Blessed Sacrament, the Holy Rosary Association, the Third Order of St. Francis,[37] and the diocesan branch of Caritas, which distributes food to the poor. He saw to it that Caritas also taught the people about nutrition. "He was always concerned with the whole person's welfare," said a woman who worked with him for years in various activities in San Miguel. Salvador Barraza, who first met him by going to hear his sermons in 1959, recalled that in his preaching he insisted on a religion that dealt with daily life and not mere piety. As time went on, he became editor of *Chaparrastique,* rector of the minor seminary, and confessor of various religious congregations. When the bishop was away, Romero governed the diocese.[38]

He made enemies as well as friends. Protestants resented attacks on them in his sermons and accused him of idolatry because of his devotion to the Blessed Virgin's image. He offended many by not letting them use the cathedral for a ceremony honoring the nineteenth-century patriot Gerardo Barrios because Barrios was a Mason. By refusing Christian burial to Masons he alienated various families.

Raúl Romero (not a relative) lived in Romero's house from 1952 to 1955 in a relationship, common in Latin America, of employee-foster son. Raúl was fourteen in 1952 and had known Father Romero through catechism class from the age of ten or twelve. The boy helped with housework and received a home, support, and education. When he was seventeen, Romero helped him enter the seminary in San Salvador, which he later left.

Raúl recalled Father Romero as both kind and demanding. In catechism class he would question the children about the previous Sunday's gospel to encourage them to listen during mass. He was generous in giving to the poor, even though frauds often abused his generosity. Raúl accompanied Romero to the local prison, where each week he offered the convicts not only mass but movies to relieve the drabness of their lives. Raúl recalled the time Romero went to visit a prisoner who was confined to his cell during the film as punishment. His parish extended into the countryside, and Raúl remembered visits to the outlying villages, where children would come running to greet him.

In the church each evening Romero held a holy hour for the people before the Blessed Sacrament exposed, always saying the rosary with them and preaching. Prayer and meditation were part of his own daily routine, and he said his masses with great care and solemnity.

Raúl remembered him as cheerful and agreeable, but capable of showing his anger if, for example, he was not given a phone message. When Raúl married in 1963 in San Salvador, Father Romero performed the ceremony and remained a friend of the family in later years, baptizing the children and giving them their first communions, and often visiting the family until his death.

About 1954 or 1955, Romero made the monthlong Spiritual Exercises of St. Ignatius Loyola under Miguel Elizondo, then master of novices for the Jesuits' Central American province. Romero stayed at the Salesians' high school in Santa Tecla and walked to the novitiate a block away each day to confer with Elizondo.[39] The novitiate building enclosed an orchard and garden that he and the novices could share with the grackles and the hummingbirds.

The Spiritual Exercises are a school of religious experience lasting about a month. The one making the Exercises spends several hours a day in prayer and perhaps an hour or so conferring with the director, whose task is to help the person recognize the promptings of grace in prayer. The material offered for meditation and prayer is designed to lead to a more generous following of Christ, who invites the person to help extend his reign through service in the church.

Romero had been at least indirectly exposed to Ignatian spirituality through his Jesuit teachers in San Salvador and Rome. There is nothing else like making the Exercises themselves, however. Notes that he made during retreats in later years as a priest and as a bishop testify that the Exercises were a fundamental force in his life. He later took a phrase from the Exercises as his episcopal motto: *"Sentir con la Iglesia"* — "To Be of One Mind and Heart with the Church."

From 1962 to 1965, Romero watched as Vatican Council II began to stir the waters of the church, and he would later show that he had read and pondered its pronouncements. During a retreat he made in January 1966, just after the close of the council, he noted the council's demand for the church's renewal, especially directed to priests, as the first reason for him to reform his life. He had been reading the statements of the council and the pope's addresses to it, as well as Pope John XXIII's spiritual account, *Diary of a Soul.* He noted in particular that Pope John used the same Ignatian Exercises and the same practices of piety as himself.

Though Romero evidently saw the council as a personal call to himself as a priest of the church, he by no means sympathized with all the tendencies that appeared in the church after the council. Young priests who appeared without cassocks, even without any sign of their priesthood, who were familiar with women, who were so restless to change the church and the world—all met his disapproval. By now he was long established as the most powerful priest in the city, with virtually all lay movements centered in his parish, besides being the bishop's secretary, rector of the minor seminary, and editor of the diocesan newspaper. Other priests resented his monopoly of power coupled with uncompromising attitudes and severe ways, and on one occasion asked the bishop to remove him from power.[40]

Shortly before celebrating his silver anniversary as a priest on April 4, 1967, Romero received the title of monsignor. But it was the beginning of his departure from San Miguel. A new bishop had taken over a year before, one more energetic and less inclined to delegate to Romero than the former one; in the notes he wrote during his January 1966 retreat Romero revealed that he had foreseen difficulties for himself. A few months after his silver anniversary celebration Monsignor Romero was named secretary-general of the national bishops' conference, which required his moving to San Salvador. Friends and supporters pleaded and signed petitions for him to stay, but to no avail.[41] On September 1, 1967, he celebrated his last mass as pastor and set out at 8:00 A.M. for San Salvador. On the way, he stopped to see friends and spent the night at the rural home of one. Without the burden of responsibility for the first time in many years, he slept soundly.[42]

Romero took up residence in the seminary in San Salvador, sharing with the Jesuits their meals and conversations. He plunged into his work as secretary, and his efficiency and dedication pleased the bishops. Jesuits of the seminary would often see his light on until late at night.[43] In May 1968 Romero became executive secretary of the Central American Bishops' Secretariat, in addition to his duties with the national conference.[44]

In 1969 El Salvador went to war with Honduras for a few days, not over a soccer game, as much of the foreign press reported, but over the expulsion by the Honduran government of thousands of Salvadoran residents. El Salvador's unequal land tenure and growing population made emigration necessary for many Salvadorans, especially campesinos, and Honduras was, and is still, thinly populated. During the life of Oscar Romero, El Salvador's population quadrupled, from 1,287,722 in 1917[45] to about five million in 1980. The closing of the Honduran escape valve in 1969 and the return of tens of thousands accentuated social and political tensions in El Salvador in the following years. With the Honduran expulsion, a momentary wave of war fever swept over El Salvador and produced bellicose statements from various churchmen, even the gentle Archbishop Chávez.[46]

Chávez had known Romero since the 1940's and now asked to have him as an auxiliary bishop.[47] On April 21, 1970, the nuncio called Romero about 6:00 P.M. and asked for an acceptance or rejection of the appointment the next day. Romero hastily consulted two priest advisers and his doctor and accepted. But in the retreat he made in June he wondered if he had acted properly, feeling that his conscience had been uncertain about the decision and his motives mixed. He endeavored in the retreat to rectify his motives, feeling reassured by the trust the pope and the nuncio had shown in him and by the positive reaction of many persons to the announcement of his naming. At the same time, he noted as his greatest fear his relations with other priests, resolving to show them his love and offer them his sincere friendship and mediation.[48]

In a retreat he made in Mexico City almost two years later, he again noted what he saw as some deficiency in his motives at both his priestly and episcopal ordinations. At the former, he felt, he had been immature and uncertain about his calling to celibacy and moved partly by fear of changing course and of what people would say if he did; at the latter, he had felt similar qualms about his calling and also motives of vanity mixed in with his desire to serve God and the church. In accord with the Spiritual Exercises of St. Ignatius Loyola, he now prayed for God's pardon for whatever was previously lacking in his motives and directed the effort of the retreat towards purifying them, saying that he wanted nothing else in his priestly life but God's glory, the church's service, and his own salvation.

Romero's comments in these retreats seem to reflect the normal qualms that anyone feels at momentous decisions, but intensified in a man who demanded perfection of himself. Even as he recognized the perfectionism of his personality, Romero continued to exhibit it in the very detailed plans for reforming his life that he outlined during retreats, plans that required him to follow the quasi-monastic daily order he had learned in the seminary, plus fulfill the responsibilities of priest or bishop; this perfectionism was also revealed in his accusing himself of sacrilege in his perceived lack of fervor in saying mass and going to confession. His self-doubts must be seen in the context of his powerful desire to serve God and the church and to conform to the ideals he set himself.

His many friends wanted to make the episcopal ordination a big event. He later explained in a radio interview that the idea was to make the ordination an occasion for the people to understand better what a bishop means to the church. The Cursillos de Cristiandad, one of the movements that Romero moderated, sponsored the ceremony, and present were the papal nuncio, Archbishop Gerolamo Prigione; Cardinal Mario Casariego of Guatemala; Bishop Luis Manresa, president of the Central American Bishops' Secretariat, of which Romero was secretary; and all the bishops of El Salvador.

The ordination took place on June 21 in the gymnasium of the Liceo Salvadoreño, a Marist Brothers' high school. President Fidel Sánchez Hernández, other civil dignitaries, and busloads of people from San Miguel were also there. Rutilio Grande spent weeks arranging the ceremony and acted as master of ceremonies on the big day.[49] Photographs, often republished, show him with Chávez, Rivera, and Romero as they left the hall, Romero with his hand raised in blessing.

Not everyone was happy with the ceremony or with Romero's naming. For some who had pondered the new direction given the church by Vatican II and the pronouncements of the Latin American bishops at Medellín in 1968, Romero seemed still wedded to the old ways and his ostentatious ordination an offense to the many who lived in dire poverty in El Salvador.[50] But, no doubt, for the many who came from San Miguel it was simply a show of respect and affection for an admired pastor and friend.

The day after Romero's ordination as bishop, the national pastoral week began. The Latin American church had held the bishops' Medellín conference in 1968 in order to apply Vatican II to Latin America. The pastoral week (really five days, Monday to Friday) was meant to bring Vatican II and Medellín to El Salvador. Priests, men and women religious, and lay workers from the whole country—123 strong—gathered in San Salvador for the discussions. Although a national event, it was dominated by the archdiocese of San Salvador. This was not surprising; indeed it was virtually inevitable. The archdiocese contained over half the clergy and the only large city of the country. An archbishop is by office the first among equals, and in the church's structure is expected to show a certain leadership among the bishops as "metropolitan." Among the bishops of El Salvador, moreover, Archbishop Chávez and his auxiliary, Bishop Rivera, had shown themselves most aware of the new life of the church and most interested in updating their pastoral methods.

Rivera had organized the week. He and Chávez participated actively all five days, but Romero registered for the week on the first morning "and was not present full time," according to the minutes, which noted in consideration, however, that he had been ordained bishop only the day before. On the second afternoon, he was present when the assembly agreed to send telegrams to the other four bishops, who were absent, asking them to come. Romero objected, according to the minutes, because Rivera, the head of the pastoral commission of the bishops' conference, was present and therefore the others were not required to be there. Besides, he said, the telegrams could wound feelings and give rise to misunderstandings. Others replied that the pastoral week needed the presence of the primary pastors, and the assembly voted Romero down.

In response to the telegrams, Bishop Benjamín Barrera, of Santa Ana, came for the last two days, Bishop José Castro, of Santiago de María, replied that he had to take care of the parishes abandoned by priests attending the pastoral week, and Bishop José Eduardo Alvarez, of San Miguel, did not reply and did not come. Bishop Pedro Arnoldo Aparicio had come to San Salvador on the first day, felt ill on arriving, and spent the day resting at the Salesians' residence (he was a Salesian, like Rivera), returning in the evening to San Vicente. According to the minutes, he did not return because priests at the meeting were not wearing cassocks.

Naturally enough, the pastoral week had less effect in the outlying dioceses, whose bishops had shown so little enthusiasm for it. In the arch-diocese it confirmed the work already begun by Chávez and Rivera. Else-where it influenced various priests, religious, and active lay people who had attended, according to Father (later Bishop) Gregorio Rosa, who served on a commission that prepared the revised form of the week's conclusions.[51]

The new pastoral methods coming into use in those years furthered the training of lay leaders, catechists, and delegates of the word (lay persons delegated by the community to lead Bible discussions and prayer services), as well as the formation of communities among campesinos. Bible study and a communitarian approach to the sacraments figured prominently. Not only first communion, but confirmation, marriage, and the baptism of one's children were to be preceded by obligatory instruction in the faith. Lay catechists as well as priests and religious would give the instruction, thus letting the laity participate in the church's ministry and extending the church's reach to many who otherwise scarcely felt its touch.

The basic ideas of liberation theology were already current in such gath-erings in Latin America and were also embedded in the Medellín docu-ments: that God does not will social injustice, but rather the opposite, and that people must work and struggle with God's help to bring about justice. Such ideas immediately challenge the social order and those in power and lead to political conflict. To a person schooled in a vision of life in which one must accept suffering and seek peace and harmony at any price, such ideas involve a considerable readjustment of attitudes and preconceptions.

It would be wrong, however, to think that Oscar Romero was stubbornly unwilling to accept Vatican II. As a man of the church, trained in Rome, devoted to the pope as head of the church, as a bishop who had taken the motto "To Be of One Mind and Heart with the Church," he meant to keep pace with the church; but he was not ready to draw from the church's pronouncements all the conclusions that others were drawing.

After the pastoral week was over, Bishop Rivera found it under attack in the bishops' conference. In their July meeting, the bishops of San Vicente and San Miguel denied that the week had enjoyed national backing and attacked its conclusions. Romero had defended the week's national char-acter during the week but now sided with the opponents. Since Rivera saw it as a national gathering, he had no difficulty in agreeing to have a com-mission named by the bishops revise the conclusions and tone them down.[52] On the commission were Rivera himself, Romero, and three priests from different dioceses. Rosa, who was on the commission, recalled that they went over every phrase.

The conclusions started off wrong, as far as certain bishops were con-cerned, by opening with the words: "We, the church in El Salvador—lay people, religious, priests, and bishops. . . ." In a hierarchical church the bishops should be named first, the critics argued. Neither did they like the way the conclusions seemed to lay down the law for the church of the nation. Rosa[53] felt that some of the objections were well founded. A vocal, clear-sighted minority had at times stampeded the voting, as can easily happen when some see their way clearly and others have not yet thought out the matter or formulated their objections.

Rivera recalled with a smile that by way of commentary a group of priests later published the revised and the unrevised versions of the conclusions in parallel columns so that all could see how they were toned down. Regardless of the fuss, he felt that the week accentuated a bolder course of pastoral action, more committed to the lines of Vatican II and Medellín.

The Jesuits at the seminary noticed that Bishop Romero did not spend as much time with them as he had as a monsignor. It seems natural that episcopal duties and social functions would take him out more. About this time, too, he became close to priests of the secular institute Opus Dei, often visiting their house near the seminary. He made priests' retreats directed by them and chose one as his confessor.[54] When he was bishop of Santiago de María, he wrote in 1975 to the pope appealing for the beatification of the founder of Opus Dei, who had recently died, adding, "Personally, I owe deep gratitude to the priests of the Work [opus Dei means work of God] to whom I have confided with great satisfaction the spiritual direction of my life and that of other priests."[55] Later, as archbishop, Romero took as his confessor Segundo Azcue, an elderly Jesuit living at the residence in Santa Tecla, five miles from San Salvador. But, while he once criticized Opus Dei during a homily, he remained friendly to it and after dinner with Opus Dei members on September 6, 1979, he praised it in his diary as "a mine of wealth for our church."

In September or October of 1970, Romero's friend Salvador Barraza found him ill one day at the seminary, where he still lived. He had caught a cold while giving a retreat to nuns in the mountains near Santa Ana and now had a fever and a cough.

"Come on, I'm taking you home," said Barraza.

"He's come to kidnap me," joked Romero as he meekly left the seminary for the Barraza home. Their little house was tucked tightly between two others of the same size. Barraza was a shoe merchant, able to afford a house and car, both small. Romero was already a frequent visitor to the home, especially since 1968, when he had often brought holy communion to Salvador's wife, Eugenia, while she spent months recovering from an accident.

Romero's sermons had attracted Barraza to his masses in 1959 when he found himself frequently in San Miguel on business. They gradually became friends, and in 1967 Barraza moved Romero's possessions to San Salvador with his truck. He recalls that Romero's chief concern was the safety of his bookcase on the trip. In San Salvador they became closer friends, especially after Romero's concern for Eugenia in her period as an invalid. Now it was her turn to nurse him, rubbing his chest and back with motherly care.

"He let himself be treated like a child," she said.

The fever passed, but the respiratory ailment hung on and he spent about two months in the Barraza home. Bishops and priests came to call, including Father Patrick Peyton, who was conducting his family rosary campaign in El Salvador. Romero's Opus Dei confessor came for confession. The dining table became his daily altar and eight-year-old Lupe his sacristan. It was the beginning of a closeness in which he became "like a second father" to her, said Eugenia.

Salvador became perhaps his most intimate friend, his companion on pastoral visits to parishes as archbishop, trips to the doctor, vacations in Mexico and Guatemala. As an independent small-business man, Barraza could find the time to be Romero's volunteer chauffeur. (Romero drove a car, "but he always did it badly," said Barraza with a smile.) The unknowing sometimes took them to be brothers. Barraza prized snapshots of the two of them on vacation trips in Mexico.

In 1972, Romero baptized Barraza's second daughter, Virginia, and at the same time became her godfather and thus her parents' *compadre* (co-parent). The relationship of *compadre* in Latin America is a sign of commitment, joining one to another more surely than that of, say, in-law. For one chooses one's *compadres,* but not always one's in-laws. For Romero, the Barrazas became in time his family, giving him undemanding love and devotion. In their tile-floored sitting room he would tease and play with the children, take off his shoes and doze in a plastic-and-aluminum lawn chair in front of the television, and open Christmas gifts as eagerly as the children. At their dinner table he would joke and occasionally talk of his sorrows, once even shedding tears when speaking of the opposition of other bishops to him. When he became archbishop, he brought the papal document to their home to show them. As archbishop, he would go on picnics with them to Balboa Park on the heights above the city or to the country house of a congregation of Sisters. Sometimes he and Salvador alone would go the Sisters' house, perched on a mountainside and accessible only by a dirt road, and he would pass the day reading, listening to his portable radio, and snoring in his hammock.

In May 1971 Archbishop Chávez named Romero editor of the archdiocesan newspaper, *Orientación,* to replace Father Rutilio Sánchez, under whom the paper had aroused controversy by focusing on El Salvador's social questions. When Sánchez went so far as to praise the Colombian guerrilla priest, Camilo Torres, Archbishop Chávez removed him.[56] Readers noticed a sharp change when Romero took over. The focus shifted to less controversial topics like drugs, alcoholism, and pornography, and to more cautious views of social questions, when they were mentioned. Romero had arranged for a layman with publishing experience, Emilio Simán, to become managing editor, but after a year and a half, Romero parted with Simán and took more direct control of the editorial content, sharing the work with a layman and an editorial staff of university students and priests.[57]

On May 27, 1973, *Orientación* published an editorial that set off an attack on the Jesuits' high school, Externado San José (the school began as an "extern" branch of the seminary), that raged for a full month. The year before, a new Jesuit administration in the school had begun to introduce into the school ideas from Medellín and recommendations by the Jesuits' Latin American provincials. Evening classes opened up the once exclusive school to youths from the poorest sections of the city. Students began to venture out on field trips in sociology courses to see the reality of poverty that they and their families had hitherto been blind to. The school magazine pointed out the conflict of the values they learned in school with those they found at home. Some of the parents reacted.

Romero lit the fuse that set off the explosion. The editorial admitted the need for profound changes in educational systems but denounced the "demagogy" of "certain pedagogs" of "a false liberating education," and the lack of charity and respect for the memory of former teachers. Apparently a few parents, friends of Romero, had convinced him that the school — unnamed in the editorial, but clearly referred to — had overstepped the bounds. The reference to old teachers suggests that some conservative Jesuits sympathized with the parents; at the time, the Jesuits were undergoing the same strains that other religious groups were, complicated by the shift from Spanish to Central American leadership. The new principal of the school was a Nicaraguan and the new Jesuit provincial was a Salvadoran.

Orientación applauded the support of the Medellín conference for liberating education but not the "demagogy and Marxism" it found in "the pamphlets and literature, of known red origin, spread in a certain school." The next day the secular papers took up the cry of Marxism, and before the month was out the attorney general of the republic had begun an investigation and called various Jesuits to testify about what was taught in the school. The newspapers overflowed with tendentious accounts, and radio and television were filled with the controversy. The Jesuits published a lengthy defense of their actions and received the public backing of the archdiocese[58] and the conference of religious.[59] At the end of all the commotion, 92 percent of all parents of students gave the school administration a vote of approval.[60]

Archbishop Chávez was unhappy that newspapers had reprinted Romero's editorial as the view of the Salvadoran church, and he named a commission of priests to investigate the charges against the school. When the commission exonerated the school, Chávez asked Romero to publish its report, but Romero put it on the last page with the headline "Archbishop Defends Externado San José" and in the same issue attacked the members of the commission as persons who followed questionable opinions instead of the sure teaching of the church. In the following weeks Romero reprinted various articles from religious magazines on the evils of "certain fashionable theologies" that invoked "dangerous Marxist positions," as well as selections of church condemnations of Marxism. In the August 12 issue, he published an article on what he saw as malicious interpretations of Medellín; the article was entitled "Medellín, Misunderstood and Mutilated."[61]

In 1973–74, *ECA* published a study of *Orientación* and of a publication called *Justicia y Paz* edited by Father Fabián Amaya under the protection of Bishop Rivera.[62] The study of Romero's editorship concluded: "The paper criticizes injustice in the abstract but criticizes methods of liberation in the concrete."[63] *Orientación,* they said, defended the established order, was directed at a public "satisfied with the present situation," concealed the roots of national problems, and took a defensive attitude before the transformation of the nation that was needed.[64] If the judgment was harsh, still no one could deny that *Orientación* had changed.

The *ECA* article stung Romero, who thought that Bishop Rivera was behind it, as Rivera recalled later. The two did not get along, though they never fought, said Rivera. As auxiliary, Romero was a part of the clergy of the archdiocese and therefore expected to take an active part in its pastoral life. Yet he never attended the monthly clergy meetings or meetings of the priests' senate, of which he was automatically a member. Romero appeared to Rivera to feel that the circle in which Rivera moved was unduly critical of authority, besides being infected with dangerous ideas. Rivera felt that Romero never trusted him while the two were auxiliary bishops.[65]

Toward the end of 1971 Romero left for a rest in Mexico. His absence stretched to four months. Father Jaime Martínez, who had been helping him in the office of the Central American Bishops' Secretariat, was named in January 1972 to fill in also for him in the Salvadoran bishops' conference. The minutes of the conference's meeting of February 8 noted that Bishop Romero was in Mexico "in search of health."

Later, when Romero was archbishop, he regularly consulted Dr. Rodolfo Semsch, a clinical psychologist, whom he had known since 1973, when Romero was rector of the seminary and Dr. Semsch gave psychological tests to seminarians. In an interview six months after Romero's death, Dr. Semsch explained that Romero did not consult him for psychotherapy, but for a psychologist's viewpoint of his life, much as he consulted his confessor for spiritual guidance. (Romero also discussed his work as pastor of the archdiocese with both men,[66] as he did with other persons.)

Members of the oligarchy, said Dr. Semsch, tried hard to prove that Romero was mentally ill, but he denied that Romero was neurotic or psychotic. He described Romero as a strong personality of great energy who experienced intense pressures in his life and reacted in a natural fashion with aggressiveness and fatigue. If he had at any time been mentally ill, said Dr. Semsch, his enemies would have discovered it. In any case, Semsch said, the proof of Romero's mental and emotional health was the balance he sustained under tremendous pressure during his three years as archbishop. Romero himself commented in his diary in November 1979 that his interviews with Dr. Semsch were "very profitable for verbalizing problems that with his help I try to solve in a calmer and surer fashion."

Long before becoming archbishop, however, Romero lived under pressure. As seminarian, priest, and bishop, he conformed to the exalted idea of church authority that reigned until after Vatican II and that he only gradually balanced with a greater evangelical freedom as archbishop. Strong-willed and seemingly born to lead, he yet submitted unquestioningly to a structure that encouraged conformity. In Dr. Semsch's view, it was only as archbishop that Romero at last found his full identity and freedom.[67]

Friends and associates remember Romero as both demanding and warm, both impatient and willing to listen to other views. The Barraza family recalls that as archbishop he once stayed away from their house for several weeks after Salvador failed to keep an appointment to drive him somewhere. He resumed their relationship without any formal making-up. He often seemed timid and insecure in contacts with individuals, though obviously vigorous, self-assured, and self-revealing when preaching. Father Fabián Amaya, who knew him well as archbishop, viewed his timidity as a fear of hurting others, rather than as shyness.[68]

Romero's retreat notes show that as early as 1966, he was consulting a doctor over the stress that he experienced in his life. He noted in January of that year that he had left the retreat house to seek his confessor and his doctor during the retreat. The latter, he noted, diagnosed him as a compulsive obsessive perfectionist, and the retreat notes show Romero fervently proposing for himself a detailed reform of his daily life, which seems to bear out his perfectionism or—in traditional ascetical terminology—scrupulosity.

In Mexico in November 1971 he noted down his faults as he saw them: avoiding social relations with others, not getting to know people, concern about being criticized, perfectionism, disorder in his work, lack of austerity, lack of courage in speaking out and defending his opinions. In February 1972, he began Lent with a retreat in Mexico City and noted down at greater length his view of himself in light of his experience of over a year as a bishop and almost thirty years as a priest, now seen with greater maturity, and after three months of psychoanalysis, which he viewed as an instance of God's providence in his life. He saw in himself a certain timidity flowing from subconscious attitudes transferred from his childhood to his adult relationships. He wanted to be more natural and spontaneous, warmer in his attitudes to others, and to overcome his timidity in expressing himself, especially when he felt he was defending the faith and the church's doctrine. (This was over a year before his editorial attacking the teaching in the Externado.) At the same time, he noted how his perfectionism produced rigidity in his character and caused him to grow angry if things were not as he wished. And the rigidity in turn produced insecurity, since it made him less natural and more fearful of mistakes. A serious effect of all this was that he would take refuge in work, which in turn kept him from better relationships with others and intensified the problem. He resolved to try to break the cycle by regulating his work and giving time and attention to his relations with people.

When Romero returned from Mexico, he seemed to Jaime Martínez more rested, slightly euphoric.[69] He plunged once again into work. In September he ended his term as executive secretary of the Central American Bishops' Secretariat.[70] He continued as secretary-general of the Salvadoran bishops' conference, however, and as editor of *Orientación*.

For several years the bishops had been discussing the major seminary of San José de la Montaña. In 1968 the Jesuit provincial, at that time Segundo Azcue, suggested that the Jesuits retire from the seminary, which they had operated since 1915 for the country's bishops.[71] The Jesuits now had to supply personnel to their new university, as well as to universities in Guatemala and Nicaragua. Although the bishops had no one to replace the Jesuits at the time, most of them were dissatisfied with the new type of training the seminarians were receiving. By 1970 the bishops were willing to supply a rector, and in their December meeting they provisionally elected Bishop Romero to fill the post if the new Jesuit provincial could not propose someone more to their liking than his candidate, Rutilio Grande. He finally proposed Amando López, who had just finished his special studies and joined the seminary faculty. They accepted the unknown Father López.[72]

López continued the policies that all the bishops but Rivera and Chávez disliked. Seminarians were no longer wearing cassocks during sports, were going out of the seminary, were even taking philosophy courses at the Central American University. At the end of 1972 the bishops voted to oust the Jesuits and selected Romero once again as rector. He and Archbishop Chávez went in person to break the news to the provincial who had succeeded Father Azcue.[73] Later, as archbishop, Romero would apologize to Amando López for his part in removing the Jesuits from the seminary.[74]

With Romero as rector, the bishops named Monsignor Freddy Delgado as vice-rector in charge of discipline, Father Marco René Revelo to take charge of the seminarians' pastoral training, Father Oscar Barahona to be in charge of spiritual formation, and Father Jesús Delgado, Freddy's brother, to oversee intellectual formation.[75] But it was a vastly different seminary that opened in February for the 1973 school year. The bishops wanted to start afresh, not only with a new faculty, but also with new students. All the theology and philosophy students had either been sent elsewhere to study or dismissed. The handful of students who now used the big gray building on the hillside were in an introductory program previous to being sent to the philosophy classes.[76]

Romero was still auxiliary bishop, editor of *Orientación*, secretary-general of the bishops' conference, and now in charge of the seminary. With so few students, however, he could leave most of the administration to Freddy Delgado. But Delgado soon began to have problems with the students, and in April Romero suggested making him adjunct secretary of the bishops' conference to get him out of the seminary gracefully.[77]

At the same time the bishops were faced with the problem of few students in a big seminary. It was costing more than they could afford, and for that reason Aparicio in particular wanted to pull his students out. The students themselves found the big, empty building unpleasant. The solution reached was to bring the minor seminarians from Santa Tecla and with them their director, Father Rogelio Esquivel, who now took Delgado's place as vice-rector of the seminary. Since the minor seminarians attended classes in a high school outside the seminary, the move involved no additional transfer of faculty.[78]

Morale remained low, however, and the financial drain proved impossible to sustain after Aparicio's students departed. At midyear the bishops decided to close the major seminary.

The failure was obviously a failure for Romero, even though the other bishops and the seminary staff shared it. Bishop Rivera thought Romero seemed dispirited about it. Besides failing to pull the team together, Romero could feel somewhat to blame for the financial failure. As the moderator of the local Serra Club (a lay organization that promotes vocations to the priesthood and supports students for the priesthood), he had turned over the financial administration of the seminary to them at the beginning. "A lot of money was spent," said Rivera when interviewed.

A national seminary that had trained most of the nation's secular priests since 1915 had collapsed as soon as the bishops put in their own team. There was blame and failure enough for many. The few seminarians remaining continued their studies in other seminaries or in private classes that Bishop Rivera and the Jesuits Amando López and Ladislao Segura provided in San Salvador for theology students of the archdiocese. The philosophy students of the archdiocese continued classes in the Central American University, and they and the minor seminarians lived in the big gray seminary building.[79]

In 1974 the bishops of El Salvador selected Romero as their delegate to the bishops' synod to be held in Rome in October. Romero, however, decided not to go and resigned the post. The bishops then chose Rivera in his place, after which Romero changed his mind and wanted to go. The bishops referred the matter to Rome, which confirmed Rivera as the delegate. Rivera recalled the incident as a moment of some tension, which relaxed when Rome named Romero bishop of Santiago de María on October 15, during the synod.

Romero saw his naming as a vindication, and he declared in an editorial in *Orientación:* "This trust of the pope in its editor must also be interpreted as the most solemn backing of the church's magisterium for the ideology that has inspired the paper's pages under this editorship. This silent approval from so high a source constitutes the best reward and satisfaction for all of us who work together for this ideal, at the same time that it determines the route to follow."[80]

The town of Santiago de María had about 10,000 people, plus another 20,000 in its environs. The diocese, which stretches from Honduras to the Pacific, had a population of 425,000 in 1975. Statistics that the diocese sent to Rome that year estimated that 95 percent of the people were Catholic. The town of Usulután, to the south, is somewhat larger than Santiago de María, but the diocese as a whole is mostly rural. It was separated from the San Miguel diocese in 1954, and Romero was only its second bishop. The diocese included his home town, Ciudad Barrios.

Romero went off to Rome to thank the pope for his naming. It would, he explained in *Orientación,* "have the same meaning as St. Paul's historic trip to Jerusalem to see Peter and to check his criteria against those of the See that is the center of Catholic unity and guarantee of the church's authentic teaching."[81] Later, in March 1977, he would invoke the same comparison when announcing his trip to Rome. In the audience of November 23, Paul VI presented him with a chalice, and he wrote to the pope on March 19, 1975, that it "continues to be in all my masses a sign of my communion and that of my diocese with Your Holiness and the whole church."

On December 14, 1974, Romero was installed as bishop by the papal nuncio, Archbishop Gerada, in the presence of high government and church officials and amid a festive populace. He set to work to organize the diocesan offices, calling on his brother, an accountant living in San Miguel, to organize the bookkeeping. The same brother had helped him in the parish accounts in San Miguel and would later become auditor for the archdiocese.

The diocese, like most of its inhabitants, was poor. When Romero wrote the pope on March 19, 1975, it was to thank him for the photographs of his November 23 audience and a much-needed gift of $5,000 for the diocese as well as to tell him he was using his chalice. He would later thank the Pontifical Commission for Latin America for paying the $550 fee for his naming as bishop, for a $3,000 gift for the diocese, and for sending a set of *Acta Apostolicae Sedis* for the diocesan office, which lacked it. *AAS* is a monthly publication of official Vatican documents of universal import. The back issues were a considerable gift, since *AAS* began publication in 1909.

On November 29, 1974, guardsmen and policemen raided a hamlet called La Cayetana, near the town of Tecoluca in the San Vicente diocese, massacring six campesinos, sacking and robbing peasant cottages, beating the wives of two of the dead, and stripping and mocking men. The bishop of San Vicente, Pedro Arnoldo Aparicio, angrily denounced the outrage, as did the whole bishops' conference.[82]

Then, on May 7, 1975, the Guardia Nacional arrested the parish priest of Tecoluca and three friends who were with him in his car. They held all four overnight and took them to San Salvador, where they blindfolded them and beat them before releasing them. The priest related that the guardsmen planted a leaflet in his mass kit and accused him of subversion. Bishop Aparicio published a vigorous and angry letter to the government authorities and declared the excommunication of those responsible for the action.[83]

Six weeks later, on June 21, a serious incident took place in Romero's diocese. Guardsmen raided a hamlet called Tres Calles at 1:00 A.M., shooting and hacking to death five campesinos and ransacking houses in search of weapons. Romero went the next day to console the families and to say mass for the victims, condemning the massacre in his homily as an attack on human rights.[84] Afterward he went to see the local Guardia commander to protest. The commander shrugged off the incident, calling the victims malefactors. Romero replied that they had a right to justice no matter who they were or what they had done.

On June 26 he wrote an anguished letter to President Molina, describing his experiences and protesting the outrage; but he did not protest publicly. The letter was deferential and respectful, in spite of the anger and pain that showed through his words.

After writing Molina, Romero wrote a memorandum for his fellow bishops. He had gone to Tres Calles to console the people, he explained, but did not wish to make a public protest for three reasons: (1) he thought it better to intervene directly with the authorities, as he had done, protesting personally to the military commander and writing to the president; (2) the church was not directly involved in the affair; (3) he was not sure of the real motives behind the killings or of what the conduct of the victims had been. He had been surprised to find several priests of the San Vicente diocese present for the funeral, but he had been glad to concelebrate the mass with them and regretted only that protest songs had been sung at the mass.

Romero's explanation of his actions shows he still believed that the public authorities were not responsible for the crimes of their subordinates and would remedy abuses, so that it was better to work things out on the level of church authorities and civil authorities. He also thought his first responsibility was to the church as an institution, and that he must avoid the embarrassment of speaking out on behalf of victims who might prove to be subversives or criminals. The events of his first weeks as archbishop would disabuse him of his trust in high government figures and impel him to take bold, public stands in defense of the victims of government violence, and he would come to see the defense of the victimized as his church's duty in the light of Vatican II's view of the church as the servant of the world.

In light of his earlier press and radio activity, it was almost inevitable that Romero would start a publication in Santiago de María. In September

1975 he published the first issue of *El Apóstol* (*The Apostle*), to become a weekly periodical of the diocese. It generally had sixteen pages (6.5 x 8.5 inches, offset, on newsprint), including a four-page pullout with the Sunday mass prayers. Romero himself edited *El Apóstol,* and the cover logo included his episcopal coat of arms. Each issue carried a page called "The Pastor's Voice" signed by "The Bishop." A sampling gives an idea of what was on his mind.

"The Pastor's Voice" for June 13, 1976, consisted of three paragraphs on saints and images, most of it quotations from Vatican II. On August 22, 1976, he used the space to thank the diocese for the birthday celebration he had been given. The October 3 issue carried an explanation of Mission Sunday and a short discourse on the mission spirit of the church, a favorite subject of his. On November 7, he gave the diocese a few words about the meeting of the Central American bishops that he had just attended in Chinandega, Nicaragua.

On November 28 he wrote, in the midst of the coffee harvest: "God, always glorious in his works, is giving us this year too that splendid rain of rubies [ripe coffee beans are red] that draws thousands of hands from everywhere to gather the rich gift of our mountains." But, he went on, "humans' sin makes the beauty of creation groan. . . . For this reason the church must cry out by God's command: 'God has meant the earth and all it contains for the use of the whole human race. Created wealth should reach all in just form, guided by justice and accompanied by charity. Whatever the form of property-holding, we must not lose sight of this universal purpose of all wealth.' "[85]

Since the harvest represented the only hope of income for many of the harvesters, who would spend the rest of the year without work, "it saddens and concerns us to see the selfishness with which means and dispositions are found to nullify the just wage of the harvesters. How we would wish that the joy of this rain of rubies and of all the harvests of the earth would not be darkened by the tragic sentence of the Bible: 'Behold, the day wage of the laborers that cut your fields, defrauded by you, is crying out, and the cries of the reapers have reached the ears of the Lord of hosts' " (James 5:4).

Romero's concern for justice for the harvesters is evident amid the flowery language, but he offers no solution for the injustice beyond wishing that the landowners were not so selfish and fraudulent. After he became archbishop, he would come to recognize that the oppressed must organize in order to pressure for their rights, and he would vigorously defend the rights of their organizations.

Romero now did what he could to alleviate the hardships of the harvesters, many of whom had come from settlements on the Honduran border. The nights are cool in Santiago during harvest time, and most of the harvesters were sleeping in the public square. He opened the cathedral rectory and diocesan offices, which occupied an old building next to the cathedral.

That was not enough, so he also gave them the hall that had recently been built at the bishop's house for clergy meetings. Hundreds of workers thus had at least a roof over their heads at night and shelter from the cold.

Romero also called on Caritas and a group of women known as the Ladies of Charity to provide a hot meal for the harvesters at the end of their long day when they came back to the town from the coffee groves. He offered catechetical films in the open air for those who wished. For the harvesters it was a diversion from the monotonous work.[86]

Besides Romero's own column, each issue of *El Apóstol* carried a feature called "The Teaching of the Pope," which was often a long quotation from some papal discourse or document, a declaration of some Roman office, or a news item about the pope. The rest of the issue was filled with news items about the diocese or the church in the rest of the world. *El Apóstol* in general gave the diocese a chance to hear the bishop's voice, to absorb a bit of catechesis, and to attend Sunday mass a little more intelligently. But it lacked the fire that Romero would show as archbishop.

On May 18, 1975, the Vatican named Romero a consultor of the Pontifical Commission for Latin America. The commission is a part of the Congregation for the Bishops, and its function is to coordinate relations between the Holy See and CELAM, the Latin American bishops' service organization. Its president was Cardinal Sebastiano Baggio, the prefect of the Congregation for the Bishops, and most of its members and consultors are Roman officials. But one member and three consultors are Latin American bishops, and Romero became one of these three. It was a singular recognition for a bishop who had just received his first diocese.

As a consultor, Romero attended a commission meeting in Rome, held October 20–22, 1975. The sessions were dedicated to the Latin American family, and a month before the meeting Romero sent the advance documents to each Central American bishop, asking for suggestions. The participants spent two days listening to talks, discussing, and preparing a statement. The third day was devoted to a concelebrated mass in St. Peter's and an audience with the pope. For Romero the experience was an introduction to the higher realms of church government and a chance to get acquainted with some of the bishops and monsignors of the Roman Curia.

Romero stayed on in Rome after the meeting. On November 5 he attended a talk by Bishop Alfonso López Trujillo, the secretary-general of CELAM, on "Priests' Political Movements in Latin America: Present Situation, Dangers, and Proposals for Remedies." After the talk, the audience of bishops added their comments, and Romero offered his observations on the clergy of El Salvador and what he saw as their politicization. The next day he expanded on the same ideas in a memorandum, "Three Factors in the Priests' Political Movement in El Salvador," and headed it "Very Confidential—for the Commission for Latin America." The document is an interesting indication of Romero's thinking at the time. Like most other bishops of his country, as well as many others in the church, he was blind to his own political stance in support of the government while worrying about the "politicization" of those who dared to question those in power.

The first factor was the Jesuits in the Central American University, the high school, the seminary (until they left it in 1972), and the Aguilares parish, and their influence on nuns and Catholic schools. He singled out the "political theology" of Father Ignacio Ellacuría, a lay professor's classes that "seem to be demonstrations against the government" (quoting the government itself), the magazine *ECA,* a book published by the university on the 1972 election,[87] the "new Christology," and the teaching of theology without consulting the bishops. "Liberating education," he said, was a slogan of the Jesuits in Central America. He recalled the 1973 "national scandal" over the supposed teaching of Marxism in the Jesuit high school and the "politicizing" of the seminarians under the Jesuits, especially the refusal of seminarians to attend a ceremony in honor of the pope "because the president would be there and they considered his election fraudulent," and their defense by the seminary rector, Amando López. A newspaper had described a Corpus Christi procession in Aguilares as "like a political rally," but the pastor, Rutilio Grande, Romero said, "does not agree with many things that his co-workers do."

A second factor, relating to "sociopolitical problems," was the Interdiocesan Social Secretariat and the Justice and Peace Commission, both under Father Juan Ramón Vega. The bulletin *Justicia y Paz* came from there, edited by Fabián Amaya, a priest of the archdiocese, with financial help from the German bishops' agency Misereor, and moral support from Bishop Rivera. "It is a biting and negative criticism against the capitalists and the government," Romero said. "The bishops' conference has several times asked the archbishop that it be discontinued; the government has complained several times because of its tendentious criticisms; and many private persons are resentful." Its editor "is one of the principal leaders of the politicizing and contestational tendency. All the priests of that tendency distribute it, as does the opposition political party." The secretariat also published polemical news releases for the international media "that have contributed towards giving a negative image of the bishops' conference" and that *l'Osservatore Romano* had refused to publish. Various Central American bishops wondered how Vega could be allowed to represent the Justice and Peace Commission "when he lacks the bishops' confidence and cannot achieve a healthy cooperation with the government towards the goals of the commission" and had even had difficulty with the government over his staying in El Salvador (he was a Nicaraguan) "because of his political activities."

The third factor was "the groups of priests, religious, and 'committed Christians' from all the dioceses but in perfect intercommunication." They spread their ideas in the peasant development centers operated by the church, which the government had pointed out as "centers of subversion," as well as on the archdiocesan radio, YSAX, and in their small communities. They used Marxist analysis in their thought, acting behind the bishops' backs and issuing public declarations. But in tight spots, Romero said, they expected the bishops to come to their help.

The ideology shown in these people's attitudes, Romero continued, was what most worried the bishops. They said the church could not be apolitical, because its actions always have political repercussions, and it is only called apolitical when it agrees with the established government. They said they were not involved in party politics but in seeking the common good, as the gospel obliges them. They said they must follow their own consciences even when against a disposition of the institutional church. They said they were not subversives, as the government alleged, but were only developing the critical and civic consciousness of the people, which was bound to annoy a repressive government.

Romero admitted that the country had "a repressive military government" and "a cruel social differentiation, in which a few have everything and the majority live in destitution." The bishops, he said, "defend their priests in all conflicts. They try to be opportune in their declarations so as to head off pronouncements of these groups. In dialog with the central government, they warn it of false information. Their greatest pastoral concern is the spiritualizing of the clergy in order to give witness of the true hope and transcendence of Christianity, but at the same time to seek the most accurate pastoral policy for joining together the social classes in a sound working with the government."

It is curious that Romero could encapsulate accurately the arguments used by those whom he opposed without feeling the need to say what he found wrong with them. That only a year and a half later his closest helpers would be some of those he pronounced suspect in this document is proof of a considerable shift by then in Romero's viewpoint. He was to become one of those who so worried him in November 1975.

Romero showed the same energy and concern as bishop in Santiago de María that he had shown as a priest in San Miguel. To attend better to the peasantry, he mounted loudspeakers on a jeep and drove to remote settlements to preach, play sacred music, hear confessions, offer mass, baptize, and marry. Unfortunately, his organization did not match his energy, according to Delgado, and he often neglected to register baptisms and marriages in the respective parishes, to the annoyance of the pastors. The clergy, however, had to admire his zeal and energy, and they also found in him a greater openness and readiness to dialog than he had shown in San Miguel and San Salvador.[88] His efforts at self-improvement were showing results.

A priest of Santiago de María recalled the day in 1976 when Romero brought in an old woman with impaired sight from a remote village. He saw that she got medical attention and housing and necessary transportation while in Santiago. Those who came in need of money always received help. He managed to provide help to needy parishes also — such things as sound-amplifying equipment or building materials. He quoted words he had heard from Pope Paul VI during his trip to Rome in 1975: "A father should always have his pockets full to give to his children." In San Miguel, he had helped found an Alcoholics Anonymous group, and in Santiago he encouraged the movement and arranged a day of recollection for it on the last Saturday of each month. As archbishop of San Salvador, he continued to encourage Alcoholics Anonymous, giving talks to groups or sending another priest in his place.[89]

Romero's two years in Santiago began to open his eyes to the reality of the Salvadoran campesino's lot. One day a Passionist priest working in the diocese told him that landowners were cheating campesinos by paying less than the legal minimum wage. Romero could not believe it. "They are good people," he said, referring to owners of coffee plantations whom he had known in San Miguel.

"Look," said the Passionist, "you can go to [such and such a plantation] and see a blackboard that says, 'Here we pay 1.75 colóns a day.'" This shocked Romero, according to the Passionist. The minimum wage was 2.50 colóns ($1).[90]

In his November 1975 memorandum to the Pontifical Commission for Latin America, Romero had mentioned the church's peasant training centers as examples of political involvement by the clergy; one of those centers was located in his own diocese. The government regarded it as subversive. The nuncio was suspicious of it and wanted Romero to take some action. He himself pondered the matter during his first year as bishop, whether to close the center or try to reorient it and, in either case, how to proceed. Los Naranjos, as it was named, was the only organized pastoral activity in the diocese and closing it would leave only the routine celebration of mass and dispensing of sacraments that prevailed in the churches of the diocese, where the clergy's average age was fifty-nine.[91]

On July 30, 1975, troops in San Salvador massacred some forty students demonstrating against the government's occupation of the university at Santa Ana. In protest, other groups, including priests and religious, occupied the San Salvador cathedral, the first of such occupations, and a priest from Los Naranjos was among the occupiers. Romero was upset, and he suspended the functioning of the center and put a new director in charge, making clear that he wanted more piety and less ideology in the training.

He called in Bishop Marco René Revelo, auxiliary of Santa Ana and head of the bishops' catechetical commission, and in early December, just after Romero's return from the meeting in Rome, Revelo came to Santiago to talk with him and the priests of Los Naranjos. Feelings were strong among the priests, who saw Romero as simply against the policies of the Medellín conference, which they were trying to carry out. Romero and Revelo felt that the training given in the center was manipulating Medellín for political purposes. They proposed that the courses be shifted from the center itself to the parishes where the campesinos lived, with the teachers from the center providing the instruction. This would mean a less intense indoctrination for the campesinos and would let Romero and the parish priests observe and influence the process. The solution satisfied the priests from the center, as well as the government and the nuncio. Romero named the new director of the center as his vicar for pastoral affairs and they began to work closely together.

Romero came out of the affair with increased stature in the eyes of the nuncio, who was already thinking of whom to suggest to Rome for the next archbishop of San Salvador. The dialog with the clergy also pushed Romero toward a more serious study of Medellín.[92] By coincidence, just when Romero was resolving the matter of Los Naranjos, Pope Paul VI published his apostolic exhortation *Evangelii Nuntiandi,* "On Evangelization in the Modern World." There Romero would find the pope himself strongly affirming liberation from temporal evils as an essential part of the church's work of evangelization.[93] Loyal to the Holy See, he would ponder it and eventually make it his own. As archbishop, he would cite it often in his sermons and writings.

August 6, the feast of the Transfiguration of Christ, is for Salvadorans the national patronal day in honor of the Savior. For the 1976 celebration Romero preached the homily at the pontifical mass in the cathedral of San Salvador. It was a carefully prepared address, and he later published the text in *El Apóstol.*[94]

Romero recalled the founding and naming of San Salvador by the Spanish conquistador Pedro de Alvarado in 1528, making the Savior the patron of the city and the future nation. He spoke of the doctrine of the human and divine natures of Christ, defined by the Council of Chalcedon in 451, and proceeded to make a swinging attack on "so-called new Christologies." Jon Sobrino, director of the Center for Theological Reflection at the Central American University, had just published a book on Christology[95] and took Romero's words as an attack on his work—as they undoubtedly were. (Though as archbishop he later called on Sobrino's theological skills, he never mentioned the sermon to Sobrino.)

Romero spoke of Christ as liberator, but most of his words were a warning about merely temporal liberation. Absent was any suggestion that Christian liberation might involve conflict. Rather, he called for harmony: "How beautiful would be this August 6 if on leaving this ancestral home after sharing a sincere return to our origins, we bore in our souls the resolve to understand one another better, each in the place where the hand of Providence has put us; if the members of the government and the shepherds of the church, if capital and labor, if those of the city and those of the country-side, the initiatives of the government and those of private enterprise— all of us—were to really let the Divine Savior of the World, patron of our nation, inspire and mediate all our conflicts and be the artisan of all the national transformations that we urgently need for the integral liberation that only he can build."

Romero's piety and his devotion to the church and its authentic teaching shine through the sermon. He attacks the new theology because it seems to him to threaten the church's teaching and belief in the divinity of Christ. He is worried that liberation will be understood in a merely material way. He calls for love, still trusting in the good will of all.

In mid-1976 Romero organized for his clergy a three-day study of the government's new land-reform program. Although the project was very small, much of it fell in his diocese and would involve campesinos for whom he had a pastor's responsibility. He took the priests' analysis of the project, which criticized it rather severely, to his friend President Molina. But the project never got going. Within three months, the same docile congress that had unanimously approved it killed it unanimously under pressure of the landowners.

During his two years in Santiago de María, Romero's attitudes and positions were still evolving. According to the Passionist priest who was his pastoral vicar the second year, in his sermons and clergy meetings he often quoted Vatican II, but never Medellín.[96] He had attended institutes on theological and pastoral topics as an auxiliary bishop in 1971 in Medellín and in 1972 in Antigua Guatemala, filling notebooks with what the leading thinkers of the day were teaching. But his own mentality was evolving only slowly. It would take the catalyst of his first weeks as archbishop to bring about a dramatic change.

❧ III ⊱

The People's Voice

June–July 1977

By 10:30 A.M. Aguilares was hot under the tropical sun. People had been gathering all morning—townspeople, campesinos from miles around, nuns and priests from the capital. The crowd, hopeful, expectant, had long since overflowed the little church into the yard.

They received Archbishop Romero with warm applause as he arrived and made his way through the throng. He was getting used to applause—when he entered the cathedral for Sunday mass, or when the people liked what he said during his homilies. Romero felt that the people's applause was their way of dialoging with him, and it made him feel closer to them.[1]

Ten priests concelebrated with Romero in Aguilares. It was June 19, 1977, just a month since the military forces had overrun the parish. They had shot down young Miguel in the square belfry above as he tried to ring the bells in warning, had carried off the three priests and expelled them from the country, had shot open the tabernacle and scattered the hosts on the floor, had rampaged through the town, killing and dragging away prisoners to be killed.

Now Romero was installing a new pastor, a priest of the archdiocese, and three Sisters who would help. They would continue what the Jesuits had begun, encouraging the small communities of campesinos, catechizing, teaching the Bible.

Romero began his homily with a phrase he would repeat in one way or another many times to come: "It is my lot to gather up the trampled, the dead, and all that the persecution of the church leaves behind." He had come, he said, to recover a profaned church, tabernacle, and people. "Your sorrow is the church's sorrow."

The first reading of the day (Zech. 12:10–11) spoke of an outpouring of grace on Jerusalem and of mourning for one who was pierced through. "You are the image of the divine one who was pierced," said Romero. "It is the image of all the populations that, like Aguilares, are pierced through, are outraged. But if your suffering is done with faith and is given a redemptive meaning, then Aguilares is singing the precious stanza of liberation. For when they look on him whom they have pierced, they will repent and will see the heroism and will see the joy with which the Lord blesses the sorrow."

Romero spoke of those who were missing, of the agonizing uncertainty being endured by their families: "For God no one is lost. For God there is only the mystery of pain, which, if accepted with a sense of sanctification and redemption, will be like that of Christ our Lord, a redemptive pain." He spoke of those who had suffered torture: "Know that all your pain and suffering is understood and that the church interprets it, as in this first reading, as a redemptive pain, a pain that will bring forth for Aguilares new streams of blessings."

The parish had been a model and leader of the new pastoral concepts. Now it was also the leader in being persecuted: "The persecution against the priests, the persecution directed against the catechists, is without doubt a sign of the Lord's favor. Today in his gospel [Luke 9:18–24] Jesus told us that those who wish to come after him must deny themselves, take up their cross, and follow." Those who offered their lives to the Lord and endured suffering and martyrdom "are giving a witness that we are taking from Aguilares to offer to all the parishes."

Warning his hearers not to "confuse Christ's liberation with false liberations, liberations that are merely temporal," Romero cited the liberation proclaimed by St. Paul (Gal. 3:26–29): "Baptism made us one body with Christ, and in Christ we are one with him and cannot betray all that flows from that: the new human being. It is a new being with a heart cleansed of all sin, a new person who does not speak with animosity in the heart, who never furthers violence, hatred, or rancor."

"Let there be no animosity in our heart," Romero continued. "Let this eucharist, which is a call to reconciliation with God and our brothers and sisters, leave in all hearts the satisfaction that we are Christians. . . . Let us pray for the conversion of those who struck us, . . . of those who sacrilegiously dared to lay hands on the sacred tabernacle. Let us pray to the Lord for forgiveness and for the due repentance of those who converted a town into a prison and a place of torment. Let the Lord touch their hearts. Before the terrible sentence is fulfilled, 'Those who kill by the sword die by the sword,' let them truly repent and have the satisfaction of looking on him whom they have pierced. And let there rain down from there a torrent of mercy and of kindness, so that we may all feel ourselves brothers and sisters."[2]

Romero spoke firmly, never shouting, letting the occasion and the message work on the hearts of the audience. At the end, the five thousand present applauded a sermon that many would remember for years. The morning stamped the figure of the archbishop on the minds of those who were there. At the offertory of the mass, Romero introduced the new pastoral team that would care for the communities of Aguilares and El Paisnal, and the people applauded their welcome. At communion time, the hosts prepared were not enough for all who wanted to receive, and after the mass the crowd accompanied the Blessed Sacrament around the town square in a belated Corpus Christi procession. As they passed the town hall, guardsmen came out with weapons, and there was a tense moment. Romero said to continue, and nothing further happened. But it was clear that the drama of Aguilares had not yet concluded.[3]

The newspaper attacks continued against the archbishop, against the clergy, especially those who encouraged grass-roots Christian communities, against Medellín and Vatican II, against land reform, against *Orientación* and YSAX, and against the Jesuits, especially those of Aguilares, the university, the high school, and *ECA.*

The most prominent attacks appeared in the form of advertisements that often filled a whole page of one or more of San Salvador's tabloid-sized papers. When not signed by FARO, the ads would appear over the name of some phantom religious organization, such as "Salvadoran Catholic Association" or "Association of Catholic Women" or "Association of Followers of Christ the King." The tactic was to make the church appear divided into two camps — loyal followers of the old doctrine and new radicals who had infiltrated and were leading people astray.

The papers also carried columns and occasional pieces with the same message, though in more reasoned form, trying to appeal to the more serious reader. *La Prensa Gráfica* regularly carried a column by the pseudonymous "Dr. Aminta Amaya," purporting to be written by an educated Catholic woman.

In more subtle form, the papers used news items for the same purpose. If the president stated that the church was not persecuted, his words appeared in large front-page headlines. Contrary statements by Romero or others would not appear at all or be buried on an inside page.

In 1977 the newspapers were still accepting ads from those who wanted to respond to the attacks and who were willing and able to pay. Occasionally the archdiocese took a page to present its side, though mostly it relied on *Orientación,* which was sold at church doors on Sundays, and on YSAX, at the time the most popular radio station in the country. YSAX's chief attraction was Romero himself. Most of the nation listened to his Sunday homilies, and he also had a weekly program on Wednesdays, when he would expatiate on topics fed to him by an interviewer.

On June 14 the Jesuits began publishing a series of statements, "The Jesuits to the Salvadoran People," in the daily press. Each of six installments covered one or two tabloid pages, and the series was later issued as a forty-seven-page pamphlet.[4] It replied to the attacks that the Jesuits had sustained and outlined their vision of the church of Vatican II and Medellín:

The church is trying to be faithful to the example of Christ, making itself one with the dispossessed and sharing their life. The church is becoming displeasing and distressing for those who have privileges and economic power. The church preaches the good news and proclaims the truth, and that truth is disturbing. The church interprets in the light of the good news the concrete situation that it lives in, and its word causes indignation. The church—that is, Christians— tries to live in agreement with the good news, and its behavior surprises and angers. The church speaks of justice, and they say it preaches hatred. The church concerns itself for the dignity of the poor, and they say it promotes fratricidal struggles. The church tries to better human society, and it is accused with fury of meddling in what does not concern it. The church, like Jesus, tries to give preference to the poor and deprived, the great majority of Salvadorans; but, curiously, when it does so they say it is harming the country.

On June 21, six days before the series ended, the "White Warrior Union" warned all Jesuits to leave the country within thirty days or become "military targets," along with all their institutions. The White Warrior Union, whoever comprised it, had taken responsibility for the murder of Alfonso Navarro the month before. Like similar names used by the violent right, the White Warrior Union seemed to have no history or identifiable members. Leftist guerrilla groups in El Salvador had founders and leaders who were known. Rightist groups were phantomlike, and to many they seemed to be simply names used by the security forces to disguise some of their actions.

Since six bombs had gone off in the Central American University during 1976 and one Jesuit had been murdered in March, the threat was taken seriously. The Jesuits immediately announced through the provincial that they would stay at their posts. They also quickly sought protection and support. The provincial went twice to see President-elect Romero, on June 24 and 27.[5] Jesuits and other people around the world wrote the Salvadoran government to appeal for protection and denounce the threat. Statements of support in El Salvador came from the Jesuits' alumni, employees, students, fellow teachers, and students' parents, and from the Catholic school federation, the conference of religious, and of course from the archbishop.

The July 21 deadline passed without violence to the Jesuits. The government had posted police guards around Jesuit houses to show its good intentions and to demonstrate that it had no connection with the White Warrior Union, which kept silent.

Archbishop Romero himself was the subject, often directly, of many press attacks. One of the milder ones appeared in *La Prensa Gráfica* on May 24, 1977, headed "Don Oscar's Family and the Archbishop" and signed by the "Committee for the Betterment of the Catholic Church." The full-page ad told of a family with twelve children in which two of the youngsters were constantly in trouble and terrorizing the neighborhood, but were always defended and justified by their father, Don Oscar. Lest anyone miss the point, it concluded:

> We see in this example a providential likeness to what is happening in the CLERGY. A FEW BAD PRIESTS ARE CAUSING MOST SERIOUS HARM TO THE CATHOLIC CHURCH AND THE WHOLE COUNTRY, AND IT IS NOT UNDERSTOOD OR GRANTED THAT THE ARCHBISHOP CARRIES HIS AFFEC-TION AS CHIEF OF THE CATHOLIC CHURCH OF EL SAL-VADOR TO THE POINT OF NOT WANTING TO SEE THE FAULTS OF THESE BAD PRIESTS. RATHER HE BLAMES THOSE WHO CENSURE THEM, WHO POINT OUT THEIR MISDEEDS, WHO DESIRE A PURIFICATION OF THE CLERGY SO THAT OUR CATHOLIC CHURCH MAY REMAIN UNPOLLUTED AND REVERENCED [capitals in the original].

Most attacks on Romero were cruder than the preceding. On May 27 *La Prensa Gráfica* published a boxed statement signed by the "Association of Religious Catholic Women" and headed "Some Shepherds More Con-fused Than the Sheep." It included the following:

> Well known are the names of certain pastors, some members of the hierarchy, who speak ill of the wealth of others but not of their own, or who point out the need to share and distribute to others the goods that each one has, but not what they have themselves.

What bothered the writers was that some campesinos had occupied lands of haciendas in a few places; one such occupation had touched off the military operation against Aguilares. The reference to the hierarchy could have been only to Romero or Rivera, neither of whom had any wealth.

FARO could be ignorant and silly as well as malicious. In a May 31 advertisement[6] it complained that Archbishop Romero had substituted an-other creed for the "beautiful, spiritual, and perfectly religious" Apostles' Creed in his mass of May 22. The writer was evidently unaware that the creed said in the Sunday mass was the Nicene, not the Apostles', and that no liturgist or canonist would question a bishop's right to drop it for a sensible reason. What Romero had actually done in his homily was to comment on the bishops' May 17 statement and then use a paragraph from it, quoted below, as a substitution for the Nicene formula.

> The church believes in God the creator, in Jesus Christ the redeemer, and in the Holy Spirit the sanctifier. The church believes that the world is called to be submitted to Jesus Christ by a gradual establish-ment of God's reign. The church believes in the communion of saints

and in the love that unites humans. The church believes in humanity, called to be God's children, and believes in God's reign as the progressive change of the world of sin into the world of love and justice, which begins now in this world and has its fulfillment in eternity.

FARO in its complaint showed its alarm by capitalizing all phrases referring to the reign of God, and then said it would refrain from getting into theological discussion about them. But it was already mired, and got in deeper when it went on: "FARO has the right to make public its INDIGNATION SO THAT ALL CATHOLICS MAY SEE THAT A PRAYER AS IMPORTANT AS THE CREED HAS BEEN CHANGED FOR ANOTHER THAT IS POLITICAL AND SOCIAL, FOR THIS IS THE REAL MEANING OF THE CONTENT OF THE NEW CREED."

The chancellor of the archdiocese twitted FARO in a reply printed in *Orientación* and headed, "Shoemaker, Stick to Your Last." "It is laughable and shameful that FARO's writers do not know even the rudiments of religion," he said. "An intelligent person does not presume to write about things he doesn't understand. I would not dare to tell FARO's members what fertilizer to use on their cotton or sugar cane."[7]

In the same issue *Orientación* warned readers that a false edition of *Orientación* had been widely distributed on the streets of San Salvador, Santa Ana, Sonsonate, and other places. The fake edition carried the authentic logo and masthead. "Those who do such a thing are desk-top criminals," said the real *Orientación*. "They intend to increase the church's persecution and legitimize a new attack on this paper, saying things that do not correspond to the teaching of the church's magisterium or to the teaching of the bishops of El Salvador, whose authentic spokesman is this weekly paper."

Some columns written for the reader willing to look beyond the large type of the ads used more subtle tactics. *La Prensa Gráfica*'s "Dr. Aminta Amaya" column of June 1 refrained from attacking the archbishop directly, but the intention is clear:

> . . . the church faces internal forces trying implacably to lead it astray, represented by the traitors within it who act with impunity and even with the complicity of high church officers who do nothing to counteract the crafty maneuver of those who have ceased loving the church and surrender to its enemies, that is, to the enemies of God.
>
> The desertion of thousands of Catholics throughout the world is not the work of a church that has ceased to exist in the spirit and the consciousness of past generations and of those who today know the problem. It is the work of a few bad leaders who have astonished the world with their enormous disloyalty and have obliged the faithful to change their place, but not to change their God, because God continues to be the same for all of us who have grown up with faith in

him and try to follow his wise teachings. There is talk of the diminishing supply of those who have priestly vocations, and campaigns are made to increase the number so that the church may not find itself, as it often admits, short of priests. But it is certain that the small number of aspirants is also the product of what society sees in the attitude of certain bishops and clerics, pitted against the heart of the Catholic church and converted into bearers of an ideology that threatens to enslave all humanity. . . .

Many within the church may fear to confront the propagandists of violent changes, but this fear will not persist, because they are not alone. The people of God is with them, with the good bishops and the good priests, joining their hearts to enlighten the minds of the wayward, that they may stop confusing people with a fake persecution of the church and so that true Christian sentiment may triumph and rise, invincible, above the false apostles.

Inauguration day, July 1, was approaching, when General Carlos Humberto Romero would become president. Traditionally, Salvadoran bishops attended the ceremony as official guests of the government. Could they, or should they, do so this time? In May the government had deported four priests over the archbishop's protests, and troops had invaded Aguilares and occupied the church for weeks, desecrating the Blessed Sacrament and killing the sexton and numerous parishioners. The investigations promised into the murders of two priests were languishing, strengthening the suspicion that the government did not want the truth to appear. After Rutilio Grande's death, the archdiocese had stated that its representatives would not attend official acts until the murder was sufficiently explained.

As early as May, Romero had discussed the matter of attending the inauguration with the priests' senate of the archdiocese. Of the thirteen senators present, only one favored Romero's attending and eleven voted no.[8] Romero prayed over the question. He spoke with the nuncio, who wanted him to attend, and with other bishops, who were divided. He consulted various priests and lay people and even Protestants.[9] His decision was not to attend and he urged the other bishops also to stay away. Romero explained his decision to the president-elect, who accepted it but did not like it.[10] He explained it to the people in his Sunday homily.[11]

The nuncio and Bishops Alvarez and Barrera attended. The other four bishops stayed away. Alvarez explained his action in his diocesan paper, *Chaparrastique:*[12]

I feel contented and happy at having performed a function of the church in attending personally the transfer of the presidency in the National Gymnasium on July 1, 1977. . . .

Aside from all politics, with a pastor's consciousness that will be translated into daily service to the people, Bishop Barrera of Santa

Ana and I, your bishop of San Miguel and military vicar, attended this magnificent ceremony.

There is no persecuted church. There are some sons of a church that, wanting to serve, lost their way and put themselves outside the law.

Behind us there is a people, and we will be a bridge of goodness for all Salvadorans, as far as we can serve them.

There is no persecuted church. There is only a church that wants to fulfill always its duty of glorifying God and serving people.

To Romero, Alvarez wrote on July 3:

Let us be of one mind with the church, with the pope, with our republic, with St. Peter. Even though they be disagreeable. 1 Peter 2:13 (civil magistrates), let us give them the warmth of our virtue, of our charity.

As a gesture of solidarity with the church, I attended the inauguration. Removed from whatever politics.

In an attitude of service to the people.

Alvarez adds that the troubles were the fault of those who suffered. "I summarize all the problems referred to as simply a safeguarding of public order." The Jesuits in particular should have stayed with their schools for the rich and not got involved in rural parishes.

It was not the first time Alvarez had lined up with a new president. In 1972, after the fraudulent election of Molina, he had celebrated a mass of thanksgiving in the San Miguel cathedral with Molina present, and had said in the homily, "We find in this designation the hand of God. The president-elect is the established authority; all authority comes from God, and we Catholics, the church, are with the established authority."[13]

In a radio interview the following Wednesday, July 6,[14] Romero explained his position: "Faithful to my promise not to attend official acts as long as the situation between the archdiocese and the government is not cleared up, I could not attend the inauguration. But this does not mean a declaration of war or a definitive break." The church maintained its good will, he said, and it was not the one that had interrupted the conversation with the government. The church was ready "to work, as the council says, in healthy collaboration with those who hold in their hands the interests and the public good of the republic." In regard to the nuncio's attendance at the inauguration, Romero observed that a nuncio is an accredited diplomat representing the Holy See before the government of the country. But the local bishop is the head of the diocese. The bishops of Santa Ana and San Miguel, who had attended, represented their dioceses but not the whole church or the archdiocese. Romero continued:

I said in my homily [last Sunday], commenting on the definition of peace that the church gives, that peace is a product of justice . . . also . . . that justice is not enough, but that love is also necessary. The love that makes us feel that we are brothers and sisters is properly what makes for true peace. Peace is thus the product of justice and love.

. . . I was pleased that in his [inaugural] address the president had coincided in this idea of peace as the work of justice. This is why I emphasized that we hope for a more just climate, a more just arrangement for Salvadorans in the distribution of the wealth that God has created for all, in the administration of the public welfare in which we all have a right to share. As long as we see no actions working toward a more just order in El Salvador, we cannot believe there is a true desire for peace. But if in fact they put their hand to the plow and work for a more just order, as those who hold the power in their hands can do, then indeed we shall believe and shall rejoice that there is a sincere aspiration for peace. . . .

Whoever has followed with true sincerity and impartiality the relations between the government and, let us say, the archdiocese, will say that there are not simply small differences or misunderstandings. From what I have just said, you can see the matter is substantial. The church preaches a just order, and if it is not so understood but, rather, interpreted as subversion, then it is not a matter of minor differences but of something substantial. I would insist that dialog, if it is to be engaged in with a truly constructive spirit, must open up thoroughly. There must be a reflection group of government and church people that learns to speak the same language so that neither side will misinterpret the other. This is where the substantial difference is. . . . It's a matter of the church's very message, as the present magisterium of the church wants it preached.

He stated further that the threat to kill all Jesuits was not a small matter either, but an unheard-of assault on human rights. Among the government's duties "is the defense of those who live in El Salvador, and it must do all it can to unmask those who make these clandestine threats."

Commenting on the archbishop's absence from the inauguration, *ECA* said: "The action of the archbishop was in complete agreement with what Vatican II said and was truly, but paradoxically, an authentic and sound cooperation with the political community, a true presence of the church, and the first step toward a genuine dialog, if the latter is to be based on the truth."[15]

From July 11 to 13 the bishops' conference held its regular semiannual meeting. One topic of discussion was the church's position in the political and social situation of the country.

Bishop Alvarez said that church and government, at least the bishops and the president, had always had warm relations and the church had received considerate treatment. But in the past five years, certain priests and lay people, backed by certain bishops and by the Jesuits, had strayed from purely pastoral action. In November 1976 rumors began that certain priests would be done away with, which culminated in the deaths of Grande and Navarro and the attack on Aguilares. Alvarez saw the Aguilares assault as a problem of defending public order and the nation's security. He had, he said, attended the inauguration out of conviction.

Bishop Barrera had also attended the inauguration. He said that although he was not indifferent to the problem the archdiocese had and to the deaths of the two priests, he did not like the pressure that some priests and laity had exerted to keep the bishops from the inauguration. He did not believe in doing anything to make the situation more tense. Rather, he wanted to contribute to a climate in which the government would take the church into account, but without the church's surrendering to the government. Therefore he went to the inauguration; he said he had done a service to the church so that it might have greater liberty of action. He had always respected civil authority and his actions had helped those in the government to respect the church's authority.

Romero's view of the situation was very different. His pastoral work was under attack. He said that one sector of society was pressuring the nuncio, who was in turn pressuring the archbishop. Many others, however, agreed with his pastoral policy, which was based on Vatican II and Medellín. He admitted the clergy and the Jesuits influenced him in part. But the church had to react to the government's persecution and to FARO's and ANEP's attacks, and its reaction was producing a flourishing Catholic life. Romero admitted that some priests had at times been imprudent or even demagogic, but in general they were going the way the church had shown in Vatican II and Medellín. Bishops should correct excesses or mistakes but not change the general direction those priests were following; their very mistakes came from their ardor in preaching what had to be preached in Latin America.

Romero cited Paul VI's document on evangelization, *Evangelii Nuntiandi,* as the text to follow. The pope had written that in the underdeveloped nations millions of people are crying for liberation. The church, Romero said, was not to be measured by the government's support but rather by its own authenticity, its evangelical spirit of prayer, of trusting, of sincerity and justice, of opposition to abuses.[16]

Some of the pressure on the nuncio that Romero mentioned came by way of Rome, though it may have had its origin in El Salvador. In a letter to Bishop Aparicio on July 3, the nuncio wrote: "The cardinal secretary of state [Jean Villot] asks me to endeavor to have the bishops that have expressed reserve in the matter [of church-state relations in El Salvador] invite the archbishop with prudence and delicacy to moderate his own position in regard to relations with the government, so as to favor the search for an understanding that may make less difficult the country's general situation." Villot's instructions, as Gerada interpreted them, fit right into what the nuncio was doing already, which no doubt was what he had been trained to do as a diplomat.

The priests' senate sent a memorandum to the Vatican secretary of state on July 18, recounting some of the things that had happened since the archbishop's trip to Rome. "In this whole painful situation . . . orthodoxy in doctrine and adherence to the faith have been the characteristic note of the archbishop . . . who is convinced that the church does not need other doctrinal support."

But moral support had come, they noted, from other churches: from the United States bishops' conference and the National Federation of Priests' Councils of the United States; from Cardinal Basil Hume of England; from the Central American Bishops' Secretariat; from the countless letters of bishops and confederations of religious, especially of Central America; from various non-Catholic churches; and from the World Council of Churches.

Within El Salvador priests and people had massively backed the archbishop, but some of the few exceptions were small groups with great power. "One cannot compromise principles or be silent about injustices without risking being branded as an accomplice in them," the senate report went on. "For this reason, the attendance of two bishops at the inauguration of the president of the country, General Romero, causes concern. . . . We are also concerned about the too partial stance of the apostolic nuncio, Archbishop Emanuele Gerada, whose advice to the archbishop coincides with the thinking of the government and of the economic power groups that oppose the church. We therefore desire and ask the Holy See to use, with its characteristic prudence, the necessary means to stop this scandal of disunion that these bishops cause."

At this time Romero himself prepared a confidential letter to Cardinal Baggio, prefect of the Congregation for the Bishops, and sent it off at the end of July.[17] The intention of the letter seems to have been to keep Rome informed on the archdiocese as he saw it. Romero wrote: "I believe I have pondered my decisions before the Lord and have consulted sufficiently over them. The abundant solidarity of my brother bishops, priests, religious, and faithful, within and without the country and the continent, I take as a worthy approval of my modest pastoral task in this difficult situation through which the archdiocese is passing. Above all, I am glad to see as a consequence of this sincere search for the gospel the luxuriant rebirth of the church's pastoral life and the confidence and credibility the church has gained among the people."

Romero was aware of the risks and the negative aspects of the first five months of his archbishopric, but he believed the positive results far outweighed them. "I do not deny the imprudences of certain priests and other elements among our pastoral workers, who are oversensitive to the political and social problems of our surroundings. But I mention this detail precisely to explain that it is an exaggeration to call them Marxists or subversives, as has been done as a pretext for their persecution by the government or as the reason for suspicion by some bishop." His own way of handling them, he said, was to talk with them and try to earn their trust.

For years the bishops had discussed with some frequency in their meetings the question of priests who got more involved in protests or peasant movements than their bishops would like. The size of the group of difficult cases depended on the viewpoint of the particular bishop who fixed the boundaries. When Romero wrote to Baggio in Rome on November 6, 1975, he had mentioned among the politicized group certain priests who by July 1977 had become his close advisers and supporters. About a dozen others of the archdiocese, however, remained a concern to Romero all the time he was archbishop, and they in turn found him too unwilling to commit himself to what they saw as the salvation of the Salvadoran people—the popular organizations of campesinos, workers, and others that gradually united to form an organized opposition to the oligarchy and the government.

"Concerning the risks that have been run in regard to the government," Romero went on, "I believe it was necessary to run them, because the reactions provoked by the government's serious abuses against the dignity and liberty of the church and against the human rights of so many defenseless people were necessary."

If, in spite of his clear conscience, the Holy See should judge that his pastoral judgments were wrong, he was ready to listen to correction or even to turn over the helm of the archdiocese to other hands. In writing this he was thinking especially of his differences with the nuncio. "With sadness I must manifest that in these circumstances, so painful and difficult for me, I have not had his support in my actions. Instead, at certain moments I have felt his very hard pressure against my decisions. On analyzing this strange attitude of his, I have concluded that he lives at a great distance from the problems of our clergy and of humble people and that with him what has most weight are the reports of Cardinal Casariego, of the politicians, of the diplomats, and of the moneyed class of the elegant neighborhoods."

Cardinal Mario Casariego, archbishop of Guatemala, where Gerada was also nuncio, had been born in Spain and had formerly worked as a Somascan priest in San Salvador, where many still remembered him as Father Mario. He was generally at odds with the other Guatemalan bishops and his own clergy, and he had provoked a strong reaction in the Salvadoran clergy by writing in an exhortation to his clergy on March 19, when several priests had been expelled from El Salvador and one killed: "It is enough to mention the recent case of El Salvador, where several priests were expelled from the country for departing from their mission and meddling in partisan and sectarian politics."

Priests and religious immediately protested. The Maryknoll superior for

Central America wrote to him: "In the case of the Maryknoll Fathers expelled I can affirm, as their superior, that neither one was involved in partisan politics."[18] FARO picked up Casariego's words and published them in all the Salvadoran dailies on April 16, and *Orientación* replied to the FARO blitz on April 24.

Romero continued, in regard to Gerada: "It is only right to confess that at present he does not enjoy the sympathy of the clergy or of our people because of his preferences." In order to keep people's trust in the church, Romero said, "I believe it opportune to keep our pastoral action more separated from the diplomatic activity of the nunciature." On the anniversary of Paul VI's coronation, June 30, the archdiocese had done just that, leaving the diplomatic protocol to the nuncio.

Romero next took up the case of the military vicar, Bishop Alvarez, of San Miguel, which, he said, "seems to me extremely serious and requires urgent solution." He was well known, said Romero, for his friendship with the government and the wealthy class, and his priests complained that he had little interest in them. He accepted liturgical engagements in San Salvador for people unfavorable toward the archbishop. "Among the faithful of his diocese he enjoys little sympathy because of his fondness for the government and for militarism." The bishops' conference considered him ineffective and even harmful as military vicar. He had done nothing for the church when a military government was trampling it, even during the occupation of Aguilares. Under the circumstances, the bishops' conference believed it would be better to abolish the military vicariate.

Romero considered Bishop Rivera, his own auxiliary, to be very loyal and humble, and to be the best candidate to take the see of Santa Ana when Bishop Barrera retired. He recommended Barrera's auxiliary, Marco René Revelo, for the see of Santiago de María, which Romero himself had left. "The advancement of these two bishops would, I believe, give force and unity to the bishops' conference, since at present I find it very shaky, given the negative attitude of Bishop Alvarez and the feebleness of Bishop Barrera."

As archbishop, Romero often presided at the local celebrations that are so dear to Latin Americans. Every church, every parish, every town or village has its patronal feast to celebrate. Dear also to the ordinary Catholic in Latin America is one or more devotions, whether a practice common to the universal church or veneration of some image in a particular place. Romero himself never lost his love of the image of Our Lady of Peace, the patroness of El Salvador, kept in the cathedral of San Miguel, or of the daily praying of the rosary. His friend Salvador Barraza recalled that when they would start a drive to any distant place, Romero would say the rosary with him or with the family if they were along. "On long trips we would say fifteen decades," said Barraza, laughing.

Vatican II and Medellín did not change Romero's devotions. Rather, he was able to synthesize the new theology with the old treasure, like the householder of the gospel parable who brings out new things and old from his storeroom. In his preaching, too, Romero combined the new and the old, taking the people's simple devotional piety as a starting point and leading them on to a deeper and more cultivated understanding of the Scripture and the church's teaching. On the way he would exhort them also to a more profound prayer and a deeper living of the gospel.

An example is the sermon he preached on July 16, 1977, for the feast of Our Lady of Mount Carmel in the church of the same name in Santa Tecla. Even though the Jesuits have administered the church since 1914, the patronal feast has a Carmelite tone, and for many people the feast is a celebration of the Carmelite scapular, which Our Lady is said to have given to St. Simon Stock and which millions of Catholics wear in a simplified form.

Only a ten-minute drive from the limits of San Salvador, Santa Tecla is a good-sized town in itself. The church of Our Lady of Mount Carmel stands near the center of town, its spires poking into the sky and its beige-painted walls rising above the one and two story houses all about. It is always filled for the festive mass.

In his sermon Romero said the Blessed Virgin gave the scapular to Simon Stock, superior of the Carmelites, as a sign of protection in time of persecution. He said those who listened to him that day should also ask her for protection in the persecution the church was enduring. "The Blessed Virgin offers us a promise of salvation. But it is not just a salvation after death. It is a salvation that demands work of us in temporal matters also, here in history. And it demands inner renewal, the kingdom of God that begins on this earth, within our own hearts."

The scapular, he said, is a sign of "the hope for salvation that all bear in their souls." It is a promise of salvation—but not a hollow promise, not a promise separated from the world each person lives in. "The promise that the Blessed Virgin wants to awaken in the human heart is an eschatological sense, a hope of the beyond—to work on this earth with the soul and the heart in heaven, to know that no one takes up residence in this world but is, rather, on a pilgrimage to eternity, that the things of the earth pass away, that the eternal is what remains. Above all, it is this: transcendence."

The Blessed Virgin, like the church, like Christ, offers us a transcendent message, and this gives the church an originality that no other promise of liberation possesses. "The Marxists, the liberation movements of the earth, are not thinking of God or of the hope of heaven, and therefore they are greatly different. Although the church speaks also of liberation, of seeking justice, of a more just social order, it does not put its hope in an earthly paradise. The church wants a better world, but it knows that perfection will never be achieved in history, that it lies beyond history. Its salvation is located there whence came the Blessed Virgin to Simon Stock. It is a destiny in that heaven where our mother awaits us."

But, the archbishop pointed out, there is another side to the Blessed Virgin's message. From childhood they all had learned that, if they wore the scapular faithfully, the Blessed Virgin promised to take them out of purgatory on the first Saturday after their death. It is not a matter of faith, he explained; no one had to believe it. "But from childhood we also learned . . . that the Blessed Virgin does not promise to save us without our making an effort on this earth." If the scapular is a message of eternity, it is also a demand to fulfill the duties of this world.

"And this is what the church is accentuating at this time. When the church demands a more just society, wealth better shared, more respect for human rights, the church is not meddling in politics or becoming Marxist and communist. The church is telling people what the scapular says: only those will be saved who can use the things of earth with the heart of God."

The gospel, he said, demands of today's Christian a greater commitment to history. "The council says all who do not work to fulfill the law of God faithfully are offending God. They are also offending against the love of neighbor . . . and are endangering their own salvation. . . . Of those who are condemned it will be said, they could have done good and did not. They had in their hands wealth that could have made happy their brothers and sisters, and out of selfishness they did not do it. They had in their hands the power that could have changed the course of the nation and made it happier, more just, more peaceful, and they did not do it. All who had in their hands such ability, such responsibility, and did not use it will also be brought to task at the last judgment and at the judgment of their own lives."

The scapular, Romero went on, is a sign of salvation, and Vatican Council II explains what salvation is. "Salvation is a concept from the gospel tradition that evolves like anything else. The tradition is the same, the one that Christ handed on to the apostles. It cannot change. But it does evolve according to the needs of peoples and times. When Christ speaks of salvation, it must be understood in the way that the church of 1977, assisted by the Holy Spirit, understands what salvation is." The council understands salvation not just as the salvation of the soul but of the whole person, as an individual and as a member of society. "Society is what must be saved, the whole world. . . . Not the soul at the hour of death, but the person living in history must be saved." If the Blessed Virgin were to give the scapular to Simon Stock today, she would tell him: "This is the sign of protection, a sign of God's teaching, a sign of humanity's integral vocation, for the salvation of the whole person, now, in this life. All who wear the scapular must be persons who live now in salvation on this earth, must feel content to develop their human powers for the good of others."[19]

From all parts of El Salvador they came, letters from the people, many laboriously traced on lined paper by hands more used to the hoe and the machete than the pen. They told of their struggles, their pains, their hopes, their faith, their confidence in him, the archbishop, the strength they drew from his words.

> I always listen to YSAX and each day my faith grows, because I had never felt that the church was so close to us poor people.

> I'm a faithful listener to the station YSAX, where I receive the voice of encouragement, I feel happy when you speak only the truth.

> We wish to tell you that your homilies and talks move us to continue stronger and more forceful in this struggle to build a more just order and beginning first with ourselves.

> We, a Christian community, committed in Christ Jesus, are one with you and very happy to have a good shepherd and prophet of our time.

> Day after day I listen to your messages on YSAX, and to tell you the truth I had never listened to that radio, or even knew where to tune it in, but now I have three favorite hours and thanks to God I have gotten my family that was so indifferent to do the same when I am absent.

> The Christian communities of the villages, conscious of the true way that Christ shows by his gospel, recognize you as the true shepherd and spiritual guide for us. And as the true defender of our Catholic teaching and religion.

> With all affection and esteem for your humble person, we greet you in the name of this community, and not only this, but at the same time we inform you that we totally agree with your consideration in the present situation, which horrifies the whole country, and especially the church, which is the bearer of the message of truth, the way and the life.

The largest number of such letters came from campesinos, most of whom cannot read or write. Many letters were signed with a collection of thumb-prints. It is not hard to visualize a group of wiry, weather-beaten men and women gathered around the light of a candle while the one or two literate members traced the words on a tablet for all to sign and one to take over the mountain paths to a distant small-town post office.

Most campesinos' letters came from grass-roots Christian communities. This was partly because few could write for themselves, but it also testified to the church life existing in many hundreds of small communities through-out the country and to the pastoral policies that had brought them about. The life of the Salvadoran peasant centers largely around the *cantón*, or hamlet. The church's parishes are centered in the larger towns and include dozens or hundreds of outlying hamlets, many of them accessible only by horse or on foot. Priests can visit them only occasionally, but the local community, with its trained catechists and delegates of the word, deepens the spiritual life of its members with its common worship and Bible study. These communities and their leaders bore the brunt of the persecution.

> Now that we find ourselves in difficult times of persecution and fleeing without any due reason but none of this will detain us we'll go on, to continue our struggle until we succeed in building the kingdom of God on earth.

> But we true Catholics are with you and with all the priests. Just as you are ready to give your lives for Jesus Christ so are we.

> Without any fear we will keep on preaching in the light of the gospel the good news to the poor, filled with an unshakable faith and a hope that renews our strength to follow without losing heart in the way of Christ.

> We committed Christians, are not frightened by so many threats, the more we are threatened the braver we feel and therefore we write you not to feel alone, we are all ready to accept any sacrifice.

Many besides campesinos also wrote. Not all were poor. Even among the upper class of society, sincere persons remained loyal to the archbishop. His enemies, in fact, were few, though powerful. For many of all classes, the time of persecution and the valiant response of the church were a call to a new life.

> I could never feel happy because my heart was full of rancor and resentment, but since the death of Father Rutilio I began to see my errors.

> Since then I feel so repentant and so ashamed before God and I want to start a new life.

Some wrote about personal matters—unhappy marriages, drink, a possible religious vocation. To these Romero would write a few lines of reply, sometimes recommending a priest to talk with. The most moving of the letters were those that recounted new outrages and persecution. Two young catechists described how they were arrested while waiting for mass in Aguilares, taken away, and beaten:

> They walked us up and down, guarded by eight guardsmen as if we were some big criminals, and then put us into the jail where we were

insulted and at the same time they kept slandering the priests and the church.

Another group wrote:

> We are victims of that ruthless persecution, we have lost our unforgettable brothers Salomé, Amadeo, and Toñito. The armed forces stole from us part of the little we had for our living and daily there appear members of the GN to keep on intimidating us, so that we won't meet any more to study the word of God, the teaching that the martyr of the gospel Rutilio Grande left us as an essence.

Misspelled, badly punctuated, unstructured, the letters nevertheless achieve the eloquence that flows from simple sincerity. For Romero they were a daily reminder of the ancient theological adage: the voice of the people is the voice of God.[20]

❧ IV ❧

The Body of Christ in History

August–December 1977

Archbishop Romero wrote his second pastoral letter to be published on August 6, feast of the Transfiguration of Christ, which is observed in El Salvador as the feast of the Divine Savior of the World, the titular patron of the archdiocese and the nation. Like his first pastoral, it was about the church, but it focused on the church as Vatican II and Medellín had begun to renew it—the church that the newspapers and FARO attacked and whose priests and catechists were persecuted. The church as it was being renewed was also the church that puzzled and disturbed many sincere Catholics used to the earlier ways. It displeased and saddened many, because it demanded that they change and be converted, "and all conversion is difficult and painful, because the change that is demanded refers not only to ways of thinking but also to ways of living."

Romero wanted to explain to people why the church of the archdiocese was acting differently from what they were accustomed to. He asked Jon Sobrino to write a first draft, and Romero then rewrote it, retaining Sobrino's basic argument and general outline. The letter brings together what Romero had been preaching in his homilies: "What I am going to say here is not at all new. But I believe it is desirable to repeat it because it has not been sufficiently assimilated and because in our country many voices, on the radio and in the newspapers, presume to judge what the church is, distorting its true nature and mission."

The fundamental change in the church in the preceding years, Romero said, was the new way in which the church looked at the world, "both to challenge it in regard to what is sinful in it and to be challenged by it in regard to what may be sinful in itself." The gospel was the foundation of this change in the church's view of the world, a change that had "helped the church to recover its deepest Christian essence, rooted in the New Testament." The church had become more deeply conscious that it is present in the world, that what happens in the world touches it and concerns it, that events are "signs of the times" for it. And it had become more

80

deeply conscious that it is in the world to serve the world, to be a sign and sacrament of salvation, "to make present the liberating love of God shown forth in Christ."

The church had recovered the insight, which fills the pages of the Bible, that God is acting in human history. Salvation history and profane history are not distinct, but the same. Medellín says: "In the search for salvation we must avoid the dualism that separates temporal tasks from sanctification."[1]

The church's relation to the world as universal sacrament of salvation "defines its firm position against the sin of the world and strengthens its stern call to conversion," Romero said. "By being in the world and for the world, one with the world's history, the church uncovers the world's dark side, its depths of evil, what makes humans fail, degrades them, dehumanizes them."

Looking at sin, the church calls for conversion, beginning with its own. And viewing the overwhelming poverty and suffering of most of humanity, in particular in Latin America, it must call for conversion of both hearts and structures. "In the encounter with the world of the poor it has found the most pressing need of conversion. The love of Christ that urges us (2 Cor. 5:14) becomes a clear demand before the brother or sister in need (1 John 3:17)."

Many attacks on the church of the archdiocese, the renewed church that the pastoral letter describes, came from a professed zeal for Catholic tradition, which was supposedly being forgotten or rejected by innovators. Romero took up the question of change in the church. "Whoever does not understand or accept this new perspective will be unable to understand the church. To keep oneself anchored, out of ignorance or selfish interest, in a traditionalism without evolution is to lose even the notion of the true Christian tradition. The tradition that Christ confided to his church is not a museum of souvenirs to preserve. It comes, indeed, from the past and is to be loved and preserved faithfully, but always with a look to the future. It is a tradition that makes the church fresh, up-to-date, and effective in each epoch of history. It is a tradition that nourishes the church's hope and its faith so that it can keep on proclaiming and inviting all toward the 'new heaven and new earth' that God has promised (Rev. 21:1; Is. 65:17)."

Change in the church is not infidelity to the gospel. Rather, it comes from the very depths of the faith and, indeed, makes it more faithful and better identified with Jesus Christ.

"This is the theme of my letter: the church is the body of Christ in history. By this I mean that Christ has wanted the church to live in every period of history. The church's founding is not to be understood in a legal, juridical manner, as though Christ had got a few men together to entrust them with a teaching and given them a charter, while remaining himself separate from the organization. Rather, the origin of the church is something much deeper. Christ founded his church in order to keep on being present himself in the history of human beings, precisely through that group of Christians who form his church. The church is thus the flesh in which Christ incarnates throughout the ages his own life and the mission of his person."

Thus the church must change if it is to be faithful to its mission as the historical body of Christ. If it ceases to be that body, it is no longer his church. "Therefore, in the different circumstances of history, the criterion that guides the church is not the satisfaction of human beings or its fear of them, no matter how powerful or feared they may be, but its duty to lend to Christ through history its voice so that Jesus can speak, its feet so that he can walk the world of today, its hands to work in the building of the kingdom in today's world, and all its members to 'fill up what is lacking in his suffering' (Col. 1:24)."

As the body of Christ in history, the church must do what Jesus did in his life—proclaim the reign, or kingdom, of God. The kingdom that Jesus preached was one in which people would live together as brothers and sisters and as children of God. He called all classes, but showed his preference for the known sinners, the prostitutes, the tax gatherers, the lepers, the Samaritans, and all the outcasts of his time. The church must prefer the outcasts of the present—the campesinos, the slum dwellers, the exploited laborers, the prisoners, those abused by the powerful.

Like Jesus, too, the church must point out sin. He denounced the commercialization of the temple, the observance of law without its spirit of justice and mercy, the rich who did not share, the self-righteous who despised sinners and Samaritans, the leaders who placed unbearable burdens on the people. Sin obstructs God's reign, keeps people from living in justice and love. The church must denounce the selfishness that lurks in every heart, the sin that dehumanizes, that unmakes families, that turns money, possession, gain, and power into the purpose of life. It must also denounce those social, economic, cultural, and political structures that oppress and impoverish people. "But, like that of Christ, the church's denunciation is inspired not in hatred or resentment. Rather, it seeks conversion of heart and the salvation of all."

This description of the church fitted also the archdiocese. "On the titular feast of this year it offers itself, marked with the painful and glorious signs of martyrdom and persecution, precisely because of its faithfulness in being the body of Christ in our history."

But just when the archdiocese was making its greatest effort to be faithful to the gospel, it was accused of betraying the gospel. Romero reduced the many accusations to three: that the church preached hatred and subversion, that it had become Marxist, and that it had gone beyond the bounds of its mission in order to meddle in politics.

That the church preached hatred and violence, he denied. The record showed that it had preached love and forgiveness in the face of persecution. "The church has not called brother to rise against brother, but it has recalled two fundamental facts. The first is what Medellín says about 'institutionalized violence' (Medellín Peace, no. 16). When a situation of permanent and structured injustice is set up, then the situation itself is violent. In the second place, the church knows that whatever it says in this situation, even when it is really guided by love, will sound violent. But it cannot refuse to say it. It cannot deny what Jesus said: 'The kingdom of God suffers violence, and the violent take it by force' (Matt. 11:12). It is the violence of struggling against one's own selfishness, against the sluggishness of a nature more inclined to dominate than to serve. It is the violence with which the violence of the situation is denounced."

As for being Marxist: "What we can call Marxism is a complex phenomenon that must be studied from an economic, scientific, political, philosophical, and religious viewpoint. Marxism must also be studied within its own history." The church says that Marxism as an atheistic philosophy is incompatible with Christian faith. "The real problem is that, to the traditional condemnation of atheistic Marxism, the church now adds in equal measure the condemnation of the capitalist system, which it denounces also as one of the practical materialisms."

The church lives amid specific ideologies and social practices. It ponders the good and the evil, the attraction and temptation that are hidden in both the socialist currents and in the capitalist ideology. "But when it examines and judges the different ideologies, it is moved first of all by the ethical concern of its faith, rather than the desire to give technical judgments on the practical measures that the different ideologies propose."

As for meddling in politics: what the church says and does can certainly have political effects, but the church does not use the mechanisms of political parties or similar organizations to do its task. In El Salvador, Romero reminded the people, the law recognized the church, but in recent months its priests and catechists had been attacked and their rights trampled, and their rights were part of the church's responsibility. The persecution touched Christ himself, because it afflicted his followers: "Saul, Saul, why do you persecute me?" (Acts 9:4).

Romero continued: "The church is persecuted because it wants to be truly the church of Christ. As long as the church preaches an eternal salvation without involving itself in the real problems of our world, the church is respected and praised and is even given privileges. But if it is faithful to its mission of pointing out the sin that puts many in misery, and if it proclaims the hope of a more just and human world, then it is persecuted and slandered and called subversive and communist."

The church's service of the gospel and the resulting persecution had given the archdiocese, said Romero, a unity unknown before.

> This unity and solidarity is for me a very clear sign that we have chosen the right road. But the events of the last months remind us that the union of Christians is obtained not by lips confessing a single faith

but by putting that faith into practice; it is achieved around a common effort, a single mission. It is obtained in faithfulness to the word and the demands of Jesus Christ, and it is built upon common suffering. There can be no unity in the church while the reality of the world we live in is ignored; and thus, although the show of unity has been impressive, it has not been total. Some that call themselves Christians have not contributed to the unity of the archdiocese, either out of ignorance or to defend their own interests. Rather, anchored in a false traditionalism, they have misinterpreted the action and teaching of today's church, have turned a deaf ear to the voice of Vatican II and Medellín, and have been scandalized at the church's new face. . . . What divides is not the actions of the church, but the sin of the world and of our society. What has happened in our archdiocese, and what always has happened when the church is faithful to its mission, is that when the church enters the world of sin with an intention to save and liberate, then the world's sin enters the church and divides it. It separates the authentic Christians of good will from those of mere name and appearance.

At the moment, he said, the archdiocese needed unity more than ever in order to be credible and effective. It had lost many priests and catechists, but the pastoral work had grown with the awareness of many Catholics who had not previously lived their faith so deeply. It was expanding its work through the radio, *Orientación*, schools, and parishes. Vocations to the priesthood and religious life were growing, but God was also calling lay people to take on responsibilities in the church. "There has never been in our archdiocese so much hope as now, in one of the most difficult moments of its history. Persecution has not produced discouragement, retreat, or faltering, but Christian hope."

He concluded with the hope that the government would understand the church's practice of integral evangelization. He was ready to converse with the government "as long as the dialog is based on common language and not on the discrediting and defaming of the church's language, and as long as a sequence of events succeeds in restoring to the church the trust that has been lost." Such events would include accounting for disappeared persons, the end of tortures and arbitrary arrests, freedom from fear for those who had fled their homes, due process for deported priests. The dialog thus begun would move toward cooperation of church and state for the creation of a just social order.

On August 9, the president's private secretary, Colonel José Napoleón Agreda, appeared unexpectedly at Archbishop Romero's office with an invitation to meet the next afternoon at four o'clock with the president in Presidential House, the official offices. Anxious not to be used for political propaganda, the archbishop asked if the meeting would be private, and

Agreda assured him it would be and that all publicity would be avoided. Hoping that this might be the beginning of the dialog he had long wanted, Romero accepted and began to prepare a memorandum to give the president at the meeting.[2]

General Carlos Humberto Romero had been president a little over a month, though many had considered him the real power in the country during the last months of the Molina government. Before his election as president he had been Molina's minister of defense and public security; as such he had brutally repressed a student demonstration, with many deaths, on July 30, 1975, in San Salvador. Besides that massacre, everyone remembered the killings at La Cayetana on November 29, 1974, and at Tres Calles on June 21, 1975.[3] Oscar Romero, as bishop of Santiago de María, had celebrated mass for the Tres Calles victims and had protested to President Molina (see chap. II).

In a press conference the day after his inauguration, the new president had spoken of "slight differences" between the government and the church and had called for dialog.[4] To this the archbishop had replied in his July 3 homily: "The church has never broken off dialog with anyone. It is others who have broken it off, others who have ill-treated the church. We would tell him there are many words that come not from the lips but must come from deeds, so as to demonstrate sincerity in this search for peace for our country. For example, the church needs to get back the priests it has been deprived of. Many families need to get back their dear ones whose whereabouts are unknown. Many deeds are needed in order to gain trust and to really seek among all and with sincerity the peace that our country needs."[5]

The government was feeling pressure for its human rights record. July 21 would be the deadline given to the Jesuits by the White Warrior Union to get out of the country, and it was also the day that the United States House of Representatives' Subcommittee on International Organizations was to hold hearings on religious persecution in El Salvador. At Romero's suggestion, the president of the archdiocesan priests' senate, Francisco Estrada, agreed to go to Washington to testify at this time about the latest developments between church and government. Not all were happy about his going, but Romero saw it as a way of showing the church's good will.

Estrada began his testimony by agreeing with all that previous witnesses had said concerning the persecution during the preceding months. "In order to be as objective as possible," he added, "in regard to so important a subject and in order to bring matters up to date as much as possible, I wish to add some facts from the first weeks of July 1977, which could possibly be interpreted as first indications and signs of a bit of hope for the near future." The new facts were that on July 15 the government had taken special security precautions to protect the Jesuits and their institutions, that a bilateral commission of church and government had been formed on July 15 and had met on July 19, and that on July 19 the government had published its first statement condemning all violence "from wherever it comes." Estrada concluded: "As you can see, the preceding consists chiefly of words and promises, even though there have been some specific actions. The question is whether the present government of El Salvador will keep its promises."[6]

The bilateral commission, which had met once, consisted of Estrada and Bishop Rivera for the archdiocese; for the government, the vice-president, Julio Astacio; and for ANEP, José Francisco Guerrero.[7]

The meeting between the archbishop and the president took place on August 10, as scheduled. The presidential offices, surrounded by tree-shaded lawns, are situated close to the southeastern edge of San Salvador, near the foot of the hills called Planes de Renderos. The president said he wished to talk with all the sectors of the country from whom he hoped for cooperation. The archbishop replied that the church was ready for dialog and for service to the people but that it hoped to recover trust in the government. Events had damaged that trust but effective actions could restore it. He handed the president the memorandum he had brought along as a basis for discussion.[8]

The memorandum outlined a three-stage process for cooperation between the church and the government. In the first, or immediate, stage the government would have to explain what had happened to the persons that had disappeared in its custody, would have to free or begin due process for those held prisoner, and would have to stop unwarranted arrests. It would also have to remove the restrictions on the reentry of priests to the country and review the cases of the priests who had been expelled, giving the church a chance to speak for them. It would have to offer protection to the priests who had left their parishes under threats, and show some action in the investigations of the Grande and Navarro murders. It would also have to use its influence to stop the defamation of the church in the media. (The daily papers were continuing a barrage of lies and distortions, and some of the most anti-Jesuit attacks had appeared while the Jesuits' lives were threatened.) Estrada's trip to Washington, said the archbishop, should be considered a show of good will by the church.

The second, or mediate, stage envisioned by the archbishop would consist of the implementation of measures designed to find a common language and to assure the confidence of the campesinos, the poor, and the church. He proposed a series of meetings with high-level military officers during which church representatives would explain the church's social documents and the teachings of Medellín. Some positive measures to better the lives of the peasants and the poor would also have to come in this stage.

The third, or long-range, stage would be one of structural change in Salvadoran society, "that is, an urgent, daring, and global change in the way the benefits of labor and of the wealth of the country are distributed."[9]

The conditions had been developed during weekly working breakfasts, lasting from 7:00 to 9:00 A.M. in the hospital where Romero lived; the archbishop had initiated these weekly meetings with a group of advisers and continued to hold them off and on through his years as archbishop.

The two Romeros went over the memorandum. The archbishop spoke of the anguished families that came to beg him to help find their loved ones. He handed the president a partial list of disappeared persons. The president looked a bit surprised but calmly promised he would ask the security forces about the cases and would inform the archbishop. The president said that prisoners were already being sent to the courts or were being released. Many though, he added, committed new offenses and were returned to jail. As for the arbitrary arrests, he objected that some parts of the country were controlled by "clandestine" groups, including FECCAS and UTC. Those who were harassed, he said, were disturbing public order, and the security forces were often those who were attacked.

The president asked Romero to supply a list of priests who had been expelled or kept from entering the country and who would not be a problem for the government if they were to return. Some priests, he said, should not return, but those who had voluntarily left the country or their parishes out of fear could return without any difficulty. The archbishop proposed the case of Father Rutilio Sánchez, who had fled the parish of San Martín, a few miles east of the capital, and was living in the seminary out of fear of the police. He also asked that the government return Sánchez's car, which the police had seized from the cathedral parking lot and had impounded in the presidential garage.

The president offered to guarantee the priest's safety and said he could have his car back, which he was surprised to learn was impounded there. He suggested that the archbishop might make up the lack of priests with foreign clergy, but they would have to be investigated before leaving their own countries, so as not to bring problems with them. The archbishop offered no objection to what seemed like a normal immigration process. (However, the priests' senate in its August 31 meeting thought it better not to give the government such an opportunity.)

They then spoke of how to arrive at a common language in the intermediate stage. The archbishop lamented that many actions of the government against priests and church workers came from misinterpretation of the church's language in its present pastoral work. His memorandum therefore proposed the high-level commission of church and government people. The president accepted the idea, and the archbishop suggested that the commission that had already met could continue. (Archbishop Romero informed the priests' senate on August 31 that he had given copies of the Medellín documents to high government and military officers.)

In regard to the church's demand for measures to better the lives of the people, the president described his public works plans, especially his plans to construct housing for campesinos.

Turning to the structural changes demanded by the third stage proposed by the archbishop, the president lamented the selfish attitudes of the country's capitalists and the difficulty of dealing with them. He favored the "humanization of capital" and said the church should talk not only with the poor but with the rich. The archbishop reminded him that the wealthy parishes of the city were well cared for and that the wealthy had long had the best Catholic schools. It was certainly urgent to "humanize capital," but the best way to do it was to let the church do its evangelizing work.[10]

After the meeting, the archbishop sent the archdiocesan chancellor to talk with the president's private secretary, Colonel Agreda, about Rutilio Sánchez and his car. The secretary knew nothing of the matter, but said he would talk to the president and send a reply. The reply never came, and Sánchez did not get his car back until the first days of September, and then several items were missing.[11]

In their next meeting with the vice-president and Guerrero, the church's representatives went over the archbishop's memorandum and gave Astacio the list of priests expelled or unable to return to the country, so that he could go over it with the president. The commission agreed to add another priest and a high-ranking military officer to their own number. They also suggested forming another bilateral commission to examine some of the events for which each side had a different interpretation, such as the recent killing of two cursillistas. The archbishop made the suggested appointment for the side of the archdiocese.[12]

On August 25, the president and vice-president met from 4:00 to 5:30 P.M. with three Jesuits. One of them had been in a meeting that morning with the archbishop, who, he said, was concerned over harassment in the Aguilares area. Delegates of the word were refused employment, and people were harassed for being associated with the church. Father Sánchez was still awaiting his car and a guarantee of his safety if he returned to his parish. The president's secretary had been informed, and nothing had been done.

The Jesuits mentioned other matters. A teacher in their high school had been arrested and had disappeared. The Grande investigation was going nowhere; a known suspect was walking free in El Paisnal, and the bodies had not been exhumed. What the church wanted was action, not just words.

The meeting produced an hour and a half of words, but not much action. The president spoke of the pressures he received from the military and the bourgeoisie, of the criticism from *Orientación* and YSAX. Traditionally, he said, the church, capitalists, and the military had aligned to hold the country together. Now the church was going its own way.[13] It was an accurate enough observation, but it overlooked the possibility that the church might be on the right path.

The archbishop wrote the president on September 13 to remind him of what had been said and done so far, going over each point of the memorandum he had prepared for the August 10 meeting.

He had left a list of disappeared persons with the president, who had promised to investigate in the security forces and inform him what had happened to them. The chancellor had reminded the president's secretary about it, but no information had yet come forth.

He had asked for freedom or due process for those under arrest and the end of arbitrary arrests and intimidation of campesino communities. "But I must confess, regrettably, that the apparent improvements do not achieve a sense of freedom and tranquility. The impression is that suspicion and surveillance continue, principally of the co-workers in the church's evangelizing work, for whom I asked you for the needed guarantees of safety."

The representatives from the archdiocese had given the vice-president the list of priests expelled from the country or forbidden to return. Nothing more had been heard about them. As for getting new foreign priests to fill in, it was not easy to find them, and he was waiting also to know how many of the others could return.

He had asked for guarantees of safety for the priests who feared to return to their parishes, in particular for Rutilio Sánchez. The chancellor had also discussed it with the secretary. Sánchez had his car back, minus some accessories, but no guarantees of safety had been received.

"With satisfaction I see that the defamatory publications against the church have lessened, although lately flyers have been circulated with the well-worn list of 'communist priests' and with offensive caricatures of me." (The press campaign had eased up at this time, but it resumed at the end of September.)

He had named his representatives to the commission they had discussed and to the second commission. He closed "confiding that the sincere desire that you have manifested and that the church has always preached of a peace based on justice and love will enlighten the way to the lost dialog."

Over a month after Romero's talk with the president, the only tangible result was the return of Rutilio Sánchez's car. The archdiocese tried to keep the process going, and Rivera agreed to continue on the commission after he was named bishop of Santiago de María in September.

However, no progress had been made by the end of the year. On December 23, 1977, the United States ambassador, Frank Devine, called on the archbishop in order to emphasize Washington's interest in bettering relations between the archdiocese and the government. He suggested several persons who might be mediators, including Prudencio Llach, the Salvadoran ambassador to the Holy See and member of a prominent oligarchic family. Romero had the records of the efforts made in August and September dug out of the files; and, when the ambassador returned on December 27, the archbishop explained to him all that had been done and the government's lack of interest in taking any positive steps to better relations.[14]

Memos were written by Llach to the president on March 14, 1978, and by the archdiocese to Colonel Agreda, the president's secretary, on March 16. Llach was trying to get something going, and the archbishop again designated his same representatives to the commission. But again nothing happened, as Romero reminded Llach when he visited the archbishop on May 29. Romero and his commission members spoke with Llach in Rome in the Vatican Secretariat of State in June 1978, along with Archbishop Agostino Casaroli, prefect of the Council for the Public Affairs of the Church. But again the effort came to naught. According to church participants, the government never showed a real interest in discussion and never even answered the archbishop's letter of September 13, 1977.[15]

On August 15, 1977, Oscar Romero celebrated his sixtieth birthday. August 15, the feast of the Assumption of Mary, is not a holy day of obligation in El Salvador, but it was a fitting occasion for the festive mass he celebrated in the cathedral at 11:00 A.M. During the mass he ordained two deacons from among the seminarians, conferring the first of the holy orders on young men who would later be ordained to the priesthood. Receiving two new helpers from the hand of God, ordained through his own ministry, was a special birthday gift.

At 4:00 P.M. the priests of the archdiocese held a "fraternal gathering" for him in the archdiocesan offices. At the same time it was his turn to give a gift to the archdiocese: the snack bar, which was opened that day. The offices occupied one wing of the seminary building. On entering the area, one came immediately upon the snack bar, and could sit at one of the small tables to watch for friends and acquaintances entering the office area. The fare was simple—instant coffee, tea, soft drinks, cookies, crackers, penny candy. The latest copy of *Orientación* and other publications of the archdiocese were on sale.

The snack bar was Romero's idea. He wanted to provide a place for people to meet informally in order to humanize the office area. It was a practical way of encouraging communication among those who worked together, whether in the offices or in the parishes and other operations of the archdiocese.[16]

His birthday was also the day Romero received his new lodgings at the Divine Providence Hospital, where he had been living in a room across from the sacristy since becoming archbishop.

The hospital was for indigent cancer patients, with a capacity of 120. Romero had taken an interest in the work about 1966, when the hospital had just opened and he was still a priest in San Miguel. He came occasionally to say mass for the patients and the Sisters who ran the hospital. He continued the practice after he moved to San Salvador, and when he was ordained a bishop in 1970 the collection taken up at the ordination mass was for the hospital. During the two years that he was in Santiago de María he used the hospital as his lodging when he came to San Salvador, sleeping in the room across from the sacristy, behind the altar of the chapel. There he took up residence when he became archbishop. He took his meals with the Sisters in their dining room, and he became the Sisters' chaplain, celebrating mass and morning prayer with them each day at 6:30.

To give him more space than the sacristy and the small bedroom provided, the Sisters had a little house built just down the slope from the kitchen and dining-room building. In the presence of the ambulatory patients they gave him the keys to the new building on his birthday. The house had two modest bedrooms, so that he could have an overnight guest, and a small sitting room. There were shelves for his books, and even hooks for his hammock. A wall in front gave him privacy in the tiny garden, and a carport sheltered his Toyota.

The Sisters refused to let him pay for his room and board, but he remained a benefactor of the hospital. When he was nominated for the Nobel Peace Prize, he promised it to the hospital if he should win, though he did not expect to. He did give them the $10,000 check he got for a peace prize from Sweden in March 1980, endorsing the check to the hospital two days before his death.

He had chosen to live at the cancer hospital instead of the seminary in order to get away from the cares of office. The hospital was about ten minutes away by car, but on the edge of a newish neighborhood and somewhat isolated and quiet. With the Sisters at table he preferred to banter and joke rather than talk of important concerns. However, his efforts to make the hospital a refuge were short-lived. Journalists, campesinos, political leaders, and others received appointments to see him there. Even the priests' senate met sometimes at the hospital. The little house, though, remained exclusively his, and only a favored few like Cardinal Aloísio Lorscheider of Brazil were invited to lodge in the guest room.

As time went on, the Sisters and employees of the hospital became his friends. Their devotion accompanied him to the end, and after his death the Sisters wanted him entombed at the hospital. But by then he clearly belonged to all the people and to the cathedral.[17]

On August 21, 1977, Romero again visited Aguilares, this time to bless the new tabernacle that had been installed to replace the one destroyed earlier by the soldiers. He found an atmosphere of tension and fear; the people were aware that their small-community meetings were watched by the police and the informers. But he also found that the members of the communities were persevering, especially the catechists and delegates of the word, who were held under greatest suspicion by the authorities and were the most persecuted by the security forces. "The church will remain faithful to its message," Romero told the people, "opposing brute force and psychological warfare with love and justice."

On August 26, security forces struck at the church in the countryside once again, killing two members of the Cursillos de Cristiandad and a young campesino. The operation was the work of a combined force of forty or fifty members of the Guardia Nacional and the Treasury Police, who arrived about 6:30 P.M. at a hamlet called El Salitre, department of Chalatenango.

They fired into the air to frighten the people and searched the houses.*

The Cursillo secretariat related that the security forces seized Serafín Vásquez, a cursillista, as he was coming back from a literacy class. They took him to a small house where Christian doctrine classes were held. At that time, a young campesino named Pablo was living there, since his own home had been flooded out by a new dam built by the government. No one knew his last name. The security forces killed the two men with machetes, leaving the bodies badly mutilated.

Another cursillista, Felipe de Jesús Chacón, a member of the national secretariat, was arrested as he got off a bus on his way home from work at the airport, where he collected taxes. He came back to his village each weekend. The police seized him as he began to walk down the dusty road toward the village. The next morning his body was found. He had been shot in the head, and the skin of his face and head cut away. His body had also been hacked with machetes.

The Treasury Police issued a report that the three dead men were cattle thieves who had attacked a police patrol and killed a policeman; apparently a policeman had been killed elsewhere in some way. The newspapers printed the police report as the truth, prompting the Cursillo secretariat to say in its statement: "Gentlemen of *La Prensa Gráfica* and *El Diario de Hoy,* you are performing a shameful role—deceiving public opinion and mocking professional ethics. . . . Have you taken the trouble to go to the scene of the events and find out from the witnesses who were there what really happened in El Salitre?"[18]

Romero offered his condolences to the grieving families in his Sunday homily, broadcast to the nation, and made a visit to the village.[19]

The news report on October 4 seemed unbelievable. Bishop Revelo, El Salvador's delegate to the synod of bishops in Rome, had declared to the synod that rural catechists in his country were influenced by Marxists. If he had really said that, it played directly into the hands of those who had been maligning, persecuting, and even killing priests, catechists, and delegates of the word. Romero opted for restraint until Revelo's full remarks

---

*A note on the principal security forces in El Salvador may be helpful to the reader at this point.

The largest of the forces is the army, which would be the principal force in a foreign war but also is used for internal security, both in the cities and in the country. Its officers come largely from the military academy and its enlisted men are recruited, usually by force. Only the poor are forced into service.

The Guardia Nacional is a military body trained and used for internal security, especially in the countryside. Although its officers come from the military academy, the ranks are filled with volunteers.

The Treasury Police is a smaller force, similar to the Guardia Nacional. Like the other forces, it is under the Ministry of Defense and Public Security, not the Treasury.

The National Police is the ordinary police force of the country, responsible for traffic direction and ordinary law enforcement. It also participates in security actions, however, especially repression of demonstrations and strikes.

could be seen. The matter justified a phone call to Rome, and on October 6 the church in El Salvador had the full text. The news report was not exaggerated.

Describing the catechetical situation in the country, Revelo had said:

In El Salvador for the past eight years five schools have functioned for training what are called celebrators of the word, or peasant catechists. From the schools have come several thousand rural leaders who carry the word of God to the most remote corners of the country. The urban areas, almost totally neglected until two years ago, are being attended now by a team of priests and lay people depending directly on the national catechetical commission. In these two years they have given thirty-three courses to 1,300 pastoral workers, including professionals, teachers, university students, and high school graduates. In broad strokes, this is the positive side of the adult catechesis situation, because the catechesis of children and young people is subordinated to it.

But there is a side that is cloudy and worrisome. The rural catechists, the best prepared, the most aware, those who always have greater capability of leadership, are rapidly falling into the nets that the Communist Party and the extreme left Maoist groups spread for them, and they quickly fill their ranks. On the other hand, the work of the national catechetical commission for the training of leaders is quickly spoiled by the lack of interest of pastors who prefer to work with campesinos, because it is easier. And no less a problem, certainly the most serious, is the group of priests convinced that the only possible solution to the oppression that the great majority of our people suffer is cooperation with Marxism.

And now the question with which I began: What to do in this situation? The answer seems obvious. The pastoral workers must receive a profoundly Christian training, and we must convince the pastors of the need to attend the urban areas with the same care they use with the campesinos.

But the question I now ask is this: In what does an authentically Christian training consist? Naturally, no one now would think of a training limited to the religious area, to the neglect of people's temporal concerns. But how to achieve a sound balance between religious training and human advancement? Is it not true that those listeners or participants in a catechetics course who are living in subhuman conditions of oppression and neglect listen more agreeably and retain more strongly any allusion to the social, political, and economic problems that distress them? Is it not true that the human problems that [need] a quick, immediate solution have a greater impact than religious problems? What stance should we take with the priests and religious who, feeling anguish before the real problem of the state of oppression and injustice that our people suffer, have opted for a way that we judge to be mistaken? Such is the question that I respectfully lay before the synodal assembly.

It was true that many trained catechists and delegates of the word had joined FECCAS and UTC or the coalitions of organizations that had formed in opposition to the government. It was also true that there were Marxists in these organizations. But to suggest that large numbers of the catechists and delegates of the word were going over to Marxism and even communism was a gross exaggeration and distortion in the view of the clergy most familiar with the question. The priests' senate of the archdiocese held a special session on October 7 to discuss the matter and observed that Revelo's address drew a picture of the situation that was "limited, exaggerated, and biased" and that his remarks unjustly attacked urban priests, rural catechetical centers, catechists, and delegates of the word. The senators present decided to query the catechetical centers, the vicariates of the archdiocese, and the conference of religious to see if they agreed with Revelo and to send the results of the query to the national bishops' conference. Meanwhile they sent the conference, the synod, and Revelo himself telegrams of protest over his remarks.[20]

The evening of the day that he spoke in the synod, Vatican Radio commented: "The words of Bishop Revelo are somewhat disconcerting, since they seem to contradict or not recognize the genuine, valiant, and even heroic apostolate that many priests and catechists are carrying out in El Salvador in the countryside, an apostolate that certainly does not seem so easy when there are threats of death, expulsions, and even martyrdom, like that of Father Rutilio Grande."[21]

Disconcerting it was, and not least of all to Archbishop Romero, who months before had asked the Holy See to transfer Revelo from Santa Ana, where he was auxiliary, to be his own auxiliary in San Salvador. He and Revelo had always gotten along well and he had thought they saw things in the same way. Perhaps they had at the time Romero became archbishop, but Romero's views had changed. Now it seemed inadvisable to bring Revelo to San Salvador, with the clergy as aroused against him as they were, even though Romero had just lost his auxiliary with the naming of Rivera to be bishop of Santiago de María.

On October 11, Romero wrote Revelo, who was still at the synod:

I think it a brotherly duty of candor to write you that your words in the synod of bishops, published here with the customary hubbub, have bewildered the priests and the people who are more conscious of our pastoral policy and only have cheered those who defame the church with exactly the accusations and suspicions with which you have regrettably judged the catechetical expanse of the country. The rejection is general in your regard, although I have tried to lessen it by exhorting people not to judge in advance and to wait for you to explain your meaning. However, the text of your words, which Father Briceño dictated by phone from Rome, has already been published, along with the unfavorable judgment broadcast by Vatican Radio.

Within me, Bishop, I am suffering very much from these painful circumstances, which for the moment do not favor the appointment of which you spoke to me in confidence. This is the principal reason for writing to you urgently—to explain to you this situation, so that you yourself can judge the utility of going to the Sacred Congregation for the Bishops to explain to Cardinal Baggio whether it might be better to wait a bit for your transfer to San Salvador, giving this bad impression time to pass. I think it would be, since I believe that just now you would suffer personally and the effectiveness of your work would be seriously impaired. But it is an opinion submitted naturally to the higher judgment of the Holy See. You can be sure I will give you my complete backing. But out of faithfulness to our pastoral policy in the archdiocese I would have to demand a satisfactory explanation of the matter.[22]

As though to assure Revelo that he had not lost confidence in him, Romero asked him to see about a delicate matter for him. "In the Congregation for the Bishops there is a section for military vicars. I would be grateful if you would use your time in Rome to speak about this delicate matter of the 'inoperativeness'—rather the counterwitness—of this vicariate. As you know, it is the opinion of the bishops' conference, and it is urgent, that the Holy See should take radical and urgent measures."

The Holy See did nothing about the military vicariate. The discontent over Revelo continued, and on October 26 Romero wrote Gerada, the nuncio, asking that the appointment be held up.

Revelo's words in the synod brought forth a letter to the Salvadoran bishops from Cardinal Baggio as head of the Commission for Latin America.[23] He took at face value Revelo's view of the catechists and priests and even carried it a step further. Revelo, he said, had lamented "that among catechists who are better prepared and made more aware there are those who easily let themselves be won over by extremist parties and groups," which Revelo had said, "and also that some priests tend to sympathize in their mental orientation and in their action with Marxist ideology," which Revelo had not said.

Baggio called for a "responsible and direct vigilance over the preparation of the catechists and the teaching that they impart." Some of the texts used in the training centers, he complained, did not conform to decrees of the magisterium and concealed ideas of "struggle, hate, and vengeance."

Certainly, Revelo's words in the synod were not the first that the commission had heard of the training centers. Bishops Alvarez, Barrera, and Aparicio had been unhappy with them for years, as their remarks at bishops' conference meetings showed, and Romero in his memorandum of November 6, 1975, had noted that the government considered them centers of subversion. By 1977, he was more aware that the government could see subversion even in the most innocent of church activities. As bishop of Santiago de María, Romero had faced the question of closing the Los Naranjos training center and had decided to work with it and the priests staffing it (see chap. II), but different pastoral views kept the centers in a state of tension with the conservative bishops.

Romero mentioned Revelo in his homily on November 27, after Revelo had returned from Rome. "There is no schism between Bishop Revelo and the archbishop of San Salvador. There is friendship from long past, and now too when we both fulfill very delicate missions. . . . I asked you from the beginning, and I do so now—let us listen to Bishop Revelo, let us not judge in advance, but let us remember that he is a bishop in communion with the pope and in communion also with the hierarchy of the archdiocese. Therefore, nothing can break this alliance and this friendship in the true message of God. And even when there may be accidental differences, which we air with complete freedom, in what is substantial we are servants of this church, which does not want to betray either the gospel or the people."[24]

During Christmas week the newspapers published the news of Revelo's appointment as auxiliary. In his homily on Sunday, January 1, 1978, Romero gave the news officially to the archdiocese: "I have already given my opinion of Bishop Revelo. He is a genuine friend, although many would distort his views. The pope has given norms for evangelization in El Salvador, and I believe that when he now names a bishop he is showing his confidence in the preaching in this land and that he trusts that the bishop designated goes along with this authentic teaching of the present-day church. I therefore ask all of you to receive with good will the new auxiliary bishop that the Holy Father has named to aid the archdiocese of San Salvador. I ask you to keep in mind the pope's way of thinking, to which every teacher in the church, every bishop, must conform in order to be a worthy minister of the church among that part of God's people to which he is sent."[25] Romero was trying to make the best of a still difficult situation, as he continued to do into the following year.

On January 8, *Orientación* published a new year's pastoral message signed by Archbishop Romero, Bishop Rivera, now bishop of Santiago de María, and Bishop Revelo, as auxiliary bishop of San Salvador. The bishops spoke of the violence that had marked the previous year, expressed their concern about the new public order law and what it might bode for human rights, and made three positive requests of the government, for (1) social legislation directed to resolve institutional injustice, (2) absolute respect for human rights, (3) "real amnesty" for all who had not returned to the country out of fear and for the disappeared persons who were still alive.

Although he signed the letter, Revelo was still in Santa Ana. He and Romero seemed to be negotiating the terms of his coming to San Salvador.

He wanted a parish, for one thing, and he wanted to be the sole vicar-general for another. Romero wrote to him on January 10 to tell him that Monsignor Ricardo Urioste had agreed to yield him his own parish of San Francisco, but that Romero himself wanted to have two vicars-general, Revelo and Urioste (who had replaced Bishop Rivera as vicar-general). He was not going to remove Urioste.

Revelo had become auxiliary bishop in Santa Ana in 1973 after serving as pastor of various parishes in San Salvador. In Santa Ana he had found the vicar-general, Monsignor José López Sandoval, counted for much more than the auxiliary bishop. He did not intend to let that happen again. Romero took up the matter in his letter.

He wanted to have both Urioste and Revelo as vicars-general, he explained,

> in order that the three of us can form the nucleus of authority in the archdiocese. I think you can understand that at this moment my substitution of Monsignor Urioste would create problems for me among the clergy, which, like other sectors of the archdiocese, will view with pleasure the presence of the two of you advising and sharing the responsibility of the archbishop. Your fear of being "nullified" by Monsignor Urioste, as in Santa Ana by Chepe [López Sandoval], I do not see as very realistic, since Urioste is not Chepe and San Salvador is not Santa Ana. In any case, much depends on your attitude. Whether alone or with another, you will receive a welcome in proportion to the pastoral love shown in your service. I harbor great hope that you and Monsignor Urioste are the two counselors and principal helps that I need right now as vicars-general. You will also have your office here where I come every day, so that every day, unless something prevents us, we can get together to plan and develop the work of directing the diocese.

Romero's hopes sound unrealistic, given Revelo's performance in the synod and the attitude that he was showing about his position in San Salvador. Romero may have hoped that Revelo could gain the support of the clergy in spite of their displeasure over the synod incident because the priests' senate had voted on December 9 to ask Romero to invite Revelo to meet with the clergy and because he himself was publicly backing Revelo and asking the diocese to accept him.

But was Revelo ready to accept them? Perhaps not, since Romero went on, "I am somewhat puzzled by some of your expressions about your low esteem for certain sectors of the clergy. I have tried to urge all the priests and religious to have feelings of respect and cordial acceptance toward you, and there is good will even though they have not digested the bad feeling over what was published about your performance in the synod. Your arrival, I think, should overcome whatever dislike they have and give them the chance also to change whatever bad will they have into friendship." He offered to have him concelebrate with him on Sunday morning in order to introduce him to the diocese.

Revelo's reply was curt. He agreed to take Urioste's parish and was waiting for Urioste to talk with him "when he has completely vacated the parish house." In regard to being vicar-general, "I am sorry to disagree with you about sharing the office of vicar-general of the archdiocese with Monsignor Urioste or with any other priest, for reasons that I reserve to myself." As for the clergy, "in regard to my way of thinking, I reserve the right to make my own judgments. In any case, my actions will speak for me. Any previous judgment runs the risk of being rash." He accepted the invitation to concelebrate.[26]

On February, 17, 1978, Revelo was present in the San Salvador cathedral at Romero's acceptance of an honorary degree from Georgetown University. He read a prayer for peace at the close of the ceremony, after being introduced as auxiliary bishop.[27] And on March 6, he formally presented his credentials as auxiliary at the monthly clergy meeting.[28] He became vicar-general, but Urioste also remained vicar-general.

On November 3, 1977, soldiers apparently skirmished with some group on the edge of the town of Osicala, in the department of Morazán, in eastern El Salvador. According to reports, the clash left some persons dead and others wounded. Immediately afterward, troops began to search houses, looking for weapons and "subversive material," and entered the church of Osicala.[29]

It being the day before the first Friday of the month, the eucharist was exposed in the monstrance on the altar. The soldiers opened the tabernacle, according to reports, to search for weapons. The bishop of San Miguel, Eduardo Alvarez, later denied that they had profaned the Blessed Sacrament, as *Orientación* had headlined.[30]

After twice searching the parish house, they returned and arrested the pastor, Miguel Ventura, and the sacristan. The priest was interrogated about his activities, his preaching, the persons that worked with him, where he had studied, and under what teachers. They demanded to know where he kept weapons and subversive literature, and for that they proceeded to torture him, tying his arms behind him and hanging him from a tree limb. Then they took him to the garage for more torture, gagging him with a handkerchief. Part of the technique was to keep insulting him and threatening to kill him.

They then took him to the police station in another town, where he met the sacristan, who had also been tortured. Both were finally released about 10:00 P.M. They were forbidden to return to Osicala until further orders.[31]

The same day in nearby villages, two campesinos were arrested, and the following day a catechist was arrested and tortured. On November 12, an advertisement signed by "Christian Communities of the Department of

Morazán" in *El Mundo* condemned the officials who had perpetrated the crimes, the newspapers that had failed to report them, and Bishop Alvarez, who had remained silent. *Orientación* of November 13 also condemned the violence, but did not mention the bishop. Alvarez later told the bishops in their December meeting that Ventura had acted in the area of politics and therefore suffered the consequences.[32]

On November 10, workers who had been striking two factories for a month without results occupied the labor ministry in order to pressure for a settlement with the employers. Romero agreed to mediate the dispute, naming as his delegate Monsignor Urioste, recently named vicar-general. The strike had taken a violent turn on October 27, when the police killed two persons during an attempt to hold a street fair in benefit of the strikers. One of those killed was a young worker, son of a woman employee involved in the strike; the other was a woman street vendor. The young man died in the cathedral, where he had been carried; Romero himself said the funeral mass there. The mediation of the archdiocese quickly ended the occupation of the ministry building and settled one of the strikes.[33]

On November 12, while the ministry was still occupied, a prominent businessman, Raúl Molina Cañas, was killed when he resisted a kidnapping attempt.[34] Two days later the archbishop celebrated the funeral mass on the cathedral steps before a large crowd. Molina had been respected and popular with his own employees and associates. But someone tried to make a political rally out of the procession from the cathedral to the crypt in the Colonia Escalón. Young men with armbands and bullhorns chanted slogans, calling on "priests of Beelzebub" to "go to Moscow" and on the government to act because "the people want peace." Like the authors of the newspaper ads that increased in size and number over the incident, they clearly wanted an increase in violence on the government's part against opposition organizations and the church.[35]

The day before Molina's funeral, a delegate of the word named Justo Mejía, who was also a leader of UTC, was found dead. He had been taken from his house by soldiers of the Guardia Nacional on November 9. The body was badly hacked, the eyes plucked out, the head cut off. The killing probably had no direct relation with the Molina case, but it was another grim reminder that the persecution continued, in spite of denials in the newspapers. The papers had been filled with news of Molina's death and tributes to him, but they ignored the death of the campesino, except for a tiny, struggling paper called *La Crónica del Pueblo*.[36]

La Prensa Gráfica carried an occasional article by Archbishop Romero, but it and the other three major dailies were principally mouthpieces for FARO and ANEP and their sympathizers. Eventually, *La Prensa Gráfica* refused to print his writing, in which he had tried to reach the minds of the wealthy class.[37] The papers continued to carry the columns and occasional ads against the church, but at this time they were directed largely to publicizing the schismatic French archbishop, Marcel Lefebvre.

On November 20 a young priest named Pedro Antonio Pineda Quinteros took over by force the church and parish house of the town of Quezaltepeque with the help of a group of townspeople. The newly named pastor, a Belgian, was forced to leave.[38] Romero quickly sent Father Quinteros, as he was generally known, a letter reminding him that he had incurred excommunication by forcibly taking over the parish and calling on him to desist. The newspapers kept the story alive for weeks, even sending reporters to interview the rebel and the legitimate pastor, who used a school chapel for mass and other services.

Pineda Quinteros was only about thirty, but he had already been in at least three dioceses. Unable to find a bishop to ordain him in El Salvador, he prevailed on one in a small diocese in Guatemala to give him holy orders.[39] Romero had taken him on probation in Santiago de María, but had withdrawn his priestly faculties and invited him to return to his own diocese of San Marcos. When he remained without authorization in the parish of Ozotlán, Romero issued a decree suspending him from priestly functions.[40] A petition with many signatures testifies that Quinteros had popularity and support among some people. When Romero became archbishop, he found Quinteros in the archdiocese.

Quinteros and the press were made for each other. They gave him headlines and he gave them wild statements to fill their columns. "We have the Salvadoran Lefebvre!" crowed La Prensa Gráfica on November 26. But Quinteros was to be no Lefebvre. He burned a banner with the word "excommunicated" on it before his congregation and "excommunicated" Romero.[41] He rambled in interviews about how Romero and other priests had it in for him.[42]

The archdiocese tried legal action, in vain, to get the parish buildings back.[43] The legitimate pastor went on using the school chapel, supported by most of the people, and on December 19 Romero celebrated the local commemoration of St. Joseph with him and the parish.[44] Quinteros stayed on in the parish for the rest of Romero's life and in 1980 finally reconciled himself with Bishop Rivera, who took over as apostolic administrator after Romero's death. Among his inconsistencies, he showed up to concelebrate at the funerals of Father Rafael Palacios and of Romero himself.[45]

One of the more picturesque backers of Quinteros was a vituperative publication called La Opinión, an eight-page tabloid that appeared occasionally, devoted to libeling Romero in particular and the church in general. A typical issue filled half the front page with the headline: "Archbishop Romero Directs Terrorist Group—Valiant Accusation Made by a Priest—Archbishop Great Ally of Agents of Subversion."[46] The priest supplying the information was, of course, Quinteros. Another issue carried a cartoon, with Romero saying from the pulpit, "If it's necessary, act with violence—kidnap—kill—long live the class struggle—up with terrorism."[47] The government sent La Opinión to the mayors of the cities and towns for distribution, according to a priest working in the archdiocese at the time.

On November 24 the government adopted a new law, called the Law for Defense of Public Order. Under it, a long list of vaguely described actions were punishable with prison sentences. For example, article 1, paragraph 2, forbade anyone to "induce in writing or by any other means one or more members of the armed forces to undiscipline or disobedience to their hierarchic superiors." Telling soldiers not to obey unlawful orders would seem to be an offense against the law. Likewise, article 1, paragraph 15, forbade transmitting "false or tendentious news or information meant to disturb the constitutional or legal order, the country's tranquility or security, the economic or monetary regime, or the stability of public property and securities." Article 1, paragraph 7, forbade spreading by any means "doctrines that tend to destroy the social order or the political and juridical organization that the political constitution establishes." Roberto Lara Velado, a leader of the Christian Democratic Party in El Salvador, observed that merely advocating profit sharing or almost any form of social change could fall under the prohibition.[48] Indeed, the provision seemed to forbid trying to amend the constitution.

Critics immediately described the law as totalitarian, not only for the all-inclusive restrictions on political activity, but also for the provision of article 15 that allowed detention of suspects for "any presumption or indication" of participation in a forbidden action. It gave a veneer of legality to many of the abuses against human rights.

Romero referred to the controversial law in his homily of November 27. "I am not an expert on law; I'm not a lawyer. I invite lawyers to make use of their legal knowledge to give their judgment on this law. . . . From the theological, priestly viewpoint, however, in the light of God's word, I do have the right and duty to cast light on this event in our land." He then explained the teaching of St. Thomas Aquinas on law: a real law must be just and must be for society's common good. Otherwise it does not require obedience.[49]

The law stayed in effect until February 1979, in spite of protests by churchmen and lawyers.[50] When the government finally repealed it, the archbishop commented, "What is most positive in this action is the government's ability to admit its mistake and begin to correct it."[51]

On December 1, Romero celebrated mass for a group of mothers of disappeared persons. The families of those who have disappeared while in the hands of authorities, who may be dead but could be alive, who may be locked in dungeons or suffering beatings and indignities, probably suffer more than the families whose loved ones have been killed. They have not even the relief of mourning, living as they do between hope and hopelessness.

Romero proposed the models of the mother in the book of Maccabees, who encouraged her seven sons to die rather than betray their faith in the living God, and of Mary, who stood under the cross of her son. "Like Mary at the foot of the cross, every mother who suffers the outrage done to her child is an accusation. Mary, the sorrowing mother, before the power of Pontius Pilate, who has unjustly killed her son, is the cry of justice, of love, of peace, of what God wills, in the face of what God does not will, in the face of outrage, in the face of what should not be."

Preaching thus, he said, is not politics but rather pointing out sin. "This is the voice of justice, this is the voice of love, this is the cry that the church takes up from so many wives, mothers, homes, forsaken ones, in order to say: this should not be, return these sons and daughters as the law of God, the law of the Lord, demands. This is to cry out against sin. This is what the church is doing, crying out against the sin that enthrones itself in history, in the life of the nation."[52]

On November 24, the archbishop spoke to the nuncio about plans to observe the beginning of the new year as Peace Day. Pope Paul VI had already proclaimed the day and its slogan, "No to Violence, Yes to Peace." Romero was planning a series of conferences for January 4–6, to be held in the cathedral, and had already invited Archbishop Marcos McGrath of Panama to give one of the talks. At the same time, the nuncio was planning a religious ceremony to take place in the Salesian church of Mary Help of Christians with the bishops and high government officials present. It looked like another attempt to paper over the differences between church and government. Romero was having none of it, especially since the efforts of August and September had produced no result and the government continued harassing the church and the people. He thought the nunciature should stick to diplomatic affairs and let the bishops handle pastoral matters.

Romero told Gerada in person and in writing that he would not attend if the nuncio went through with his idea. The presence of a government that kept trampling the church and the people would be a mockery. "For those who would promote such an action, it seems to me an expression lacking in solidarity with the sufferings of this church and people and with the concern and efforts of its pastor. For the people it would be a negative sign, and the ambiguity of such a stance would in fact discredit the church." Since Romero would not attend and other bishops might, the event would needlessly publicize the bishops' division and "supply new arms for the heavy attacks to which our archdiocese is subject in these days." The conference he was arranging would be "more in keeping with the desire of the Holy Father."[53]

Romero wrote to Cardinals Baggio and Villot to inform them of this latest tiff with the nuncio.[54]

Gerada replied to Romero with a laconic note saying that he had planned his celebration as a national observance, with the agreement of the president of the bishops' conference, Aparicio; but, "clearly, on my part, no celebration will be organized after your refusal."[55]

Romero's series of conferences went off as planned.

On December 12 Romero sent letters to Cardinals Baggio and Villot, summing up what had happened since he visited Rome in April. He continued: "Our evangelizing and pastoral mission has continued in our archdiocese on the part of priests, religious, and lay people, even in the midst of definite dangers, threats, and surveillance, and of course with the limitations that this supposes. Even members of Bible study groups are regarded with suspicion and apprehension, and at times are arrested and treated with violence. Salvadoran priests have recently had to leave the country to avoid worse misfortunes, due to threats. In spite of all, we continue to spread the work of the church, which does not feel completely free to preach its word."

Romero was concerned by an increase in terrorism, as persons tended to become radicalized. "We are worried likewise by the hardness of heart of those who could do something more for the tremendous poverty of our people." The church's cries for justice based on the gospel continued to be attacked by those who felt themselves affected. But he was cheered to think that his position agreed with the gospel and with the words of the pope. The solidarity of the priests and nuns and of the faithful, especially the poor, also encouraged him. He did not wish to confront the civil authorities, but he had not been able to reestablish normal communication with them, "not having yet the physical and moral security needed for all our priests and catechists, especially in the countryside."

In closing, Romero quoted words of the pope from a recent issue of *l'Osservatore Romano*[56] calling on bishops to be "untiring teachers of the faith." That, he said, was the kind of pastor he was trying to be. He sent the letter to Rome through the bishop of Brugge (who had priests working in El Salvador) rather than through the nunciature.

Villot replied cautiously on February 18. "I read with great interest the report you sent, in which what most stands out are the concerns and aspirations you express for the certainly delicate and complex reality that your country presently lives in. I want to assure you that the Holy See, thanks to the reports that reach it regularly, always follows with special concern the development of the situation in that nation, seeking to evaluate the data objectively and in the light of the judgments and information expressed by all the bishops joined in the bishops' conference and by the apostolic nuncio."

The archbishop, he said, "would not fail to consider how urgent and necessary it is in the present circumstances that through the efforts of the pontifical representative and seeking always agreement with your brother bishops you contribute to the effective reestablishment of a constant understanding with them looking toward an effective dialog with the government authorities, as you yourself desire. All this could indeed help to obtain a more serene, balanced, and impartial vision of the conditions of the country and could also effectively favor the search for a fair and peaceful solution for the many problems that afflict the nation."

The nuncio and the majority of the bishops were clearly influencing Villot's vision of the church in El Salvador. That the Vatican wanted to improve relations with the government of El Salvador is natural and understandable, but Villot left unsaid what price it was willing to pay.

❧{ V }❧

Pastoral Fortitude

January–June 1978

The new year opened with a statement of support for Archbishop Romero by clergy and religious of the archdiocese, who stated their "clear, decided, and total support" for his actions as bishop. "We make our own his word, we commit ourselves to his pastoral policy, and we feel in our own beings the slanders cast at his person. Whoever touches the archbishop touches the heart of the church."

From January 9 to 13, Romero made a retreat with seventeen members of his clergy. In notes he made he observed that the special circumstances he had been living in since taking office made it difficult to turn inward, and he lamented that he had lost somewhat the power to turn to God easily in prayer, although he could still do so when he set about it seriously. He resolved to be firmer with himself about fulfilling his regular times for prayer and reflection and about seeing his confessor regularly. The retreat itself seems to have been one not given to silence and reflection, but he noted that he had found great value in being with the younger priests, whose good will and priestly spirit he was able to know more deeply, and he realized that the Holy Spirit does not need human ascetical methods to bring about transformations.

Abroad as well as at home, Romero was becoming known as a defender of human rights, and those who supported and admired him realized that international support could strengthen his hand and even protect his life in El Salvador. It was such considerations that led to his receiving an honorary degree from Georgetown University of Washington, D.C. Since the murder of Rutilio Grande and the death threat against the Jesuits in El Salvador, various Jesuits in the United States had taken a special interest in El Salvador and its archbishop. Out of that interest grew the concept of an association between the Central American University and Georgetown, and the decision to award an honorary degree to Romero.

Although Georgetown routinely notified the apostolic delegate in Washington about two months in advance of what it was going to do, it was only two weeks before the scheduled award ceremony that the Vatican showed qualms about it. Archbishop Jean Jadot, the apostolic delegate, called the president of Georgetown to ask if Georgetown could withhold, or at least delay, the honor for Romero in view of the political situation in El Salvador. Meanwhile, Cardinal Gabriel Garrone, prefect of the Congregation for Catholic Education, was writing to the Jesuit superior general to try to stop the degree. The Jesuits in Rome, however, agreed with Georgetown that it was too late to change the plans, and the Vatican made no further effort to prevent the honor for Romero.[1]

On Tuesday, February 14, near the end of Romero's first year as archbishop, people filled the San Salvador cathedral for the conferring of the honorary doctorate on Romero. Archbishop Chávez and Bishops Rivera and Revelo were there, as was the president of Georgetown, who had come to El Salvador especially for the event. But it was the people—the humble, the poor—who filled the cathedral. Few had heard of Georgetown University before or knew what an honorary degree is, but they understood that their archbishop was receiving recognition from afar because he spoke for them.[2]

Romero accepted the honor as a "solid support for human rights, . . . a world-resounding applause for the new humanism that the church of today teaches and practices after reflecting on it chiefly at two solemn moments of its present ministry: the Second Vatican Council and the meeting of Latin American bishops at Medellín." For those very reasons he could not accept the degree for himself alone. "I feel it is right to share it in communion with all of our local church, and also with those who even not belonging to the church have made this cause their own by their sympathy, their support, and their collaboration. They are uncountable priests, religious communities, lay Catholics, Protestants with a sincere sense of the gospel, and other persons of good will who have incarnated this cause and defended it even unto the heroism of bloodshed and persecution."

Romero saw the degree also as "a gesture and a voice of solidarity that inspires and gives hope to those who here suffer violence against their fundamental rights in so many and such humiliating ways." The church's voice "of defense and denunciation, which out of self-interest has often been silenced, distorted, and slandered or naively misunderstood by some even within our borders, feels itself today clarified, strengthened, and stimulated by an action serenely contemplated in the cultural surroundings of a prestigious university."[3]

Applause from the crowd interrupted Romero many times, and at the end an announcer had to ask the people to wait until Bishop Revelo could read a prayer for peace concluding the ceremony and then to go to the square outside to congratulate the archbishop.[4] It was clear that a year after becoming archbishop Romero belonged wholly to the people. For the moment everyone could overlook the absence of three bishops and the nuncio, and few were aware that some in the Vatican had tried to prevent Georgetown from giving Romero the degree.

After the ceremony, Romero and a small group shared a supper prepared by the Sisters in the Colegio de la Asunción. It was late when two Jesuits drove him home, and the gate at the hospital drive was closed. Romero got out of the car at the gate and walked up the drive alone, the honorary doctorate in his hand. One of the Jesuits, watching him, remarked how easy it would be for an assassin to lie in wait for Romero on such an occasion.[5]

In a curious sequel to the Georgetown degree, Romero received a letter shortly afterward offering him a degree from Loyola University of New Orleans. It came from the president of Loyola, Father James C. Carter, whom Romero had met briefly the preceding November. Carter had felt concerned about the Jesuits in El Salvador when they were threatened in June 1977 and had written to the Salvadoran consul in New Orleans, Mario Osorio. Osorio asked to meet him and in the interview invited him to visit El Salvador, where he met President Romero. The president asked Carter to try to get the archbishop involved in talks with the government, and Carter brought up the subject in his interview with the archbishop, who explained the history of the attempts to talk with the government and the conditions the church had set down as minimal proof of good faith.

Romero was now wary of Carter's offer of the degree. The Salvadoran press had recently featured a photograph of Father Carter with President Romero at a trade conference in New Orleans, but the media had almost ignored the Georgetown degree, even though the event had filled the cathedral. Carter, the archbishop soon learned from him, had been photographed when a small gift was unexpectedly presented to him and he was called forward to receive it during the conference. The idea for the honorary degree had come from officials in the United States Department of State, who thought New Orleans would be a good place to arrange a meeting between President Romero and Archbishop Romero. To promote the degree and the meeting, the Salvadoran government had made an offer to Loyola to provide free passage on the Salvadoran airline for the archbishop and a companion to travel to New Orleans.

Once he understood how he and Loyola were being used by the two governments, Carter backed off from his involvement. He renewed the offer of the honorary degree, whether Romero spoke to the president or not, with Loyola paying the plane fare. But Romero did not accept the degree.

Recalling the incident almost three years later, the Jesuit provincial remarked that President Romero once asked him in one of their talks, "Why does the archbishop want to talk with me outside the country?" Perhaps even he did not understand all that his consul and the United States Department of State were up to.[6]

In his Palm Sunday homily, March 19, Romero called the week before "a week of bloodshed." Police had killed two persons at checkpoints in

San Salvador. In the department of Chalatenango the caretaker of a rural chapel was found dead after having been arrested. In the capital the government violently broke up a demonstration of campesinos when they arrived at the Agricultural Development Bank to keep an appointment to discuss a reduction in the prices of land rent, fertilizers, and insecticides. "Our people are hungry," said Romero. "They need land to work, they need to talk with someone about finding a solution to their problems. Killing and wounding are the response to that desire."[7]

Romero was recounting events of the week before, but Holy Week itself and the week of Easter were to outdo the sorrowful events he lamented. The new sorrows began on Palm Sunday and embraced a wide area centering on the town of San Pedro Perulapán, twelve miles east of San Salvador.

According to newspaper and government reports, peasants of FECCAS and UTC were "terrorizing" people in the area. Refugees filled the school in San Pedro Perulapán and, according to the government, the security forces entered the area to keep peace and protect lives. Dozens of campesinos, practically all of them members of FECCAS and UTC, were arrested. The two weeks ended with at least six dead, sixty-eight missing, fourteen wounded, many peasants' homes destroyed, and a continuing climate of fear.

The version of events that witnesses and refugees soon began to give the archdiocese was very different from that of the government and the newspapers. Members of ORDEN, the government's paramilitary organization to keep the peasantry in line, had begun by harassing members of FECCAS and UTC with threats, looting and burning houses, clubbing and beating men, women, and children. They soon progressed to shooting and hacking with machetes. They abducted a campesino named Tránsito Vásquez, and the next day he was found decapitated and hacked, with the head grotesquely hanging on a tree and facing the body.

Events followed on events, and some of the FECCAS and UTC peasants began to fight back. Three of the murderers of Vásquez were forced to beg pardon of his corpse and dig his grave. But ORDEN and the troops carried the day, and dozens of FECCAS and UTC people were taken away under arrest.

An archdiocesan ad hoc commission examined the events and reported on April 7: "After hearing the testimony of numberless eyewitnesses and victims, and having analyzed the conflict attentively, we believe that the events were provoked mediately and immediately by ORDEN in close collaboration with the security forces." The commission also accused the government of using and perhaps preparing the incident in order to discredit and undo the campesino organizations. The press coverage was directed to discredit the church as well as the organizations.[8]

On Easter Monday the archdiocese took in the first refugees in the parish house of San José de la Montaña. Increasing numbers soon overflowed into the seminary, whose students were on Easter vacation. Romero formed a commission with three subcommissions, for investigation, publicity, and aid. The investigation subcommission set about getting the facts and later published the report quoted above. The aid group fed, housed, and cared for the refugees, who stayed in the seminary until April 15.[9]

By then the Popular Revolutionary Bloc (BPR), a coalition of popular organizations, was occupying the cathedral and several embassies, demanding the release of the campesinos arrested in connection with the San Pedro Perulapán troubles. Concerned that the police were preventing even food from getting to the cathedral, Romero tried to go himself to see the situation there on April 14. Prevented by the police, he sent Bishop Revelo to talk with President Romero and request a guarantee of safety so that the campesinos in the cathedral could go to their villages and homes. The president said they could go, but the police remained at the cathedral. That evening, however, Romero and Revelo were able to enter the cathedral and talk with the people. Romero spoke to them of Christian liberation from sin and love of Christ, "which excludes all resentment, all hatred," and promised to return and say mass for them the next day. However, Romero was concerned that some of the BPR refugees at San José de la Montaña had used the site to plan the occupations. He defended the cause of the popular organizations, but wanted to keep the church autonomous from them at all times.[10]

Romero was pleased with Bishop Revelo's performance in the crisis. The next morning, Romero had breakfast with Revelo, Urioste, the chancellor, and the archdiocesan treasurer, and they agreed to breakfast together each Saturday. Romero noted with satisfaction in his diary that Revelo was trying to work as part of the team. The archdiocese was also facilitating talks between the BPR and the ambassadors of the countries whose embassies were occupied, and Revelo spent most of that day trying to talk with the ambassadors and the BPR. Three days later he was able to get the two sides together at the archdiocesan offices, and the occupiers left the embassies and the cathedral.

During the San Pedro Perulapán crisis, another event was causing a stir in the church of El Salvador. It started with a letter to the papal nuncio, Emanuele Gerada, originating with a group of priests who met weekly with Romero's knowledge and occasionally with his presence, although he knew nothing of the letter until the nuncio made it known to the bishops.

The group set about gathering signatures among the clergy and religious of the nation. Even after the letter was delivered, more signatures of priests and nuns were sent to the nunciature. Some two hundred (some sources say three hundred) finally signed, out of a total of 1,125 priests and religious in the country. A poll of the nuncio's popularity would surely have produced still more negative votes: some who disapproved of the nuncio did not sign the letter.

The letter began by saying that the signers felt "the grave pastoral obligation" of telling the nuncio how they viewed his public actions. "After calmly reflecting in the light of the gospel, we reach the conviction that Jesus, the Lord of history, urges us to call attention to those aspects of your activity that mean grave scandal for the people of God and are destructive for the church and its evangelizing mission."

They listed the more notable examples of his actions that they saw as antievangelical, including his open disagreement with the "pastoral and prophetic policy" of the archbishop and the archdiocese; his public support of a "repressive and unjust government"; his concelebration of a farewell mass with Father Rogelio Esquivel, a priest whom Romero had removed as pastor of San José de la Montaña parish and allowed to leave the diocese for a parish in Miami; his insensitivity "to the silent sorrow of the oppressed and persecuted peasantry, to the tears of the widows and mothers of the disappeared for political reasons, and to our people's hunger for bread and for truth"; his apparent sympathy for policies of FARO, ANEP, Cardinal Casariego, and the military vicar, Bishop Alvarez, and lack of support for Romero and Rivera and those "who opt for the unconditional service of the gospel and the truth."

They felt obliged, they said, to declare that he had placed himself "outside the faith, hope, and charity that our local church in El Salvador lives and professes in communion with the universal church." They repudiated "the negative sign" of his actions and his collaboration with those who persecuted the church, and asked him "not to make more difficult the communion of our local church with the Holy See." They prayed that God would help him to "hear the cry of a whole people in which Jesus continues to die and rise again each day," that the blood of their martyrs would enlighten him "not to keep struggling against the light and the truth in the service of Caiaphas, Herod, and Pilate," and that he would have the strength "to renounce the human wisdom of politicians and to enjoy the freedom of the children of God."

"For the love of God," the letter concluded, "do not make more bitter our calvary in the hour when the powers of this world have let loose their malice against the church and against the saints of God."[11]

Gerada sent a copy of the letter to the bishops' conference, and they discussed it in their March 15 meeting at the seminary.

Aparicio announced that he would take drastic measures with those of his priests who had signed the letter. They already had a record of defiance and rebellion against their bishop, he said. Rivera objected that such measures would not deal with the problem proposed by the letter. The question was whether what it said was objectively true or not.

In the discussion that followed, Rivera and Romero appealed for calm consideration of the letter, while Aparicio called for action against the signers and Alvarez attacked Romero and all the clergy who agreed with him. Romero said that although he had not written the letter and did not care for the form of expression used in it, he did think it brought up matters that called for consideration. After all, he said, Bishop Aparicio, "who today shows so much zeal to defend the nuncio," had said on another occasion, "We don't have to let the nuncio lead us by the nose." The nuncio, continued Romero, should try to understand people's suffering. An old woman had remarked how the nuncio was present at Esquivel's farewell but not at Alfonso Navarro's funeral. And before condemning the authors of the letter, one should converse with them and try to understand them.

Aparicio complained about priests from other dioceses meddling in "problems of the archdiocese." He seems to have been annoyed that some of his priests went to Romero for advice and comfort.[12]

The newspaper *Excelsior* of Mexico City somehow got a copy of the letter and published it. *El Gráfico* of Guatemala City then printed it, and finally it appeared in *La Crónica del Pueblo* of San Salvador, a paper of only three thousand circulation.[13] But it was the bishops themselves who publicized it the most.

Aparicio suspended ten priests of the San Vicente diocese who had signed it, leading to a great deal of reaction and commotion among the clergy, religious, small communities, and lay organizations throughout El Salvador. Statements of support for the signers began to appear, and letters landed on the desks of the various bishops.

In the midst of the hubbub, Aparicio, Barrera, Alvarez, and Revelo called an emergency meeting of the bishops for April 3 in order to approve a statement of support for the nuncio that they had prepared. Rivera could not attend, and the meeting opened with the reading of a telegram from Rivera asking for postponement of the meeting until he could be present, since it was so important. Romero asked that Rivera's wish be followed and the meeting changed to another time. The question went to a vote and Romero lost, four to one. He asked that the vote be registered in the minutes.

Romero protested that the bishops' statement had been written without previous discussion. Aparicio answered that it was normal in an extraordinary and urgent session for some bishops to meet in advance and draw up a statement. Romero then objected that they had already discussed the matter in the previous meeting. Aparicio and Revelo replied that the situation was more serious now that the letter of the priests had been published in the press.

Aparicio then read the proposed statement, entitled, "Condemnatory Statement of the Bishops' Conference of El Salvador in Regard to a Letter Sent to His Excellency, the Apostolic Nuncio, and Statement of Allegiance to the Representative of the Holy Father, Paul VI." It said that the bishops were "grieved by the attitude of a group of priests and women religious shown in a letter of March 7 to the apostolic nuncio of His Holiness, Paul VI, Archbishop Emanuele Gerada."

The letter, said the bishops, "arbitrarily and ignorantly" accused the nuncio because of his diplomatic labor with the government. It presented him as an obstacle to the pastoral policies chosen by the archbishop of San Salvador; it accused him of not sharing the sorrow of Christians who suffer; it aligned him with Cardinal Casariego of Guatemala, Bishop Alvarez of San Miguel, and certain groups in society in an open struggle against the archbishop of San Salvador and the bishop of Santiago de María; and it attempted to make "the parameters of the division" the service of the gospel and of the truth. Further, it declared "in an ignorant and malicious misuse of the right of the teaching authority that belongs to the Sacred Congregation for the Doctrine of the Faith" that the nuncio was "outside the faith, hope, and charity that our church lives and professes in communion with the universal church." It "insolently repudiated" him as "a negative sign and a collaborator with the persecutors of the church and the gospel." It called him an obstacle to the communion of the local church and the Holy See. It reviled him as "contrary to the light and the truth, with cutting, grotesque, and offensive metaphors," and accused him of submitting to politicians, to the detriment of the freedom of the children of God. Finally, it made him "responsible for the time of confusion and violence that the country lives in."

Anyone who had not seen the original letter—and few had—now would know a good deal about it.

The statement went on to say that the bishops condemned "with all the energy of our mission as pastors this haughty and irreverent posture as unjust, antievangelical, and disrespectful to the Holy See in the person of the Supreme Pontiff's representative." They rejected the charges against Gerada and deplored "the effrontery of publishing the letter in the press of the country in violation of canon law." The zeal of many of the persons who signed the letter "does not agree with the witness of their lives as Christians, ecclesiastics, or religious." The bishops pledged their fidelity to the nuncio and the pope and prayed for "these children who have caused so much sorrow."

Aparicio finished reading the statement and the discussion began.

Romero asked whether or not it was opportune to publish such a document. He asked them to prescind from his own person and to consider its opportuneness with the clergy and the people. A history of events lay behind the letter. Gerada was only seen at receptions and not at church affairs like Navarro's funeral. The concelebration with Esquivel had been a scandal. And his reputation in Guatemala was just as bad. Defending him was not a matter of defending the pope.

As for the letter itself, Romero did not like the style, but the signers should not be condemned without being heard. It was not clear that they had given it to the press, as the bishops accused them. "If they are condemned like this, it seems to me very unjust, just as it seems unjust to me to suspend ten priests without a hearing."

That set off Aparicio. He accused Romero of meddling, of ruining the bishops' conference, of supporting dissident priests, of putting a fifth column in other dioceses. "They come to you for anything," he said. "They bring recordings of what has been said in San Vicente."

Romero tried to return to the subject of the nuncio; if he had done what the letter said, he did not merit the bishops' defense. But Aparicio would not be diverted from his attack on Romero, accusing him of harming the country and the church with his sermons, YSAX, and *Orientación*: "You're dividing the country. You've confused the nation."

"I don't think so," replied Romero. He said he was following his conscience and the people were begging the bishops' support. Aparicio said they had given their support, but Romero said it had been inconsistent and that Aparicio wavered because of the favors he obtained from the education ministry. Aparicio then said he had only demanded rights and accused Romero of using the Catholic school federation. Romero replied that as archbishop he had authority over the federation, and Aparicio countered that Romero meddled in the rest of the country, saying, "We know your underhanded maneuvers. And then you appear as the victim, as if they're doing you every wrong. We're on to you."

What were the bishops going to gain, asked Romero, with this sort of atmosphere?

Revelo intervened to say it was more important to analyze the letter of the priests and nuns. "Let's see if there is reason to answer them this way or not."

Romero said that before analyzing the letter they should call in those responsible for it.

Aparicio interrupted. Since Romero insisted so much that the author of the letter be called in, "does that mean, then, that you are the author of the letter?"

"No."

"Then you told them to write it and send it," countered Aparicio.

"That is a slander," said Romero.

Since Romero kept insisting that the authors of the letter should be called in before the bishops pronounced on the letter, the question was put to a vote. Four voted no, Romero voted yes.

They then proceeded to discuss the content of the letter of the priests and nuns, wandering from the actions of the nuncio mentioned in the letter to the pastoral practice of the archbishop and back, with several digressions from both. It was getting toward noon when they finally put to a vote whether to approve the text of their statement and publish it in the press. Four voted yes, Romero voted no.[14]

The day left a sour taste, Romero noted in his diary. He considered the resolution imprudent and felt it had only deepened the bishops' division. Moreover, his own auxiliary, Bishop Revelo, had openly challenged him, disagreeing with his interpretation and application of Vatican II, Medellín, and the papal encyclicals. The next morning his clergy gave him a vote of confidence in a pastoral meeting. The day following was Wednesday, and he had his usual breakfast meeting with representatives of the priests' senate and the Justice and Peace Commission. They discussed the bishops' declaration and advised him to make no public statement, since his failure to sign the declaration made his position clear.

The newspapers published the statement that day, April 5. That kept the matter alive and brought forth more statements of support for the signers of the letter to the nuncio, especially for the ten priests whom Aparicio had suspended. It also publicized the division among the bishops. Four had signed it, two had not. The decision to publish it had probably deepened the division that already existed, and almost certainly gave more publicity to the original letter to the nuncio.

Romero sent an explanation of his own position to the nuncio and to the other bishops on April 24, putting on record what he had already said to the nuncio personally and to the bishops in the two tense meetings. He had nothing to do with the letter itself, he reiterated, and knew nothing about it until the nuncio showed it to him. He saw no disrespect for the pope in the letter, which dealt only with the actions of the nuncio. He disapproved whatever disrespectful language the letter might contain, but "I could not condemn the priests without making with them a calm analysis of the facts mentioned, since they are matters that regrettably a goodly sector of the people of God remark about in the same way as the letter. It seems to me that according to the spirit of the postconciliar church, holy and at once needing conversion, this kind of fraternal correction should not scandalize but invite one to reflect and to examine humbly one's own acts, especially when these personal acts can compromise the successor of Peter himself."

It seemed unjust to him to disapprove publicly the priests' action without a hearing to determine their intentions in writing the letter and their responsibility in publishing it, which they might not have intended at all. He thought the bishops' statement would further publicize the criticism of the nuncio and "would further a bad atmosphere among the bishops, who would appear disunited and more concerned for an intrachurch problem while the people expect rather a show of unity and a pastoral word of encouragement and guidance before the serious situation that the country is in."

Finally, Romero said, he did not sign because the session in which it was signed seemed to him to be rigged by the president of the bishops' conference. He had the impression that the four signers had already met and drawn up the statement, which was not revised or amended in the meeting. They had disregarded Rivera's request to delay the meeting so that he could attend, and when Romero had supported Rivera he had had to "endure inexact and offensive accusations against the pastoral work of my archdiocese."

Certainly, the meeting must have been a rough session for Romero without Rivera's calm, steady support. The Barraza family recalled that Romero had at least once wept when mentioning his problems with the other bishops after one of the conference meetings, and this may have been the occasion.

Sixty-three of the signers of the original letter to the nuncio sent a letter to the four bishops in May, which is the closest the signers got to a hearing. Their intention, they said, was to help the nuncio "to fulfill in a more Christian manner his task as representative of His Holiness, Pope Paul VI."

Of the bishops' statement they said: "It does not reproduce faithfully what we affirmed in our letter. For example, you say, 'He is made responsible for the time of confusion and violence that the country lives in.' This is false. We did not say that. We are aware that the causes of the multiple tensions that the country lives in have deep roots in economic, social, and political imbalances. We did affirm his support for the present government, which is immediately responsible for so much killing and repression. It contains other imprecisions and simplifications that make it appear before the reading public of the country's press that our letter was composed out of pure passion and with no objectivity, which is not true. For each affirmation we make we have proofs. They are not made 'arbitrarily and ignorantly,' as you seem to us to proceed when you say, 'We deplore that the zeal of many of the persons that signed the letter does not agree with the witness of their lives as Christians, ecclesiastics, or religious.' "

On April 17 Romero wrote to Freddy Delgado, secretary-general of the conference, asking him to amend the minutes of the March 15 meeting. "I am attributed the phrase, 'We are not going to let the nuncio lead us by the nose.' This is not correct. I quoted the phrase, but in recalling that its author was Bishop Arnoldo Aparicio, who today is such a defender of the prestige of the nuncio."

On April 21 he wrote again to Delgado, who had now simply omitted the phrase from the minutes. Romero wanted it corrected, not omitted. Delgado checked with Aparicio, who replied, "At first I gave no importance to what Archbishop Romero requested in the correction of the minutes. Now I see his intentions, and to accept it I demand: (1) that he prove I said it; (2) with what intentions and in what circumstances."[15]

It was the secretary's task, of course, to record faithfully what Romero said in the meeting, whether the statement was accurate or not. Aparicio was demanding that Romero prove it in order to have it in the minutes. Romero therefore wrote again to Delgado, on May 22, appealing for the correction. "The assertion and my request for correction were said in plenary sessions and no one offered any objections to them, not even Bishop Aparicio. It is therefore a duty to record them faithfully in the respective minutes. If afterward Bishop Aparicio wants to engage in polemics, as he indicates in the letter that he sent you on April 26, of which

I received an unsigned copy, it would then be a matter for the agenda of a later meeting."

The final version of the minutes reads (Romero speaking): " 'Bishop Aparicio may not agree with being led by the nose; we are not always going to have the nuncio lead us by the nose — that is what you said,' he replied to Bishop Aparicio."

Since mid-1977, at least, Bishop Aparicio had been urging that the archdiocese vacate the space it was using in the seminary building in San Salvador.[16] Archbishop Chávez had moved the archdiocesan offices there in 1971, when the old office building was torn down. The seminary building had plenty of room then, and even more after the Jesuits left at the end of 1972 and the seminary closed in 1973. Although it had reopened in 1977, the building still had vacant space, even though the archdiocese occupied part of the front.

The major seminary, which began as the seminary of the archdiocese, had been made interdiocesan, that is, national, in the mid-1930's. The archdiocese built the present building, where the seminary moved from its downtown quarters in 1938. The archdiocese remained owner of the new building, as it had been of the old one, and continued to use it for its minor seminary while letting the interdiocesan major seminary use it also. With the Jesuits administering both seminaries under a single rector, there was not much conflict, even though the minor seminary was under the archbishop and the major seminary under the bishops' conference. They were split only in 1969, when a large influx of students caused the minor seminary to move to Santa Tecla.[17]

Aparicio was also unhappy that the rector of the seminary, Father Gregorio Rosa, was interviewing Romero each Wednesday on YSAX. Rosa had studied communications and had volunteered to help the radio in his spare time. Because of Aparicio's complaints at the bishops' meetings, Romero spoke with Rosa about relations between the archdiocese and the seminary, and Rosa discussed it with the other priests of the seminary administration.

The difficulties that they reported back to Romero on January 10, 1978, were minor. Romero's correspondence secretary, a priest from Santiago de María, was living in the seminary, and they thought he should move out. Two other priests who had taken refuge in the seminary during the year still had the keys to their rooms and should return them. There should not be permanent guests in the seminary, only transients. The offices were no problem, but one gentleman from the office for the laity was rather intrusive. They thought it better to restrict to the weekends the meetings that the archdiocese often had. The parish church that the Jesuits had built next door was building its own rectory now and should be careful to leave behind the seminary's furniture when it moved. At times lay people, usually campesinos, had spent the night in the seminary when afraid to go home in the dark after a meeting; the seminary people thought that those planning meetings should have more foresight and not assume that the seminary was there to take care of such problems. Finally, some adjustment should be made in sharing the cost of electricity and housekeeping.[18]

Most of the points touched on concerned arguments that Aparicio was using to urge the archdiocese to get out of the seminary building. He seemed to feel that the archdiocese influenced too much the type of training the seminarians were getting, and he wanted them more isolated. In this he had support from Alvarez, who disliked even the seminarians' helping in parishes on weekends.[19]

On January 12, Aparicio, Barrera, and Alvarez sent a letter to Romero, and copies to all the bishops, to the nuncio, and to the seminary rector, in which they set out demands that they proposed to discuss in the meeting of the bishops' conference scheduled for January 16–18: All the offices should vacate the seminary building. "All outside influence and interference that could obstruct the work of training the seminarians" should be banished. The administration should be careful not to allow in the seminary training "progressive" tendencies "of a political-commitment type that would lead to political reductionism." Members of the administration should not take jobs that could bring difficulties on the seminary or their specific task of formation.

At the meeting, the five members of the seminary administration were present with the bishops to give their report on the second semester of 1977 (the school year in El Salvador runs from February to October). Besides the letter of the three bishops, the meeting also had a letter that had come from the Sacred Congregation for Catholic Education through the nunciature, in which the congregation said it kept receiving reports of "the continuous and well-known politicization and Marxist tendency" of the seminarians.[20]

Romero, Rivera, and the seminary staff regarded the reports sent to the congregation as grossly distorted and exaggerated. The letter from the three bishops produced a long and lively discussion, during which Rosa, to satisfy Aparicio, agreed to drop out of the radio program.[21]

Aparicio had gained a point, but he was not resting. On February 14 he wrote Romero and again demanded that the archdiocese vacate the seminary. The building, he said, had been constructed for the use of the bishops' conference, and the offices and minor seminary had been allowed to use it when the major seminary closed. Now it was time for both the offices and the minor seminary to get out. He also demanded that Romero stop reconditioning the former convent of the Sisters who had taken care of the seminary kitchen until 1973. (The building is on the street and several yards removed from the seminary building. Archbishop Chávez had made it a print shop, and now the archdiocese was preparing it to be used as radio studios.) Aparicio made clear also that he was taking the whole matter to the Holy See.

"The bishops," he summed up, "hereby present to you and to the Holy See formal request to suspend the aforesaid installation and, for the tranquility of all, set a date by which the seminary building will be completely vacated, including the transfer of the archdiocesan minor seminary to a different locale from the major seminary." Romero delayed sending his reply in order to have a study made of the ownership of the building.

On April 4, while the refugees were still arriving at the seminary from San Pedro Perulapán, and the day after the bishops' second bitter discussion of the priests' and religious' letter to Gerada, the nuncio transmitted to Romero the contents of a letter from the Sacred Congregation for Catholic Education.

The congregation's letter, directed to the nuncio, said it was well aware of the problems Romero had faced with the government and the other bishops, and that these had been reflected in the national seminary: "rooms occupied, political refugees, persons interfering, lack of personnel and teachers, some of whom are overbusy with other functions." Because of their confidence in the archbishop's interest in the seminary and his devotion to the Holy See, it continued, they asked that he remove from the seminary the offices of the archdiocese, of the conference of religious, and of the commission for the laity, and also the radio studios and offices, and that he free it of "permanent guests, political refugees, parish meetings and activities, and all that is not strictly connected with priestly formation." They also asked him, because of the leadership position of the archdiocese, "to use all efforts to have the staff and students abstain from all political activity and, in view of the increase in students, see how to increase the staff and teachers."

The letter ended with the scarcely veiled threat: "Any delay in the measures mentioned above could occasion the risk of another closing of the seminary of unforeseeable duration, and all know how much harm this would cause the local church."[22]

The letter clearly reflected things that Aparicio and company had been saying. Romero immediately began drafting a reply, but he delayed sending it in order to confer with the seminary staff and to prepare also his reply to Aparicio and the bishops' conference.

In January he had asked the seminary to inform him of what frictions existed between the seminary and the archdiocese in order to eliminate them. He now asked for a report on what problems had arisen from the temporary housing of refugees from San Pedro Perulapán in the parish quarters next to the seminary. Their number had made necessary some use also of seminary facilities.

The staff gave him a four-page report on April 18, the day the last refugees left the parish. They had left the seminary three days before. The staff acknowledged that the situation had been a real emergency and said that the interference with the seminary routine had been minor, since the refugees had used only a small part of the huge building. There had been some frictions with the people taking care of the refugees, but the staff said Romero had been eager to avoid difficulties and to correct them when they happened. In brief, the emergency had not been a serious problem for the seminary.

On May 2 Romero sent the staff copies of the letters from Aparicio and the other bishops and from the nuncio, asking them to let him know how they felt the archdiocese had complied with their observations of January and what difficulties they might have noted in the school year that began in February.

The rector reported back to him on May 12. Most of the minor problems noted in January had been resolved. Romero's secretary had moved out, and only one priest still had the key to the room he had used. The head of the laity commission still interfered somewhat in seminary affairs. Regular meetings had stopped, and weekend meetings were held only with permission, as they had asked. Relations were good with the new pastor of San José de la Montaña. The archdiocese was now paying a satisfactory amount for common expenses. The refugees from San Pedro Perulapán were the only lay guests there had been, and that was an emergency already ended.

The problems so far in 1978 were minor. People left open the door between the seminary and the office area. Others used the seminary entrance to enter the offices. Some ex-seminarians from the archdiocese came around the seminary at times to visit and were not wanted. Priests at times had meetings in the minor seminary area and disturbed the major seminary. The refugee aid committee had used the vacant seminary garage as a warehouse without asking permission. Almost all this, they concluded, was inevitable with the offices in the same building. "It therefore seems reasonable to suggest that, little by little, the archdiocese transfer its offices to another place. Let the record show, however, that the staff does not affirm the foregoing as an ultimatum to the archbishop but as a consideration that it deems valid."

Romero had been preparing his replies to Aparicio and to the congregation. Aparicio had asserted that the archdiocese was seriously interfering with the functioning of the seminary. He had ample testimony from the seminary staff by now that it was not doing so and had not done so. Aparicio was demanding that he get the archdiocese out of the seminary building, but he now had a detailed study of the property to show that it belonged to the archdiocese. And since the offices, minor seminary, and radio were not interfering with the seminary, they had no reason to leave. Romero was convinced that the whole incident was principally a means of harassing him and the pastoral approach he had chosen.

It was June before Romero finished revising the letter for the congregation's prefect, Cardinal Gabriel Garrone.[23] By then he was planning to go to Rome and was able to take it, together with all the correspondence with the bishops and the seminary staff, along with him.

"You refer to my 'known devotion to the Holy See.' That, Your Eminence, you may take as certain," he wrote to Garrone. "What I would also like to be certain about is that this sacred congregation is well informed about the reality of what has been and is the life of our central seminary. I have very well founded reasons to think it is not." The nuncio and Bishop Aparicio, the congregation's primary sources of information, did not hide their aversion to his pastoral policies.

The archdiocesan offices, he said, had functioned for seven years in the seminary building, which had space to spare and, moreover, belonged only to the archdiocese. The archdiocese did have the land, the plans, and part of the money to build a new office building, but neither he nor Chávez had rushed to build while they had space to spare at the seminary. "It seems to us inconsistent with the spirit of a poor church to get involved in putting up a new building if need does not demand." Nevertheless, they did plan to build whenever it became necessary.

Taking up the congregation's request that he use the leadership of the archdiocese to see that staff and students refrain from political activity, Romero observed that this "seems to assume that the staff and students devote themselves to political activity. It also seems to suggest that the archdiocese has a lot to do with this." If, he went on, the statement "contains a veiled censure of this archdiocese for political activity, I believe the best answer is the pastoral action of this local church. A dispassionate examination of our pastoral activity will show clearly that in our actions and in our social teaching we have tried to follow faithfully the apostolic exhortation *Evangelii Nuntiandi*." As far as he knew, he said, the staff of the seminary had never engaged in, taught, or allowed any forbidden activities. The seminary tried to instill in the students correct norms, both doctrinal and practical, "which is not easy to achieve in this atmosphere so charged with social tension."

During his time in Rome, Romero left his letter at the Congregation for Catholic Education. Later he and Rivera returned and spoke with Cardinal Garrone and two of his aides. One of the aides, at Romero's request, read to them the text of the letter the congregation had sent to the nuncio and that the nuncio had then conveyed to Romero in translation on April 4. The negative comments on the situation now appeared not as the judgment of the congregation but, rather, as what the congregation "had heard." The nuncio had also omitted the congregation's decision that sending an official inspector to the seminary was not called for, which implied that someone had suggested one, and had omitted the congregation's words of praise for Romero's efforts in the country's difficult situation.

Bishop Rivera was able to make clear in the interview that as a member of the bishops' seminary commission he did not agree with the reports that

Aparicio had been giving them. It was clear enough that Romero also did not agree.[24]

The note was scrupulously correct and icily menacing:

San Salvador
May 5, 1978

His Excellency
Oscar Arnulfo Romero
Archbishop of San Salvador

By special instructions of the Honorable Supreme Court of Justice, I most respectfully beg Your Excellency to express the names of the "venal judges" to whom you referred in the homily you pronounced during the celebration of the mass of Sunday, April 30 of the present year, in the metropolitan cathedral church, broadcast by radio station YSAX, in order to proceed to trial and judgment of those responsible, if your accusations should prove correct.

Respectfully yours,
Dr. Ernesto Vidal Rivera Guzmán
Secretary, Supreme Court of Justice[25]

The note was sent not only to the archbishop but also to the newspapers, which gave it full coverage. It was a clever trick. If Romero should send them names of individual judges, he would be dragged into a messy judicial procedure and expose himself to charges of slander or contempt of court, with no hope of justice from the corrupt system he was attacking. If he backed down, he would lose face. If he kept silent, his enemies would hound him as a liar and a coward.

This is what Romero had said in his homily on April 30:

We cannot forget that a group of lawyers is struggling to obtain an amnesty and have published the reasons that have led them to ask this favor for so many who perish in the prisons [the archdiocese was also supporting a general amnesty for those arrested in San Pedro Perulapán]. These lawyers also report anomalies in the procedures of the First Criminal Court, where the judge does not allow lawyers to enter with their defendants, while the Guardia Nacional is allowed to be present and intimidate the accused, who often bears evident marks of torture. A judge who does not report signs of torture and lets himself be swayed by its effect on the testimony of the accused is not a just judge. I think, brothers and sisters, in view of these injustices that are seen all about, even in the First Court, not to speak of many other tribunals, judges that sell themselves — [interrupted by applause]. What does the Supreme Court of Justice do? What of the function, so transcendent in a democracy, of this power that should be above every other power and should demand justice of everyone that violates it? I believe that the key to a great part of the malaise of our country is in the president of the Supreme Court and all his co-workers, who with greater integrity ought to demand of the courts, of the tribunals, of the judges, of all the administrators of that sacred word *justice* that they truly be agents of justice. I wish to congratulate the lawyers, Christian or non-Christian but with a great sense of justice, who are putting their finger on the sore. May all our lawyers be truly a hope for justice, which is so ill treated in our surroundings.[26]

Romero had not used the words "venal judges" that the secretary of the court attributed to him, but he had spoken of "judges who sell themselves." The words were certainly not too strong for the components of a judicial system that connived with the most blatant forms of injustice, that allowed the security forces to imprison without due process, to torture, and to murder. Attempts to secure habeas corpus relief for persons who had disappeared in the clutches of the Guardia Nacional were fruitless.

Some twenty-five lawyers offered their services to Romero in the preparation of his reply. He conferred especially with the legal aid office of the archdiocese, Socorro Jurídico.

On Pentecost Sunday, May 14, the whole nation was waiting for Romero's reply to the note from the Supreme Court. He saved it for the end of his homily and read a carefully prepared statement, speaking rapidly but firmly. The crowd listened attentively to what must have been hard to follow in parts, as he avoided legal pitfalls and still reaffirmed and expanded what he had said before.

He first read what he had said on April 30 and then went on:

The secretary of the Supreme Court begs me "most respectfully to express the names of the 'venal judges'" to whom I referred in my homily.

In regard to this honorable communication I should explain the following, principally to avoid the possible confusion of public opinion occasioned by the Supreme Court's publication and by the commentaries in the press of the country.

First of all, I am thankful and happy to have the opportunity that the Supreme Court affords me to expand what I said in my homily on April 30 in the cathedral mass. I am thankful and happy because at last, after speaking out for so long about these things, I see the Supreme Court declare publicly its intention to begin to remedy what is wrong in that supreme power so transcendental for the peace of our national life.

The court's note, he went on, was not a legal instrument like a subpoena, since it did not follow the legal requirements for such actions. "Therefore, my reply is a spontaneous reaffirmation of my pastoral commitment in defense of justice, truth, and the people." The battlefield that the court had chosen was not the law, but public opinion, and there he would answer it.

The note, Romero said, "has mutilated the wording and deformed the spirit" of what he had said, calling on him to name "venal judges" when he had not used the expression. "If, indeed, I did mention in my homily 'judges that sell themselves,' it was a merely incidental term in the whole context of my message, which spoke of more general irregularities that concern the whole system of judicial administration. To put an exclusive emphasis on this accidental term without mentioning the general context that frames it is an illogical and unjust procedure that one might even suspect is malicious. By it the Supreme Court gives the impression that it wishes to hide, or distract public opinion from, the central point of my message. That was and remains, I repeat, to point out a social evil rooted in the institutions and procedures that are the responsibility of that honorable tribunal."

The court had tried to trick him and public opinion by focusing on a few words of his taken out of context and reworded to make them more compromising. He was turning the spotlight where it belonged, on a body, entrusted with the administration of justice, that failed to render justice.

Venality in the technical sense, he said, was one of the hardest charges to prove, since the only witnesses are generally the guilty parties. He was not a jurist but a pastor, who was simply pointing out the existence of an evil that needed correcting. As overseer of the judicial system, the court had the means to investigate and end the violations of the law and the abuses of the other powers of the state — "to proceed to trial and judgment of those responsible," as the court's secretary had said. The court might conduct its investigation, "taking into consideration the known groups of mothers or families of political prisoners or disappeared persons or exiles, and the many reports of venality published under the responsibility of the communications media, not only at home but abroad. Furthermore, at least from my theological perspective, I believe the concept of venality is fulfilled by any functionary who receives from the people a salary to administer justice and instead becomes the accomplice of injustice, moved by sinful purposes. This phenomenon can be investigated with greater facility by those who have the adequate means, the mission, and the grave duty to do so."

But more serious still than cases of venality, Romero went on, were others that showed the Supreme Court's "absolute contempt for the obligations that the political constitution gives it, which all of its members have obliged themselves to fulfill." He then went on to list some of the violations of fundamental human rights. Habeas corpus, a right recognized by article

8 of the Universal Declaration of Human Rights and by article 164 of the Salvadoran constitution as a recourse against arbitrary restrictions of individual liberty, was useless. "Various judges have honestly and valiantly informed the Supreme Court that they have found it impossible to carry out their sacred constitutional mission in the case of the security forces."

The constitution provided in its article 164 that no one could be deprived of life, liberty, or property without due process of law, and yet "mothers, wives, and children, from one end of the country to the other, have walked a way of the cross searching for their dear ones without finding any answer whatever. We know of about eighty families with some member arrested without having charges brought in any court so far. Before this most serious situation, which day by day tears the hearts of these mothers, wives, and children, I invoke only one rule: 'No one can be arbitrarily arrested, imprisoned, or exiled' (article 9 of the Universal Declaration of Human Rights)."

Both the Universal Declaration of Human Rights and the Salvadoran constitution, he went on, forbade forced exile and allowed all Salvadorans to return to their homeland, and yet exiled Salvadorans were not allowed to return. The constitution provided for the right to petition and to have one's petition attended to, and yet a petition for amnesty for the prisoners of San Pedro Perulapán and an appeal for the annulment of the public order law as unconstitutional were simply ignored.

Even the press, he went on, had published accusations of irregularities against administrative and judicial functionaries, and yet the authorities showed no interest in investigating the matters. "I am convinced that if there really existed a concern for public administration, the facts would be investigated exhaustively in order to bring about a true and genuine wellbeing of society and to lay down precedents."

The Universal Declaration of Human Rights and the constitution "consecrate the sacred right to liberty, which has been violated in various ways," Romero continued. The security forces seized people without warrants and held them for more than a week and even more than a month without bringing them before a judge, in open violation of the constitution. "These situations are publicly known, are reported in the news, and are at times dolorous, like the events of Aguilares, El Paisnal, and San Pedro Perulapán." These things happened even though the law required the security forces to turn over their prisoners to the courts and forbade them to use violence and intimidation against prisoners. Yet many prisoners appeared before the tribunals "with evident marks and signs of ill treatment."

Furthermore, the constitutional right to form labor unions was violated in many ways, "from restricting the freedom of labor leaders to subtly giving favors and concessions to those workers who reject the union organization." The right to strike was "repressed and treacherously distorted" by calling most strikes "subversive," saying that they were managed from outside the country, "even though as a legal measure they are used by the worker to defend collective contracts, wages, and vacation days recognized by the labor laws, and to protect their occupational interests."

Since both the Universal Declaration and the Salvadoran constitution recognize the right of unionization, "it is impossible to understand all the detailed inconveniences, hindrances, and obstacles put in the way of the farm worker to achieve the practice of that fundamental right."

The Supreme Court had generally retreated from its obligation to protect legal rights. This failure was what Romero had called attention to in his homily and which he now repeated. "This accusation is inspired in a positive *animus corrigendi* and not in a malicious desire to defame. I believe it my duty to make it as pastor of a people suffering injustice. It is a duty placed on me by the gospel, for which I am ready to face trial and prison, even though they would only add another injustice."

He thanked all the persons, especially lawyers and law students, who had told him that they shared the church's concern for the administration of justice. "Their cooperation is a positive building of peace. This church of the Holy Spirit has proclaimed from the distant times of the prophet Isaiah and today repeats with the renewed youth of this Pentecost amid the shocking condition of our people: 'Peace can only be the product of justice' (Is. 32:17)."[27]

The people applauded long and warmly, and he added, "Thank you for the seal of approval that you have placed on my poor words." He had read rapidly at times, perhaps nervously.[28] The moment had been tense. But at the end no one doubted that he had not only emerged unscathed and shown up the trick used against him but had turned the light of truth and the eyes of the nation on the fundamental corruption of the powers of justice.

The Supreme Court did not reply.

On May 21, 1978, Romero directed a twenty-three page letter to Cardinal Sebastiano Baggio, prefect of the Sacred Congregation for the Bishops. Its length and detail show that it must have been in preparation for some time, and its opening words suggest that it may have been begun as early as March or even February: "A little over a year after receiving the archdiocese of San Salvador on February 22 last year . . ." Its purpose was "to open my heart to you once more, as I did in my letters of August 1 and December 12, 1977, in order to express to you my vision of the church in this archdiocese, my joys, and my sufferings."

As he had done in his earlier letters, Romero reviewed the events of his time as archbishop of San Salvador, his understanding of the church, and his view of his own role. He gave expression to his worries about the danger of Marxism and the harshness of capitalism in El Salvador and the repression of human rights among his people. He reviewed, finally, the joys and hopes that he found in his work. Signs of Christian faith flourished in both the city and the countryside: "Bible study groups, grass-roots communities, the Legion of Mary, the Catechumenate movement in various parishes, prayer groups, the parish work of priests and religious, the widespread eagerness of groups of lay people to also be bearers of the word of God, the awakened interest in the Bible and the church's teaching, and what is so significant: the sharing in the eucharist and the uncountable Catholics that receive the body of Christ."

Romero could say frankly and honestly that the diocese was better organized pastorally and better united, and priestly vocations had increased. Expressions of support arrived constantly from inside and outside the country.

"This is the way I have wanted to open to you my heart as shepherd of this diocese. I beg the Lord to give me strength always to continue the work he has entrusted to me. Nothing is more encouraging for me than to know I am closely united to the pope and the Holy See."

Romero had not yet sent his letter to Baggio when he received one from the cardinal inviting him to Rome.[29] Letters about El Salvador, the archdiocese, and Romero himself, said Baggio, came to the Congregation for the Bishops "with a frequency that knows no precedents and with the most contrary reports, both good and bad." Since the Holy See was worried that the situation seemed to be getting worse all the time, they would like him to come and talk about things "in a brotherly and friendly conversation" sometime in June.

It was the year for the bishops of El Salvador to make their visit to Rome, which they were to do every fifth year. Romero had proposed to the other bishops in April that they all go together, as many national hierarchies often do, but Aparicio was not interested.[30] Having been archbishop less than two years, Romero was not obliged to make the visit, but advisers[31] had urged him to go there to explain his position and he decided to do so. He would visit the various congregations and the pope, in addition to talking with Baggio. Bishop Rivera also wanted to go, although he was not required to do so either, and the two left El Salvador with Monsignor Urioste on June 16, a Friday, arriving in Rome the next day. Romero had sent ahead his long report to Baggio[32] and had also sent a copy of it to his friend Cardinal Eduardo Pironio, prefect of the Congregation for Religious.[33] Pironio was probably the highest-ranking person in the Roman Curia whom Romero could count on to be favorably disposed to him. Romero had known him at least since 1972, when Pironio had given some meditations at the beginning of a month of reflection and study for bishops that had been sponsored by the Central American Bishops' Secretariat and that had been held in Antigua Guatemala.[34]

The afternoon of the day they arrived, they went to visit St. Peter's basilica. "Before the tomb of the first pope," Romero recorded in his diary, "I prayed intensely for the unity of the church, for the pope, for the bishops, and for all of the universal church, especially for our archdiocese, commending to St. Peter the interests of our church and the success of this dialog with the Holy See."

The next day was Sunday, and Romero went to hear the pope speak to the people in St. Peter's Square. Later he visited the tomb of St. Paul. "It was the hour of vespers," he recorded.

> The basilica was fully lighted. The sound of the organ and of the monks' choir singing Gregorian chant filled the surroundings. Kneeling at the tomb of the Apostle of the Gentiles, the great St. Paul, in those prayerful surroundings, I relived in my memory, in my heart, in my love, all those emotions of my days as a student. On my visits to Rome as a priest, my prayers before these tombs of the apostles have always meant inspiration and strength—especially so this evening, when I realize that my visit is not just a visit of private devotion. In making my official visit I bring with me all the interests, concerns, problems, hopes, plans, and afflictions of all my priests, religious communities, parishes, and grass-roots communities. A whole archdiocese comes with me to kneel, yesterday before the tomb of St. Peter and today before the tomb of St. Paul.

On June 20 he spoke at length with Baggio in private—the "brotherly and friendly conversation" he had come for. Baggio was severe, and Romero emerged dejected from the interview, though he observed in his diary, "I think I was able to attenuate" much of the incorrect information sent to Rome. He went to his quarters to begin a memorandum, which developed into a nine-page document that he sent to Baggio three days later.[35] It recalled what they had discussed and offered his further reflections on it.

As Romero recalled, Baggio began by expressing a feeling of frustration that he said was shared by several respected persons who had backed the selection of Romero for archbishop over Rivera, who had been preferred by Archbishop Chávez and even, as Romero recalled, by Baggio himself. Among Romero's backers, Baggio had mentioned Cardinal Casariego and Carlos Siri, a prominent Salvadoran layman. The other Salvadoran bishops were also disappointed, according to Baggio, as were many priests who hoped to work with Romero and now felt left out while another group held him captive with their flattery and made him do whatever they wanted. Among the latter group he mentioned three diocesan priests who were Romero's closest advisers "and others who do not merit trust." The disappointed ones had expected a steady, calm, and discreet attitude, not the aggressiveness that he was showing. He had heard that Romero himself described his change as a "conversion."

Romero said he was grateful for the support people had given to his appointment. "I recognize Bishop Rivera's superiority, as I expressed at the time to you and to Bishop Rivera himself. This recognition has grown before the loyalty and humility with which he continued to help me as auxiliary and with which he has continued to support my pastoral policy. I see this intelligent and unselfish support of Bishop Rivera as a sign of trust in me and as a powerful attestation that I am not standing alone against the bishops' conference."

He denied that he had ever said he had been converted. "What happened in my priestly life, I have tried to explain for myself as an evolution of the same desire that I have always had to be faithful to what God asks of me. If I gave the impression before of being more 'discreet' and 'spiritual,' it was because I sincerely believed that thus I responded to the gospel, for the circumstances of my ministry had not shown themselves so demanding of a pastoral fortitude that, in truth, I believe was asked of me in the circumstances under which I became archbishop."

He also denied that a few priests had coopted him or that others were left out. "What happens here too is that faithfulness to the gospel brings about the division that Christ announced even among members of the same family. If someone complains that he is excluded, it is because he has excluded himself, since he is not ready to give up the comfort he gets from friendship with a power that does not respect the church."

Baggio had the idea that Monsignor Urioste, Romero's vicar-general, was a Jesuit, and Romero remarked that the mistake was a sign of how distorted was the information he had received. Urioste was a member of the diocesan clergy, and Romero had named him vicar-general with the approval of Rivera, who was leaving for Santiago de María at that time, and of former Archbishop Chávez.

Recalling their discussion of the group of so-called politicized priests, Romero said he was disturbed by the pejorative judgment that Baggio had formed of them, and he supposed it showed the influence of Aparicio and Freddy Delgado. The group, with members from all the dioceses, met openly and invited all the bishops and priests to its discussions on pastoral matters in the country. Romero himself had attended meetings, and his relations with them had never involved him in "incorrect positions."

Romero greatly regretted "that your mistrust of our clergy has touched also the memory of our two murdered priests, Fathers Grande and Navarro, whom our Christian people love for their supreme witness of self-sacrifice in preaching justice." He shared Baggio's circumspection about their "limitations, their deficiencies, and especially the atmosphere surrounding their pastoral work," and he agreed that they were not martyrs of a higher grade than those of old. "But I can affirm their sincere love for the church's truth and for our people, and I do not believe that the meaning of our reflections on their deaths has gone beyond the simple affirmation that *they too* merit the Beatitude of the martyrs because 'they suffered persecution for justice' sake' and that *today too* the church is persecuted."

The next topic was Bishop Revelo. Baggio had passed on Revelo's complaints—he could not make contact with Romero, the other vicar-general left him nothing to do and was the one who gave orders—and had urged Romero to develop a more cordial relationship with his auxiliary.

Romero explained his various attempts to approach Revelo and the response they had got. Revelo had demanded he be the only vicar-general when Romero felt he could not remove Urioste. To Romero's request that he try to get along with the clergy, he had replied with "a vigorous call to respect his way of thinking." He did not come to clergy meetings or senate sessions or the meetings of his own vicariate. He stopped attending the meetings of the chancery staff until they were held at a time and place to suit him.

"You understand," wrote Romero in his memo, "that working together cordially, as you recommend and I desire, requires a basis of sincere trust. With brotherly candor, I must tell you that the Holy See itself and my brother bishops have undermined the basis of that trust, for Bishop Revelo himself admits, and you confirmed, that his appointment was 'to rein me in' and the nuncio and bishops use this same mandate to stir up antagonism that destroys any cordial relation.[36] How can a cordial relation exist if we both know there has to be rather a relationship of surveillance and restraint? On the other hand, I have very confidential testimonies that his relations with the government, with priests, and with other persons who do not agree with me are putting this fellowship in danger."

Romero added, surprisingly, that in spite of all this he did not regret asking for Revelo as his auxiliary. He hoped that their history of friendship could still "motivate the cordial cooperation that I need of him."

They had not discussed the matter of the nuncio at length, since it concerned more the Secretariat of State. Baggio called it "an almost irreparable scandal." Romero went over once more his reasons for wanting to separate diplomatic and liturgical functions so as not to appear to be blessing the government and why he had not signed the bishops' condemnation of the priests and religious who had written to the nuncio.

Among other subjects, Baggio had mentioned Romero's homilies. He said he had read some of them and found no doctrinal errors, but they were very long and contained very concrete judgments. Many people no doubt listened to them, he said, out of political rather than religious interest.

Romero said that he never used to go over fifteen or twenty minutes in his homilies, but he noticed how eagerly people listened to them in spite of their length, not only in the cathedral but on radios everywhere. It seemed to him he should take advantage of the chance to proclaim the reign of God and make known the teaching of the church. "If indeed I do refer to particular events of the week, it is to 'incarnate' in our life the Lord's word, explaining to my listeners that thus they should get used to enlightening their own lives and problems with God's light. I always insist that the main thing in my homilies is not the circumstantial framework but the word that has been read and the theological teaching of the comments on it and above all the preparation to celebrate that particular eucharist."

He said he had asked prudent and well-informed persons to point out and correct any impropriety in particular applications or accusations. They had always assured him that no one could be reasonably offended, since he praised whenever he could just as he also pointed out sin where he found it.

He was not bothered that many might listen out of political interest or mere curiosity. "Rather, it spurs me to ignite faith where it perhaps has been extinguished." He had been consoled by knowing of many who had lost interest in the church and now found it closer to their "joys and hopes, troubles and sorrows," in the words of Vatican II.[37] He had also demanded that no political group use the church for its own objectives and struggles. This had caused displeasure, "but it has defined the autonomy and originality of Christian liberation as *Evangelii Nuntiandi* presents it, which is what guides me in this problem."

The day after speaking with Baggio, Romero was to talk with Cardinal Garrone, of the Congregation for Catholic Education, about the seminary. He and Baggio had touched only lightly on the topic, therefore. Baggio said he was "terrified" to think of what sort of vocations were being fostered there, which left no doubt about what sort of information he had been fed. He had also heard that the members of the staff were Romero's "own people" and he said he thought the archdiocesan headquarters should get out of the building.

Romero reminded him that Bishop Rivera was a member of the bishops' seminary commission "with equal rights and responsibilities" along with Aparicio, whose opinions Baggio had just repeated. Rivera took a diametrically opposite view from Aparicio's. "I hope that my explanations have been able to diminish those negative judgments," wrote Romero. "You may be sure that we strive to seek genuine vocations and to train them according to the renewed mind of the council, that I have always backed the training staff in their recommendations to remove students when they do not offer guarantees of becoming good priests, and that I respect to the full the autonomy of the staff, which I value highly, because I consider it one of the best groups of priests that our church has."

Finally, Baggio had taken up the request for Romero's removal that other bishops had made. "With the same simplicity as in our talk," Romero wrote, "I put in writing that, if it is for the good of the church, with the greatest pleasure I will turn over to other hands this difficult governance of the archdiocese. But while I have it under my responsibility, I will only try to please the Lord and serve his church and his people according to my conscience in the light of the gospel and the magisterium."

Romero ended his memorandum on his talk with Baggio with these judgments and conclusions:

From your invitation of May 16, I expected to hear "the most contrary reports, both good and bad—both of them, genuine and spontaneous." But I am left with the impression that among the reports that you had in mind the negative ones prevailed almost exclusively and that my explanations or answers did not receive official support. Naturally, I return with the worry that you will continue to receive only one-sided reports that coincide exactly with the tendentious comments of the powerful sectors of my country.

This gives me the impression that you have certain ready-made judgments on these matters, which makes me wonder what effect my explanations have. I get this impression from the way you spoke of the vocations of our seminarians ("it horrifies me to think"), of my honorary doctorate ("evidently" a political trick, "it does you no honor"), in defense of the nuncio ("an almost irreparable scandal"), of the incompatibility of the seminary and the archdiocesan headquarters in the same building ("it has to get out"), in defense of Bishop Revelo ("he was criticized with ill will"), and from other expressions that leave the impression that there is no other way to think.

Romero stated that he would continue to keep the congregation informed, especially by sending his homilies, and asked Baggio to invite him again to Rome, as he had done this time, before making judgments or a serious decision. He asked Baggio's help "to think out and put into practice a sound autonomy of pastoral-liturgical functions of the bishop over against the specific functions of the nuncio, to get rid of the idea that there are two churches and that both types are supported or discredited according to the advantages of different groups." He also asked Baggio's cooperation in achieving a cordial union with Revelo, so that Revelo might not misinterpret the Holy See's backing as authorizing antagonism toward Romero.

"My thanks for having called me to dialog," he concluded. "I consider this happy opportunity the beginning of a more frequent correspondence that will help you to have objective information and will help me, as this talk has helped me much, to keep on trying with love to serve our holy church. The special audience that the Holy Father granted me on Wednesday has been a new charism that has put a note of greater optimism in my life to try to fulfill this purpose."

The audience with Pope Paul VI, on the day after the talk with Baggio, was for Romero the supreme moment of the trip to Rome. Paul took both his hands while "he spoke words of encouragement and understanding and made me the messenger of his great pastoral affection for our people," Romero wrote later. "The natural emotion of being close to the universal shepherd and especially his cordial and positive welcome did not let me record and repeat textually his words. I am sorry, but I believe it should be so, because more than words they were for me a new breath of the Spirit, which 'has strengthened' [Luke 22:32] my faith in the church of Jesus Christ and my shepherd's love for my people."[38]

The pope, Romero said in his diary, told him that he understood how difficult his work as archbishop was and that it was often misunderstood.

He encouraged Romero to be patient and courageous. The people were seeking their rights, he said, and Romero should work for them and help them to see the value of their suffering and to avoid hatred and violence. The pope himself loved them and prayed for them and for their archbishop. Romero replied that he was trying to preach peace as the pope said, calling for the conversion of sinners, and he affirmed his adherence to the pope's teaching.

Romero left with the pope a private letter setting forth the purpose of his visit to the Roman secretariats. It was so hard, he said in the letter, to carry out his duties in El Salvador. He was leaving documentation in the Vatican that showed how the church was defamed in his country and also how other persons supported his own line of action. He regretted that some of the admonitions he had received from Roman offices coincided with the views of the forces that were trying to impede his apostolic work. The next Monday, when he and Bishop Rivera visited the Secretariat of State, he saw the letter on the desk of Archbishop Agostino Casaroli, secretary of the Council for the Church's Public Affairs. It had notes on it, apparently in the pope's hand.

Casaroli asked them about the division among the bishops. Romero explained that the other bishops had seen Marxism and politics in the grass-roots communities since the time of Archbishop Chávez. The meetings of the bishops' conference were superficial, not really analyzing what was going on. Rivera said that Bishop Barrera was overage, and Romero remarked on Alvarez's military connections. "Everyone calls him the colonel," he said. Aparicio was intent on getting advantages from the government, like payment for teachers' salaries in the Catholic schools. President Romero had said of him, "He wags his tail when you give him something."

Secretary Casaroli expressed concern that the church might become politicized or be used by political groups. Rivera admitted the danger, since groups were cut off from other means of activity and would try to shelter themselves with the church. But the church was aware of the danger.

Casaroli wondered also if they were seeking the best way to bring about justice. Rivera explained that they were not preaching revolution but peaceful change. This brought the talk around to the bishops' conference again, and at that point they were joined by the Salvadoran ambassador to the Holy See, Prudencio Llach.

The discussion went off on a tangent: whether or not the parish priests could give their catechists an identification card to protect them. Romero was not sure whether it would be a protection or a danger and asked for time to consult about it. Rivera recounted the long history of efforts at conversation with the government, and how the government failed to follow up possibilities. They agreed to get the bilateral commission going again, which the government had let languish.[39] But nothing further happened, and the dialog remained stagnant (see chap. IV).

Romero left Rome feeling contented, in spite of the tense session with Cardinal Baggio. The pope had understood and encouraged him, as had his friend Cardinal Pironio, prefect of the Congregation for Religious. He had corrected false reports about the seminary at the Congregation for Catholic Education, and the Secretariat of State had listened to him. Ambassador Llach, with whom he had dined on Sunday, was trying to restart the dialog with the government. Romero had spoken to the Congregation for the Clergy about his problem with Father Quinteros and about the priests suspended by Bishop Aparicio, and the congregation had said it was sending instructions to Aparicio. Romero had attended the pope's public appearances and the solemn mass in St. Peter's on June 29, the feast of Sts. Peter and Paul.

"I feel sorry to leave Rome," he recorded in his diary. "It is home for one who has faith and who has feeling for the church. Rome is the homeland of all Christians. The pope, the true father of all, is there. I have felt him so near to me, I leave feeling so grateful to him, that my heart, my faith, my spirit continue to draw nourishment from that rock where the church's unity is so palpable." He had time to reflect during the flight home, "the immensely long night over the ocean," on all that had happened in Rome. Bishop Revelo and a crowd of people welcomed him at San Salvador's Ilopango airport on Friday, June 30, and took him to the cathedral for a mass together. On Sunday morning, at his regular cathedral mass, he told the people about his trip. In his diary, he called the mass "a homage to the pope from all the communities of the archdiocese. . . . Blessed be God for the love our people feel for their shepherds."

❧ VI ❧

The Church and the Organizations

July–December 1978

By mid-1978 the Latin American church was caught up in preparation for the third general meeting of the Latin American hierarchy, scheduled to be held in October at Puebla, Mexico. The preparations were in the hands of CELAM, the service organization of the Latin American hierarchies. CELAM had also prepared the 1968 meeting at Medellín, which had so dramatically changed the course of the church in Latin America. But the CELAM of 1978 was different from the CELAM of 1968. The change of administration in 1972 had made a young Colombian bishop, Alfonso López Trujillo, the secretary-general, and he had begun replacing the more forward-looking personnel with conservatives. Ten years after Medellín, those who were most fervent in following Medellín's guidelines saw the coming conference as an attempt to slow down the process or even to reverse it.

A thick preparatory document that CELAM sent around the continent early in 1978 confirmed the fears of many. It portrayed a Latin America suffering from rapid urbanization and underdevelopment, but not from the oppression of the poor by the rich, and it viewed the military rule that dominated most of the area as a natural reaction to the power vacuum of nonfunctioning political systems. Missing was the fire of the prophets before injustice, and ignored were the martyrs — in El Salvador, Panama, Honduras, Brazil, and Argentina — of the renewed church growing out of the Medellín conference. Priests, grass-roots church communities, and even bishops' conferences roundly criticized the document. To CELAM's credit, however, it must be said that it had proposed the document precisely to be discussed and criticized.

The Salvadoran bishops had begun to study the document early in 1978 and had convened several special CEDES meetings to deal with it. On April 17 they elected Bishop Revelo to be their delegate to the Puebla meeting, with three votes in his favor against two for Rivera and one for Romero. Bishop Aparicio, the president of CEDES, would go ex officio. They also chose as an observer, to represent the clergy of the country, Monsignor Freddy Delgado, the secretary-general of CEDES.[1] The choice went down very badly with most of the clergy, who were irked at not being consulted and at the choice.[2]

Like many Latin American bishops, Romero consulted his people on what the Puebla meeting should do. In the first months of 1978 he had a questionnaire prepared for the archdiocese, especially for the small communities, which were ideally suited to such a discussion. A group of specialists in theology, sociology, and pastoral practice then prepared analyses of the people's responses.

Cardinal Baggio wrote Romero on May 26 to tell him that as a consultor of the Pontifical Commission for Latin America he was entitled to go to Puebla, but without the right to vote enjoyed by the elected delegates and episcopal-conference presidents. Romero had been a consultor of the commission since 1975, when he had attended a meeting of the commission in Rome (see chap. II). Romero shared the general dissatisfaction with the preparatory document and the suspicions of what was being prepared.[3] All the more reason, then, for him to attend, even without a vote.

In September Romero received the working paper for the conference, a new document prepared following the discussions and reports from all over Latin America by small communities, pastoral workers, bishops' conferences, and regional meetings of bishops. It was somewhat more pastoral than the first document but still open to many of the same criticisms. Romero called a series of meetings in a retreat house in Planes de Renderos, on the wooded mountains overlooking San Salvador from the south. Theologians, priests with long experience in pastoral organization, and social scientists like Héctor Dada of the Central American University engaged in daylong studies and discussions. The new pope, John Paul I, who had just succeeded Paul VI, had reconfirmed the October meeting date. But suddenly the new pope died, and everything was up in the air. A conclave would take place in October and a new pope would have to confirm the whole idea and approve a new time for it. As it turned out, John Paul II decided to have it begin at the end of January 1979 and to open it himself, as Paul VI had opened Medellín.

Romero had been planning a pastoral letter for many months, to be issued for El Salvador's patronal feast of the Divine Savior of the World, August 6. It would be his third pastoral as archbishop, and Bishop Rivera would also sign it as his first pastoral as bishop of Santiago de María.

Two related subjects, Romero felt, called for a word of guidance. One was a subject that campesinos, especially catechists and delegates of the word, often asked about: the relation of the church to the popular organizations, especially the peasant unions, FECCAS and UTC. FECCAS had begun in the early 1960's as a part of the international Christian trade union movement of the Christian Democrats. Like the rest of the movement, it had secularized but still paid homage to its Christian beginnings and ideals. UTC had begun in San Vicente in 1974 under Christian leadership and had federated with FECCAS in 1975.[4]

Many priests encouraged FECCAS and UTC, and many members of small church communities belonged to them, including community leaders, catechists, and delegates of the word, who tended to become leaders in the organizations as well. At times it was hard for those who belonged to both entities to see the difference between the Christian community and the popular organization. Then, there was the question of the Marxist thought that the organizations were now using. Was it compatible with Christianity? For many persons a Marxist label was enough to condemn anything.

The second subject was that of violence. Could one resist with force the violence of repression, the denial of human rights, the institutionalized violence of unjust structures? If so, in what way? The questions were not merely theoretical. Members of FECCAS and UTC had clashed with campesinos of ORDEN, the government's repressive counterorganization, in the San Pedro Perulapán incidents and elsewhere, and members of the BPR had begun to carry small arms to demonstrations in order to fight back if fired upon. Police as well as demonstrators had died in some cases.

As early as April, Romero began meeting with various advisers, both clerical and lay. At least the first draft of the text was given to Bishop Revelo for his comments. Romero himself worked over the final draft, and Bishop Rivera made some final suggestions as late as August 22. Although dated August 6, it was not actually published until August 26, by which time the public was expecting it, since Romero had summarized it in his homily on August 6.

But by August the other four bishops were also thinking about a statement on the organizations. The bishops had discussed the subject at their regular meeting in July.[5] Romero had read a paragraph from the pastoral being prepared and suggested that the other bishops might want to sign the letter. He sent them copies on July 24, but none besides Rivera cared to sign it or, apparently, even discuss it further.

On August 16 the bishops' conference met to discuss whether they should issue a statement. The nuncio had urged them to say something about the organizations, as a consequence of the Vatican's reaction to Revelo's remarks at the bishops' synod the previous October. The discussion was long. It was evident that Romero and Rivera were the only ones who wanted to avoid a condemnation of FECCAS and UTC. To the other four, they were tainted with Marxism, and that was enough. They voted to draw up the statement, four to one; Romero had left the room before the vote. Aparicio was chosen to write the text and have the others look it over before approving it.[6]

The long-awaited pastoral letter that Romero and Rivera published on

August 26 was followed two days later by the unexpected statement of the other four bishops, issued in the name of the bishops' conference. The latter was far shorter and evidently less thought-out, and it naturally looked like a hasty reply to the former. Though it agreed to some extent with the pastoral letter, for instance in asserting the natural right to organize, its overall tone and direction were utterly different. It ended with a virtual condemnation of the organizations, which their enemies immediately seized upon. On the heels of the carefully nuanced treatment by Romero and Rivera, the statement issued by the other four publicized dramatically the division in the hierarchy.

Romero foresaw some of the public reaction when he wrote to Freddy Delgado on August 26, asking for more time to study the statement and suggest changes before deciding whether to sign it (he had received it on the 24th and Delgado wanted an answer by the 27th; meanwhile the pastoral letter was already being distributed on the 26th). "It seems to me," Romero wrote, "that it would be prudent to await the reaction and the results that the letter produces in the people before offering them another document on the same subject. If both publications appear at the same time, we are liable to confuse rather than orient and to offer a new demonstration of further disunion."

Anyone in El Salvador who had not yet noticed the split in the body of bishops could hardly miss it once the two documents appeared. The notoriety extended beyond the national boundaries to the rest of Central America and even to church circles overseas.

The ones most affected by the four bishops' statement, FECCAS and UTC, reacted with a statement of their own. They recounted at length their efforts to obtain better wages and working conditions and to struggle so that "one day not far in the future we can end forever this system of exploitation and injustice and build a society based on solidarity, equality, working together, and peace." They detailed the brutal efforts to suppress their movement. The bishops, they said bitterly, had taken a stand in a class struggle against them.

That is the only way to explain why these four bishops expressly deny to FECCAS-UTC the right to "claim the protection of the church" because they are "leftist organizations" and have never denied this protection to ORDEN, a paramilitary government organization that has committed hundreds of crimes and outrages against the working class. That is the only way to explain why these bishops forbid their priests and religious to "work directly or indirectly" with FECCAS-UTC on the grounds that we carry on an activity "in the strictly political field," the taking of power, while one of them, Bishop Eduardo Alvarez, is part of the forces of repression, a colonel in the army. The military forces in our country likewise exercise an activity in the strictly political field, being in power through fraud and violence, and they have carried out military operations against the people and against the church.

They reaffirmed that they were organizations completely independent of the Catholic church: "Being a Christian is not a requisite for belonging to our organizations. Nevertheless, many of our militants are Christians, since most of the poor peasants and day laborers of our country are." And they noted with satisfaction that "in El Salvador there are some bishops, priests, religious, and lay people who in various ways have joined us in our people's just struggle."[7]

The bishops met to discuss other matters on September 13, but they could not help talking about the storm that their declaration had brought on their heads. Romero left the meeting early, and after Alvarez launched into a long attack on Romero and the pastoral letter, Rivera moved that the discussion be off the record. The motion was approved. Alvarez was angry about the series of commentaries on the two documents that YSAX was making during September. Aparicio said that the letter had been published to counteract the bishops' declaration, and Rivera replied that the opposite would be closer to the truth: the letter was not improvised but had developed over months. He himself had been concerned about the challenge of the popular organizations for a year before Grande's death. He had signed it because it agreed with his own way of thinking. Alvarez said that he was convinced of that, but in Romero's case the group of Jesuits had given him those ideas.

But many others besides Jesuits contributed to the pastoral letter. All told, some twenty-five people worked on the letter, which went through at least four drafts, each one subject to suggestions and criticisms. The idea for the letter came from Romero himself, who had met at various times with leaders of the popular organizations, especially FECCAS and UTC, beginning in 1977. His policy was to be available for dialog with everyone. The talks with the organizations, and his contact with campesinos and the priests and nuns who worked with them, convinced him that he should make clear the church's position.

In Romero's schedule for a while was a weekly breakfast meeting with a group of advisers, principally members of the priests' senate and the lay Justice and Peace Commission.[8] Many of these two-hour sessions were spent in going over the drafts of the letter. Various persons, priests and lay people, received drafts of the letter to read and criticize. So many changes were made that one adviser urged Romero not to pass the final draft to more than a few, lest it should never be finished. Although many hands and minds were involved, in the end it was Romero who decided what would be said and how it would be said.[9]

The pastoral letter became the text of many study groups in the archdiocese and beyond. The first edition published by the archdiocese contained an outline and questions to guide groups in studying and discussing it. The archdiocese published a booklet of background material giving some basic facts about the country (e.g., government statistics showing that a large proportion of Salvadorans consumed an average of only 1,435 calories a day, far less than the recommended 2,200 and even less than the survival level of 1,500) and about the church's social teaching, from Leo XIII to the Salvadoran bishops. Although concerned primarily with Salvadoran problems, the pastoral also attracted interest elsewhere in Latin America and was even translated into English.[10]

Calling the Salvadoran popular organizations one of the "signs of God's presence and purposes" that Vatican II[11] spoke of, the letter recalled that the right of workers to organize is embodied in the Universal Declaration of Human Rights and in the Salvadoran constitution and is asserted by John XXIII's encyclical letter *Pacem in Terris* and by Vatican II. Yet, in practice, El Salvador denied this right to the majority of its citizens, the campesinos, both by legislation that denied legal recognition to their organizations and by actively repressing them through the security forces and its own hostile campesino organization, ORDEN. "Groups agreeing with the government or protected by it function freely, while organizations that represent a voice out of harmony with the government's, whether speaking through political parties or industrial, trade, or peasant unions, in fact find it difficult or simply impossible to use their right to organize legally in order to work for their objectives, even though these be just."

On the other hand, the economically powerful had complete freedom to organize and to spend vast sums on publicity campaigns in order to get the government to do what they wanted. "This state of affairs shows the enormous inequality of citizens in their ability to participate in political life, according to whether they belong to a powerful minority or to the needy majority and according to whether they enjoy official approval or not." Yet the purpose both of laws and of organizations was to protect those who needed protection of their rights.

By setting up its own counterorganization, ORDEN, the government created a confrontation between campesinos. It was not ideology, said the letter, that divided the campesinos, but their very poverty and need to provide for their families. "Some let themselves be seduced by advantages that progovernment organizations offer them while using them for various repressive activities that frequently involve informing on, intimidating, capturing, torturing, and in some cases murdering their own fellow campesinos." The letter did not mention ORDEN or any other organization by name, but the reference was obvious.

Since the peasant organizations and the coalitions of popular organizations were not political parties and yet sought political change, they presented a new question for the church. This was the core of the letter, which set out three principles as a basis for the church's stance:

1. The church's mission is religious, but from its mission "flow functions, lights, and energies that can serve to establish and consolidate the human

community according to the divine law," said the letter, quoting Vatican II.[12] The church's nature is to build community. The grass-roots ecclesial communities springing up, especially among the poor, are the foundation of the church (the Spanish term for them, *comunidades de base,* means *foundation communities*). Since the word of God that feeds the community is a word that awakens and makes demands, it is not only to be listened to but acted upon. And that can awaken in a Christian a political commitment.

2. The church has a mission to serve the people, that is, to use its "functions, lights, and energies" to "establish and consolidate the human community according to the divine law." The church does not choose one political organization over another, "but it can and must give a judgment on the overall intentions and particular mechanisms of parties and organizations precisely because of its interest in a more just society, since people's economic, social, political, and cultural aspirations are not foreign to the definitive liberation through Jesus Christ that is the church's transcendent hope."

3. The church must enlighten the legitimate efforts of organizations for human liberation with the light of its faith and Christian hope, with its vision of integral liberation. That liberation "embraces the whole human being in every dimension, including openness to the absolute that is God." It is centered on the kingdom of God and proclaims salvation in Jesus Christ. "It proceeds from a gospel vision of human nature and is based on deep motives of justice in charity. It has within it a truly spiritual dimension and has as its final goal salvation and happiness in God. It demands conversion of heart and mind and is not satisfied with merely changing structures. It excludes violence, which it considers 'unchristian and unevangelical,'[13] ineffective, and not consonant with the people's dignity."

The letter applies these three principles of the church's mission to various questions that arise about the church's relation with the popular organizations. Some organizations had arisen from Christian communities, naturally enough, but that did not make the church responsible for all their actions. The problem was that faith and political commitment exist in the same person, the Christian who has a political commitment. Indeed, all Christians should have both dimensions in their lives, and faith cannot be separated from life. But the work of faith cannot be identified with a specific political task. "The Christian with a political vocation must manage to achieve a synthesis of Christian faith and political action, but without identifying them. Faith must inspire the Christian's political action, but the Christian must not confuse them."

Christians in any organization must be aware of the autonomy of faith and politics and of what they can demand and not demand from the church. They can ask that it defend their rights but cannot ask that its liturgy or preaching be the vehicle of political action. In their political life they must also profess their faith and not use methods inconsonant with it. Political life may produce tensions with one's faith, but a Christian's ultimate loyalty must be to the faith and to the poor of Jesus Christ, and not to the organization as such.

Not every Christian has the vocation to political activism, and much less to any particular organization. Some will struggle for justice in other ways, for example, in promoting the "liberating education" advocated by Medellín or the "evangelization not foreign to human rights and the liberation of peoples" of Paul VI's *Evangelii Nuntiandi.*

One of the most critical and most delicate points that the letter had to deal with was the position of priests, religious, and lay workers identified with the church, when such people dealt or worked with the popular organizations. The letter had to offer guidelines and yet allow room for prudent decisions in individual cases. It recalled that Paul VI's *Evangelii Nuntiandi* was the pastoral policy of the archdiocese, and went on: "We urge all our priests and lay people to guard the gospel purity of this policy and, thus guarding it, not to fear the boldness that it will often demand. It is normal and frequent that priests themselves and their closest lay co-workers feel political problems keenly, precisely because they are concerned for an incarnated and committed evangelization. As persons and citizens they will feel more sympathy for one party or popular organization than for others. It is even understandable that, when asked, they cooperate in giving a Christian orientation to the leadership of Christians' political activities in favor of justice." But in any priestly or pastoral work that persons, parties, or organizations ask of them, "let them always keep as first objective to be animators and guides in faith and in the justice that faith demands."

In exceptional cases, a priest might be called on to take on some further political role, but "it is up to the bishop, in sincere dialog with the priest in the light of faith, to arrive at a Christian discernment over the apostolic value of such work."

In the case of lay people like catechists and delegates of the word, who "have been taken into the service of the church for a special hierarchical mission," they must recall that they are representatives of the hierarchy and therefore a "sign of the unity of all the children of the local and universal church." They should thus be prudent about joining a popular organization and "if active participation in an organization deprives the pastoral worker of credibility or efficacy before God's people, there is a strong pastoral reason to opt for one of the two leaderships, after making a serious discernment before the Lord."

The question of violence comes up naturally when people organize to claim their rights. Organization suggests force, whether moral, economic, social, or physical. In El Salvador in 1978, physical force, violence, was already a tradition on the part of those who would keep the peasants in their place. The massacre of 1932, in which thousands of campesinos were slaughtered after an attempted insurrection was crushed, still lived in the national consciousness. The more recent operations in Aguilares and San

Pedro Perulapán were small-scale replays of what had once happened and could happen again. But the organizations were determined also to defend themselves by violence if necessary. In addition, small extremist groups of revolutionaries were active, bombing, kidnapping, and killing to gain their objectives. Romero had spoken out many times against both the violence of the government and the rich and the violence of the leftists.

The letter's treatment of violence reads almost like a manual of moral theology, and indeed its teaching is largely what moralists have said for centuries. It formulates the ideal of peace and nonviolence, but goes on to say that violence will not disappear until its causes are rooted out. And to get at the causes, it distinguishes various types of violence, in textbook fashion but using a modern division of the subject suggested by Medellín.

"The most acute form of violence on our continent and in our country is what the bishops at Medellín called *institutionalized violence,*[14] the product of a situation of injustice in which the majority of men and women—and, especially, of children—in our country are deprived of what is needed to live." This violence, the letter continues, is expressed in the day-to-day working of a system that takes as normal that progress is possible only by using most of the people as a productive force managed by a privileged sector. Those responsible are both the international structures that condition the national economic structure and those persons who jealously hang onto their privileges, even by violent means. Responsible also are those who sin by omission, by doing nothing in favor of justice.

"Usually arising parallel to institutional violence is *repressive violence,* that is, the violence used by state security forces as the state tries to contain the aspirations of the populace, violently stifling any show of protest at the injustice we have just mentioned." This violence is unjust, because with it the state defends an unjust system and hinders any chance for the people to use their right to govern themselves and to find their way toward institutional justice.

What some call revolutionary violence, "we prefer to call *terrorist* or *seditious* violence, since the term *revolutionary* does not always have the pejorative sense we intend here." Paul VI, in Bogotá in 1968, had spoken of it as "explosive revolutions of despair."[15] It is usually organized in the form of guerrilla warfare or terrorism and "mistakenly is considered the ultimate and only effective means of social change." The letter rejects it, because it "produces and provokes sterile and unjustified bloodshed, leads society to explosive tensions, uncontrollable by reason, and spurns in principle every form of dialog as a possible instrument to solve social conflicts."

Another kind of violence is that which arises *spontaneously* when persons are attacked while exercising their rights by demonstrating, striking, and such. Because it is a desperate and improvised reaction, this violence is ineffective "and therefore cannot be effective in obtaining one's rights or achieving just solutions to conflicts." Legitimate *defense* is also a type of violence; it seeks to stop or bring under control an imminent danger.

Finally, "to complete this classification of violence, it is fitting to add the power of *nonviolence,* which today has conspicuous students and followers. The counsel of the gospel to turn the other cheek to an unjust aggressor, far from being passive or cowardly, is the showing of great moral force, which leaves the aggressor morally overcome and humiliated. 'The Christian is able to fight but prefers peace to war,' said Medellín, alluding to the moral force of nonviolence."[16]

The letter's judgment on the different types of violence follows the classic teaching of the church: violence is wrong when sought for itself or when used against a human right or when used as the first and only means to defend a human right; it is allowed for legitimate defense, provided one does not use more force than necessary, has exhausted all other means, and does not bring about a greater evil than the one being averted. Institutional violence, repressive violence, terrorist violence, and any violence that could provoke a legitimate violent defense are all wrong.

On the complex type of violence involved in insurrection, a form of defense that can set off chains of further violence and other evils, the letter limits itself to quoting Paul VI and Medellín. Insurrection might be justified, said Pope Paul, in the very exceptional case "of evident and prolonged tyranny that seriously attacks the fundamental rights of the person and dangerously harms the common good of the country."[17] Medellín added, "whether the tyranny proceeds from one person or from clearly unjust structures."[18] Like Paul VI and Medellín, the letter adverts to the danger of causing further violence and injustice, which would also make the insurrection wrong. Because of the dangers involved in insurrection, the church teaches that a government must strive to make recourse to violence unnecessary by protecting the fundamental rights of its citizens.

To its careful and traditional treatment of violence, the letter adds a few practical considerations for El Salvador:

> We proclaim the supremacy of our belief in peace and we call upon all to strive positively for its construction. We cannot put all our confidence in violent methods if we are truly Christians or simply persons of honor. But the peace in which we believe is the product of justice. Violent conflicts will not disappear until their fundamental causes disappear, as a simple analysis of our structures shows and as history confirms. While the causes of the present misery persist and the factions in power remain intransigent, refusing to tolerate the least changes, the explosive situation will become worse. If repressive violence is to continue, unfortunately it will simply intensify the conflict and "make less hypothetical and more real the case in which recourse to force as legitimate defense can be justified."[19] We believe our most urgent task is to establish social justice.

The letter warned further that the fanatical violence of certain groups and individuals was harming the country by divinizing violence as the only source of justice. "This pathological mentality" made it impossible to stop the spiral of violence. Even in legitimate cases violence must always be a last resort. "We fraternally invite all, especially the organizations that labor in the struggle for justice, to continue courageously and honestly with just objectives and to use legitimate means of pressure and not put all their trust in violence."

Paul VI died suddenly on August 6, the feast of the Transfiguration, and Romero took note of it in the introduction to the pastoral letter that appeared twenty days later. Paul had been a support to the archbishop, who often quoted the pope's encyclical "On the Development of Peoples" (*Populorum Progressio*) and his instruction on catechesis, *Evangelii Nuntiandi,* in his own writings and sermons.

Paul's successor, Albano Luciani, took the surprising name of John Paul I. No one foresaw how short his reign—or his ministry, as he preferred to call it—would be. He would be remembered for his refreshing departure from the stiff protocol of the papacy, bringing in a relaxed humanness that recalled John XXIII and that the second John Paul would build on. Instead of a coronation, John Paul I had an inauguration of his papal ministry. But old terms often die hard, and it was to celebrate the "coronation" that Archbishop Gerada invited Romero to the nunciature.

Romero replied by letter[20] that in spite of his fidelity and love for the pope, he could not attend the reception that the nuncio was giving. "Unfortunately, the publicity given to these acts is eagerly used to give the public an image of the relations between this government and our local hierarchy that, in my opinion, makes us bishops lose trust and credibility with our people, to whom we are principally committed." One could be sure that the next day the papers would carry pictures of bishops smiling and chatting with generals and cabinet ministers, even with the president himself.

The archdiocese, Archbishop Romero said, would show the pope its solidarity and devotion with a concelebrated mass of all the clergy on the occasion of the next clergy meeting, the first Tuesday of September. He would send Monsignor Urioste to represent him at the nuncio's reception.

A few days later Romero received a confidential message from a government employee advising him that the nuncio and Cardinal Casariego, who were to travel to Rome for the papal inauguration, had agreed with the president and the government to seek his removal, and warning him not to give them any document for the pope because it would not be delivered. A handwritten postscript to the memorandum told him to destroy it after reading it.

Romero was shrewd enough not to believe everything he heard, but experienced enough not to disregard everything that sounded extreme. He already knew well enough that the government, the nuncio, and other bishops wanted him removed. Cardinal Baggio had discussed his removal with him in Rome in June. And he seems to have avoided using the diplomatic pouch of the nunciature to send important documents to Rome.

Whether the present warning was important or not, it was an example of the sources of information that were offered to him. He had been a much-admired churchman for many years, with many friends among rich and poor, powerful and lowly. Hundreds of thousands in all walks of life now hung on his words and saw him as the leader and symbol of honesty in the land, beset by ruthless enemies out to destroy him. If the government and the oligarchy had their sympathizers and informers among the bishops and the clergy, he also found support in government offices and even in the barracks and officers' quarters of the military.

John Paul I died suddenly at the end of September, leaving as his legacy a new papal style. After his death it would seem impossible that, before John Paul I, popes were crowned like kings and spoke with the royal "we."

John Paul II became pope on October 16. Taking his loved predecessor's name and following his personal style, John Paul II immediately began to imprint his own mark on the papacy. Perhaps sensing the dynamism of the new pope, Romero moved swiftly to lay his own case before the pope in a six-page letter dated November 7. Romero sketched briefly the history of his time as archbishop: the institutional injustice in the country, the persecution of people and church, the murders and expulsions of priests, the dispersal of Christian communities, the tortures and disappearances.

"From the beginning of my ministry in the archdiocese," he wrote, "I genuinely believed that God asked of me and gave me a pastoral strength that contrasted with my 'conservative' inclinations and temperament. I believed it a duty to take a positive stand in defense of my church and, on the part of the church, at the side of my oppressed and abused people. In all my actions I have prayed for much light from the Holy Spirit so as not to depart from the gospel or the guidelines of Vatican Council II or the authorized documents of Medellín. The exhortation *Evangelii Nuntiandi*, especially, has been a providential norm for me."

This pastoral practice had produced in the archdiocese greater unity in the clergy, a flourishing spirituality in the Christian communities springing up everywhere, apostolic zeal, priestly vocations, and the conversion of many estranged from the church. He had also received the encouragement of support from many bishops and people of other lands.

Romero then told the pope about his fears, arising from the "systematic and incomprehensible opposition" of the nuncio and most of the other bishops. The nuncio "has shown himself influenced more by government, diplomatic, and capitalist sectors than by the sufferings of the people." Romero found the nuncio's efforts to show a unity between archbishop and government "not very intelligent," since an apparent friendliness with the government would cost Romero his credibility with the people. "I have not rejected dialog with the government, but I have placed as a condition for it that an atmosphere of trust be developed by ceasing to repress and outrage the people and giving signs of respect for their rights."

Various actions of the nuncio had also given the impression that there was a church of the nuncio and one of the archbishop, "which is called 'political, communist, and subversive.' " The nuncio had shown his public support for certain priests estranged from the archbishop. "The most scandalous case is that of Father Rogelio Esquivel, who in spite of his disagreement with his bishop has found complete support in the nunciature and even was part of the diplomatic mission that attended the inauguration of your pontificate."

Of Bishop Rivera, Romero wrote: "His mind open to change in the church and his great spiritual and intellectual capacity have seen nothing to reproach in the pastoral policy of the archdiocese. Rather, I enjoy his full support and solidarity." In the other four bishops, Romero found "a continual rejection." The cause of their aversion was partly the "personal pettiness that has almost always existed in suffragans toward the metropolitan," but each also had his particular reasons.

Bishop Alvarez "is also the military vicar and his pastoral policy is to prefer to maintain privileges with authorities, high-ranking military, and powerful persons. The bishops' conference itself has complained of his pastoral inefficiency in the army. Clergy and people of his diocese complain of the lack of diocesan pastoral practice."

Bishop Barrera "is an old man of seventy-six and he has never chosen a pastoral policy of serious evangelical commitment to his people."

Bishop Aparicio "is supremely fickle, vain, and self-seeking. He has acted very valiantly against abuses of power and wealth when it was in his interest. But today his advantages are on the side of the government and he makes himself accomplice of its policy of persecution. Some of his actions as president of the bishops' conference have been very arbitrary and very disloyal, even compromising the church's autonomy before the government and manipulating the bishops of the majority against the policies and interests of this archdiocese."

(Romero left unmentioned that on October 5 the Guardia had arrested two priests and an employee of YSAX, who recounted after their release that Aparicio had appeared before the police and, Romero recorded in his diary the next day, "instead of defending the church said the police were right—which seems dangerous for the archdiocese, since it tends to give the impression that the archdiocese exaggerates and that in fact there is communist infiltration and that we are unjust when we report so much abuse committed against the people and the church.")

Romero reviewed the history of his problems with Revelo, including Baggio's instructions to him to rein in the archbishop. Baggio, he said, defended Revelo as if he were treated unjustly and argued in his favor that the bishops had elected him to the synod and to the forthcoming Puebla conference. "But this is explainable when one knows the regrettable divisions in our conference and the animosity of the majority toward Bishop Rivera and me."

In regard to Puebla, Romero wrote:

We all see its importance and have great faith and hope in the Holy Spirit and in the great prayer and work of our churches. But, humanly speaking, fears and even convictions prevail that human machinations could be "extinguishing the Spirit" [I Thess. 5:19]. The clergy in our country are unhappy with the representation that will go to Puebla. Bishops Aparicio and Revelo are not believed to reflect the opinions of all of our church. Monsignor Freddy Delgado was named by the majority of the bishops' conference without taking into account his lack of acceptance among priests. The religious are dissatisfied because those elected by them were not considered. We believe that the whole preparation for Puebla was managed with great "human prudence" and that in large part the bold and creative elements with which God has gifted the church of this continent in order to walk evangelically with our peoples have been set aside.

Romero concluded the letter with the request that, when new bishops were named, they not reinforce the "negative views of the present majority of the bishops," but that "our hierarchy be enriched with attitudes of genuine church renewal," and he rejected two candidates whose names had been bandied about. He asked that Revelo be made auxiliary of another diocese "more in accord with his way of thinking."

The letter was bold and simple. Romero spoke bluntly but in confidence, impressed, he said at the beginning, by the pope's own "love, strength, and simplicity" in the service of the church. He was not afraid to open his heart before this stranger whose experience had been so far removed from his own in place and culture, and yet not so different in that both had to care for a flock while facing a hostile government.

As auxiliary bishop, Revelo remained a problem. Romero had wanted him to be a binding force among the clergy, but he had remained withdrawn and sullen. By signing the declaration on FECCAS and UTC issued by the bishops who opposed Romero and by not signing Romero's pastoral letter, Revelo had publicly placed himself on the side of the bishops who were working against the archbishop. At the monthly clergy meeting on September 5, those present voted to ask the priests' senate to write to Baggio of their dissatisfaction with Revelo, sixty-two voting in favor and nine abstaining. The senators sent the letter on September 14.

The crowning blow, however, came in November, when it became clear that Revelo had committed a public act of insubordination that could not be overlooked. The national office of Caritas, the church organization that distributes relief supplies to the poor, was incorporated under civil law in

El Salvador with the archbishop of San Salvador as its head. Without Romero's knowledge, Revelo as vicar-general signed away the archbishop's rights in favor of the president of CEDES, who was Aparicio. According to a priest who worked closely with Romero, this occurred at a time when Romero was interested in tightening up the distribution system, in which the government was heavily involved, in order to prevent it from using food aid as a payment to members of ORDEN.

Revelo's action was against church law, since he acted against the known mind of the archbishop. The action was probably illegal also under civil law, since the civil bylaws of Caritas said nothing about the vicar's acting for the archbishop.

Romero protested to the government, but to no avail,[21] since the government was a party to the collusion. Justice from the courts was unthinkable. They were under the government's thumb, and Romero had humiliated the Supreme Court in May.

The priests' senate formally requested Romero on November 17 to remove Revelo as vicar-general. He did so on November 23. Four days later he wrote a weary but stern letter to Revelo reminding him of his duty as pastor of San Francisco parish to cooperate in the joint pastoral efforts of the vicariate to which it belonged: "I have never thought that the parish was to be only a place of residence for you and your family. Neither do I believe that being a bishop exempts you from trying to offer your help to the pastoral efforts the church demands. Rather, being a bishop imposes a greater obligation to be the one who puts life into the joint pastoral work."

Reviewing the incident, the priests' senate noted in its minutes for November 17, "Once again is seen the ill will of the country's bishops, presided over by Bishop Aparicio, toward Archbishop Romero. This has become scandalous and crippling for the Salvadoran church's evangelical and evangelizing vigor. And the government gladly lends itself to such affairs."

Romero threatened to replace Revelo as pastor if he did not see improvement, but he never carried out the threat. Revelo stayed on the sidelines of archdiocesan life, firmly allied with the bishops who opposed Romero. A year after Romero's death, he became bishop of Santa Ana when Barrera retired.

In November 1978 Romero's name was sent to the Nobel Peace Prize committee by 118 members of the British Parliament, from both the House of Commons and the House of Lords. According to *The Times* of London,[22] it might never have happened had not the British government planned to sell secondhand armored cars to El Salvador. Public protest prompted Parliament to take a hard look at El Salvador, and the plan was dropped; but enough interest remained to bring about Romero's nomination. A group of United States congressmen added their plea to that of the British when Congress convened in January 1979. Editorials in many places seconded the idea. All this was a sign of Romero's growing international renown, and it made him more widely known, even though the prize went in due course to the better-known Mother Teresa of Calcutta. In retrospect, one wonders if all the publicity harmed rather than helped Romero's chances. But the nomination itself and the publicity were a way to educate the world to conditions in El Salvador and Latin America.

A delegation of British parliamentarians, composed of Lord Chitnis, Peter Bottomley, and Dennis Canavan, visited El Salvador December 2–9, meeting the archbishop and attending his Sunday mass. They also visited the president, ministers, political leaders of the opposition, relatives of prisoners and those who had disappeared, persons who had been tortured, the head of the Supreme Court, the president of the legislative assembly, and campesinos. In the Guardia Nacional headquarters they found a torture chamber. After their visit they issued a report that left no doubt that human rights were grossly violated in El Salvador.[23]

In spite of the continual problems and controversies, Romero as archbishop was mostly busy with pastoral activity, as his diary and those who knew him attest. Visits to parishes or village chapels often filled his Sundays and some of his weekdays. Monthly meetings with the clergy focused on matters of catechesis, sacraments, and the spiritual life of parishes and grass-roots ecclesial communities. His homilies provided long commentaries on the readings of the mass, and his comments on current events were meant simply to help the people integrate God's word with real life.

Pastoral policy in the archdiocese insisted on solid instruction in the faith and understanding reception of the sacraments. An index of the direction followed is the pastoral instruction on the sacraments that Romero promulgated for the archdiocese on the first Sunday of Advent, December 3, 1978.

The instruction insisted on catechesis as a necessary preparation for the sacraments. In order that an infant might receive baptism, parents and godparents had to attend instruction on Christian doctrine and on their obligations to rear the child in the faith. This was a practice already widespread in the archdiocese, as it was in other places in Latin America.

With the beginning of Advent, the archdiocese ceased the practice, centuries-old in Spanish-speaking countries, of infant confirmation. In the future, only children of at least eight years would receive confirmation, and the pastors of parishes would be encouraged to prepare adolescents for the sacrament so that it would be a mature commitment to an adult Christian life.

The instruction insisted also on adequate preparation for marriage, both to deepen the couple's understanding of the sacramental aspect of their union and to strengthen the marriage bond itself. This was a reassertion of a requirement already imposed in the time of Archbishop Chávez.

Pastors were to see that children were properly prepared for first communion. The anointing of the sick was not to be only for the dying, and pastors were encouraged to have occasional communal celebrations of the sacrament for the sick of the parish. The instruction encouraged occasional communal celebrations of penance also, as well as private confession. It exhorted pastors to encourage vocations to the sacrament of holy orders.

The instruction is not startling, but it is evidence of a diocese alert to the emphases in the church's sacramental life since Vatican Council II. Along with the special commitment to the poor and to the life of grassroots communities, it documents a diocese striving to keep pace with the church of Vatican II.[24]

The visit of the three British parliamentarians coincided with a crisis arising in the archdiocese over the death of Ernesto (Neto) Barrera, a young priest working closely with laborers and their unions. He died on November 28 under circumstances that remain somewhat mysterious. According to the version published by the government, he was one of four members of the Popular Liberation Forces, or FPL, who died in a five-hour shoot-out with security forces that besieged them with bazookas, grenades, and machine guns until all were dead and the house in which they held out a ruin.

At least part of the government story was clearly a lie. One man was not killed in the shoot-out, as affirmed, but came out with his hands in the air, as shown in a newspaper photograph, and television reporters were able to interview him briefly on camera before guardsmen and police led him away. He had a wound in his throat but gave some answers in writing. The next day he was dead of a bullet in the head that, according to the coroner's report, shattered his brain. Even though thousands had seen him alive on television, the police declared he had received the mortal head wound in the shoot-out.

The coroner did not attempt to fix the time of death of the other men, as he should have done. It would not have been the first time that security forces staged a fake shoot-out and dumped bodies of prisoners killed beforehand. Moreover, Neto Barrera's body showed signs of beating, as though he had been tortured first. The whole government story would have seemed a fabrication had not the FPL itself quickly claimed the four as its own.

Barrera, said the FPL, was a full-fledged member, with the nom de guerre "Felipe." A second was an aspirant to membership and the other two were active collaborators of the organization. The FPL hailed all four as heroes who had bravely held off a far superior force for five hours while they destroyed printed materials. The FPL's statement said: "The heroism with which Father Barrera struggled and died as a revolutionary combatant, defending the interests of the working masses with his weapons in his hands, is an imperishable example for all working people and for all Christians, who now more than ever will understand that there is room in the ranks of the revolution for all those persons who consciously try to struggle against oppression and against class injustice." The statement called "unfitting" the attitude of those who "with good intention or out of ill-understood momentary interest try to hide or put in doubt the heroism shown by the combatants up to the last moment of their lives, offered on the hard road to the attainment of our people's future happiness."

Two questions arose immediately. Was the FPL's declaration genuine or was it put out by someone trying to embarrass the church and justify all the accusations that it promoted violence? And, if it was genuine, could the FPL be trying to cash in on some of the church's popularity by claiming a slain priest as its own?

The archbishop faced the immediate question of Neto's funeral. Should he preside? Should Neto be buried as a priest? Should the church make the same public display that it had for Grande and Navarro? Meetings of priests and advisers were hurriedly called.

Romero quickly decided on his line of action, and he maintained it steadily during the following weeks of doubt and controversy. Neto was his priest. He knew him as a faithful, devoted priest, who followed his bishop's pastoral directions and was open with him. He had blessed Neto's work with the labor movement. Any other Neto was outside his ken—the burden of proof was on those who asserted that he was an FPL militant.

Romero presided at Neto's funeral mass and burial in the church in Mejicanos where Neto's brother was pastor. In the cathedral on December 3, Romero expressed thanks for the condolences received and spoke of the impressive funeral, but gently chided the BPR for using it to chant slogans. He announced that a church commission had made a preliminary report impugning the government version of the deaths. "In regard to the membership and the political activities of Father Ernesto Barrera, whom they have tried to defame, I tell you with all sincerity: I have no personal knowledge." His thought on the subject was in his third pastoral letter: if a priest felt called to political activity in some organization, he should discuss the subject with his bishop. Romero added that he had also discussed and condemned terrorist or seditious violence in the same letter.

The following Sunday, December 10, Romero spoke at greater length about the Neto case. "Every time that I conversed with Father Ernesto Barrera, we spoke about the important challenge presented to him to be an animator in faith and the justice demanded by faith in his pastoral care of working people. He never told me that he was involved in any further collaboration in political mechanisms by way of exception, or that for that purpose he had joined the FPL. I have no proof. There was never any information on that." He went on to quote at length the norms set down in his third pastoral letter for the possible participation of a priest in a political organization: he should enliven faith and the justice demanded by faith and he should dialog with his bishop about the apostolic worth of any more material participation by way of exception.

If it was true that Neto belonged to the FPL, the archbishop did not know or approve of it. "And let this be a notice to all pastoral workers: the policy of the archdiocese is clear and definite and will not change." Any priest who might be involved in any violent group did a poor service to the archbishop, the church, and the cause of the poor; and so did any such group that boasted of attracting a priest to its ranks. They were making more plausible all the accusations that the church's enemies had been making against it and against the archbishop. "Any shrewd observer of the situation," a commentator on YSAX had said, "will realize that if anyone wants to harm the archbishop at this moment the best way to do it is to say that Father Barrera belonged to the FPL." But at least, it said, it should be clear not only that the archbishop was not on the side of the FPL but that the FPL was not on the side of the archbishop. "If they were, they would have tried to protect his image."

The next evening Romero met with a group of friends whom Neto had counseled and, he noted, none of them had noticed a "violent attitude" in him and all had praised his work as a priest. Reports, he said in his diary, had tried to defame him.

In response to what Romero had said in his December 10 homily, the FPL sent him a six-page letter dated December 14. It confirmed that Neto was a full-fledged member of the FPL and defended their decision to make his membership public. Their policy, they said, was to tell the people the truth and to withhold it only when necessary to protect lives. To protect families or friends, they occasionally withheld the identity of fallen members, but that was not necessary in this case. On the other hand, they cited a recent case in which they had refuted a government claim to have killed eight members in a confrontation when in reality the security forces had staged a fake gunfight with bodies of prisoners killed beforehand. "In the case of our fellows who died struggling heroically in the Colonia La Providencia in this city, we are obliged to make the truth prevail. Otherwise, we would commit a historic injustice toward their sublime heroism and immortal example of struggling for the interests of the people to the last moment of their lives, against greatly superior forces of tyranny and under the storm of projectiles and tear gas that in no moment bent their iron revolutionary morale."

That Barrera was a priest, the FPL said, was no reason to deny him his aspiration to struggle "for the happiness of the poor, the lowly and oppressed. We believe we have no right to deny to any honest and conscientious person entrance to the revolutionary struggle for our people's social liberation. In his case it represented not a contradiction but, rather, an extension and a qualitative leap within his religious convictions in regard to the poor and within his understanding of the steps that must be taken for the definitive victory of the revolutionary aspirations of the oppressed and exploited working masses. Neither could his being a priest prevent our organization from recognizing at the proper moment that high revolutionary quality."

Neto's example, said the letter, should make everyone reflect honestly that being "an abnegated and loyal member of the church does not argue against the duty to struggle against the tyranny the people suffer from and to achieve the highest acts of heroism in defense of the people's interests, of their definitive liberation, of their happy future, free of oppression and the exploitation of one person by another." The contrary would be to put the church against the people and at the service of the dominant classes, as in the past.

Like much revolutionary writing, the letter is long-winded and repetitious. It is intelligent, however, and courteous. If it was a forgery, it was a clever one. Romero had it examined by a priest who had studied the popular organizations and the political-military groups like the FPL in detail, knew many of their leaders, and was a frequent liaison with them, arranging and attending meetings of their leaders with the archbishop. He said he saw no reason to think the letter was not authentic, and it confirmed for him that Neto was indeed a member of the FPL, though not necessarily a combatant. Two years later, when interviewed, he had not changed his mind. He said leftist leaders had confirmed Neto's membership privately, and his knowledge of the FPL as a serious and truthful organization left him unable to doubt what they said in this case. He did, however, believe that Neto had been killed before the supposed shoot-out and that the FPL had mistakenly believed the government story.

Romero did not mention the FPL's letter in his diary, and so it is not clear whether he had read it by December 17, when he spoke again in his homily about what a good priest Neto was, saying: "I believe that if a tree is known by its fruit, then this fruit says something about Father Neto's priestly work." A month after Neto's death, however, he had some doubts. After speaking with a group of working people whom Neto had guided, he observed: "I sincerely feel that Father Neto did not always convey a message that was altogether priestly and that he yielded considerably to the political and revolutionary ideals of these organizations. Nevertheless, they always noted in him, they told me, an effort to guide them in a priestly way. What the fundamental ideology of this priest was, remains unknown."[25]

When his commission submitted its final report, concluding that the government had faked the confrontation but that there were no reasons to doubt that Neto was a member of the FPL, Romero was not convinced, and he did not publish it. He expressed his skepticism about the government's version again in his homily of January 21, 1979, when he mentioned the murder of "the only witness who could have explained the truth to us," the wounded man seen on television.

❧ VII ☙

The Church, the People, and the Government

January–May 1979

There were no doubts about what happened on January 20 in El Despertar. About thirty young men were gathered for a weekend retreat called a "young people's Christian initiation gathering," sponsored by the parish of San Antonio Abad, which operated the retreat center, which was owned by the archdiocese. With them, in addition to kitchen workers, were a Belgian nun and a laywoman, who were the coordinators of the weekend. Father Octavio Ortiz, thirty-four years old, temporarily in charge of the parish in addition to his own parish of San Francisco in the Mejicanos district of the capital, vicar of the parishes in the area, and member of the priests' senate of the archdiocese, had conducted the first exercise of the weekend on Friday evening and was spending the night with the group.

El Despertar was a plain, rough-brick building on a narrow, unpaved street in one of those new and poor neighborhoods that abound in Latin America. The neighborhood is hilly, the tiny streets were rutted and alternately muddy or dusty. A vehicle would have some trouble using them, but the security forces were able to enter with an armored car, with which they battered open the sheet-metal gate, like a garage door, that led into the yard. Rifles and machine guns blazing, police and guardsmen rushed into the grounds.

It was about 6:00 A.M. and the occupants had been sleeping. Father Ortiz fell in the yard, where he must have gone to investigate the first noises. When the archbishop saw his body in the morgue that afternoon, one side of his head and face was crushed, as if the vehicle had run over it. Four young men died of gunshots, two of them fifteen years old, the others twenty-two; most of the group were teenagers, the rest a little older.

The police arrested the survivors, even the small children of one of the cooks. Later that day the women were released and could tell the story.

154

The young men were held in jail for the time being.

Meanwhile the security forces set about an attempt at a cover-up. Soldiers lugged the bodies of the dead youths to the roof of the building and pressed pistols into their hands. Photographs of the bodies on the roof appeared in the next day's newspapers with an elaborate story of a gun battle issued by the Guardia Nacional.

The government's only casualty was the small hope that things might be better under the new commander of the Guardia Nacional, who had been named at the beginning of January. In the official communiqués and the press, El Despertar became a guerrilla training center, its guitars weapons, its songbooks subversive literature. Its occupants, said the government, had answered a knock with gunfire, which the security forces had to return. Several subversives had fled, others had died on the roof where they were firing. It was, Romero said in his homily the next morning, "a lie from beginning to end."[1]

Over a hundred priests gathered for the funeral mass in the cathedral at eight o'clock that next morning. An altar was set up outside the front door of the cathedral, and a crowd of ten thousand to fifteen thousand people gathered under the sun in the street and square below. The archdiocese had asked priests to cancel other masses at that time in order to concelebrate with the archbishop. The scene recalled the mass for Rutilio Grande and his companions which had caused such a stir less than two years before.

As the long file of priests began to emerge from the doorway, the crowd burst into applause. They applauded again as six priests bore the body of Father Ortiz on their shoulders and placed it with the others before the altar. They applauded loudly when the archbishop emerged, mitred and bearing his shepherd's staff surmounted by a crucifix.[2]

Before the archbishop began his homily, Jorge Lara-Braud, representing the United States National Council of Churches and the World Council of Churches, spoke to the congregation. He had arrived in El Salvador the day before to celebrate Church Unity Week with the archdiocese. He was a visible sign of the solidarity that the archdiocese and its pastor had achieved with Christians, Catholics and non-Catholics alike, outside the country.

Archbishop Romero opened his homily by taking note of the universal character of the gathering, which included not only the thousands present, but many more in the radio audience—all centered on the cathedral and the bodies of those who had given their lives, all gathered to celebrate the Sunday liturgy of the death and resurrection of the Lord. Romero, who was to leave the following day for Mexico to attend the Puebla meeting, symbolically asked his people's permission to leave them for a moment "in order to take along your wealth and bring back the strength of the pope and of my brother bishops who are to meet at Puebla." The crowd applauded its approval. He read a telegram received from a parish priest in

Chalatenango: "POOR ELDERLY WOMAN HAD MASS SAID FOR GOOD TRIP ARCHBISHOP MEXICO." He warned the people to beware of manipulated news from Puebla. "Puebla is like a savory prize for those who distort the truth of things; and after seeing the brutal disfiguration of the events that we are lamenting this morning we also have reason to fear that an event so sacred and of such great hope could be spoiled by our selfish political and economic interests and communications media."[3]

But he spoke mostly about the five deaths that had brought them together that morning. He read the testimony of an eyewitness and denied all that the government had published. "Our security forces are incapable of recognizing their mistakes, and they make them worse by slanderously falsifying the truth. They are destroying the credibility of the government and of our communications media day by day, making us resort to international organizations and to publications from other countries, because we no longer believe in the justice and the truth found in our own surroundings." The people applauded when he called for "a cleansing of the corrupt security system of our country." Once again, he said, the wrongness and the danger of the public order law was evident. It legalized the sort of acting on mere suspicion that had caused the deaths in El Despertar. He called for an end to the brutality that had saturated the environment and "a return to the reflection that makes us feel ourselves reasonable beings, able to search for the roots of our ills and bring about fearlessly the daring and urgent changes that our society needs."[4]

He spoke briefly of the life of Octavio Ortiz, born of campesino parents in a village of Morazán, not far from where Romero himself was born. He was the first priest Romero had ordained. Ortiz had worked in poor neighborhoods around San Salvador, active until the last dawn of his life in El Despertar (which means *The Awakening*).

The message of the day, drawn from the readings of the mass (Jonah 3:1–5, 10; 1 Cor. 7:29–31; Mark 1:14–20) and the circumstances of the occasion, "could bear this title: a murder that speaks to us of resurrection. In the readings I find the presence in this world of a new world summed up in the resurrection of Christ." To live in that new world, "Christ calls us today to conversion. And . . . to grow in that new world and to be light of the world, salt and light of the earth, we must believe." That new world is the kingdom of God proclaimed by Christ in the words, "The time is fulfilled; the reign of God is at hand." Octavio and his companions were witnesses of that kingdom of God and models of conversion and of belief.[5]

"I am happy to tell you, dear fellow Christians," Romero continued, "that today, when it is more dangerous to be a priest, we are receiving more vocations in the seminary. This year will break the record: twenty-seven young high school graduates are entering in the new seminary class. This reign of God in the world is a reign of God that makes the noble, the young, truly say, like the one in the gospel: 'Let us go with him and die with him'" (John 11:16).[6]

He turned to other events of the week: another businessman kidnapped by leftist groups, three others still held. He appealed for their safety and their release and for the release of five disappeared prisoners for whom they were held hostage. He noted also that FAPU, one of the coalitions of popular organizations, had occupied the Red Cross offices, the Mexican embassy, and the Organization of American States offices in the city to ask for repeal of the public order law and a general amnesty. Romero had tried to mediate the conflict, as requested by the Washington headquarters of the Organization of American States, but "when I sent the delegation of priests, their passports and identification papers were taken away and they were disregarded. Here the church is not recognized as a force that loves the rights of human beings."

He paused and then continued firmly: "The president, in spite of all this, said in Mexico that there isn't any persecution of the church. And he compromises our newspapers, putting in front-page headlines something which the cathedral here makes evident is a lie." The people applauded and he went on: "The president charged in Mexico that there is a crisis in the church because of 'third-world clerics.' He asserted the archbishop's preaching is political preaching and it does not have the spirituality that other priests do still preach. No, I am not using my preaching to promote my candidacy for the Nobel Prize. How vain they think I am!" The crowd applauded again, and a note of bitterness entered his voice as he continued: "To the question whether or not the fourteen families [a popular name for the oligarchy] actually do exist in El Salvador, the president said, no, none of that exists, just as he also denied that there are disappeared persons and political prisoners."

The night before, Romero said, a journalist had phoned him from Mexico and asked about the president's statements. He had told the journalist that the best commentary was what had just happened: a priest and four youths killed. And he spoke of the defamation of the archbishop and the clergy, the harassment of the ecclesial communities, the violence to human rights. "The church feels that this is its ministry: to defend the image of God in man. And I told him finally: Note that the conflict is not between church and government; it is between government and people. The church is with the people and the people are with the church, thanks be to God!"[7]

The people applauded enthusiastically at that point. They had applauded often during the sermon, increasingly so as he progressed, sensing the drama and the importance of the occasion and of his words. He had boldly given the president the lie and had aligned the church with the people against the government. It remains today one of Romero's most memorable sermons.

Romero flew to Mexico the next day for the Puebla meeting. In El Salvador, five hundred priests and religious held a silent march of protest through the streets of the capital. On February 1, one of the guerrilla groups, the People's Revolutionary Army, boldly set off several bombs, one in the central police barracks, killing twenty persons and wounding many others. The guerrillas said the attacks were in revenge for the martyrs of El Despertar.

The archdiocese immediately issued a condemnation of the bombings, calling them "one more violation of human rights." It repeated the words "No more!" that the archbishop had cried out in his homily on January 21 and that the clergy and nuns had carried on a huge banner in their silent march. "Stop the violence and the bloodbath that threatens to engulf us all. The church of the archdiocese reaffirms its opposition on principle to revenge, hatred, and violent methods to solve the nation's problems."[8]

On his flight to Mexico, Romero had to change planes in Guatemala City, where to his surprise a reporter recognized him in the airport. It was the first of uncountable times that reporters would question him in the next three weeks. He always answered them softly, frankly, and directly. Only his plain-spokenness carried over from his pulpit manner. With individuals he was shy and quiet, though somehow relaxed at the same time if he sensed no hostility in the interlocutor.

At the Mexico City airport, the press was waiting again, and another brief interview occurred. Sisters of the same community that operated the cancer hospital where he lived in San Salvador met him and took him to their novitiate until it was time to go to Puebla. It was an old building in an old neighborhood of two-story houses built flush against the sidewalk somewhere in the vast sprawl that is Mexico City. The conference organizers had arranged for bishops to stay with affluent Catholic families for the few days the bishops were to be in Mexico City, but Romero had declined the courtesy.

Archbishop Romero had arrived early because he hoped to confer with bishops of a similar mind with him before the conference began. The Saturday before, he had received a letter from Leonidas Proaño, the bishop of Riobamba, Ecuador, encouraging him and anticipating meeting him in Puebla. The day after he arrived, he spoke with Bishop Sergio Méndez Arceo of nearby Cuernavaca, who was not a delegate to Puebla.

Mexico was feverish in expectation of Pope John Paul II's visit during those days. He would arrive on Friday, January 26, open the bishops' meeting on Saturday with a mass at the shrine of Guadalupe in Mexico City and send the meeting on its way on Sunday with a field mass and an address to the bishops in Puebla. Romero had little to do meanwhile but relax and collect his thoughts.

The present writer interviewed Romero on Tuesday evening at the Sisters' novitiate. He sat in shirtsleeves and spoke slowly and sadly of the persecution in El Salvador and how other bishops denied that it existed. Asked if he felt isolated and alone, he answered quickly, "No," adding that he had the support of bishops and many others in many countries and, in his own country, of Bishop Rivera and of his own clergy and people. He smiled when he recalled how the people had given him their permission to leave for Puebla by their applause and when he was told that a campesino community had sent his office $80 for his trip with the message that they gave him their permission to go to Puebla. He had come to Mexico to be their voice, whatever the legal technicalities of his position in the conference. Told of rumors in El Salvador of a plot to kill him in Mexico, he looked solemn for a moment.

"I suppose it's not the first threat?" he was asked.

"No," he replied, recovering his smile.[9]

On Friday the pope arrived in Mexico City to a tumultuous welcome. Meanwhile, Romero traveled to Puebla, where he visited a family whom he had known in San Miguel. Puebla is about two hours by car or bus from Mexico City and is an old city, its center still dotted with colonial churches, its cathedral filling one side of the central plaza, the Zócalo. An undistinguished modern city sprawls out from the center. Romero knew the city already from vacation trips to Mexico. He registered and took the room reserved for him in the huge seminary building, where the bishops would be closeted for over two weeks. The building was modern and comfortable, in an institutional way, with the long corridors that characterize traditional seminaries. He spent each night there during the conference, except for a weekend spent in a hospital because of an eye disorder.

The pope celebrated mass with the participating bishops at the shrine of Our Lady of Guadalupe in Mexico City, as scheduled. By the time the bus carrying Romero and other bishops reached the basilica, the crowd so jammed the vast esplanade in front that the prelates had to climb over a railing, cassocks and all, to reach the church. Romero laughed at the momentary loss of episcopal aplomb. The next day, Sunday, January 25, Pope John Paul II arrived at the seminary after the largest triumphal march in history in Mexico City and after greeting immense crowds along the road to Puebla. He concelebrated again with the participants before a crowd of some two hundred thousand on the seminary athletic field. After the mass he addressed the delegates inside the seminary building, and the conference officially began its work.

To the surprise of some, who knew Oscar Romero only by the fame he had gained as a vocal defender of human rights and social justice, he did not take a leading role in the conference or make any memorable pronouncements. He worked quietly on the commission on evangelization and human development—most of the work of drafting the conference's document was done in committees—and left to others the debating and the parliamentary strategy and tactics. Such meetings were not Romero's strong point. He was a country pastor at heart, shy, direct, and simple, like a campesino. He was most eloquent when addressing his flock, most at ease with those who accepted him without making more demands than that he be what he was.

Yet, the event that was Puebla would not have been the same without him, even though no one can point to a passage of the final document that was his. His presence was felt more outside the assembly hall, where the people and the world were, than within. Reporters found him easy to talk with, direct and simple in his answers when they could catch him outside the barrier that shut off the press from the conference. They often interviewed him. After the Puebla meeting ended, the head of the archdiocesan communications office calculated that, at least in the Mexican press, Romero was one of the three bishops most written about, along with Helder Câmara and Leonidas Proaño.

Midway through the conference, Romero gave a memorable press conference at a hotel on the Zócalo in downtown Puebla, arranged by the Ecumenical Studies Center of Mexico City. Reporters and many others jammed the hall, where he shared the dais with Plácido Erdozaín, a Spanish priest whom the Salvadoran government had suddenly expelled in Romero's absence, and José Luis Ortega, also Spanish, one of the Jesuits expelled in the May 1977 attack on Aguilares. But Romero himself was the center of attention. He answered simply and directly, yet shrewdly avoiding the traps unwittingly set by a few questioners, advocates who had come to Puebla with journalists' credentials, intent on enlisting his support for their own agendas. He declined to oppose the nunciatures and military vicariates as institutions, saying only that the nuncios and military vicars too should be converted to the gospel. To a questioner who would have had the Vatican strip itself of its property, he replied that the church needs money for its work but should give what is superfluous to the poor. Without money, he pointed out, the pope could not have come to Mexico.

One questioner focused on Romero's supposed conversion through his contact with the poor and the persecuted. "Would that I were converted!" he said, getting a laugh from the audience and gaining a moment to form a more careful reply. The previous June Cardinal Baggio had objected to the term and Romero had denied using it of his changed attitude as archbishop; he admitted that the events of the preceding two years had changed him, but he did not see the change as a radical break with the past, especially not a turning toward God from a state of estrangement. "To be converted," he explained to the questioner now, "is to turn to the true God, and in that sense I feel that my contact with the poor, with the needy, leads to a growing sense of need for God." The poor, aware of their own need and weakness, teach even preachers that without God one can do nothing. "In this sense, then, I too seek conversion, in order to be able to put my trust in God and through God be able to provide a word of consolation, a response to the poor's anguish, and if possible point out the way to those who can resolve these predicaments." The latter, he said, must not look out for their own selfish advantages, must not worship the world's idols, but must search for the God of the poor, who could teach them to "seek the satisfaction of being human only in the true God and not in idols."

He spoke of the families of political prisoners and persons who had disappeared in the hands of police and security forces. Among the people who had come to Puebla were mothers, wives, and sisters of the disappeared and imprisoned of El Salvador and Argentina. He had often had to speak with such persons in El Salvador, and he often spoke of their suffering in his sermons. "The church must echo their anguish," he said now. One of the things he wanted to do at Puebla was to tell the assembled, "If we want to be a church that responds to the people's sufferings, we must make our own these cries. If we do not, we are not giving all the response that God wants to give to those who suffer."

After the long press conference, Romero escaped from the reporters—who were also tired by then, 9:30 P.M.—and he wandered across the Zócalo in the cool of the evening and entered the massive cathedral. There he knelt alone in prayer for a few minutes, got up, and left.[10] He went back to the hospital where he was staying because of the eye ailment.[11]

Outside the conference sessions in the seminary building, a group of about thirty theologians and social scientists, mostly priests, was also working on the same matters as the bishops inside. Among them was Jon Sobrino, who had come to Puebla from El Salvador at Romero's urging. He was not, however (as some supposed), Romero's theological adviser or secretary, and they saw each other only once or twice during the conference. Romero visited the group of theologians several times, most notably one evening with several bishops invited by the group for their openness to the new theology and their commitment to the church of Medellín. For Romero it was an evening of joy, being with bishops who shared his views and concerns and who eagerly gave him their support. It was a pleasure he could not enjoy in the constant tension of the Salvadoran bishops' conference.

Out of the evening came the idea for a letter of support for human rights in particular situations in Latin America. The ideas discussed were made concrete in letters addressed to Romero, to the bishops of Nicaragua (where the struggle to overthrow the Somoza dictatorship was in progress), and to the bishops of Guatemala. The Guatemalan bishops proved to be too divided, however, and eventually only the first two letters were sent. Some thirty signatures were obtained for each, impressive in itself but disappointing in view of the number present in Puebla: over two hundred bishops.

The letter to Romero was a simple, personal message of support and encouragement. Addressing him familiarly as "Dear Brother," it spoke of his labors as pastor, of his defense of the poor, of the cross and persecution that he and his church were suffering, of the spirit of unity he had built up in his archdiocese. "We encourage you to continue on this narrow and steep way of building permanently the kingdom that Jesus Christ presents to his church as the gift of the Spirit and as its mission. With you we pray the Our Father, sharing together the bread of our commitment and of our hope. And the hope of the poor will not perish, for theirs is the promise."[12]

Bishop Aparicio was also making news at Puebla. In remarks to reporters he said that Jesuits were responsible for the violence in El Salvador, that Romero had let Marxist priests influence him, that the persons who had disappeared in El Salvador had simply hidden or joined the guerrillas, that rebel priests were training children to be guerrilla fighters. The Salvadoran press immediately picked up his words, and the priests' senate sent him a letter. They reminded Aparicio that he had signed the bishops' statements of March 5 and May 17, 1977, which attributed the country's violence to the social injustice in the country.[13] Romero did not reply to Aparicio except to defend the Jesuits in his own February 9 press conference, saying he agreed completely with the defense that Father Pedro Arrupe, the Jesuit superior general, had made earlier at another press conference. Arrupe was also in Puebla for the bishops' meeting, as president of the Union of Superiors General.

Romero addressed the assembly once to give his recommendations for the final document. He expressed gratitude for the "expressions of solidarity and understanding" that he had received during the conference, noting that a report of the Organization of American States had just recognized the systematic persecution of his church. He went on:

> I believe that our document will not reflect all the gospel commitment that the church ought to take on so as not to lose its credibility in our lands if it does not emphasize an evangelization that effectively responds to the unjust distribution of the wealth that God has created for all and the noble longing of all to associate freely and participate actively in the politics of the common good of their country. It should be an evangelization that denounces with candor arbitrary arrest, political exile, torture, and above all the sorrowful mystery of the disappeared. It should indeed underline transcendence and hope of heaven, but for this reason it requires the commitment to work for a more just world that will reflect that transcendence and that spirituality. I believe too that our pastoral vision of reality would not be complete if it ignored and did not evangelically encourage new phenomena like our campesinos' efforts to organize, at times merely in order not to die of hunger. It should note especially the heroic deaths of our priests and pastoral workers, all the more heroic in that slanderous official declarations try to discredit their work of awakening evangelical consciousness in the community.[14]

The conference ended on Tuesday, February 13, and Romero stayed in Mexico until Friday. He visited a national meeting of members of grass-roots ecclesial communities, where he made a strong plea for a group of refugees from El Salvador. Puebla had just made a firm endorsement of grass-roots communities, and they were an important element in the pastoral work of his archdiocese in the countryside and the poorer areas of the capital. The communities were the most visible sign of the new church in Latin America. The Mexican community members responded warmly to this bishop, who was also a sign of a new church.[15]

Romero returned home to a large reception in the Ilopango airport and a crowded mass in the cathedral. On the following Sunday, February 18, in his homily, "Christ, the Word Ever New of the Church" (he had long since taken to giving his homilies titles to emphasize their central thought), he spoke of God in history, sending his message through his prophets, through his Son, and now through the word of Puebla. The bishops had published, on the last day of the meeting, a brief, hard-hitting pastoral message to the people of Latin America, a message more accessible and more immediate than the longer, complicated general document. Romero quoted extensively from the pastoral message in his homily.

"I have found on arrival," he said, "many false interpretations of Puebla and of the pope's speeches. I am glad that before I left I told you that I appealed to your growing sense of discernment and maturity not to believe everything you read in the press or see on television or hear on the radio. The communications media are very much manipulated, very much conditioned, and even a speech of the pope and a meeting as sincere as that of the bishops at Puebla can be slanted to become a support for the injustices and the disorders that neither the pope nor Puebla can tolerate."[16]

The bishops at Puebla had chosen the cause of the poor, calling on the rich also to be converted and make that same cause their own. "When we say 'preferential option for the poor' we do not mean exclusion of the rich, but rather a call to the rich also to feel as their own the problem of the poor and to study, in dialog with the government, with specialists, with those who can resolve this dead end in El Salvador. They have the duty to study and use every means they have as though it were a matter of solving their very own problem. You don't solve the problem by sending capital abroad. It has to be put to work with a genuine social sensitivity. The pope expressed it quite beautifully: 'Don't forget that a huge social mortgage weighs on private property.' "[17]

Christ and Puebla call for a personal conversion, Romero said. The bishops' message stated: "We pastors also beg pardon of God and of our brothers and sisters in the faith and in humanity for all our faults and limitations. We wish not only to convert others but also ourselves with them, so that our dioceses, our parishes, our institutions, our communities, and our religious congregations may not be obstacles, but rather incentives to live the gospel."

"Believe me, I say this with all sincerity," continued Romero. "One who accuses must be ready to be accused. From the beginning I have said that I gladly accept criticism when it is constructive and means to improve whatever bit of good there may be in me. I truly ask pardon of all those to whom I have not succeeded in conveying the message as I should have. But let them understand that there is no pride or ill will or distortion of what the gospel bids me preach to this archdiocese entrusted to me."[18]

In their message to the people the bishops asked: "What have we to offer you in the midst of the serious and complex questions of our era?" Romero reflected: "I have often been asked here in El Salvador: What can we do? Is there no way out of this situation in El Salvador? And filled with hope and with faith, not only divine faith but human faith, believing also in human beings, I say: Yes, there is a way out! Let those exits not be closed off." The bishops answered their own question by recalling St. Peter's words to the lame beggar who asked for alms and by telling the people: "We have no gold or silver to give you, but we give you what we have: in the name of Jesus of Nazareth, get up and walk." The wealth of the church, they said, is the wealth of Peter: "Jesus of Nazareth, dead and risen, ever present through his divine Spirit, in the apostolic college and in the inchoate communities formed under its direction."

"In the message," said Romero, "there is a passage that says, 'The wealth of the men and women in Latin America is their Christian hope and faith.' Let's not misspend it! If my words can serve for something, let it be for this. I have no pretensions of anything else. And this would be my greatest pride: that the treasure we have inherited from the evangelization of past centuries not be ossified, not be paralyzed, not become an invalid. Let us not lose hope in our church. The church is a living organism; it is you, baptized and anointed by God's Spirit."

Romero addressed Christian political leaders, capitalists, specialists, and professionals: "You have the key to the solution. But the church gives you what you cannot have by yourselves: hope, the optimism to struggle, the joy of knowing that there is a solution, that God is our Father and keeps on urging us. He needed men to take the paralytic up to the roof and lower him before Christ so that he could cure him. Christ and God could bring about by themselves our people's salvation, but they want also to have stretcher-bearers, people to help pick up that paralytic called the nation or society — so that with human hands, with human solutions, with human ideas, we can put him down before Christ, who is the only one who can say, 'I have seen your faith. Get up and walk.' And I believe that our people will get up and will walk."[19]

In the midst of the crisis set off by the death of Neto Barrera, on December 14, 1978, Romero received a note from the nuncio telling him that the Congregation for the Bishops had named Bishop Antonio Quarracino, of Avellaneda, Argentina, as apostolic visitor to the San Salvador archdiocese. Bishop Quarracino, Gerada added laconically, had just arrived and would get in touch with the archbishop.

A "visitor," in church law, is a troubleshooter sent by a superior to look into a situation. Visitors often are armed with wide power to set things right. Quarracino seems to have come only to investigate and report back to Rome. He did apparently have the authority to order the archdiocese to make no announcement of his presence.

Romero immediately ordered his staff to provide Quarracino with piles of reports and other papers: studies of the situation in the country and the archdiocese, correspondence about Revelo, statistics and documentation on violations of human rights, letters of solidarity received by the archbishop, press clippings on the division among the bishops of the country, all the bulletins and statements published by the archdiocese under Romero, transcripts of his homilies. Quarracino also interviewed a number of people around the archbishop. He told the president of the conference of religious that he feared for the archbishop's life. His visit seems to have been cordial and even deferential. "Well, I was sent here," he half-apologized to one person.

The next month Romero went to Puebla, and he seems to have heard no more about Quarracino's visit until he went to Rome four months later and spoke to Cardinal Baggio and to John Paul II. He made the trip to attend the beatification on April 29 of Francisco Coll, a Catalan Dominican who had founded the Dominican Sisters of the Annunciation, a congregation that had several schools in the archdiocese. The Sisters had invited Romero as their guest. But it was also an opportunity to put his case again to Baggio and to talk with the new pope.

Romero explained the coming visit in his April 22 homily:

Naturally, for everyone who goes to Rome, especially a pastor, the great desire is to see the pope. I'll see the pope and speak with him. I've never been opposed to what the pope proposes; I'll follow everything the pope says. I know there are many accusations against me over there, many reports telling about my pastoral deviations, and I know the pope will ask me about that. I'll tell him: Holy Father, you sent an apostolic visitor who was able to consult many witnesses, to consult the people, and I do no more than consent to whatever Your Holiness disposes. But, for my part, know that I have preached the gospel and I am ready to keep on preaching that gospel of the Lord in defense of the beloved people that the Lord has entrusted to me.[20]

It was a bolder, more mature note than Romero had sounded two years before when speaking of going to see Peter. Two years of leadership, of resisting attacks from inside and outside the church, of support from people, clergy, and other bishops had matured his attitude toward the church's government.

Even so, on arriving in Rome on Saturday he noted in his diary, "Being in Rome is always a blessing of the Lord for me," and the next morning he added: "This early morning in Rome calls up so many memories. These scenes that I knew when I studied my theology, when I was ordained and lived my first months as a priest, renew my spirit. Now, with new responsibilities, I feel that Rome is a blessing of the Lord confirming my mission, my work. God bestows on me the happiness of being able to work modestly with him in founding his kingdom in the world."

That morning he was thrilled by the beatification ceremony in St. Peter's basilica, which was filled to overflowing.[21] The next days were largely taken up with ceremonies and visits. "I felt joyful," he noted in his diary after a mass with the Dominicans, "for the church's life, which is ever abundant in holiness." On Thursday, after visiting the tombs of the popes in the crypt of St. Peter's, he noted: "At the beloved altars of St. Peter and of his present successors in this century, I prayed very much for faithfulness to my Christian faith and for the courage, if need be, to die as did all these martyrs, or else to live consecrating my life as these modern successors of Peter consecrated theirs. The simplicity of Pope Paul VI's tomb impressed me more than all the others."

On Wednesday, Romero attended the pope's public audience in St. Peter's Square among 130,000 pilgrims. At the end the pope received each bishop present, and when Romero asked his blessing for El Salvador, the pope said he would like to speak with him in private. But, in spite of the pope's personal invitation, an appointment proved hard to get. Romero spoke to Vatican officials after the Wednesday audience and was put off, even though weeks before he had asked the Salvadoran ambassador, Prudencio Llach, to try to arrange an audience for him with the pope. Romero returned to the Vatican on Thursday and Friday without success. On Friday he remarked in his diary: "I am very much concerned about such an attitude shown toward the pastor of a diocese. I requested the audience well in advance and yet the reply is put off. I even fear they may not give me the appointment, since there are many bishops on their *ad limina* visits and there are also other criteria for giving preference to other requests. I have placed everything in God's hands, telling him that for my part I have done everything possible and that in spite of everything I believe I love this holy church and will always be faithful, with his grace, to the Holy See, to the pope's magisterium, and that I understand the human, the limited, the defective part of his holy church. It remains the instrument of salvation for humanity, and I will serve it without reserve."

He went again to the Vatican on Saturday morning and was told he would have his audience with the pope on Monday. Armed with four reports of foreign investigation commissions on El Salvador, with various letters of solidarity he had received, and with a copy of his own letter to John Paul of the previous November, Romero entered the pope's office at 12:20 on Monday, May 7. Romero suggested following a memo that he had prepared as an agenda for the interview, and John Paul agreed.

The pope asked about conditions in El Salvador. He stressed that pastoral work is very hard in circumstances like those Romero was working under and advised him to be very prudent and balanced, especially in making accusations in particular instances. It is better, he said, to stick to general principles because of the risk of error in speaking of concrete cases. Romero explained that sometimes he had to be very specific because the outrage had been very specific, as was the murder of Octavio Cruz and his companions. The pope agreed. He spoke of his own experience in Poland, where the church also had problems with the government. He said the unity of the bishops was very important—in Poland, that was what they had to insist on most of all. Romero explained that he also wanted very much to be united with the other bishops but that unity could not be feigned but had to be based on the gospel and on the truth.

John Paul told him that Bishop Quarracino, who had visited the archdiocese in December, had recommended the naming of an apostolic administrator *sede plena* for the archdiocese. That is, Romero would remain archbishop in name, but another would govern. Such a recommendation, said the pope, showed that Quarracino regarded the situation there as extremely delicate. "He gave me a chance," recorded Romero, "to present my thought and he also expressed his views."

Romero left the Vatican satisfied that the pope had listened to his ideas, but he was worried that the pope was receiving such negative reports about him. He recalled, though, that John Paul had recommended boldness and courage along with balance and prudence. "Although my first impression was not altogether satisfactory, I believe it was a most useful visit and talk, since he was very frank, and I have learned that one should not always expect a resounding approval, but rather it is more useful to receive admonitions that can improve our work."[22]

The next morning he had a talk with Cardinal Baggio, prefect of the Congregation for the Bishops. Baggio was cordial and eager to talk with him. He was concerned about the division among the Salvadoran bishops and especially the split between Romero and his auxiliary. He admitted that Revelo had been wrong to approve the new statutes for Caritas against Romero's wishes, but he thought Romero had been too harsh in removing him as vicar-general. Romero tried to explain that the reasons adduced by Revelo—that Caritas was falling into the hands of guerrillas and that Romero was in the hospital with a stomach infection for a few days—were not valid reasons for his action.

The suggestion of naming an administrator, said Baggio, remained under study but it did not seem like a practical idea. What other bishop could undertake it? Romero said he would continue to do the best he could and spoke of the reports he had left with the pope, especially one by the Organization of American States that spoke of a real persecution of the church in El Salvador. Perhaps sensing tension in Romero, Baggio remarked at one point that they were not enemies but were 90 percent in agreement.

Romero left the congregation feeling satisfied and hopeful.[23] However, the naming of an administrator for the archdiocese remained a possibility, and back in San Salvador on May 30 he wrote to Baggio his considered opinion of the idea.

"It seems to me that Bishop Quarracino's proposal not only is ineffective for solving our church problems, but would, rather, be prejudicial to the archdiocese and even to the Holy See." Romero gave four reasons to explain his opinion.

First, "the roots of the present problems are not to be found only in the character and personality of the persons, but in the country's highly unjust and therefore conflictual situation and in the directions that the church has given us since Vatican Council II and the Medellín and Puebla conferences. The church tries to be faithful to these directions, and hence any relationship of the church with the government must in large measure involve conflict. Likewise, the serious conflicts existing in the country must also crop up in the bishops' conference, even though we bishops all intend only pastoral and not political action. These roots of the problems will not change with the sending of an apostolic administrator. Sooner or later his activity would lead him to take an unavoidable and definite stand, and once again the consequences would not improve the bishops' unity or ease tensions with the government, if his behavior is to follow the church's directions mentioned above."

Second, an apostolic administrator would be likely to make matters worse. His coming would cut the ground from under the archbishop and further weaken his standing with the other bishops and the nuncio. Neither would it help the church's relations with the government. "Although the government wants to center the root of the tensions in the person of the archbishop, it understands very well that the archbishop is only the visible voice of the majority of priests, religious, and lay people. Even supposing that an apostolic administrator should succeed in bettering his personal relations with the government, its real relations with the church would not change in any way. An indication of this is the 'good relations' with the other bishops that in no way convince or benefit the faithful of their dioceses. The incapacity and loss of credibility of a government that, to sustain itself, can only distort reality and repress the people are no secrets to anyone in El Salvador."

Third, confusion would spread among the clergy, religious, and faithful who had been following Romero's pastoral policies. He saw this as the strongest reason not to impose a change. "The pastoral work of the archdiocese tries to be a unified ministry. It attends directly to the religious aspects of the gospel's and the church's message, through catechesis, sacraments, liturgy, and education. But because of its evangelical nature and our country's conditions of extreme poverty, it cannot overlook the other aspects of an evangelization that seeks integral liberation. Therefore, within this unified ministry, aspects of social betterment are developed, and the church's pastoral action is maliciously viewed as political activity."

Quarracino apparently meant to leave the archbishop with authority over the "religious" aspects of the archdiocese and to have the administrator handle relations with the other bishops and the government, for Romero goes on to say: "That within a unified and necessarily complex pastoral activity two types of authority should exist, one directly responsible for the religious message and another for relations with the government and the other bishops, would cause confusion and perplexity among the faithful and loss of efficacy. I honestly believe that in the long run the church itself and the Holy See would lose credibility. Such a measure would be interpreted as a step backward in the church's gospel commitment and as a way of maintaining its own security and privileges by abandoning the poor masses of the country. This result, the loss of pastoral efficacy and of the church's credibility, is what would most worry me as the one responsible for the church in the archdiocese."

Fourth, the church's unity in the archdiocese, which had taken much time and work to accomplish and which was difficult to maintain, would be threatened. The archbishop had been able to hold together those who wanted to go faster and take more radical positions and those who were going at a more measured pace. Putting in an administrator would probably exacerbate the tensions, and the unity that had been achieved would begin to fall apart. Breaking down the unity in the archdiocese would shatter the church of the whole country. The archdiocese, even before Romero, exerted leadership over the rest of the church, as was natural in a small country, both through its size (in 1979, the archdiocese had 37 percent of the country's Catholics and 60 percent of its priests, diocesan and religious)[24] and its position as metropolitan see and center of national life. "Breaking the unity of the archdiocese would mean a much greater rupture and disunion than the one presently existing, with incalculable consequences for the future. It would mean the official sanction of disunion, and in practice the renouncement of the directions of Vatican II, Medellín, and Puebla. This worries me deeply."

Besides arguing the harm that the change would work, Romero also suggested that the problems it was meant to solve might be dealt with in other ways. He himself had continually tried to engage the government in sincere dialog and demanded only that the government show its sincerity. High-ranking members of the archdiocese, such as the vicar-general, the president of the priests' senate, and, at times, Romero himself had attended meetings with high-ranking members of the government, army, political parties, and business. He planned to continue the attempts made so far to lower tensions. President Romero only days before had called for a dialog with various national leaders, civil and ecclesiastical, and Romero planned to participate in it and support it.

The problem of disunity among the bishops was indeed difficult, wrote Romero. Aparicio had attacked him publicly at Puebla, and he had not replied. He had tried to give Revelo a good reception in spite of the latter's remarks at the synod of bishops. He tried always to avoid any action or statement that would emphasize publicly the lack of unity. "Under the circumstances it is not easy to bring about the unity of the bishops' conference, but one must try to maintain and not break off dialog among us and to practice charity toward persons, and I mean to do so."

Romero saw the solution for the church's problems in the naming of new bishops who would follow his and Rivera's line of pastoral action, rather than appointing an administrator. He rejected some candidates and suggested several others, as he had done in his letter to the pope the previous November.

Before leaving Rome, Romero had a "long, brotherly conversation" with his friend Cardinal Eduardo Pironio. The talk, he recorded in his diary, "was enough to fill me to the brim with joy and strength." Pironio, an Argentine, said that he too felt keenly the problems of Latin America, which were not completely understood at the highest level of the church. One had to go on working, making known as well as one could the truth about Latin America. " 'The worst thing you can do is to get disheartened,' he told me. 'Courage, Romero!' he said to me many times." Leaving Pironio's office, Romero paused in St. Peter's Square, where the pope was preaching to the people. Around the outside of the crowd, people were going about other affairs without paying attention. Romero reflected that it was the pastor's task to keep on preaching, as the pope was doing, whether people chose to listen or not.

He flew from Rome to Barcelona to spend a day in the homeland of Francisco Coll, the last stage of his pilgrimage. From Madrid, he boarded the plane for home, aware of new troubles in El Salvador. During the long night as he flew westward across the Atlantic, he turned to prayer, "placing myself deeply in God's presence, asking him to enlighten me and to help us resolve the serious situation that I am going to encounter in the country."[25]

The annual rains begin in May in El Salvador. In May 1979 it did not rain, as if the heavens refused to wash away the blood from the streets and sidewalks of San Salvador and from the fields of the countryside, leaving it, in the words of a writer in *ECA*, "to blend into the earth and the cement as a witness of the most tragic and bloodiest month in the last forty-seven years."[26]

In the last days of April the government arrested five leaders of the BPR. On May 1, Labor Day, the labor unions and various other groups, including opposition political parties, held a rally. In the afternoon the BPR held its own rally, demanding the release of its leaders. The separate rallies showed each one's own strength, but also the division of the popular forces.[27]

Meeting a cold denial from the government that it had captured the leaders, and fearing for the prisoners' lives, the BPR a few days later began to occupy embassies and churches in order to draw international attention. Members moved into the French, Costa Rican, and Venezuelan embassies, holding hostages in each to keep the security forces from attacking. Others occupied the San Salvador cathedral and various churches around the country. Various protesters began to block streets and burn buses, to call strikes and rallies. Shops in downtown San Salvador began to close, bus lines to shut down.

As the security forces killed protesters, the FPL began to take reprisals, killing policemen and guardsmen and setting off bombs. The security forces in turn began to unleash greater savagery against the demonstrators and sympathizers of the BPR.[28]

On May 8, while Romero was in Rome, a small demonstration stopped in front of the cathedral, occupied by the BPR. Suddenly the police opened fire, as foreign journalists watched and television crews filmed. As bullets struck the crowd and glanced off the cathedral steps, people desperately ran for the safety of the cathedral. For a time the police kept the Red Cross and other medical help from the cathedral, as the wounded lay bleeding inside. The total was twenty-five dead and seventy wounded in the action. Millions around the world later watched the scene on their television screens.[29]

Romero spoke of the violence in his first homily after his return from Rome. The cathedral was still occupied by the BPR, and he spoke in the Dominicans' church of El Rosario, a modern arch-shaped building a block away on the Plaza Libertad, the scene of the February 28 massacre in his first days as archbishop.

While he was in Europe, he recalled, "I received the news of the sad situation of our land. It is painful to feel oneself pointed out abroad as one who lives in a country where violence seems like everyday breathing. Abroad you see versions of events that we can't see back here. You have crueler impressions of the things we see here. At times the insensibility of Europe toward Latin America makes your heart ache more and makes one from Latin America in Europe feel like a missionary, like an awakener of conscience, of universal brotherhood, begging for understanding and love for our huge and complex problems in Latin America."[30]

Toward the end of the homily, Romero turned again to the violence of recent days. "How painful it is to travel about representing a diocese embedded in a land so convulsed!" he said. "But how much good one can do as a missionary from that diocese to clear up distorted news, to awake the insensitive, to promote communion in prayer and solidarity with other communities! This has been my pilgrimage in these days that I have been absent from the diocese. And, coming back, the great comfort of finding oneself once again with one's family, the family of the diocese, is a comfort that turns into a sharing in the anguish and tension."[31]

He reviewed what had happened, including the president's ritual promise of a thorough investigation of the massacre and his threat to declare a state of siege. Romero read with approval part of an analysis issued by the governing board of the national university attributing the crisis to the inequality of wealth and the tendency toward authoritarian government in order to keep down the poor. "The church is quite in agreement with this statement and believes that there lies the ultimate reason for this situation. The proximate cause, as everyone knows, is the illegal capture of five leaders of the Popular Revolutionary Bloc."[32]

The government had released two of the leaders, but denied having the other three. Romero reminded his listeners that these now made 127 persons who had disappeared after arrest. "They are our brothers and sisters, and we want to know where they are," he said to applause. "An exhaustive investigation has been promised. How that would please us! It is only just. But we fear that if an investigation is to suffer the fate of the investigation that the Inter-American Human Rights Commission was asked to make last September 14, when it was asked to observe and investigate the human rights situation in El Salvador, then there is not much to hope for. Certainly, it's the right thing to do, but with the purpose of accepting responsibility, of punishing the guilty, and of correcting mistakes. For me, this is what is most serious: mistakes are made and are not admitted. We must all recognize our mistakes and not distort the truth for an apparent saving of honor."

He also condemned the violence of the other side. "I want to speak with candor; it is my duty to reject the forces of violence and such violations of liberty of action as the burning of vehicles, the machine-gunning of residences, the occupation of offices and locales set aside for the people. There is an unshakable moral principle that says one cannot do evil in order to achieve good."[33]

The violence continued. On Tuesday, May 15, security forces fired on demonstrators in Soyapango, on the outskirts of San Salvador, killing one person and sending the rest running for refuge in the church. On the same day Romero told a press conference, "The people are no longer willing to keep on enduring the deep structural crisis that the country is suffering."[34]

On Sunday, May 20, Romero noted that the cathedral was still occupied, as well as the French and Venezuelan embassies, both with hostages; more churches were occupied, in the capital, in Apopa, Suchitoto, San Antonio Los Ranchos in Chalatenango, Aguilares, and Santa Ana, besides a school and a bread company. Fifty-four persons were dead, seventy injured, twenty-five arrested, three exiled. Thirty vehicles had been burned.[35]

The archbishop had published a statement on the situation, and he read parts of it. He did not mention the obvious: that the bishops' conference had made no pronouncement. "It is not enough," he said, "to keep denying that they [the BPR leaders] are in the security forces' jails. Sufficient reasons exist to think that these three persons have been arrested by them." But he also read the words addressed to the BPR: "In case the government should erroneously and unjustly remain obstinate in not recognizing this abuse of power, we propose to the leaders of the BPR that they soon put an end to this conflict. They have already achieved the objectives they proposed when they organized the means of pressure that they have been carrying out in these days. They obtained the freedom of their secretary-general and of the student of the Central American University, they have made known on the national and international levels that the security forces have 'disappeared' three more persons arrested, they have had the support and solidarity of thousands of persons who accompanied them to bury the victims of the May 8 massacre. If the government does not yield by charging or freeing the other three leaders, it is probably because something fatal has occurred, which we fear. Of this fact the majority of the people are already informed and convinced."

Romero continued, "We need to create a climate that lets us expound, study, and solve the structural problems that are at the root of the growing popular discontent. . . . To keep on with the occupations and to keep stirring up the country seems to us out of proportion to the objectives they have not yet achieved. We want to tell them [the BPR] clearly, we do not approve of it."[36]

On May 17 President Romero had made his call for a "national forum," a consultation with a spectrum of organizations on the country's problems, but not with the all-important people's organizations, an omission that presaged little success for the effort. Opposition parties and other organizations were skeptical and suspicious. "We are glad," said the archbishop, "that this time the president has not reacted by increasing repression, and we hope that events will proceed to give credibility in face of the skepticism with which many have received his words. For our part, we would have liked to hear a concrete reply to the petitions made concerning the disappeared, who are the immediate motive for the strong political tensions of these days."[37]

On Tuesday, May 22, a group of demonstrators tried to reach the Venezuelan embassy with food and water for the occupiers. The security forces opened fire, leaving fourteen dead and sixteen wounded. Others were arrested and disappeared. The next day the minister of education and his chauffeur were ambushed and killed. The government imposed a state of siege. On May 27, Romero was back in the cathedral (the other churches had also been vacated), but he looked back on a week of violence. Besides the massacre at the Venezuelan embassy and the assassination of the education minister, Romero recounted two murders in the name of the White Warrior Union, a skirmish that left three dead near the Chilean embassy, more buses burned, and operations by military and security forces and ORDEN in the countryside that killed four campesinos and left several others disappeared, two of them later found dead.[38]

Bishop Barrera had issued a call for peace, and Archbishop Romero quoted part of it. He himself had issued a statement after the violence at the Venezuelan embassy and the assassination of the education minister, in which he said, "As archbishop of San Salvador, I call on the consciences and hearts of those responsible not to continue their unyielding and intransigent position, but to yield and seek a way to break as soon as possible this endless chain of bloody deeds. What matters now is not to show the nation and the world who is the stronger or the winner but who is the more responsible and humane, capable of stopping this growing spiral of violence."

He called on those who might influence either the government or the BPR to use their influence to persuade them and offered the services of the archdiocese for the cause of peace.[39] The National Forum had held its first session, with Bishop Revelo and Monsignor Freddy Delgado representing CEDES. The archbishop had abstained from voting on who would represent the conference,[40] perhaps because of skepticism about the whole affair. Many others felt doubts, and all the opposition parties and groups were refusing to participate. Romero stated his attitude in the homily: "My desire is that the credibility and trust that must be the basis of dialog be constructed with deeds. . . . Deeds speak better than promises."[41]

June 3 was the feast of Pentecost, and once again the cathedral was occupied, as was the nearby church of El Calvario, this time by members of FAPU. May had left 115 dead, 55 arrested (of whom 30 had increased the list of disappeared), 92 injured, 64 vehicles burned, 28 buildings either burned, machine-gunned, stoned, or destroyed. The archbishop had just issued a call to respect the persons of foreigners especially and to try to avoid pressuring their countries to violate the principle of nonintervention. But he also called on the diplomats to use their influence to defend human rights: "They can work with our people in their just defense of human rights. Because these rights are human, universal, and explicitly accepted by all civilized peoples, their defense is outside the borders of nonintervention."[42]

Oscar Romero was born and lived his early years in the house on the left corner. It is now the office of a cooperative.

The cathedral in San Salvador, which remains unfinished. Romero decided not to spend more money on construction.

Newly ordained a bishop, Oscar Romero blesses the people, accompanied
by Archbishop Chávez, Bishop Rivera, and Jesuit Father Rutilio Grande,
whose assassination in 1977 was a turning point for Romero.

Brockman

Archbishop Romero lived in this small house on the grounds of a cancer
hospital from August 1977 until his death.

The archbishop's crozier rests on his bed. Romero's little house is kept as it was when he lived in it.

"I am a shepherd who, with his people, has begun to learn a beautiful and difficult truth: our Christian faith requires that we submerge ourselves in the world."

AÑO 1
SAN SALVADOR,
EL SALVADOR, C. A.
DICIEMBRE 1977
No. 11

La Opinión
Voz de un pueblo al servicio de la verdad
y defensora de los derechos humanos...

10 CENTAVOS

Se Descorre el Velo

MONS. ROMERO DIRIGE GRUPO TERRORISTA

- Valiente Denuncia hace un Sacerdote
- Arzobispo Gran Aliado de los Agentes de la Subversión

No hay duda que la Iglesia Católica está atravesando una seria crisis. Sin embargo lo que más llama la atención es que algunos de sus dirigentes estén llevándola al despeñadero. Monseñor Romero tiene mucho de culpa en esa situación porque ha venido sembrando la cizaña y promoviendo el odio de clases. Para colmo de males ahora se le denuncia como dirigente de un grupo terrorista de esos que han venido cometiendo asaltos, asesinatos y sembrando la zozobra en el país. Una revelación que es necesario conocer.

MONSEÑOR OSCAR A. ROMERO

¡LEA MAS INFORMACION SOBRE ESTE IMPORTANTE TEMA EN PAGINA 4!

La Opinion was published solely to attack Archbishop Romero. This headline accuses him of directing a terrorist group.

"There can be no church unity if we ignore the world in which we live."

Ch. Poveda

"Whatever political issue we take up we must look at it in terms of the people . . . the poor."

"If God accepts the sacrifice of my life, my hope is that my blood will be like a seed of liberty and a sign that our hopes will soon become a reality."

Brockman

The chapel of the Divine Providence cancer hospital in San Salvador where Romero was shot while saying mass. The assassin fired from the rear of the chapel.

Publicaciones Pastorales del Arzobispado

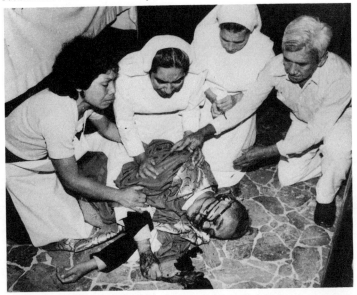

Friends rush to Archbishop Romero's aid as he lies bleeding.

Brockman

Women pray at Archbishop Romero's tomb in the San Salvador cathedral. Plaques on the tomb thank him for favors.

Pope John Paul II visits Archbishop Romero's tomb during a trip to
El Salvador in March 1983.

The Church in the Nation's Crisis

June–October 1979

The month of June saw no end to the violence in spite of the state of siege, or perhaps because of it. No massacres like those of the Tuesdays of May caught the world's attention, but the month ended with 123 killed, 47 arrested, 18 disappeared. Thirty of the dead were teachers, and the national teachers' union reacted with protests and strikes. Labor leaders, campesinos, and political figures also fell victim to right-wing groups, security forces, and paramilitary forces. Corpses, mostly of young people, often mutilated from torture, appeared in various places in the country. The armed leftist groups responded with assassinations, skirmishes with the military, arson, bombs, and seizure of radio stations.[1]

One of the dead was Rafael Palacios, a forty-year-old priest who was working with grass-roots church communities, especially in Santa Tecla, and who had also taken charge of the parish of San Francisco in the Mejicanos district after Octavio Ortiz was killed. Jesús Delgado says that the way Palacios guided the communities in regard to political activity was exactly what Romero himself advocated. "This priest was fully convinced that Christian lay people should commit themselves to political struggle in order to bring to it the light of the gospel and the salt of God's word. Nevertheless, Father Palacios did not accept that a grass-roots church community might opt for a particular party or political tendency. The organization was one thing and the grass-roots church community was another." Some other priests, Delgado adds, confused the two and so deprived the community of its own evangelical identity.[2] Romero had dealt extensively with this subject in his third pastoral letter.

On Saturday night, June 16, Palacios went to see the archbishop to tell him of his fears for his own safety. Two days before, someone had printed a threat from the White Warrior Union on his car. On Tuesday Romero met him again at a meeting of priests, and Rafael told him, "Today they killed a military officer and I've had that threat. Something serious is going to happen in Santa Tecla." The officer, a major, had been killed by leftist guerrillas in Santa Tecla. Romero thought that Rafael's fears were somewhat exaggerated, but the next day Palacios was shot down in the street in Santa Tecla, the fifth priest to be killed in a little more than two years.

"If it is true that the death of Father Palacios is in revenge for the death of the day before—as was said of the death of Father Navarro also, that it was in revenge for the abduction and murder of the day before—what basis have these retaliations?" asked Romero at the funeral in the cathedral the next day. He called on the authorities to control "these forces of hell and murder" and recalled that "when the same phantom organization threatened the Jesuit Fathers, the president of the republic called for rationality and the threat was stopped. It can be done when there is a will. How long are we to endure these crimes without any just atonement? Where is our nation's justice? Where is the Supreme Court of Justice? Where is our democracy's honor if people are to die in this way like dogs, with their deaths left uninvestigated like Father Rafael's? I ask and demand in the name of the citizenry that this be investigated and that an end be brought to this growing spiral of violence."

Rafael, he said, was a victim of "the structural sin built into, embedded in our society," and had thus paid for his ministry of calling attention to that sin. He praised Rafael's faithfulness to his vocation and his faithfulness to the poor. His death, Romero said, was a message of hope: "In him we see the new man and the zeal he had to fashion those new human beings that Latin America needs today—not just by changing structures but above all by changing hearts. It is the voice of conversion, the voice of genuine evangelization."[3]

Bishop Rivera and many priests from all parts of El Salvador concelebrated the funeral mass with Romero. He accompanied the body to Suchitoto, where Rafael had grown up, and where they laid him to rest in the parish church. At the urging of his clergy, Romero had all the church bells tolled each night at eight o'clock for nine days, followed by a noon mass in the cathedral on Saturday, June 30. Other masses were canceled that day in the archdiocese as a sign of the church's unity and of the loss of a priest.[4] In his homily that day Romero spoke of the eucharist. "The presence of this single mass in the cathedral is meant to be the torch that enlightens the Christian communities, that they may learn to feel the beauty of their masses—consciously, well celebrated, felt as an impulse of holiness and redemption for ourselves and others." He condemned abuses of the mass, "out of selfishness, when it is subject to one's convenience . . . as though God were a servant of the family or of the social class . . . or the mass subject to the idolatry of money and power, used to condone sinful situations, used to suggest to the public that there are no differences with the church . . . where what most matters is to have it publicized in the newspapers and to make mere political advantage prevail. . . . And the mass is also prostituted within our church when it is celebrated out of greed, when we make the mass a business. It seems incredible that masses should be multiplied just to make money. It is like the act of Judas selling out his Lord, and it deserves that the Lord take up the lash he used in the temple, saying, 'My house is a house of prayer, and you have made it a den of thieves.' "

He spoke of the priesthood and the need for priests. "It's as if a community were decapitated when it has no priest to celebrate the mass and make divine all that is human. . . . The absence of Father Palacios among the priests that concelebrate today affects us all." But the offering of the lives of five priests was a sign. "The priesthood in our archdiocese can bear this seal of Jesus: 'If they persecuted me, they will also persecute you.' I believe that we stand before a characteristic mark of the authenticity of our church's preaching. Of Rafael Palacios I can say with the communities that knew him at first hand that he was far from provoking violence, from sowing hatred. . . . He preached love; a man of deep meditation, he always believed more in the force of love than in the force of violence. . . . His ideal was to create communities inspired in the love of Jesus Christ." The deaths of the five priests were joined to the deaths of many others. "We can present along with the blood of teachers, of laborers, of peasants, the blood of our priests. This is communion in love. It would be sad, if in a country where murder is being committed so horribly, we were not to find priests also among the victims. They are the testimony of a church incarnated in the problems of its people."[5]

The violence continued through July. The government let the state of siege expire in the third week of July, two months after it had begun. If it had been meant to stem the violence, it had failed.[6]

On May 18, Romero mentioned in his diary a document that Bishops Aparicio, Alvarez, Barrera, and Revelo had prepared for Rome early in May.[7] The document fills ten closely typed pages, bears the signatures of the four bishops, and is headed "Political-Religious Situation of El Salvador." It is, however, simply an attack on Romero, portraying the archbishop as at once naive and wily, imposing a politicized, Marxist idea of pastoral ministry on the church and the country, interfering in other dioceses, led by a group of radical priests, associated with the "Marxist" FECCAS-UTC and BPR, blessing terrorism, and defaming the government.

In the document Rutilio Grande and Alfonso Navarro become turncoat leftists killed by their former leftist associates, Octavio Ortiz dies "pistol in hand" while indoctrinating young recruits for the BPR and FAPU "in order to infiltrate them into grass-roots communities," catechists and delegates of the word become "genuine guerrillas and terrorists, some of them; others, activists of the different organizations that form the BPR and FAPU." Radio YSAX, *Orientación*, and the Jesuits, according to the bishops, have managed to deceive the world media with a story of a government that violates human rights and persecutes the church, whereas "the present government dares not act with the firmness demanded by the security, tranquility, and peace that the state has the obligation to guarantee the nation, so as not to feed the international smear campaign that presents it as a trampler of human rights and persecutor of the church."

Romero, according to the document, was the centerpiece of the campaign against the government, with his Sunday homilies broadcast to the nation, "making a display of his impunity with continual accusations against the government of trampling human rights and persecuting the church, accusations shown on more than one occasion to be false or exaggerated, and with his disrespect toward the chief of state, whom he publicly called a liar, and toward the Supreme Court of Justice, which he accused of being venal." He openly showed his sympathy with the popular political organizations, and the purpose of his and Bishop Rivera's pastoral letter on them "seems to be to undo" the declaration of the other bishops condemning FECCAS-UTC. He had criticized Bishop Aparicio's suspension of his priests for signing the letter to the nuncio and had usurped "the right to interfere in any conflict arising in the other dioceses."

At Puebla, they said, Romero had "spent long hours giving statements to journalists about the violation of human rights and the religious persecution in El Salvador and his own stance of valiant prophetic accusation in defense of trampled human rights," and frequently met with the "anti-Puebla" liberation theologians and supplied them with secret documents from the conference. He was presently meeting secretly, they said, with the Christian Democrats, ANEP, and perhaps with the president himself to seek a middle way out of the political impasse, but the archbishop himself was the chief obstacle to the dialog "because of his connection with the BPR, FAPU, and other radical groups." (Representatives of the archdiocese were indeed engaging in talks with the Christian Democrats and ANEP, though not with the government and not in secret, and Romero himself had attended a meeting on the previous December 6.)[8] At the same time, said the bishops, the archbishop seemed to be conspiring with the government and ANEP to have his own radio transmissions jammed in order to prevent the left from knowing he was participating in the talks. (Romero had protested the government's jamming of the radio in his homilies and had complained to the government.)[9]

The pastoral practice emanating from the archdiocese, said the document, "incites to class struggle, to the radicalization of the peasantry and the laboring class, to revolution and taking power for the establishment of 'a socialist government of peasants and laborers.' It manipulates the Bible, adulterates the figure of Jesus Christ our Lord, portraying him as a subversive, a revolutionary, and a political leader." It distorts the dogmas of the divinity of Christ, the resurrection, the eucharist, and the church. Grassroots communities dare to criticize bishops, and the elected vicars and deans dare to complain to the bishops' conference and the nuncio, and even ordered the churches closed for three days when Octavio Ortiz was killed. Radical groups of priests and religious, said the four bishops, criticize and ridicule bishops who do not go along with them, use the mass to indoctrinate and politicize, and even invite everyone at mass to receive holy communion.

"The politicized pastoral stance of the archbishop and its underlying ideology," the document continued, has produced an alarming crisis of faith in El Salvador among priests, nuns, and lay people. "A factor in this crisis has been the sympathy and commitment of the archbishop toward the radical political groups. People ask how it is possible that a shepherd of the church should support cold-blooded criminals who openly declare themselves Marxist-Leninists."

The division of the bishops' conference, the four bishops admitted, was also a reason for the crisis of faith, but that division was the result of the rejection by the four bishops of "the ideology of the popular church, which underlies the pastoral practice of the archdiocese," and which the archbishop refused to give up. This ideology, the document stated, "has infected a great part of the clergy and nuns of the archdiocese, and the archbishop not only permits it but he shows by his attitude, and more than once in his homilies, that he is himself infected by that ideology."

How does he show this? The letter states:

In his Sunday homilies he receives with satisfaction the applause with which the people interrupt his talk; this applause always coincides with his charges and attacks against the government and with his support and defense of subversive groups. Is this the archbishop's vanity? . . . We think not. Rather, it is the assurance that he is interpreting the sense of "the church" in the applause with which the people united in the cathedral approve his stand. Repeatedly, on speaking of the magisterium of the church, he has said that this magisterium is in the people of God—a correct affirmation if what is meant by "people of God" is the church made up of hierarchy and laity. But when he is heard to say to the politicized audience that he has before him, "You are the people of God," or that the bishop in his teaching is the interpreter of the sense of the people, or when in speaking of the infallibility of the pope he affirms that it consists in the pope's taking on the infallibility of the people of God, he gives cause to suspect that the ideology of the popular church has got into his theology.

When the priests' senate, the vicars' commission, the vicariates, the pastors, the nuns, and the grass-roots ecclesial communities have taken to themselves an authority that is not theirs, reproving the bishops or the apostolic nuncio, instead of correcting them for such an abuse, he has supported them in CEDES meetings and justified their stand.

Despite the history of conflict and accusations on the part of the four bishops, the document is shocking. It ignores most of what Romero had been saying and doing publicly, in order to present a warped view of his teaching and practice. It distorts beyond recognition his attitude and actions in relation to the popular organizations. It accepts wild theories about the priests and lay workers killed in order to explain away the persecution of the part of the church that was trying to follow Medellín and Puebla. That some bishops should have a different vision of what the church should be is understandable. That they should search so hard to find fault and should rely on such a hollow argument seems small-minded and mean.

After discussing the document with Bishop Rivera, Romero observed that in spite of its seriousness he felt at great peace. "I recognize before God my deficiencies, but I believe I have worked with good will, far removed from the serious things I am accused of. God will have the last word, and I calmly hope to keep on working with the same enthusiasm as ever, since I serve our holy church with love."[10]

Romero sent a letter to each of the four bishops on July 6. He said he was writing because of the accusing document they had signed, because of the approaching election of CEDES officers, and because he had promised his priests that he would convey their criticism of the bishops to the bishops themselves. The clergy had held their monthly meeting on July 3; the death of Rafael Palacios on June 20 was still on everyone's mind, and the silence of the conference in the face of the violence of the previous two months and the murder of another priest was scandalous. Romero had wanted to write them before, but had put it off for "fear of not being well received and because of the hope that something or someone might move us to recover the unity that has been lost among the bishops."

He reviewed the violence of May and June just past and said: "We know very well that the government and the oligarchy indiscriminately call subversives all those who have become conscious of injustice and all those who try effectively to correct it. But if we forget for a moment the problem of ideologies, in the name of which justification is sought for the most atrocious crimes, I believe that for all of us, as bishops, Christians, and plain Salvadorans, it is clear what is the reason for our anguish: the masses of the poor and all those who take their part are systematically exterminated. At times there may be questionable actions on the part of some, and there will always be human limitations in helping and defending the masses of the poor. But all that does not seriously lessen the fundamental fact that in our country God's children are being murdered with impunity, especially the poor, God's favored, for whom at Puebla we made a preferential option."

He then asked them if it was not true that their disunity was making the spiral of repression and violence worse. "Two years ago, in the messages of March 5 and May 17, 1977, we had a single message. The church spoke with a single voice, and thus the Christian people, the government of the republic, and the shadowy bands of murderers understood it. But since then, our message has been divided and even contrary, and we have divided our forces instead of uniting them for the cause of peace and justice."

He asked whether the cathedral massacre of May 8 did not merit a word from the bishops that might have lessened the subsequent killings and the retaliations of the leftist extremists. "What have we done to prevent the murder of more than twenty teachers and the recent death of our fellow priest Father Rafael Palacios?" he asked.

"Is not this the moment to overcome our own differences and show ourselves united before the nation and thus defend and save human lives?" asked Romero. "It is for us as bishops to preach conversion, further the preferential option for the poor, and promote communion and participation," he said, citing key expressions of the Puebla conference. "It is urgent that we show ourselves united and that this unity empower our voice of the gospel and of the church to better our country's situation and save lives. If we do not do it, we too will have to hear the frightening word of the Lord, 'What have you done with your brother?' The blood of so many Salvadorans should move us to begin again as a bishops' conference, leaving aside our own differences and limitations, which appear small in comparison with the magnitude of our land's tragedy."

Romero suggested that they postpone the elections scheduled for their three-day meeting in July in order to devote the time to reflection on what to do. "If we do not act quickly and boldly, the country's situation could degenerate further and we could come to experience the atrocities that we see and lament in our sister nation of Nicaragua."

Nicaragua had experienced the heavy bombing of several of its cities as the Somoza dictatorship tried to put down the people's insurrection. It was now in the midst of the final Sandinista offensive, which overthrew the dictatorship on July 19. The Salvadoran bishops did put off the elections until November, but they did not act quickly and boldly. Their disunity was never healed, and historians can only wonder how the history of El Salvador might have been affected if they had been united. Would a stronger, united church have been less vulnerable to attack? Would the lives of many, including Romero, have been saved?

On Saturday, August 4, another priest died violently. He was Alirio Napoleón Macías, pastor of the town of San Esteban Catarina in the San Vicente diocese. A week before, without naming him, *Orientación* had published information that he had supplied on repression in his parish: raids and killings by the security forces, seven persons arrested and later found murdered, four others arrested and not heard of again, others under threat.

He was tidying up the sanctuary of his church when the three killers entered. Apparently recognizing them, he called to the people present,

"Look out, they're police." Witnesses said they recognized the killers, dressed in civilian clothes, as members of the Guardia Nacional. As he fell between the altar and the sacristy, his mother ran to him and saw him open his eyes as blood poured from his nostrils. He died there.[11]

Macías was the first priest killed from a diocese other than San Salvador. Aparicio, his bishop, was outside the country, but the bishops of the other four dioceses issued a public expression of condolence and protest, their first joint statement since May 1977. They called for an investigation, asked the nuncio to intervene, and called on the government to deal with church superiors if it had any complaint against a priest.[12] When Aparicio returned, he issued a strong statement condemning the killing and publishing the murderers' excommunication, though the statement made him seem almost more upset by the profanation of the church than by the murder itself. He did, however, end his statement by announcing succinctly that the bishops' conference was recalling its two delegates to the president's National Forum.[13] This made quite clear who he thought was responsible for the killing and undercut the government's pretense at dialog with the church.

Romero went to the funeral at 4:00 P.M. on August 6,[14] after the mass in his cathedral for the national feast day, the Divine Savior of the World. On Saturday, August 11, a nationwide meeting of priests and religious was held, with 110 priests and 131 nuns present.[15] They comprised one-third of the nation's priests and over one-sixth of the Sisters. Almost all of them— 108 priests and 118 nuns—signed letters to the pope, the bishops' conference, and the governments of Latin America, begging them to speak out for human rights in El Salvador. "We are convinced that the deaths of many innocents would have been avoided if the apostolic nuncio and all the bishops had protested energetically and unanimously against this abuse of power."[16]

The same day the bishops met in the nunciature with the nuncio. They discussed the death of Father Macías and agreed to start legal action. The nuncio offered to speak with the president. Romero tried to discuss the reasons behind the murder, but the majority took up the theme of a Marxist infiltration of the church. Romero tried to explain that the church's fidelity to Vatican II, Medellín, and Puebla was bringing it persecution, but the others said he was to blame for most of the country's and the church's troubles.[17]

Although Bishop Aparicio had virtually blamed the government for the murder of Father Macías, on September 9 he reversed his position in a swinging attack on FECCAS-UTC during the course of a homily in his cathedral. He branded the peasant organizations as communist and said their members were excommunicated. Fathers Grande, Navarro, Palacios, and Macías were all killed by leftists, he said, when the priests tried to break away from the organizations. Various priests of his own diocese were also implicated with leftist groups, he said, and "I won't be able to save them, I won't be able to do anything for them, because they've made a commitment that won't let them turn back." His homily appeared in full in the national press[18] and caused an immediate reaction. Romero noted in his diary that Aparicio's words could expose priests to assassination. A commentator on radio YSAX called the homily "monstrous," saying that Aparicio had made accusations without a semblance of evidence and had virtually invited further murders of priests.[19]

In his homily the next Sunday, September 16, Romero did not mention Aparicio by name, but he could not ignore the attack in his comments on the events of the week. "I want to recall with affection the priests who have been murdered and express my faithful solidarity with them," he said. Investigations by the archdiocese and the Inter-American Human Rights Commission of the Organization of American States had made clear that the four priests were not killed by leftist groups but by the White Warrior Union or by government agents. In the case of Navarro, even the government had blamed the White Warrior Union in its reply to the Inter-American Human Rights Commission. Romero went on: "I want to express my solidarity with the priests, nuns, and other pastoral workers whose lives are in danger. I know that their actions and teachings respond to the demands of a church that asks of us precisely what we have been reflecting on today: a commitment to the true messianic work of Christ, which leads us, as it led Christ, to the limit of death, even to Calvary."

He reported a death threat from the White Warrior Union to another priest and added his support to the letter the assembly of priests and religious had sent to the bishops' conference on August 11. He read from it: "Let priests and religious be ordered to abstain in their homilies and meetings from defaming priests and their pastoral co-workers. When civilian or military authorities make complaints about persons, let the persons be spoken to directly so that they can explain their apostolic work and show the truth or falsity of the accusations." He spoke also of threats and harassment against the Catholic radio station, the director of the legal aid office, and two nuns working in Arcatao, in the Chalatenango area.[20]

The same Sunday Aparicio again attacked FECCAS-UTC, plus unnamed priests and nuns whom he accused of following "the communist line." No one was persecuting the church in El Salvador, he said, except the members of the popular organizations who occupied churches and interfered with worship. *Orientación*, he said, "is disorienting the people. I wish it didn't come into our Catholic homes; I wish it didn't get to the campesinos; I wish priests . . . wouldn't poison them in this way." If anyone had a genuine complaint against the government, he said, he himself would take it all the way to the president. "But if they've already gone to San Salvador and they've been shouted about in some pulpit and had their case published in *Orientación*," then they should not come to him, because in that case the government would not pay attention to him.[21]

The San Salvador priests' senate met the next day to discuss Aparicio's attacks and spoke of visiting Aparicio and of preparing a report for Rome.[22]

A commentator on YSAX pointed out that Aparicio was repeating the arguments of the large landowners and of the government, who "need to make the country and the whole world see that what is happening in El Salvador is nothing more than the resolve of a few communists to subvert the established order and submit the country to Soviet imperialism by way of Havana." Rather, as the United States Under Secretary of State for Latin American Affairs had just testified before Congress, the unequal distribution of property, income, and power was the problem in El Salvador. Bishop Aparicio, said YSAX, "is mistaking the leaves for the roots."[23]

Central America was once one country, and the citizens of the five small nations still feel a common bond somewhat greater than that of mere geographical closeness. The struggle to overthrow the forty-five-year-old Somoza dictatorship in Nicaragua raised the hopes and enthusiasm of people all over the isthmus.

The Sandinistas had been fighting a guerrilla war for years, but the fight had taken on national proportions in Nicaragua in January 1978 with the murder of the newspaper editor and publisher Pedro Joaquín Chamorro. The opposition began to grow. In September rebels seized several cities, and Somoza's forces put down the inhabitants' uprisings with heavy damage and heavy loss of life. The city of Estelí rebelled again in Holy Week of 1979, and once again Somoza crushed the rebellion. But the insurrectional forces were growing steadily and by June had mounted a general offensive, taking the war into the capital, Managua. The final victory came on July 19.

Romero often asked for prayers and material aid for those suffering from the war in Nicaragua, and Caritas, the relief organization, collected money and sent food. He began his homily on July 22 by speaking of the overthrow of the dictatorship and the euphoria of the people of Nicaragua. "I believe I interpret the feeling of all of you if our first greeting this morning is for our sister republic of Nicaragua. I salute it in a sense of fraternal prayer and solidarity, because today more than ever it needs that spiritual support. The joy that the beginning of its liberation gives us also makes us concerned that this dawn of freedom not prove a frustration but that the Lord, who has been kind, may continue to be the Nicaraguan people's inspiration. They must also consider, in their Christian inspiration, the cost of this moment. Over twenty-five thousand dead are not a trivial matter; the gift of God offered at this moment is not to be cast away."

The gospel for the day included the words, "Upon disembarking, Jesus saw a large crowd. He pitied them, for they were like sheep without a shepherd" (Mark 6:34). Romero entitled his homily "Christ, the True Shepherd-King of All Peoples," and Nicaragua was the background for the message. "The gospel says of the feelings of Christ in the midst of his people: he had pity, he had mercy, because they seemed a people dispersed, like a flock without a shepherd. The same figure applies to us, where our people too give that impression. But like a flock that looks for unity, for the solution of its problems, they find in the gospel message of today God's answer to their hopes. God grant that Nicaragua and our country and all the countries of the world that have problems, that are in crises, may look to the Good Shepherd, the Shepherd-King promised by today's prophecy in the first reading [Jer. 23:1-6] and fulfilled in the gospel read today [Mark 6:30-34]."[24]

Romero spoke of Jeremiah's difficult mission of calling to task the corrupt rulers of his day. "Woe to the shepherds who mislead and scatter the flock of my pasture, says the Lord. . . . I will appoint shepherds for them who will shepherd them so that they need no longer fear and tremble; and none shall be missing, says the Lord" (Jer. 23:1,4). Jeremiah, continued Romero, condemned the dispersion of the people. "The authority that should be a moral force to unite becomes by its errors a force of dispersion — a flock without a shepherd." Jeremiah condemned too the expulsions, the repression, the ruling by fear. "A frightened flock, a people under terror, a people intimidated. I lived it yesterday in the villages of Chalatenango — what fear people feel! There are men who don't go to their homes; they have to stay in the hills — truly dispersed, fearful sheep. And finally the prophet speaks of the sheep that are lost. Don't you seem to hear in this the cry of the disappeared? The sheep that should be cared for in the fold with a shepherd's love are persecuted, are 'disappeared,' are cast out."[25]

The bloodbath of Nicaragua showed what happens when power is made an absolute, a god, Romero said. It showed also that power could not be sustained by repression or with the corruption of its wielders. "There comes a moment when the people tire of being exploited and oppressed [the people applauded] — a wonderful lesson for those who believe in that force which cannot be maintained."

Nicaragua's struggle was also a lesson for the church of El Salvador. In Nicaragua, "not only the archbishop, but the whole bishops' conference was able to unite and to denounce together the injustices and to support and enlighten the people. Without identifying itself with the Sandinistas, the church played a very important role, because it kept itself close to and faithful to the people. That is why the Sandinistas now trust the church. They do not consider it to be allied with Somoza, or with any revolutionary forces either. They see it as a mother that is able to understand, and in this moment of reconstruction they know they can count on it for its Christian enlightenment."

Romero offered a further reflection for the ruling class of El Salvador. "It is very sad to realize that, in the midst of the great joy, enthusiasm, and hope that this dawn of liberation in our sister country of Nicaragua has awakened in our people of El Salvador, our government and the ruling classes do not yet want to join in this gladness for Nicaragua's liberation. But the church has the joy and the happiness and the satisfaction of having been one in thought with Nicaragua's church and also of now feeling very close to its joy and sharing its responsibilities through prayer and through the light of the gospel."[26]

He praised the new Nicaraguan government's guarantees of human rights and quoted parts of its program intended to correct the same kinds of abuses that were rife in El Salvador. "A regime of effective democracy, justice, and social progress" would be established. The judicial power would be independent and would guarantee the full exercise of civil rights. Freedom of expression and information, of worship, of association would be guaranteed. Murders, disappearances, tortures, arbitrary arrests, and searches of homes would be outlawed. Repressive "security" forces would be abolished. Graft and corruption would be wiped out. Justice would be applied to those military and civilian officials who had committed crimes, and the new army would have no place for corrupt and criminal personnel. Exiles would be welcomed home. "These things," he said, "are not a favor but simply the rights of the human person. May we not have to endure a bloodbath to obtain them. There is still time to win them by rational means if only the government shows the good will to be what the Bible says today: the people's understanding shepherd."[27]

Sometime after returning from Puebla, Romero mentioned to his psychologist friend, Dr. Rodolfo Semsch, that he felt a deep sense of calm, of peace, underlying all the problems and conflicts of his life — a sense of peace that took nothing away from his energy, from his driving sense of duty to denounce crime and injustice, to visit every town or village that invited him to its local feast, to have meetings continually with various groups of people, from the priests' senate to the seminarians.

Romero's energy always amazed those who knew him well, especially since it seemed to increase after the burdens and conflicts of governing the archdiocese became his. The Sisters at the cancer hospital, with whom he took most of his meals, recalled that he took pills for his nerves and that his hands shook when he first became archbishop. After a few weeks, he stopped the pills, his hands steadied, and the problem did not return. The Barraza family recalled that he could follow a conversation with one eye on television while eating a meal and monitoring YSAX on his portable radio. A day off was rare, and a few hours or an afternoon was usually all the relaxation he managed at any one time. His diary often records two or three public masses with their sermons, each in a different place, on the same day. He especially amazed the many among the clergy who had pegged him as a weakling before he became archbishop.

Yet in the midst of constant activity, he remained a man of reflection and prayer. He rose early and prayed before saying mass for the Sisters at 6:30. He would sometimes slip away from a meeting to go to the chapel and pray. What went on in those moments of silent prayer only the Spirit of God can say. But a biographer can suspect that the deep sense of peace that came upon Romero during the last year of his life was a fruit of his union with God. Dr. Semsch told Romero then, and repeated over a year later in an interview, that he could not explain it as a psychologist. Dr. Semsch also mentioned, but did not try to explain, the cosmic experience — a sense of oneness with the universe — that Oscar Romero reported that he had once had.

Such clues, along with others in his retreat notes and occasionally in his homilies, suggest some of the depth of Romero's inner life. For example, during the retreat he made with some of his priests in January 1978, he observed that he was finding it hard to turn inward, but "thanks be to God, I see that when I put myself to it seriously I achieve concentration and the elevation of prayer. God is good, and I find him easily." In his homily of July 23, 1978, he told the people: "We all have a church within ourselves, our own consciousness. There God is, God's Spirit. . . . Blessed are those who enter often to speak alone with their God." And in preaching on Jesus at prayer he said: "He wanted to teach us . . . that we must lose ourselves in the beauty, the sublimity, of God. . . . How can a person spend a whole life without thinking of God, leave empty that capacity for the divine and never fill it?"[28] In the tragic days of May 1979, he said: "Christians must always nourish in their hearts the fullness of joy. . . . I have tried it many times and in the darkest moments . . . when slander and persecution were strongest, tried to unite myself intimately with Christ, my friend, to feel more comfort than all the joys of the earth can give — the joy of feeling close to God, even when humans do not understand you. It is the deepest joy the heart can have."[29]

On El Salvador's patronal feast day, August 6, Romero announced in beginning his homily that his fourth pastoral letter, "The Mission of the Church in the Nation's Crisis," was soon to be published. He devoted his homily to the subject.

As with the third pastoral letter, Romero consulted various persons in the preparation of the letter, though fewer experts than in the case of the third. But the letter also grew out of wide consultation within the archdiocese, so that Romero could say to the people, "You and I have written this fourth pastoral letter."[30] He had sent a questionnaire to the grass-roots ecclesial communities and Catholic organizations in the archdiocese, and their discussions and comments provided part of the material from which he formulated the letter. All told, several thousand people were involved. He called on the grass-roots communities especially, which had recently received strong support from the bishops at Puebla, to study the three-page questionnaire carefully, discuss it at length, and reflect on it in prayer before sending their replies to the archdiocese.

The object of the fourth pastoral letter, Romero told the people, was to "present officially to the archdiocese the total spirit of Puebla."[31] Puebla had pointed the way for the church in Latin America, had turned on a light that the letter would direct on El Salvador, now in the midst of a grave political and social crisis.

The basis of the country's crisis, as reported in the letter, was social injustice—and all that Puebla had described about social injustice in Latin America could be said of El Salvador. Romero summarized it in his homily: "children who from the earliest age must earn their living, young people who have no chance to get ahead, peasants who lack even basic necessities, laborers whose rights are bargained away, the underemployed, the throngs of outcasts, the aged who feel useless."[32]

Along with this picture of injustice, "we could have written just for El Salvador what Puebla says: 'Organizing of laborers, of peasants, and of the lower classes is regarded with suspicion, and repressive means are taken to hinder it. Such regulation and limitation of action is not imposed on the owners' associations, which can use all their power to assure their interests.' "[33] As an example of what Puebla said, Romero cited statistics of the archdiocesan legal aid office: in the first six months of 1979 it listed 406 persons killed by the government's military or paramilitary forces, 107 of them campesinos, not one a large landowner; 307 were arrested, 129 of them campesinos, not one a large landowner.

The government, continued the letter, showed itself unable to restrain the escalation of violence in the country. "Moreover, a suspicious tolerance of armed bands that, for their implacable pursuit of the government's opponents could be considered its servants, contradicts in practice the government's emphatic statements against every kind of violence. Rather, it seems to declare repression against all political opposition and against every organization that makes a social protest."[34] Both the bishops at Puebla and John Paul II in his opening speech to the conference declared that the church must lift its voice and condemn such abuses, "particularly when the responsible officials or rulers profess to be Christians."[35]

The questionnaire that the archbishop had sent to the clergy and grass-roots ecclesial communities listed "an even more frightful inventory of infidelities and betrayals of our ethical and Christian values, and even of our political constitution," the pastoral letter explained. It gave as examples the entire judicial system's failure to demand the observance of the law and its prostitution as an instrument "at the whim of a government of force"; the violation of human liberty and dignity shown in the impunity of so many crimes, "many of them committed by the security forces openly or, in the popular saying, camouflaged as civilians"; the indifference to the anguish of families of persons who had disappeared while under arrest; the uselessness of appeals for writs of habeas corpus; the silent complicity in violations of the constitution and other maneuvers to advance party or class advantages; the fraudulent elections; "the impudent propaganda and imposition of antibirth policies that are practically castrating our people and undermining its moral reserves."[36]

The pastoral letter also enumerated examples of what Romero in his homily called "the dreadful rule of the mystery of sin in Salvadoran society."[37] Employers maneuvered to deprive workers of their rights or bought off union leaders; unions at times used strikes for unjust claims; employees at times loafed or skipped work or demanded gratuities or bribes for work they were paid to do; persons in authority used their positions for friends or relatives or even to enrich themselves by padding payrolls or expense accounts; human dignity was bought and sold in various ways, such as demanding sexual acts in exchange for employment, or running places of prostitution and drug use; the communications media were manipulated through pressures and bribes to libel and defame; there were forms of extortion such as kidnappings and threats from real or phantom secret organizations, at times with seeming official connivance.[38]

In the letter he went on to discuss the internal crisis in the Salvadoran church, and of this he said in his homily: "We want to be truly candid. Whoever accuses must be ready to be accused. If the church does its duty of accusing, it expects also the accusation that you can make against it." He admitted that many Christians had not followed the Christian principles of the gospel and preferred to follow only the principles of their political commitment, "believing themselves wiser than the wisdom of the gospel and of the church."[39]

But the "most visible sin"[40] mentioned by the respondents to the questionnaire was the hierarchy's disunity. "We cannot hide it," said Romero in the homily, "and I for my part want to beg pardon of the church and tell you in explanation, so that you can perhaps understand and help us find the causes and resolve them, that what is happening among us is a reflection of what is happening in our society and that what society and priests and bishops and all Christians must do is be converted"[41] to what Puebla called the preferential option for the poor. This preference for the poor, said the pastoral letter, "which the gospel demands of Christians, does not polarize or divide, but is rather a force for unity, because 'it does not try to exclude other representatives of the social picture in which we live . . . but is an invitation to all, regardless of class, to accept and take up the cause of the poor as though accepting and taking up their own cause, the cause of Christ himself.' "[42]

In the second part of the letter, Romero asked what the church could do for the people's liberation from the evils mentioned in the first part. The answer came largely from Puebla. The church must be true to itself and to its evangelizing mission—it must preach the liberating message of the gospel, teaching God's truth about Christ, the church, and humanity. It must point out error and sin and preach conversion. It must expose the idols of society: property and "national security" on one side, and the popular organization on the other, because persons committed to an organization dedicated to the people's liberation can become so involved in the organization that it becomes more important than the people it is meant to help. The church must promote a liberation that emphasizes both the transcendent aspect of human spirituality and eternal destiny and the here-and-now establishment of God's reign on earth. The church's evangelization must press for "urgent and profound" but nonviolent social change, without which the roots of the present evils would remain. The church must be on the side of the poor, but direct its call for conversion to poor and rich alike.

The third part of the letter took up three special questions of the day: violence, Marxism, and the government's call for national dialog. Romero had devoted the last part of his third pastoral to the subject of violence, and now he merely added a few touches to what he had already said, "given the increasing violence that brings grief to many families of our land."[43] The church, he wrote, sought peace that was the "work of justice." It condemned the "structural" or "institutionalized" violence that was "the product of a situation of injustice in which the majority of men, women, and—most of all—children in our country are deprived of what is necessary to live." It also condemned "the arbitrary and repressive violence of the state." In El Salvador, every form of dissent was repressed "more and more violently, treacherously, and unjustly."[44] The church, wrote Romero, also condemned the terrorist violence of bands of the extreme right,[45] which were part of the state's violence, and the violence of the leftist groups "when they intentionally victimize innocent persons or bring about consequences out of proportion to the positive effect that they wish to obtain in the short or medium run."[46] These words seems to contain a guarded and conditioned recognition of the guerrilla organizations that, in the third pastoral, Romero had practically dismissed and condemned as fanatics and terrorists.

The previous March 26, Romero had talked with two members of the guerrilla forces who came to see him. He tried to persuade them of the "Christian idea of nonviolence," but he noted in his diary: "These people are quite convinced that the force of love will not repair the present situation, but only the force of violence. . . . I felt deeply the difference in thinking between the extensive section of our country represented by these speakers and Christian sentiment. I ask the Lord to illumine his church's ways so that they may be understood even by those who seek the nation's good by ways very different from those that Christ pointed out."

In the pastoral letter, Romero repeated Paul VI's guarded approval of the right of insurrection enunciated in the encyclical "On the Development of Peoples" (*Populorum Progressio*) and repeated by the Medellín conference. He had cited it in the third pastoral, but this time he called it "the classical teaching of Catholic theology"—as it is—and then quoted Paul's statement: an insurrection can be legitimate "in the very exceptional case of evident and prolonged tyranny that seriously attacks the rights of the person and dangerously harms the common good of the country," to which Medellín had added, "whether it proceeds from one person or from evidently unjust structures."[47] Similar to the right of insurrection is that of defense, "when a person or group repels by force an unjust aggression of which it is the object."[48]

But to use the right of legitimate defense, including that of insurrection, one must also see that other conditions are fulfilled: the violence used must not exceed what is needed; all peaceful means of redress must first be exhausted; defensive violence must not bring about greater evil than what it seeks to correct. "In practice," said the letter, "it is very difficult to take into account all these theoretical principles when justifying violence. From the experience of history, we know how cruel and painful is the price of blood and how hard to repair are the social and economic damages of war." It is more reasonable and effective for the government to use its power not to defend an unjust order but to guarantee the fundamental rights of all. "Only thus can those cases be made more distant and unreal in which recourse to force by groups of individuals can be justified by the existence of a tyrannical regime and an unjust order."[49]

For the guidance of Christians in the violent surroundings of El Salvador, Romero offered the words of Medellín: "Christians are peaceful and are not ashamed to be. They are not simply pacifists, for they are capable of fighting; but they prefer peace to war. They know that 'sudden and violent changes of structures would be deceptive, ineffective in themselves, and certainly not consonant with the people's dignity.' "[50]

The question of Marxism was, and remains, an intellectual and practical one for Christians in El Salvador and Latin America. Romero's pastoral letter sketched some basic distinctions that need to be made, rejecting the simplistic condemnations that so often replace discussion. "Puebla itself teaches us to distinguish between what can be Marxism as a dominant ideology of total behavior and what can be a working with groups that share that ideology. Naturally, if by Marxism is meant a materialistic and atheistic ideology enveloping human existence and giving a false interpretation of religion, it is completely inadmissible for Christians, whose faith guides their lives from the existence of God toward a spiritual and eternal transcendence that becomes possible in Christ, through the Holy Spirit. The two interpretations of life are diametrically opposed."[51]

The term "Marxism," however, also has other meanings; Romero mentioned two that bear on the present discussion: Marxism as a theoretical — or, as the Marxists say, "scientific" — analysis of the economy and of society; and Marxism as a political strategy.

Of Marxist analysis, Romero wrote: "Many in El Salvador, as in all Latin America, use this analysis as a scientific resource that, they say, does not affect at all their religious principles. The magisterium of the church, which recognizes this distinction between Marxist ideology and scientific method, nevertheless prudently warns about the possible ideological risks (*Octogesima Adveniens,*[52] for example).

"Likewise, in the sense of a political strategy," the pastoral letter continued, "many use Marxism as a guide in the struggle for power. Perhaps in this latter use lie hidden the greatest practical dangers, because this Marxist political praxis can lead to conflicts of conscience in the use of means and methods, which do not always agree with what gospel morality prescribes for Christians. This Marxist political practice can lead to the absolutizing of the popular political organizations, to the cooling of the Christian inspiration of the organized, and even to departure from the church, as though the church had no right to exercise, from the standpoint of its transcendent ideology, a critical function in human political activity."[53]

Marxism was a delicate and important matter to try to give right guidance on, because much anti-Marxism was a thinly veiled support for the evils of capitalism. Romero cited Puebla: "The fear of Marxism keeps many from confronting the oppressive reality of liberal capitalism. Before the danger of a system clearly marked by sin, they forget to denounce and combat the reality implanted by another system equally marked by sin."[54] Romero concluded this part of the letter with a thought expressed by one of the respondents to the archdiocese's questionnaire: "The best way to overcome Marxism is to take seriously the preferential option for the poor."[55]

The third special topic that Romero took up was the government's call for dialog among the various forces struggling for advantage in El Salvador. Unfortunately, the call had been coolly received, because the government continued to harass and fight the very organizations with which it should have been conversing. President Romero's National Forum had been accompanied by two months of state of siege and fierce violence by the government, and even the bishops' conference had withdrawn after the murder of Father Macías.

Archbishop Romero set down some common-sense conditions for a successful dialog. All sides—"at least those that have not gone underground"—should be present, not just those that really did not want any change in the country. All violence should cease, especially the government's repression of public protest and its political assassinations, arrests, and deportations. The subject matter of the dialog should be the reexamination and change of the structures that constituted the institutional violence from which the other violence flowed. "Naturally, once the terrorists and proponents of violent solutions find a serious and sincere will for dialog, they must give up their attitudes and collaborate in creating the calm atmosphere needed for a genuine dialog antecedent to the profound change of the country's structures." Dialog should also focus on freedom of organization. "Our inclinations and our Christian sensibility lead us to prefer methods of seeking social justice based on the organizing of the populace in keeping with constitutional and preeminently peaceful principles. I believe labor organizations are a crowning achievement of the working classes of all democratic countries and they must not and cannot be rejected outright for El Salvador."

The last part of the letter dealt with Puebla's application to the pastoral ministry of the archdiocese. Romero observed in his homily that Puebla would simply give a further impulse to what was already being done from the time of Archbishop Chávez with the help of Rivera as auxiliary bishop and of the clergy. The letter discussed several aspects of pastoral practice that Puebla had emphasized, for instance, an attitude of search, of openness to change. "New language, new attitudes are needed,"[56] said Romero in his homily. The archdiocese had long ago made the preferential option for the poor now recommended by Puebla. But, said Romero's letter, "I recognize there is still much to do,"[57] in particular, "to perceive and to point out the mechanisms that produce poverty,"[58] joining forces with "those of good will, to uproot poverty and create a more just and brotherly world,"[59] supporting "the aspirations of workers and campesinos who want to be treated like free and responsible persons called to share in the decisions that concern their life and their future,"[60] defending "their fundamental right to freely create organizations to defend and further their interests and to contribute responsibly to the common good."[61]

At least since January 1976, and to a great extent before that, the archdiocese had followed a common pastoral plan, as Puebla now urged all dioceses to do. Romero had only to recall a few important norms from the January 1976 archdiocesan pastoral week: the urgency of evangelization on all levels of society, the need to train pastoral workers, especially lay workers, the building of communities, and the creation and updating of pastoral mechanisms.[62]

Puebla urged the church to adapt its pastoral practice to the times and situations, and Romero now urged the archdiocese to pay special attention to three areas where he felt that adaptation was needed.

First, it had to consider the church's attention to the mass of the people. In his August 6 homily Romero spoke of the crowd before him for the feast-day mass — "a multitude that we cannot neglect" — and the huge crowd at the traditional procession the evening before.[63] The church's ministry, said the letter, "must find concrete ways to give all Christians a critical outlook, an ability to value themselves as persons and images of God, persons in control of their own destiny." It must be "a liberating response of the church to our peoples, helping them to progress from being a mass to being a people, and from being a people to being God's people."[64] Most of Latin America's Catholics practice a religion centered on popular devotions, which can be means of evangelization. Puebla urged: "The people's religion, like all of the church, should always be evangelized anew. . . . It will be a labor of pastoral pedagogy in which popular Catholicism is assumed, purified, completed, and dynamized by the gospel."[65] Romero's letter urged much patience on the part of pastoral workers involved in this kind of ministry, and also "creativity, imagination, and respect, even in the manner of expounding, so as not to wound people's sensitivity, but at the same time being extremely exacting against abuses."[66]

Second, Puebla had insisted on the importance of grass-roots communities in the Latin American church. In the archdiocese the communities were flourishing, especially in the countryside. "Living in community," wrote Romero, "is not a matter of choice but of calling. Christianity demands, by vocation, the forming of community." The communities must embody the values of the gospel, must be consciously a part of the universal church, and must be a leaven in the world to extend God's kingdom.[67] "We are aware," wrote Romero, "that the more Christians assume the role of adults in the faith and of joint responsibility for the church's course, the more will conflicts arise with parish priests and other church authorities who will not want to proceed at the present-day church's pace, seeing their own authority shaken with the regular criticism and evaluation made of them. But, even in these cases, a good Christian keeps in mind the supreme values of charity and unity."[68]

Finally, Romero recommended to the archdiocese a "pastoral accompaniment" of those Christians who had found their individual Christian vocation in political activism in a popular organization. "The church cannot abandon Christians who, moved by good faith in their understanding of the gospel, wish to participate in a political party or organization," he said in his homily. "We must follow them, but according to the church's way, following as pastors, so that these Christians may know that wherever they go they carry the germ, the word, the seed of salvation, the light of the gospel."[69]

The letter defined pastoral accompaniment as the ministry of evangelizing those "who have made a political option that they conscientiously see as their faith commitment in history."[70] It was not, he said, a politicized pastoral activity, but rather a type of pastoral work that guides Christian consciences according to the gospel in a politicized environment. "Political life, like all human activity, needs pastoral guidance. Our situation is made all the more difficult when many Christians, in an environment as politicized as the one in our country, make their political options before finding their identity as Christians."[71]

This type of pastoral work, wrote Romero, would require in the minister much spirit of prayer and discernment in the face of events, much clarity and firmness of gospel principles, respect for diverse choices and charisms, spirit of sacrifice and generosity, spirit of hierarchy and teamwork. "In encouraging priests to this type of pastoral work and in giving them my support and understanding, I ask them, for the honor of the church and the good of our people, that it never be a work taken on superficially and with personal judgments, or impetuously—perhaps very generously but at times naively and imprudently. Rather, let them submit to planning in communion with their bishop so that it may be a response coming from the church as church."[72]

Romero recognized that risks were involved. "I understand that this type of pastoral work involves risks and brings on complaints and false accusations. But I believe it is necessary for the demand of these times."[73] He would continue to speak of pastoral accompaniment for the remaining months of his life, and shortly before his death he asked Father Fabián Amaya to begin outlining a pastoral letter on catechesis that would include some further development of his thoughts on pastoral accompaniment.[74]

The fourth pastoral letter did not break as much new ground as the third, and therefore it did not attract the same wide attention and study. But it summed up Romero's pastoral view and plans for the post-Puebla church in the archdiocese.

In his July 22 homily, speaking of his trip to a small town fifty miles north of San Salvador, Archbishop Romero said:

Yesterday I was at San Miguel de Mercedes, simply doing my duty of encouraging the Christian communities that are fostered there. The military posted at either end of the town kept many people out and made them go back. They made me get out of the car too, and they searched it. They even suspect the bishop. And afterward they said it was for my [Romero paused as though searching for the word or controlling his emotion] security. If it was for my security, I thought, why are they suspicious about where I'm going when I'm seated here? And I said to them, "Why don't you let those people that you have stopped go in with me? I'll walk in with them." They were women; the guards wouldn't let them enter. Afterward I had the chance to meet the people at San Antonio Los Ranchos [a town nearby] — they were there waiting for me, because they were very eager to converse with their pastor.

I believe that here, as in the case of the military cordon they put around the cathedral for our vigil [the month's mass and prayer vigil for Rafael Palacios on July 20],[75] they are trying to hamper our church's freedom. I would like to beg respectfully that these actions not be repeated, because they are an injury to our church even though they be under the pretext of its pastor's security. I will repeat what I said before: the shepherd does not want security while security is not given to his flock.

In the same homily Romero reported the exiling of two priests, a Salvadoran and a Belgian, who were kept from reentering the country. "There is no freedom for our priests to fulfill missions that at times require them to cross borders."[76]

Four weeks later, Romero told the archdiocese of another incident, this time in the town of Chalatenango. At the entrance to the town, security forces made him get out of his car while they opened everything, including letters, and even searched under the car's hood. The mass in the town was kept under surveillance, and the departmental commander and his officers even brought in tape recorders. At the end of the homily Romero asked the people: "Do you think I have said anything subversive? If I have, say so, because I want to correct it. Have you understood anything subversive in my words?" All the people said no and applauded, and he said, "Those who have this ceremony under surveillance, notice how the people have understood it. Don't go and tell it any other way."[77]

The following week, as he approached Arcatao, in the Chalatenango area, to officiate at a local fiesta, guardsmen stopped the archbishop and made him put his hands on the roof of his car and searched his pockets. In his homily the next Sunday Romero complained especially about the military's insensitivity to the people's local celebration. "They even took away the firecrackers, and in a village there's no celebration without fire-crackers. But they confiscated them. Someone has said," he went on, "that when I speak about how I was searched and inspected that I am seeking my own acclaim. Well, when I visit these towns, I don't go there to strut and show off. I go because my pastoral duty calls me and the community asks me. And I think it is proper for an archbishop to protest when they make him get out of his car again, and even do what they had never done before—search me like a common suspect, my pockets and all my effects. I protest because a pastor has the right to visit his flock wherever they are and also not to have gatherings be thwarted that the people have devotedly prepared for him."[78]

On August 16 President Romero had told a press conference that he would hold free elections supervised by the Organization of American States and let the International Red Cross enter the prisons to see that there were no political prisoners; also, that he would let all political exiles return, reform the election code, and order an exhaustive investigation of the murder of Father Macías.[79] The president's words, said the archbishop in his homily the next Sunday, "would give us great encouragement if, on the other hand, we did not see the contrary reality." The president had spoken of the need for change in the country, but, said the archbishop, "why is a person or organization that urges precisely those changes called subversive?" He read the list of persons arrested and disappeared that week and of villages raided, and also a letter from a woman whose husband, son, and brother had been arrested on May 29 and had vanished. "This is the voice that is not heard and that we must make heard. It would not be a true gospel if we were indifferent in the presence of such anguish, especially when attempts are made to smooth things over with promises and an-nouncements that do not tell the truth but always hide what we so much fear." If the Red Cross now finds jails without political prisoners, he asked, "What have they done with them? Where are they?"[80]

The rest of the country was just as skeptical of the president's words. Political parties pointed out that elections were impossible when the citi-zenry lacked even the minimal conditions of freedom.[81] The archbishop continued to speak out in his homilies about the killings, arrests, disap-pearances, bodies found, and harassing searches, especially in the country-side. On September 2 the cathedral, the church of El Rosario, and various churches outside the capital were occupied by popular organizations, and Romero had to say mass and preach in the Sacred Heart basilica, a large church a few blocks from the center of San Salvador. He complained in the homily about the leaders of the organizations who were so often depriving the people of their churches, but he recognized that their cause was just and that they resorted to the occupations because they had no normal channels for public protest. He reminded his hearers that they themselves, not the buildings, were the true temples of God.[82]

Later in the homily Romero read a letter he was going to send to the president and to the defense minister, objecting to hostility and harassment against the church's pastoral workers in the Chalatenango area and especially against the two Sisters who were working in the town of Arcatao, near the Honduran border. Things had become so difficult, he said in the letter, that he had asked the Sisters to leave for a while

> in order to let you think this question over better and give orders to those responsible to respect the Sisters and stop harassing them. After this time, they will return again to Arcatao with my full support. I have received no evidence against them to demonstrate to me that they are instigating acts of vandalism, and I do have many testimonies of the excellent church work that they are performing in the area, the results of which I have personally witnessed.
>
> I expect that you will guarantee the free pastoral activity not only of the Sisters but of all the pastoral workers approved by the archdiocese, and will take means to end the harassment and repression of the church and people in Chalatenango and the whole country. We wish to believe in the verbal promises of the president regarding the democratization of the country. But unfortunately, these actions tend to contradict those promises.[83]

Romero sent the letters, and in the one to the defense minister he included a crudely written death threat that he had received from the White Warrior Union. It had arrived by mail in an official Defense Ministry envelope. The minister replied that the envelope could have been stolen from the ministry or printed by others, which would have been a plausible explanation coming from a government with some credibility. Coming with the minister's bland denial that the security forces were doing anything to harass the church's workers either in Chalatenango or anywhere else or were bothering the campesinos anywhere, the dismissal of the threatening note is less convincing. And his lofty assertion that "there exists evidence that [the Sisters'] work is not confined to pastoral ministry, as it should be," verged on the insulting, as Romero observed in his homily on September 16.[84]

Meanwhile, the president suffered a personal loss in the murder of his brother, Javier Romero, a teacher, by the Popular Liberation Forces. The archbishop condemned the crime in his September 9 homily and praised the president's reaction. Recalling that previous political crimes by the left had been against officers of the government or businessmen, President Romero had said: "Now they have struck at my own family in open provocation, as though trying to force me to react so as then to justify their actions. But they will not achieve their objective."

"It is a magnanimous expression," said the archbishop. "Let us not continue this violent race of stupid reprisals in which the victim is an innocent person."[85]

It was not often possible to praise the Romero government, which had been responsible for many times more crimes than those committed by the armed opposition. And by treating any dissidence, or even suspicion of it, as justification for seizing, torturing, and killing whomever it wished, the government was driving even peaceful opponents toward taking up arms. By October the country seemed to be slipping into a civil war.

On October 7 the archbishop had his own personal loss to lament in his homily. His friend Apolinario Serrano and three other peasant leaders were killed, and a story was put out that they were trying to attack with two pistols a post of three hundred heavily armed soldiers. "Polín" Serrano had sought out the archbishop months before to talk with him about FECCAS and had gained Romero's respect. From their discussions, says Jesús Delgado, Romero "discovered the Christian roots of the popular and revolutionary commitment of those people. From this he discovered quite clearly that the revolution of these leftists drew its life much more from Christian teaching and ideals than from Marxist or communist ideology," and these talks were more convincing to Romero than the theories of experts or the advice of counselors.[86] Of Polín, Romero said: "He was a man much loved, of great hope for achieving justice for the peasantry. I believe one of the gravest errors and one of the injustices that most cry to heaven has been committed. The people are deprived of their hopes and of the voices that denounce their oppression."[87]

The next week the archbishop cited some statistics in his homily: in 1978, there were at least 1,073 political arrests; from January to August of 1979, there were some 444. In 1978, an average of 80 political prisoners were held in the jails; now there were only 15. "The government has emptied the prisons of political prisoners," he said, "but unfortunately the cemeteries have filled with the dead. Look, in 1978 there were 147 murders for political reasons. And from only January to September of this year there are already 580 murdered—four times more than last year. The disappeared have also increased in alarming numbers. In 1977 there were 39 disappeared for political reasons, in 1978 we counted 23, and in the months of this year there are now 65 disappeared."[88]

Archbishop Romero continued his October 14 homily with the usual litany of particular cases of dead, captured, and disappeared, of cases of injustice like the new minimum wages for farm workers, of strikes, with hostages held in factories to prevent violent repression by the government. He cited the words of a nine-year-old boy asking for the release of his mother, who had disappeared: "Please, her freedom!"

"In this suffering land," he commented, "even freedom must be begged."[89]

❈ IX ❈

October 15 and After

October 1979–January 1980

On September 25, 1979, a military officer called on Romero in his office to discuss the country's situation and what Romero in his diary called "very secret intentions." Two weeks later, October 7, two officers visited him in the evening to speak of plans for a new government that they hoped to see installed within a week. Romero promised them his prayers "and all the moral collaboration that the church can offer in such delicate circumstances."

Three days later, October 10, he met with several priests and two lay advisers, Román Mayorga and Héctor Dada, to discuss what posture the church should take in the event of a coup d'état. They advised a wait-and-see attitude; the church should not make any show of solidarity that could compromise it. The church, though, should set out certain minimum objectives for a new government: it must purge the military forces, it must set out to change the structures of society, and it must let the people participate in a beginning of genuine democracy. The church would voice the people's desires and hopes for the new government.

The next day, the United States ambassador, Frank Devine, called on the archbishop with the embassy's political officer. The State Department wanted to know how the church viewed the country's situation and what it saw as the solution. Romero replied that in theory the church wanted a democratic opening but that in practice the repression and the government's weak credibility prevented it. He asked the United States government to use its influence to further an opening toward democracy. Otherwise, only a violent revolution or a coup d'état could be foreseen.

On October 13, Romero heard that something had gone wrong with the plans for the coup, perhaps a betrayal. The situation was tense. However, shortly before 8:00 A.M. on Monday, October 15, a priest telephoned and told the archbishop that the military organization would take over the army posts at eight o'clock. Romero had asked the Sisters and patients at his

200

early mass in the cancer hospital for special prayers for the country that morning.

He spent the morning in a biblical study session at the parish in Cojutepeque. The capital was quiet, with only rumors of a coup at midday. At 5:00 P.M., at last, the radio told the news. President Romero had flown to Guatemala and the nation was in new hands. The coup had been scientifically prepared and carried out. That evening the archbishop discussed the situation with priests and lay advisers. They suggested that he wait to see what would happen but that meanwhile he call on the people to avoid any extreme reaction and at the same time call on the new government to keep its promises of economic and social reforms.

Romero began preparing a public statement that evening. The next morning, the governing junta, two young colonels named Adolfo Majano and Jaime Abdul Gutiérrez, asked him to call on the people to be calm. In Mejicanos and Soyapango, two working-class suburbs of the capital, violence had broken out in reaction to the coup. The archbishop himself went on the radio during the morning to discuss the situation, and at noon the radio began to broadcast a recorded statement of his, which he termed a "pastoral appeal in the country's new situation." It was not a political message, he said, but "a deliberation in the light of our Christian faith." The church's first reaction to the coup, he went on, was to lift up its prayer to the Lord of history, giving thanks that the coup was bloodless, offering to God all the people's previous suffering in the hope that "God may furnish us a future of genuine justice and peace."

He called on the populace to be patient in looking for changes, "for the prudent observe and wait before judging and acting." He asked the privileged, "who have been guilty of so much evil and violence," to listen to the voice of the poor "as the cause of the Lord himself, who calls to conversion and is to be the judge of all." He asked the political parties and popular organizations to show "true political maturity, flexibility, and capacity for dialog." The church in turn would "continue to provide its disinterested service on the people's behalf."

In the first pronouncements of the new government Romero recognized "good will, clarity of ideas, and clear consciousness of their responsibility." However, the new rulers would have to show the people that the beautiful promises were really the beginning of a new era. As a pastor of the church, Romero was ready for dialog and collaboration with the new government. "We lay down only one condition: that we both, government and church, be conscious that our reason for being is to serve the people, each in our proper capacity."[1]

The two colonels visited the archbishop at 1:00 P.M. to thank him for his call for prudence and restraint. Romero exhorted them to show their good faith by their actions, in particular by an amnesty for political prisoners and exiles and by an investigation of the fate of the disappeared. They said they would.

The next day, Román Mayorga, the young president of the Central American University, came to speak with Romero. He was the first layman to head the Jesuit university, an engineer and economist, and one of the archbishop's frequent advisers. Romero regarded him highly. "He is a man we can trust fully," he observed in his diary. "He genuinely represents the church's mind."

The military wanted Mayorga to join the government junta, and he wanted Romero's advice. The archbishop told him he was the man for the job. His academic background would add intellectual weight to the junta and as a civilian he would balance the military men in the new government. Mayorga said he recognized the voice of God in the archbishop's words. Romero added that entering the government would not be an unconditional commitment. If things went wrong, he might have to leave, and if he, the archbishop, saw that things were wrong, he would tell him so. Mayorga knelt and asked for the archbishop's blessing.[2]

Mayorga proposed to the military that the Popular Forum, a coalition formed a month before that had united much of the opposition to the previous government, name another member to the junta, and it chose Guillermo Ungo, a leading figure of the political opposition. Ungo had run for vice-president in 1972 on a coalition ticket with the Christian Democrat José Napoleón Duarte, but a fraudulent vote count kept them from winning. Besides being active in politics, Ungo was also on the faculty of the Central American University. The Chamber of Commerce and Industry chose the third member, Mario Andino. By the end of the week, the junta had recruited its cabinet, a blue-ribbon collection of mostly young but prominent citizens.[3] The only military man was Colonel José Guillermo García, minister of defense and public security.

The coup caught the popular organizations by surprise. Their first reaction was to denounce it as simply a maneuver of the right wing to replace the incompetent General Romero with some new faces and make some cosmetic changes in order to undermine the popular opposition. A movement of young military officers who genuinely wanted a government that would respond to the people's needs did not fit their mental categories. The BPR and FAPU mostly contented themselves with angry denunciations, but the LP-28 and People's Revolutionary Army took to arms in Mejicanos and in the nearby towns of Cuscatancingo and San Marcos. The security forces put down the uprisings, leaving at least thirty-one dead and eighty wounded on Tuesday and Wednesday. In his Sunday homily, Archbishop Romero called the premature uprising "irresponsible and precipitate." At the same time, he said, the security forces must learn to confront such outbreaks in a less violent way.[4]

While condemning the hasty attempt of the LP-28 and People's Revolutionary Army because "insurrection is licit only when rational means have been exhausted," the archbishop gave his judgment that the coup of October 15 was a legitimate insurrection, because he believed that the conditions for a lawful insurrection against General Romero's regime existed. The archbishop declared that he had not blessed the coup, as a local radio station said he had; rather, he had called for calm judgment in his pastoral message. He added in the homily that the events of the week had not changed his views from what he had expressed in his message on Tuesday. "Among the members of the government junta there are persons who have my full confidence," he said, meaning no doubt Román Mayorga, Guillermo Ungo, and perhaps Colonel Majano. But it was the people, he said, who would have to judge the new government's performance and give it legitimacy. Both in its pronouncements and in the junta's press conference he found promising attitudes. Mayorga had spoken of "achieving a new society, more just and united," of "the church, which has been punished for defending the cause of human rights," and had called on God "to give us a climate of justice and peace, in order to forge a new and better nation, that he may help us rid ourselves of irrational hatred and greed." And Majano had said: "We have a new and different government, which will demonstrate its break with the past. Human life will be respected."[5]

But the promises would have to be kept, Archbishop Romero said, and therefore he was calling attention to the abuses that had continued after the coup: striking laborers brutally expelled from several factories, the search of the church and rectory of Soyapango and the arrest of the pastor, who was mistreated, and the sacristan, who had not been seen again; attacks by the Guardia Nacional on Arcatao, with one man reported dead and another captured, a helicopter terrorizing people, and the parish rectory raided. Some of the new appointments of military and civilian officials also gave cause for concern. And past violations of human rights must be righted. The disappeared must be accounted for, the guilty must be brought to judgment, and restitution must be made to victims or their survivors. Romero read with approval from a letter he had received from a citizen: the communications media also owed an explanation and satisfaction to the public for "their demonstrated complicity in the murders and corruption of the previous government."[6]

He agreed with the writer of the letter that the new government ought to return 50 million colóns ($20 million) that had been given to the armed forces from the budgets of other ministries, and he asked the United States not to resume military aid to El Salvador. He cited with approval the words of the letter he had received: "We are tired of weapons and bullets. Our hunger is for justice, for food, medicine, education, and effective programs of fair development. If human rights come to be respected, we will have no need at all for weapons or methods of death."[7]

The second half of October was a time of turmoil as the new junta tried to get the government and the country under control. The BPR seized the labor, social service, and economy ministries, with a large number of hostages, including the three ministers. FAPU had a demonstration broken up by the security forces on Monday, the 22d. The following Monday the security forces massacred seventy persons in an attack on a demonstration of the LP-28, and the next day United States marines used tear gas on the LP-28 in front of the United States embassy. On Wednesday, October 31, security forces killed twenty persons while breaking up a BPR parade. The People's Revolutionary Army set off bombs in a bank and two newspaper buildings, and killed a Guardia lieutenant accused of being a chief torturer. The FPL ambushed a Guardia patrol near Zacatecoluca, killing six guardsmen.[8]

Serious as the opposition of the large popular protest organizations and small guerrilla groups was, the junta's biggest problem was its own armed forces. They were acting even more savagely than before. Various persons arrested in the latest repression disappeared, and no word was forthcoming of the hundreds who had disappeared before. Romero reminded the military in his homily on October 28 that the constitution required them to guarantee the people's constitutional rights. He called for "the courage to judge and fix responsibilities and to punish those responsible."[9]

At the same time he criticized the "fanaticism" of the popular organizations. He agreed with their broad objectives and thought that they had done much for the people in arousing their awareness, but they should give the new government a chance, since it had virtually the same objectives as they did. He had warned in his fourth pastoral letter of the danger of making the organization itself an absolute, and the danger was present here. The organizations, instead of looking to the good of the people, feared losing their own following if the government's reforms succeeded.[10]

Romero wondered in his homily of November 4 if the security forces were not also trying to weaken the government, robbing it of credibility by their brutality. He himself had mediated a serious crisis the previous Thursday, November 1, which reveals some of the tension that prevailed. The LP-28 were occupying the church of El Rosario, the Dominican church a block away from the cathedral on the Plaza Libertad. They had captured a guardsman who had tried to force his way in, and the Guardia Nacional was ready to go in after him, even though it would likely mean his death and that of many others. Romero was asked to mediate, and it was night when he arrived at the big arch-shaped church. The attorney general and several priests were also present.

It turned out that the LP-28 had called the attorney general in order to turn over their prisoner to him unharmed. But a rumor had reached the Guardia that they were torturing him and were going to kill him slowly, and guardsmen had surrounded the church in preparation for an attack when the man was finally handed over at almost 1:00 A.M. "Along with the intermediaries, I urged the LP-28 to turn over the man quickly, and they did so in fact and the storm that was seen coming was calmed. But what I'm talking about here is the aggressiveness, which I felt at close hand—though I noticed in the younger officers an eagerness to calm people and a capacity for dialog. But in the others, an almost uncontrollable aggressiveness."

The night was not over. The Guardia was satisfied, but another rumor had it that two policemen were also captive, and the National Police force was now threatening drastic action. Romero himself went in with policemen whom the occupiers allowed to enter and search. "There was no policeman, either among the living or the dead—there were twenty-one bodies there. So the second phase of Thursday night's storm was also calmed."[11]

The tension in El Salvador caused Romero to cancel a trip to New York to address the National Council of Churches. They had planned three days of activity, including a service in Riverside church next to their headquarters and a mass in St. Patrick's cathedral.

On November 5, Romero received a message from the papal nuncio in Costa Rica, advising him of a rumor that a far leftist group was plotting his assassination in order to cause problems for the government. Similar rumors had circulated before, accusing the left of the deaths of the murdered priests, and the bishops who opposed Romero had seized upon them to exonerate the government and the far right (see chap. VIII). Romero thought the present rumor was probably just one of the usual ones that this time had reached the Vatican, but he decided to take "prudent care, but without exaggeration," as he had done with threats coming from the right. As early as the previous January 4 he had been threatened, and in May he had received the written threat, complete with swastika, in a government envelope (see chap. VIII), besides anonymous phone calls at various times. Considering that this warning had come from the Vatican, however, he went to see Archbishop Gerada, the nuncio in San Salvador, to report it. They also discussed the bishops' disunion and the country's situation. Romero noted in his diary that Gerada was concerned that the Vatican had not yet recognized the new government.

Romero spoke of the threat in his November 11 homily, observing that there had been considerable publicity about it but questioning why the publicity accentuated that it came from the left. Some, he said, wondered if it was not all a maneuver of the far right to get him to keep quiet. "I leave the question open," he said. "I have indeed said that if I am in danger, it could be from the extremes for whom I am a nuisance. But I want to assure you, and I ask your prayers to be faithful to this promise, that I will not abandon my people but will share with them all the risks that my ministry demands of me."

After the incident at El Rosario on November 1, the security forces restricted their actions for the rest of the month. It was a sign of hope. An investigating commission was formed to look into past abuses of human rights, especially to learn what had happened to the two hundred or so persons arrested and disappeared. Unfortunately, some had also disappeared under the junta, and Romero repeated each Sunday his call for an explanation of the disappearance of the sacristan of the church of Soyapango, who had been arrested on October 16. On November 25, he read to the people an account of the discovery of a secret cell hidden under loose floor tiles in the headquarters of the Treasury Police; prisoners had written their names on the walls of the cell. "I go," one had written, "but my hatred remains."[12]

Yet Romero saw encouraging signs. Various organizations had held demonstrations without incident. People and groups were speaking out publicly. A different political climate was forming, even though injustice and abuse still abounded. On the feast of Christ the King, November 25, Romero concluded his homily: "Those who govern have a great challenge thrust at them not only by the suffering of the people but above all by the justice of God, who made us all equal, his images, sharers in the dignity of Christ the Redeemer, so that we might enjoy with him the same happiness, while making this earth an antechamber of the kingdom beyond. The feast of Christ the King fills us with hope, because he lives; and from our prayers, our work, and our solidarity, relying on that faith and that hope, we will keep on seeking a better world."[13]

The bishops' conference had postponed its elections at its regular meeting the preceding July, and on November 19, 1979, it met at 10:20 A.M. in the seminary of San José de la Montaña to elect its new officers. The six member bishops were present, along with the apostolic nuncio, Archbishop Emanuele Gerada, and the CEDES secretary-general, Monsignor Freddy Delgado.

The nuncio addressed the bishops, underscoring the importance of the two main items on the agenda, the election of new officers and the discussion of the state of the country. He informed them that he would probably be leaving his post as nuncio to El Salvador and Guatemala within a few months. He had tried to improve relations between the church and the state and to unite the bishops of El Salvador, he said, though so far he had not succeeded. He remarked on the new government's good intentions and the high quality of its members, on the determination of secret opposition forces that sought to take power by an insurrection, and on the destruction being wrought by the continued violence. The church of the archdiocese had made its voice heard, but the conference had not. The circumstances demanded greater unity among the bishops. He warned them to keep the church out of politics and suggested that they name a conciliating commission, for example of Bishops Rivera and Revelo, to try to find ways to unify the church's activity.

The president, Bishop Aparicio, replied to the nuncio's remarks, thanking him for his service as nuncio and apologizing for the conflicts they had had with him. He suggested that the disunity of the conference might be due to outside elements, beginning with a French priest who had worked in El Salvador some years before. He called on the bishops to each recognize his own faults, as they seemed to him disposed to do, asking the nuncio to inform the Holy See of their attitude and of the outside forces that had tried to divide the bishops and the clergy.[14]

After Gerada had left, Archbishop Romero backed the nuncio's suggestion that a conciliating commission be named to look for ways to unite the bishops. Aparicio said it did not seem very necessary to him but they could take it up after the elections. The bishops proceeded to vote for the president and vice-president of the conference. Under the norms of canon law, they would be elected on a single vote, the president to be elected by a majority vote and the runner-up to be vice-president.

On the first ballot, no one received a majority: Aparicio 3, Alvarez 1, Rivera 1, Romero 1. The second ballot gave exactly the same result. Since one cannot vote for oneself in canonical elections, it seemed that Romero and Rivera were voting for each other, Aparicio was voting for Alvarez, and the rest were voting for Aparicio.

Romero renewed his plea to form the commission suggested by the nuncio. The voting showed that the conference was polarized, he said.

Alvarez objected. There was no polarization, he said.

"We see it," said Romero.

"Let's take another vote," said Alvarez.

Romero objected that the voting had already shown how things stood.

The only one with any support was Aparicio, said Alvarez.

Romero agreed, but the vote showed they were stalemated. "It's better that the commission that was suggested should get to work."

"What reason does the nuncio have—he can't—" spluttered Alvarez.

"It's a suggestion."

"He can't even suggest."

"Why not?"

Aparicio interrupted to remark that he had foreseen such an impasse when the elections were postponed in July. Alvarez remarked how the nuncio had insisted on their staying out of politics. Barrera wanted to consider the nuncio's suggestion. Aparicio insisted on continuing the elections, and he proposed that Alvarez be elected president. Alvarez demurred and said Aparicio was the better choice for the crucial times they were in.

"The nuncio's suggestion seems to me a solution that would enable us to get to work," Romero said.

"It all depends on if the nuncio had consulted with each one about it," objected Alvarez. "I don't accept it. As I see it, there is no division."

"It offers possibilities," countered Rivera.

"There are no possibilities as long as YSAX keeps calling us bishops liars, and *Orientación*—" declared Aparicio. "That's too much for any kind of unity. When Father Colorado came I complained to him about the way they insult the bishops."

According to canon 101, a mere plurality, not an absolute majority, would suffice to elect a president on the third ballot. Monsignor Delgado, the secretary, read the result: Aparicio 2, Alvarez 2, Rivera 1, Romero 1. A tie.

They took more votes to break the tie. The fourth and fifth ballots yielded the same result as the third. The sixth ballot: Aparicio 2, Alvarez 2, Barrera 1, Romero 1. Still a tie.

Delgado asked if the election of president and vice-president could not be left pending and the members elected to the conference's working commissions. The uncertainty, he said, was keeping the commissions from getting anything done and Rome was constantly making inquiries and sending documents needing replies that could not be given.

Romero agreed with the idea of turning to the commission elections. Rivera reminded them they had other business to consider also.

Aparicio objected: "This is what we are here for."

Delgado suggested they stop after ten ballots. They already had six.

The seventh ballot: null; seven votes were cast. They voted the seventh ballot again: Rivera 2, Barrera 2, Aparicio 1, Romero 1. The eighth: Rivera 2, Barrera 1, Alvarez 1, Aparicio 1, Romero 1.

The tie was broken, but no one had a majority. No one had realized that a majority was not needed after the first two ballots. They continued balloting. The ninth and tenth ballots yielded another tie: Aparicio 2, Rivera 2, Alvarez 1, Romero 1.

"It's twelve noon," Rivera pointed out.

"We still have to discuss the state of the country," said Romero.

"I understand the importance of this for the archdiocese and the clergy of the other dioceses," Aparicio said. "I called for the elections to eliminate this impasse."

Rivera said, "It's been clear from the first two votes that the lineup has not changed. I think that people are expecting something also in the bishops' conference."

"Well," said Alvarez, "we still have what the nuncio proposed. People are expecting—."

"Well, yes, that there be a change of president in the conference," said Rivera.

"Well, I think if you two [Romero and Rivera] are chosen that will take care of everything," said Alvarez.

"No," said Rivera, "we expressed a desire."

"Let's skip the diplomacy," Aparicio said. "You have to look at the truth as it is. I'm not—only God knows how much this has affected me, and the attacks they have made on me, and the way the vicariates of San Salvador have treated me. If the other bishops agree, I agree that one of them should be president and the other vice-president. Even if they have both offices, I don't think that will take anything away from us."

"It has nothing to do with attacks or anything of the sort," Romero stated. "Impartially, Bishop Rivera is the president. I feel the conference is discredited."

"But, who has discredited it? I want you to say so if I have."

"Not everything is your responsibility," Romero replied to Aparicio. "You're getting irritated."

"No, no—we're alone," said Aparicio. "Let's speak clearly."

"Let's rather—"

"I'm not going to get sore," Aparicio broke in to Romero's words.

"It's just something objective that I think we all see: they want a change," Romero continued.

Aparicio said, "I have never spoken from the pulpit against you, never. I told you the last time: let's speak clearly to each other. I like to be told clearly: this or that."

Delgado interrupted to suggest that they choose among those who had received the most votes on the ten ballots.

Ignoring him, Alvarez intervened to tell Romero that a group of priests was influencing him, as the other bishops had said right along. The problem, he said, all stemmed from the letter that the bishops had issued against FECCAS-UTC the year before and because they would not sign Romero's letter on the popular organizations. Now, he said, "those organizations have turned against you too."

Revelo supported Delgado's suggestion. They could choose among Aparicio, Rivera, and Alvarez, the three who had received the most votes.

They voted for the eleventh time: Alvarez 3, Aparicio 1, Rivera 2. Was Alvarez elected? They recalled canon 101: after the first two votes, a plurality was sufficient.

"Then, on the eighth vote, Bishop Rivera has two votes and we each have one," said Romero.

Aparicio replied that as president he had the right to vote twice and that he would give his vote to Alvarez. Rivera explained that the president had a second vote only to break a tie, and there was no tie on the eighth ballot. He, Rivera, had a clear plurality.

Then, said Delgado, on the third ballot there had been a tie and the president had a right to break it. No, said Rivera, not when the president was a party to the case. They went over the results of the ballotings again. Delgado suggested another vote to settle it.

"I'm more and more convinced," said Romero, "that this matter should be prepared ahead of time."

"Look, Your Excellency," said Alvarez. "The election would be done with already. We know quite well that the principal city of El Salvador is the capital. It would be more suitable that the archbishop of San Salvador should also be the president of the assembly, but since you are involved in such a conflictive situation, without giving pastoral care, and monopolized by all those things and those groups— But we have seen the results; at least speaking personally, that's why I do not vote for you. No, it would be natural; San Salvador is the principal city. I could show you all the papers they have sent me from here, those guerrilla papers. No, well, says the archbishop, sincerely, this has to be prepared with more care and devotion."

They took a twelfth vote: Alvarez 3, Rivera 2, Aparicio 1. "Bishop Alvarez is elected," said Revelo.

"I think so," said Aparicio. "Now for the vice-president."

Alvarez and Revelo explained that he was already elected. The runner-up was vice-president.

"Oh—all right," said Aparicio. "I didn't understand that at all."[15]

With Alvarez now presiding, and with better attention to canon 101, they elected their treasurer (Revelo), secretary-general (Delgado), permanent committee (Revelo—the archbishop was a member ex officio), and heads of commissions: catechesis (Revelo), liturgy (Rivera), missions (Barrera), vocations and ministries (Aparicio), laity (Rivera), education (Aparicio), communications media (Romero), Caritas (Revelo), social action (Aparicio), faith (Rivera), ecumenism and nonbelievers (Rivera), administration and church patrimony (Revelo), justice and peace (Romero), seminaries (Revelo), bilateral commission of CEDES and the conference of religious (Rivera). As delegate to CELAM they elected Rivera and as substitute Revelo, whom they also elected to represent the conference in the priests' cooperative.

The discussion of the state of the country was left for their January meeting, and they adjourned at 5:00 P.M.[16]

A commentary on YSAX the next day noted that the election results were disturbing but not surprising. "It is quite disconcerting that the new president is Bishop Alvarez, an armed forces colonel at present and, particularly, in the past. It is very disconcerting that, with the exception of Bishop Rivera, the bishops who have acquired greater power have not made their own the guidelines of Medellín and Puebla, have not been distinguished for furthering the preferential option for the poor but have even rejected it, have not been distinguished for being on the side of the people in the hard times of repression and persecution." They had rejected the archbishop for the leadership posts even though the people viewed him as the best qualified spokesman for the church and the firmest proponent of a church of and for the poor. While it was encouraging that he would head the commissions on communications media and justice and peace, "it is surprising that they have not entrusted to him areas that concern the very life of the church, such as evangelization, liturgy, faith, and seminaries." It seemed as if the other bishops recognized in Romero "a good bishop in his relations with society, but not so good—or dangerous—for determining what the church itself is."[17]

The day after the election, Romero wrote to the nuncio, who had left before the voting, that the conference had acted illegally in conferring the presidency on Alvarez instead of on Rivera, who had received a plurality on the eighth ballot. Further, he said, since Alvarez was not elected, he acted illegally in breaking tie votes for the later elections for three of the commissions. Romero wrote:

Besides the legal aspect, I think that the country's ecclesial and political circumstances require for the office of president of the episcopate the personality of Bishop Rivera. You yourself recommended him, along with Bishop Revelo, to make up a commission to work for the lost unity of our episcopate. I supported this opportune suggestion of yours and proposed that this work of peacemaking be done before the elections, but Bishops Aparicio and Alvarez, principally, roundly rejected it. Indeed, the person of Bishop Rivera seems to me the most conciliatory for overcoming the differences in CEDES. I believe too that his critical ability and his prudence make Bishop Rivera the most suitable bishop to give a new face to our collegiality. Politically and socially, a feeling of change and hope is abroad in which the voice of a church identified with the sufferings and hopes of our people can be heard with attention. The disrepute into which our conference has regrettably fallen, inside and outside the church, occasioned by events like the one I am writing about, will keep increasing if, to preside over it and represent it, one is chosen who is well known for the frivolity and superficiality of his judgments and words and for his notorious involvement with the political and social situations that we are trying to overcome in the whole country.

He requested the nuncio to ask the Congregation for the Bishops to intervene and make Rivera president. As though anticipating disappointment, he added: "In any case, I have the satisfaction of having done my duty in conscience in reporting this arbitrary injustice."

On December 2, the bishops and the nuncio all found themselves present in Santiago de María for the silver anniversary of the diocese, and they decided to have a meeting to settle the matter of the election that Romero had challenged. They gathered at 11:00 A.M. in the dingy diocesan offices next to the little cathedral.

Romero explained his objection, on the grounds that Rivera had been elected on the eighth ballot. Aparicio replied: "If the problem is canonical, then according to canon 101 I am the one elected. The canon expressly says: 'If on the third vote there is a tie, the president will break it with his vote. If it is an election and the president does not want to break it with his vote, the senior by ordination or first profession or in age will be elected.' On the third vote, Bishop Alvarez and I tied; and since I am the senior by ordination and by age, I am elected."

Rivera and Revelo discussed the canon, and Romero suggested that they let everything stand as it was.

Aparicio said: "I renounce my right in favor of Bishop Alvarez. Anyway, we officially announced the naming of Bishop Alvarez as president. It would be embarrassing to change at this point."

They all agreed, and at twelve noon they adjourned.[18]

The next day Freddy Delgado sent Romero a note convoking another meeting of CEDES on December 5 to consider once again the validity of the election. Aparicio, Barrera, and Revelo had called the meeting.

Romero replied immediately and with evident irritation that he would not attend, "first, because I have a previous commitment, but especially because I judge that there is no reason for the convocation and meeting. The matter indicated for the agenda was already treated and resolved in the legal meeting that we held last Sunday in Santiago de María."

In spite of his objections and his conviction that Rivera was really elected, Romero said he had yielded "for the sake of peace" and agreed to the election of Alvarez. "It seems to me a lesser evil." Aparicio, he went on, "out of honesty and especially for the good of our church, should give up his evident desire to continue as president. It would likewise be decent and consistent that he give up the education and seminary commissions," which he had held on to. "If the meeting in Santiago de María is invalidated, that will be a new arbitrary action, such as I have said have discredited our conference. In that case, let all the documentation be sent to Rome, including my two letters, the one I wrote to the nuncio and this one."[19]

Four bishops met on December 5, with the nuncio and Freddy Delgado present, but without Romero and Rivera. The bishops decided that in the light of canon 101 Aparicio was elected president and Alvarez vice-president on the third ballot taken on November 19. They did not discuss the validity of the actions taken by Alvarez as president, and they voted to ask the Holy See to make the final decision on their action. They voted, furthermore, to register in the minutes their formal protest before the Holy See and their vote of censure of the archbishop of San Salvador "for the discourteous and offensive letter against the bishops' conference and against certain bishops with which His Excellency, Oscar A. Romero, archbishop of San Salvador, replied to the invitation to the present meeting made to him by the secretary-general of CEDES, of which he sent copies to the nunciature and to the bishops. They object to the threat that he makes in the letter, because they consider this stance creative of greater tension among the bishops and hardly fraternal."[20]

The conference made no public announcement of the change in the election results. Church people knew, of course, that the bishops had reversed themselves.

On March 12, 1980, the bishops met at a retreat house outside of San Salvador at the instance of Archbishop Lajos Kada, papal nuncio to Costa Rica, who had been sent by the Vatican to unify the Salvadoran bishops. Romero suggested that they confirm Alvarez as president, which they did. But when they elected a vice-president, they chose Aparicio instead of Rivera.

Romero was disappointed, as he wrote to Kada later: "I believe that the same reasons that supported my suggestion to confirm Bishop Alvarez as president would be valid also to confirm Bishop Rivera as vice-president: to give unanimous witness of our good will and effort to be united and to conceal from outsiders the anomaly of the former election. It is also fitting to have represented in the executive both of the 'two fractions' that you mentioned with such candor at the beginning of our discussion."[21]

The day after the meeting and new election, Kada spoke with Romero about moving his offices from the seminary building, apparently another mission Kada had received from Rome. While Romero did not agree that the offices seriously hampered the seminary, he had been having meetings with staff members for some time about building a separate building and he assured Kada that he planned to do so as soon as the means could be found. Romero took him to dine with him and the Sisters at the cancer hospital, and afterwards they discussed the bishops' meeting of the day before. Kada admitted that Aparicio and Alvarez had attacked Romero with considerable animus at the meeting, but he insisted that Romero himself was largely responsible for the bishops' division and that he should cede wherever possible. Romero remarked in his diary that he was willing to do so, but not when it was a matter of faithfulness to the gospel, to the church's teaching, and to the people.

Romero rarely missed his 8:00 A.M. Sunday mass in the cathedral (or in another downtown church if the cathedral was occupied by some protest group). He restricted his travel in order to celebrate the principal mass of the diocese and address his people. The whole archdiocese, and indeed the whole nation, listened to him, and even those without radios could usually get near enough to an open window or to a market woman's portable so as to listen. During his three years as archbishop, Romero never took an extended vacation, but he did occasionally miss the Sunday mass for an important, brief trip.

One such trip was the occasion of the twenty-fifth anniversary on December 2 of the diocese of Santiago de María, where he had been the second bishop and where his loyal associate Bishop Rivera was now the third. It was a happy homecoming for Romero, in spite of the rather unpleasant bishops' conference meeting that took place (see above).

The short trip to Santiago was hardly an escape from duty or a rest, but Romero managed to combine duty and pleasure in a brief trip to Guatemala a few days later. The Sisters who operated the hospital where he lived invited him to receive the first vows of several young Sisters at their novitiate in Guatemala, on the shores of a picturesque lake. He drove to Guatemala with his friend Salvador Barraza, who often accompanied him on similar excursions. Barraza recalled that they passed a light truck that was stuck by the roadside and, a few miles beyond, Romero said they should go back to help. They tried to help the driver push the truck free, and Romero dropped and broke his eyeglasses in the effort. They then drove miles out of their way to take the driver to his destination. The trucker never suspected that one of his helpers was the archbishop of San Salvador.

In Guatemala City Romero and Barraza shopped for books while they waited for Romero's new glasses and tried to find a cassette to use in learning French. Romero was to travel to Belgium in February to receive an honorary degree from Louvain University and wanted to brush up on his French. He had to settle for a book on French instead, but he bought a cassette of marimba music, one of his favorites, to use in the tape deck in his car. He witnessed the young Sisters' vows on Saturday, December 8, feast of the Immaculate Conception, and then hurried back to San Salvador to prepare for Sunday morning mass. Although he enjoyed getting away, eating a late supper and drinking a beer peacefully with Barraza in a place where he wasn't known, nevertheless it was as bishop with his people that he felt most at home, in spite of the strains and the burdens.[22]

In his homily of December 9 Romero could still speak of the new atmosphere of freedom in El Salvador: "The church no longer has to be the voice of those who have no voice. Today many can speak out and are speaking." But he noted also that the previous days had been filled with conflict. The oligarchy, surprised at first by the coup d'état, had now reacted vigorously. They were calling production stoppages, and labor and peasant unions were reacting with sit-down strikes and in some cases holding hostages. The oligarchy had begun mobilizing women for its demonstrations, taking their cue from their counterparts in Chile in 1973, when affluent women banged saucepans in the streets in an effort to weaken the Allende government. He rejoiced that the investigating commission was looking into human rights violations and was making recommendations for the future.[23]

But the oligarchy had reasserted itself in public with its demonstrations and with a publicity campaign that began in the media in mid-November, and right-wing officers had gained control of the army, beginning with the naming of Colonel José Guillermo García, before the junta was even named publicly. In the first days of the new government Romero had told García that he had been named illegally, since only Majano and Gutiérrez had named him, and that he should resign. García offered his resignation on the spot to Majano, who refused it, no doubt fearing that the army would follow García.[24] Romero continued to urge García to resign, even doing so in his homilies.

Through García, the right was able to place its military sympathizers in key spots. At a meeting in the military academy on December 18, it restructured the entire high command, placing its own people in charge. In effect, it was a countercoup, and the days of the junta were numbered.[25]

The formula for the future would be repression with reforms. The most needed was land reform, and a program was announced in mid-December. In speaking of it, Romero cited for his listeners on December 16 some of the government's own statistics: 67 percent of peasant women gave birth with no medical assistance; sixty of each 1,000 campesino children died in their first year; only 37 percent of rural families had access to springs of water; 73 percent of campesino children were undernourished; half the rural adult population could not read; over 250,000 rural families lived in one-room dwellings, with an average of five or six members in each family; 99 percent of the landowners shared only 51 percent of the land, and 0.7 percent held 40 percent—and the best land, at that. He praised the beginning of the land reform process but warned that it was only a beginning and a promise. He called on the government and the landowners who would be affected by the reform to fulfill the promise of eventual justice for the campesinos.[26]

On December 19, militants of the LP-28 seized the archdiocesan offices and the entire seminary building and held them for three days. It was the low point of Romero's relations with the popular organizations. One of the occupants accused him to his face of having swung completely around and aligned himself with the powerful, because of his support of the junta. Romero's diary shows that he was pained by the accusation and by the evidence that a few priests and members of grass-roots church communities identified with the occupiers. A public statement a month before from some priests, nuns, and grass-roots community members had expressed discontent with the policy the archdiocese was following. Several meetings of the priests' senate and the archdiocesan pastoral commission had taken up the subject, and Romero found a majority with him. For him and his supporters the statement and its defenders evidenced the danger of pastoral workers' becoming committed to the popular organizations, which he had warned of in his third and fourth pastoral letters.[27]

The reason alleged for the occupation was to pressure the archdiocese to speak out against the violence used by the security forces in recent evictions of protesters and to intercede for the release of those arrested. The archdiocesan legal aid office was already working on the cases, and the incident ended with the abandonment of the offices and seminary on December 22. But it dramatized that once again El Salvador was in the midst of strife and repression.[28]

In his Christmas sermon on the night of the 24th, Romero called for hope: "The country is giving birth to a new age, and therefore there are pain and anguish, blood and suffering. But as in childbirth, says Christ, the woman whose hour has come suffers, but when the new child has been born she then forgets all her pains. These sufferings will pass. Our joy will be that in this hour of childbirth we were Christians, that we lived clinging to faith in Christ, that pessimism did not overcome us. How I would like to cry out over all the fields of El Salvador this night the angels' great news: Fear not! A Savior is born! What now seems insoluble, a dead end, God is already marking with a hope."

The military high command had begun treating the junta as its servant since the meeting of December 18, calling it to meetings at the military's convenience. On December 26, the high command summoned the junta and the cabinet once again, and several high officers bluntly told the civilians that they were in the government at the military's pleasure. It was now clear to the civilians that they could not continue in the government under those circumstances. The military leaders were willing to permit some reforms but would not share power or relinquish their presumed right to kill, beat, torture, or imprison anyone they chose.[29] Within days, the cabinet, Supreme Court, and heads of various government bodies sent an ultimatum to the military calling for a reassertion of the government's power over the armed forces.[30] But it was too late.

On the last day of 1979, the minister of health asked the archbishop to intervene, and Romero invited the junta and the officials who had signed the document to a meeting in the seminary on January 2, 1980. He called it an informal, friendly meeting in which his position "was that of a representative of a great part of the people who trusted in the church."[31]

But Romero was also the pastor of those present at the meeting. He quietly advised them to consider carefully what was best for the people and then each one decide according to his own conscience and not out of emotionalism or group spirit. Before the meeting was over, radio and television stations were broadcasting the military's reply to the government challenge. The military leaders conceded some points and held firm on others, but they were clearly not submitting to the government's authority.

That afternoon the ministers of agriculture and education and three other high officials resigned together. The next day, all who had signed the ultimatum resigned—cabinet members, the Supreme Court, and the other high officials. The same day Mayorga and Ungo resigned from the junta. All of them explained their leaving as a protest at the impossibility of carrying out the reforms promised by the October 15 movement. The other civilian, Mario Andino, also resigned from the junta, in order to leave the military free to form a new government, and various other officials did the same. Besides the two colonels on the junta, only one high official remained—Colonel José Guillermo García, minister of defense and public security.[32]

The human rights investigating commission hastened to complete its work and its report. The failure of the attempt at a reform government was ominous. What would become of the reforms begun, such as the land reform and the nationalization of the exportation of coffee and sugar? Romero raised the questions in his homily on January 6 and observed:

At this moment, I want to restate my conviction, as a man of hope, that a new ray of salvation will appear. And I want to encourage those who have the kindness to listen to me to have the same conviction. No one has the right to sink into despair. We all have the duty to seek together new channels and to hope actively, as Christians.

These events and these questions lead me to make the following pastoral appeal, which is my intent in what I am about to say to you. What must be saved before all is our people's movement toward liberation. The people have begun a movement which has already cost much blood and which must not be wasted. The crisis in this movement must be resolved by making the movement succeed. That is what we must seek. Using a comparison from today's gospel [the story of the Magi], we might say that the star that must today guide the people, the government, and the various sectors must be this: how to keep the people's movement toward social justice from becoming stagnant and atrophied, how to save it and further it.[33]

Already on December 31 the Christian Democratic Party had offered to form a new government with the military, a fact that may have stiffened the latter's defiance of the first junta and its ministers. Two Christian Democrats of renown, Antonio Morales Ehrlich and Héctor Dada, and a physician with no political experience, José Ramón Avalos, joined the two colonels on the junta. Dada had been foreign minister for the first junta and constituted virtually the only civilian link with it. The head of the Christian Democratic Party, José Napoleón Duarte, preferred to remain off the junta. This time it was harder to find ministers and officials, and the new government spent most of January 1980 getting organized. On paper, the Christian Democrats demanded and got guarantees from the military as stringent as those demanded by the government officials who had resigned.[34] But in fact the military would continue to repress opposition with violence.

In his January 6 homily Romero called on the new government to seek the nation's unity in the common good of the people and in the people's organizations, not only in the armed forces. He praised the officials who had resigned for their efforts on behalf of the country, and he reminded the military that they were to serve the people. He said that Colonel García should also resign "out of honesty and as a sign that he seeks the genuine good." The people applauded that.[35] Four days later García came to see Romero to protest his view of him. They spoke for nearly two hours, Romero recorded in his diary.

On the last day of 1979 Cardinal Aloísio Lorscheider arrived in San Salvador to make a brief visit on behalf of the Holy See. It was a fact-finding mission rather than a canonical visitation, "in order to render a personal account of the church's situation amid all that was happening," as Lorscheider later described it.[36] He came from Nicaragua, then only six months into the Sandinista revolution after the overthrow of Anastasio Somoza, and after three days in El Salvador he left for Costa Rica. Romero met him at the airport on his arrival, where he also found the nuncio and Bishop Revelo. Romero had arranged for Lorscheider to stay in the home of the secretary of the Christian Democratic Party, but Lorscheider preferred to stay with Romero in the little house at the hospital, one of only a few who did so, saying, "This way I show that I am with you." Romero regarded his visit as a support and a chance to convey his views to Rome rather than as a sign of Roman misgivings.[37]

Lorscheider had been president of CELAM at the time of the Puebla conference and was one of the three presidents of the Puebla assembly. He was an important leader of the Brazilian hierarchy and of the Latin American church, and he and Romero saw pastoral matters much the same way. He told Romero he had read his pastoral letters and some of his homilies and found them perfectly correct. "I feel in this visit of this new envoy of the pope a further confirmation of the work our archdiocese is doing," Romero told the people in his January 6 homily.[38]

Besides talking with the archbishop, Lorscheider conferred with a number of priests and religious, and asked for written reports on the church and the country. Romero followed up the visit with a letter to him, dated January 4, in which he reiterated some of the chief concerns they had discussed during the visit. He recounted all the problems with his auxiliary: Revelo's failure to come to meetings, his baptizing in his parish without the parents' instructions required in the diocese, his continuing to confirm infants when the archdiocese had dropped the practice in favor of a program of catechetical preparation of adolescents followed by confirmation, his omission of marriage instructions in his parish, his signing of the Caritas document against Romero's wishes, his private and public statements against the archbishop. "In view of these past and present attitudes," he wrote, "I do not know how I can work with him in the mission that the Lord and the church ask of us. I thought this problem was solved when I visited Cardinal Baggio last May and he assured me he would be changed to another diocese. I think that is best, and as soon as possible."

The disunion of the bishops' conference, he continued, was "very painful and sad, and a scandal for the faithful." Rivera, he said, fulfilled completely what Vatican Council II and Puebla demanded of pastors, but the others did not. Even though 60 percent of the seminarians pertained to the archdiocese, the conference had just named Aparicio, who had sent all his own seminarians to Mexico, to the seminary commission, along with Revelo, the archbishop's problematic auxiliary. At the December meeting, in the absence of Rivera and Romero, the other four had made changes in the seminary staff, rejecting four teachers, even though Rivera and Romero were content with the staff. At the same meeting they had named as executive secretary of the bishops' social action commission a retired priest of the archdiocese who had written articles for the newspapers attacking the archbishop and calling him a Marxist. "I cannot understand any of this," wrote Romero.

The church in the country needed new and different bishops, Romero said. He suggested five candidates. "All of them, in my judgment, are balanced priests who are truly of one mind with the church and sense what the church demands of a bishop in its conciliar and other documents."

He concluded: "I think very much about the future of the church and the country, and with concern. It is a crucial moment in our church and in our land. In the measure that we manage to respond to what God and the church hope of us, we make grow the message of the gospel—or we can perhaps, God forbid, be rejected."

For Romero, Lorscheider's visit was a comforting sign of concern and support. "I saw how much Archbishop Romero was committed to his people," Lorscheider later wrote, "and the force and authenticity of his witness. He was a true shepherd who was ready to give his life for his sheep—which is what happened, as could well be foreseen."[39]

The Christian Democrats spent all of January 1980 without putting together a complete cabinet. Few persons of note wanted to try to govern with them and the military after the failure of the first junta. The first junta's education minister, Salvador Samayoa, announced that he had joined the FPL and went underground. On January 11 the three coalitions of mass movements, FAPU, the BPR, and the LP-28 joined with the leftist National Democratic Union to form the Mass Movements Revolutionary Coordinating Commission to coordinate their political activity. It was the beginning of the union of the left, bringing together the political forces that were closest to the people. Ten days later, Guillermo Ungo's social democratic Nationalist Revolutionary Movement also joined the Coordinating Commission. Meanwhile, two of the three armed resistance organizations, the FPL and the National Resistance, joined forces with the Communist Party to coordinate their military activities.[40]

In his homilies of January 13 and 20, Romero analyzed the political options proposed to the country by different forces and divided them into three: the program of the oligarchy, that of the government, and that of the leftist popular forces.

The oligarchy wanted no social change, and its answer to those who did was simply violent repression. It had with it part of the business and commercial sector and part of the military. It was also behind the activities of forces like the White Warrior Union. Recalling words of John Paul II at Puebla, Romero plainly condemned the oligarchy's program: "The church does defend the lawful right of private property, but it teaches with no less clearness that all private property is under a 'social mortgage' "—under lien to the common good.[41] Romero called the oligarchy to conversion: "Again, in the name of our people and our church, I call on them to hear the voice of God and joyously share their power and wealth with all, instead of provoking a civil war that will bathe us in blood. There is still time to take the rings from their fingers before they lose the hand."[42]

The government of Christian Democrats and military forces was promising change and reform, Romero said, but so far it was providing mostly bloody repression. Each week in his homilies Romero was still reading a list of murders and disappearances carried out by government forces. He urged the Christian Democrats and others in the government to heed a statement published by a group of former officials of the previous government.

According to these ex-officials, possibilities have been exhausted for establishing reformist solutions in alliance with the present leadership of the armed forces, dominated by pro-oligarchic elements, and without real participation of the people. The solution that these former officials propose is to set up a democratic regime, one of genuine social justice, that demands as a fundamental element—these are their words—"as a fundamental element it requires the participation and direction of the people, their popular and democratic organizations, and genuine confrontation of the oligarchy and its allies."... No government can ever become established that, along with its promises of change and social justice, is staining itself more each day, with the alarming reports that come to us from everywhere of repressive cruelty at the expense of the people themselves.[43]

The popular forces that were growing in unity shared an ideal of a democratic government and social justice, but differed in their ideologies and methods. Romero viewed with approval the growing unity, which he saw as a sign of political maturity, and he approved their goals of justice and democracy. But he criticized them for refusing to cooperate with the government in carrying out reforms—most of them had opposed the first junta as well—and for using violent means, a criticism that fell especially on the armed groups. He also condemned examples of antireligious ideology—he deplored a flyer given to children that said, "You waited in vain for God above to send you your daily bread." He pleaded for the kidnapped persons held by extremist groups and pointed out the inconsistency of condemning imperialism but not mentioning the Soviet intervention in Afghanistan.[44] "I want to tell them the same thing I tell the government: words and promises are not enough, especially when they are shouted with frenzy and demagogy. Deeds are needed. For my part, as pastor, I will watch to see if these deeds really show that the popular organizations are able to further their broader unity with the traits I have just indicated."[45]

Romero ended the January 20 homily with an appeal to all to avoid civil war and to achieve justice in the land. "It is indispensable that we all be ready to share with the rest what we are and what we have, and to participate in the measure of our possibilities in creating the politico-economic structure that according to God's plan will favor all Salvadorans fairly." He called especially on the large nonorganized sector of the people to "act in favor of justice with the means they have and not remain passive out of fear of the personal sacrifices and risks that every daring and truly effective action implies. Else they will also be responsible for injustice and its harmful consequences. But let it be quite clear, also, that in making this appeal to the people to organize, I am not saying that they enter one or another organization. I simply mean they should use their critical sense, each one, and put it at the service of the common good, just as St. Paul tells us today when he says that the Spirit gives his gifts not for personal use but for the good of all" (1 Cor. 12:7).[46]

Romero noted in his diary the following Saturday that the United States government had shown some alarm at his discussion of the political program of the popular organizations, since the United States was backing the junta of Christian Democrats and armed forces. He was unconcerned. It was not a matter, he said, of pleasing the United States but of seeking the best solution for El Salvador.

That evening he was visited by a representative of the clandestine guerrilla groups, whom he had always criticized for their violent methods. Romero spoke of the church's view of the "violent solutions that these organizations sponsor, which have done so much harm in recent times." But, he said, it was hard to get them to change their ideology, and all anyone could do was to pray for them.[47]

As January passed, the violence grew. The newspapers listed over three hundred dead from political violence. Other sources counted more than five hundred, besides many persons disappeared or wounded. ORDEN (officially abolished by the first junta, but still functioning), the White Warrior Union, the army, the security forces—all took their toll. Some victims were guerrillas killed in skirmishes; most were not. Three bodies were found beheaded in Usulután; a small-town mayor was killed after being freed from charges of subversion; two members of the Nationalist Democratic Union were killed and one was wounded when their car was machine-gunned; three mutilated bodies were found in San Salvador's Liberty Park, another on a ball field of the national university; two nurses in Aguilares were arrested and their mutilated bodies found days later; a military operation in the Aguilares area left twenty-two dead; Arcatao and Las Vueltas in Chalatenango were left almost deserted, the population dead or fled. Churches occupied by protesters were fired upon in Ahuachapán, Santa Ana, Ilobasco, Santa Rosa de Lima, and San Miguel. Several died when El Rosario church in San Salvador was machine-gunned.[48]

On January 22, the anniversary of the peasant uprising of 1932, when thousands of campesinos had been massacred by the army, the newly unified opposition planned a giant manifestation in San Salvador. It would be the Coordinating Commission's show of organization, efficiency, and political strength. It also proved to be its baptism of fire and a sign of its political maturity and moderation.

For days before the scheduled march, rightists filled the air with propaganda and threats, and even machine-gunned leftist offices. On the day itself, the bus companies suspended service in San Salvador. But over 100,000 from all parts of El Salvador gathered in the capital for the huge march.

From early morning they began to fill Cuzcatlán Park, Roosevelt Avenue, 25th Avenue north and south of Roosevelt, several blocks of Arce Street,

23d Avenue, and 7th Street. They included campesinos who had come to the city a day or two before, laborers, housewives, market women, office workers, professionals, students, intellectuals. The Nationalist Democratic Union brought out 25,000 persons, FAPU 40,000, the LP-28 15,000 (along with twenty-two buses taken for the day from the unwilling bus lines); the BPR had over 55,000 persons. Thousands more cheered from the sidewalks. Huge banners and flags of many colors added to the holiday atmosphere on this bright Tuesday morning.

The BPR's 55,000 waited on Roosevelt Avenue, stretched out from Cuzcatlán Park to the monument to the Divine Savior of the World near the seminary, about twenty blocks, as the other delegations began the march and emptied the side streets and marched down Rubén Darío Street, around the market area, back again to Rubén Darío, past the National Palace and its government offices on the main square, past the cathedral and around its corner, and on and on. At 11:10 the march had begun, and by 1:00 P.M. the BPR was still waiting to take its place as the other thousands moved ahead. At that time part of FAPU was passing the National Palace and the cathedral, when riflemen of the security forces opened fire on the column from the palace and other buildings nearby. The people ran for cover, into the cathedral, to the Plaza Libertad a block away and its church of El Rosario. Twenty lay dead on the street, 120 wounded.

The leaders of the BPR, still waiting far up the avenue, began to move their people in order to the national university campus over a mile away. Near the shooting, sympathetic householders opened their doors to refugees. Radio announcers who had been covering the event began to transmit calls for help and continued to describe the scene, converted so quickly from joy to sorrow. Within minutes, the government interrupted the programs and put all the stations on a single network, making them broadcast the same program as the government radio. Until 4:00 P.M. listeners could hear only light music, as the Red Cross and other workers carried the wounded to hospitals. About that time the government began to broadcast its version of events: the security forces had been confined to barracks, the marchers had attacked various buildings, and so forth. For the next two days, the radio blackout continued. The press published pictures of marchers with arms, but not of those who attacked them.

Thousands of marchers reached the university campus and spent the night there. But the army encircled the campus, and exchanged shots with security guards of the various organizations during the night. Archbishop Romero asked the government several times to end the radio blackout. He opened the archdiocesan offices to shelter campesinos who had fled to the cathedral and El Rosario. With the Red Cross and the Human Rights Commission, the archdiocese arranged for the army to retire from the university and let the people go home.[49] On Sunday Romero told the people:

> As pastor and as a Salvadoran citizen, I am deeply grieved that the organized sector of our people continues to be massacred merely for

taking to the street in orderly fashion to petition for justice and liberty. I am sure that so much blood and so much pain caused to the families of so many victims will not be in vain. It is blood and pain that will water and make fertile new and continually more numerous seeds — Salvadorans who will awaken to the responsibility they have to build a more just and human society — and that will bear fruit in the accomplishment of the daring, urgent, and radical structural reforms that our nation needs. This people's cry for liberation is a shout that rises up to God and that nothing and no one can now stop.

When some fall in the struggle, provided it be with sincere love for the people and in search of a true liberation, we should consider them always present among us — not only because they stay in the memory of those who continue their struggles, but also because the transcendence of our faith teaches us that the body's destruction does not end human life. Rather, we hope that after death by God's mercy we humans will achieve full and absolute liberation. Temporal liberations will always have to be imperfect and transitory. They are sound and are worth struggling for only insofar as they reflect on this earth the justice of God's kingdom.

The gagging of the radios Archbishop Romero called "out of proportion and therefore unjust." He noted that the press and television had given only the official version of the events. And he called once again on all to leave the ways of violence.

In response to the armed forces' violence, I must recall their duty to be at the service of the people and not of the privileges of a few. . . . In response to this intransigent violence of the right, I repeat once more the church's severe admonition, when it declares them guilty of the people's anger and despair. They are the real source and the real menace of the communism that they hypocritically denounce. . . . To the government junta, I must say with my people that it is urgent to show by ending the repression that it is able to control the security forces, which at present seem to be a parallel government that is doing great harm to the junta. Each day that passes, marked by the security forces' repression, is a further weakening of the government and a new frustration for the people.

The archbishop praised the popular organizations for their "maturity and good sense" in not letting the attack provoke them to greater violence. The church, he told them, "expects of you, the organized, that you be reasonable political forces for the people's common good. Making the revolution is not killing others, because only God is the master of life. Making the revolution is not painting on walls or shouting outrageously in the streets. Making the revolution is thinking out political programs that better build a people of justice and brotherhood."[50]

If the rightists had intended to provoke the organizations into widespread violence or insurrection, as many believed, then they had failed. Their moderate, disciplined reaction to the provocation was a sign of the maturity that Romero had so often looked for in them. They also drew the practical lesson that they could no longer hope to demonstrate peacefully. A few with pistols had tried to return the fire of the snipers. In the future the organizations' members would take more care to be well armed.

The January 22 massacre forced Archbishop Romero to postpone for a week a trip to Europe to receive an honorary degree from the University of Louvain in Belgium. The degree from one of Europe's ancient universities was a singular honor, which he said he would receive in the name of the archdiocese and its people.[51] In Belgium he would be able to visit the bishop of Brugge, who had priests helping in San Salvador, and the families of the Belgian priests and nuns. He would also visit Cardinal François Marty, the archbishop of Paris, and the pope.

Romero's first stop was Rome, where he attended the pope's general Wednesday audience on January 30. That evening he told the archdiocese by phone and radio about the experience: "I went in with some bishops that were there. As is customary, the Holy Father called to the bishops to give the blessing to the whole crowd; and when he greeted me, I told him I was from El Salvador. 'Yes,' he said, 'I know you. I want to have a talk together after the audience. Wait for me, please.' It was a pleasant surprise."

Romero had to wait about an hour. An Italian circus troupe in the audience put on a show, which everyone enjoyed. Then a Polish choir sang, which delighted John Paul II. And the pope spent more time talking with people.[52]

Then came the private audience. The pope said he understood that Romero's apostolate was very difficult. He told Romero to continue to defend social justice and love for the poor but to be careful of ideologies that can seep into the defense of human rights and in the long run produce dictatorships and violations of human rights.

Romero said that was precisely what he was trying to do, to be with the poor in their claims of justice and at the same time to defend the people's Christian values. "But, Holy Father," he added, "in my country it is very dangerous to speak of anticommunism, because anticommunism is what the right proclaims, not out of love for Christian sentiments but out of a selfish concern to preserve its own interests."

The pope observed that he agreed, but that the church does not preach "anti," does not preach anticommunism. "Holy Father," said Romero, "that is why I don't present it that way but, rather, positively, praising the spiritual, Christian values of my people and saying that we must always defend and preserve them."[53] He added that he preached what the pope himself had preached in Mexico. John Paul, he felt, approved of all that he said. At the end the pope embraced him and said he prayed every day for El Salvador. "I felt here God's confirmation and his force for my poor ministry," Romero entered in his diary.

Shortly before his audience with the pope, Romero had spoken with his friend Cardinal Pironio, who told him that Cardinal Lorscheider had come directly to Rome after his visit to Central America and had given the pope a favorable report on him.[54] Feeling that he had Pironio and Lorscheider on his side may have emboldened Romero in speaking with the pope.

The next day he spoke with Cardinal Casaroli, the secretary of state, who told him the American ambassador (whether the ambassador to Rome or to El Salvador is not clear from Romero's diary) had visited him to express informally his government's concern that Romero was supporting a revolutionary line of action while the United States backed the Salvadoran junta. Romero replied that he had not made a political option but was simply seeking justice in the solution of the country's problems. He and Casaroli agreed that the church must proceed in accord with its conscience and the gospel and not so as to please earthly powers. They agreed also that Romero should continue to support what was sound in both the government and the popular organizations, at the same time encouraging dialog between the two. Romero noted in his diary that this was a confirmation of what he was doing.

He also visited the Congregations for Catholic Education and for the Bishops, where he spoke with undersecretaries who were understanding and encouraging. It was, he recorded, "another day filled with great satisfaction and much pastoral accomplishment."[55]

The following Saturday, February 2, Romero was in Louvain, where he spoke on the political dimension of the faith, beginning with the option for the poor. He began with a few words in Flemish: "I would like to use your own language, but unfortunately I cannot. I will speak, then, in my own language, the language of the poor of my people, whom I wish to represent."[56] The assembly applauded his effort, and he went on in Spanish, thanking the university for the honor, which he chose to interpret not as given to himself but, rather, to the people of El Salvador and their church "as an eloquent testimony of support and fellowship toward my people's sufferings and their noble liberation struggle and as a gesture of communion and sympathy with the pastoral action of my archdiocese."

He then thanked the church of Belgium for the priests and religious whom they had sent to labor in his archdiocese, "for joining so generously your lives, your labors, and your economic contribution with the concerns, the works, the labors, and even the persecutions of our pastoral ministry."

The discourse on faith and politics that he now read was the story of what his archdiocese was doing: turning to the poor to proclaim the good news, serving and defending the poor, and therefore sharing their persecution—and in that commitment finding a deeper understanding of the mysteries of sin, incarnation, and redemption, and a deeper faith in God and Christ. As he had done with the second pastoral letter, Romero had asked Jon Sobrino to prepare a draft of the speech. But, instead of rewriting it, this time he simply added an introduction and lightly touched up Sobrino's text. He also noted in his diary that other priests had helped him "express better the pastoral sentiments in the speech." Its language was more theological than that of his homilies, but the thought was the same.[57]

❧ X ❧

The Final Weeks

February–March 1980

Archbishop Romero returned from his European trip to the same violence in El Salvador that he had left. The government kept speaking of reforms, and the security forces kept killing perceived or suspected enemies or subversives, while no one tried to curtail the activities of the oligarchy's terrorists.

Romero was disturbed when he read in the newspapers that the United States was planning to send military aid to El Salvador and in fact during the previous November had already sent gas masks and bullet-proof vests for crowd control worth $200,000, along with six experts in their use. He thought of writing to the president of the United States, Jimmy Carter, to express his concern, but wondered if it would be prudent to do so. After consulting various advisers and praying, he wrote the letter.[1] During his homily on February 17 he read the draft of his letter for the people's approval, which they gave with their applause, and he sent it.

"Your government's contribution," Romero wrote Carter, "instead of favoring greater justice and peace in El Salvador, will undoubtedly sharpen the injustice and the repression suffered by the organized people, whose struggle has often been for respect for their most basic human rights." The present regime, he pointed out, had produced a far greater tally of dead and wounded than the previous government, which had been denounced by the Inter-American Human Rights Commission. Since the time when the security forces had reportedly received the United States equipment and training, "the security forces, with increased personal protection and efficiency, have even more violently repressed the people, using deadly weapons."

He asked Carter, who professed making human rights a cornerstone of his foreign policy, "if you truly want to defend human rights," not to send more military aid and "to guarantee that your government will not intervene directly or indirectly, with military, economic, diplomatic, or other pressures, in determining the Salvadoran people's destiny."

227

Although El Salvador was in crisis, the people were growing in awareness and organization and had begun to prepare to take charge of the nation's future, Romero said. They were the only ones able to overcome the crisis. "It would be unjust and deplorable for foreign powers to intervene and frustrate the Salvadoran people, to repress them and keep them from deciding autonomously the economic and political course that our nation should follow. It would be to violate a right that the Latin American bishops, meeting at Puebla, recognized publicly when we spoke of 'the legitimate self-determination of our peoples, which allows them to organize according to their own spirit and the course of their history and to cooperate in a new international order' (Puebla, no. 505)."

The next evening Romero learned that the Vatican Secretariat of State was quite upset about his homily and especially the letter to Carter. The news had come from the Jesuit headquarters in Rome to the Jesuits of Central America, and Romero asked the Jesuits to call the provincial, who was in Panama, and suggest he go to Rome to explain the situation in El Salvador. The letter, he recorded in his diary, was prompted by the "proximate danger" that he saw in military aid in view of the "new notion of special warfare, which consists in eliminating in murderous fashion all the endeavors of the people's organizations under the pretext of fighting communism or terrorism." This type of warfare, he said, means to do away with "not only the men directly responsible but with their whole families, which in this view are all poisoned by these terroristic ideas and must be eliminated." The danger he saw as serious. Military aid would mean great harm to the people and would snuff out many lives.

Two days later the chargé d'affaires of the United States embassy visited the archbishop to try to explain the State Department's position. Even though President Carter had not yet received the letter, it had quickly attracted international attention. On March 14, Robert E. White, the new American ambassador, delivered Secretary of State Cyrus Vance's reply. "We understand your concerns about the dangers of providing military assistance," wrote Vance, "given the unfortunate role which some elements of the security forces occasionally have played in the past."

Romero summarized Vance's reply and offered his comments to the people in his March 16 homily. Vance had written that the present government's reform program "offers the best prospect for peaceful change toward a more just society." Romero replied that Vance was offering a political judgment that was open to discussion. To Vance's admission that the security forces had "occasionally" gone too far, he observed: "It's at least something that they would recognize it and would be afraid to provide help indiscriminately: 'We are as concerned as you,' says the letter, 'that any assistance we provide not be used in a repressive manner.' It is a matter of 'maintaining order with a minimum of lethal force.' It also speaks of the need for a less belligerent and confrontational environment in order to implement a reform program."

Vance had said that the United States would not interfere in the internal affairs of El Salvador. "We hope," said Romero, "as we have always said, that the events will speak better than the words." Vance had concluded by mentioning the threat of civil war, seemingly as the alternative to the government's program. Romero observed: "I believe that there can be other alternatives, and I would like to say to all . . . that we should not be so moved by the idea of an impending civil war. . . . I believe that there are still reasonable solutions that we must sincerely look for."[2]

Romero was continuing to look for alternatives and keeping open his channels of communication with all parties. His diary shows that during his last weeks he spoke personally with junta and cabinet members, the Co-ordinating Commission, leaders of the popular organizations, intellectuals, diplomats, bankers, and even with the FPL. After talking with several members of the LP-28 and FPL on March 6, he was impressed with their "quite profound analysis" of the government's reforms, which they said did not go to the heart of things and only sewed patches on the country's social injustice in order to look good abroad, while allowing United States intervention. "These workers and campesinos in politics" answered questions with great conviction and left the archbishop with no doubt that they understood profoundly "our country's true condition." He prayed to God to avert the violence that he nevertheless foresaw, "since the left and the popular political groups see no other way for the country's genuine transformation."[3]

Romero's last Sunday homilies are among his most memorable. The country's growing violence, the disappearance of alternatives to violence, his anguished, driven response, and his growing realization that the violence would almost surely touch his own person, as it had struck down so many friends, so many of his priests and co-workers—all this gave his words an eloquence that drew frequent applause from his hearers. To read his words today, or better, to listen to them, is to feel the drama of those moments when his figure in the pulpit of the Sacred Heart basilica held the faithful before him and the thousands listening by radio in eager attention.

February 17 was the Sunday before Lent and Ash Wednesday, and Romero preached on the gospel Beatitudes and on the poor. He reminded the congregation that they were assembled as the people of God. A visitor from Venezuela the week before, said Romero, had come thinking that the mass would be a political rally—such was the impression he had gathered from the media. Instead, said the visitor, he found "a true Christian assembly—these people sing, they pray, and at communion time I was greatly impressed by that long procession of people who approached the eucharist."

"I do not intend in any way to engage in politics," said Romero. "If for a need of the moment I am casting light on my country's political situation, it is as pastor, it is from the gospel. My preaching is a light that is obliged to enlighten the country's ways, to offer as church what the church has to offer."

He spoke of Lent as a time of renewal and of Ash Wednesday as a call to conversion. In the communities where there was no priest, the person in charge, whether catechist or nun or ordinary lay person, would bring the ashes from the parish church and in a simple ceremony calling for conversion would put the ashes on each one's head. The archbishop's office would supply a mimeographed sheet for the ceremony, but "if you can't obtain the sheet, read a passage of the Bible, explain what the imposition of the ashes means, the meaning of Lent, and draw near humbly and enter Lent hearing the words of Christ, who tells us that God's reign is near and we should be converted to the gospel." Those who could not get to the village ceremony should have a ceremony at home. "The father of the family can take home a bit of the ashes and celebrate with his family the beginning of Lent and there impose the holy ashes like a true priest of the family. It's not a sacrament, just a simple rite to recall that you are dust and are to return to dust and that what is important is to be converted to the Lord."[4]

Romero spoke of the poor, who, Christ said, were blessed. He read parts of his Louvain speech. The church lived in the polis, in the city, that is, in the world; and in El Salvador it was a world of the poor. It had to be incarnated there among them, like the Savior himself, and proclaim to them the good news. It had to defend them and share in their persecution. From its experience with the poor, the church was understanding better what is sin, whose fruit is death, "the death of Salvadorans, the rapid death of repression or the slow death of structural oppression."

The mystery of poverty, Romero continued, had also taught the church to understand better the redemption brought by Christ. "God wants to give us life, and everyone who takes away life or damages life — mutilating, torturing, repressing — is showing us also by contrast the divine image of the God of life, of the God who respects the life of humans."

Poverty is also a call to the church itself: "Everyone who accuses must be ready to be accused. If the church accuses others of injustice, it is ready also to hear itself accused and is obliged to be converted. And the poor are the constant cry that points out not only social injustice but also our own church's scant generosity."

But besides being an indictment, poverty also means a Christian spirit of openness to God: "Blessed are you poor, for yours is the kingdom of God. You are the ones most able to understand what is not understood by those who are on their knees before false idols and who trust in them. You that do not have those idols, you that do not trust in them because you have no money or power, you that are destitute of everything: the poorer you are, the more you possess God's kingdom, provided you truly live that spirituality. The poverty that Jesus Christ here sanctifies is not simply a material poverty, not just having nothing — that is bad. It is a poverty that awakens consciousness, a poverty that accepts the cross and sacrifice, but not out of mere compliance, because it knows that such is not God's will."[5]

Poverty also means a commitment, and hence a force for liberation. Romero quoted Medellín: "Poverty as a commitment that assumes voluntarily and out of love the condition of this world's needy in order to bear witness to the evil it represents and to spiritual freedom before possessions continues in this the example of Christ, who made his own all the consequences of the sinful condition of the human race and who, being rich, made himself poor in order to save us." This is the Christian's commitment, said Romero: to follow Christ in his incarnation among the poor.[6]

In this homily Romero read his letter to President Carter. He also spoke of the continued violence by the military and security forces. "The promises continue without taking form in deeds. What has become more evident this week is that neither the junta nor the Christian Democrats are governing the country. They are only allowing that impression to be given nationally and internationally. The February 12 massacre of the demonstrators belonging to the Salvadoran Students' Revolutionary Movement and the bloody eviction of the occupiers of the Christian Democrats' headquarters show clearly that it is not they who govern but, rather, the most repressive sector of the armed forces and the security forces."[7]

He asked the Christian Democrats to reconsider their place in the government. "I ask them to analyze not only their intentions, which no doubt may be very good, but also the real effects that their presence is occasioning. It is covering up, especially on the international level, the present government's repressive character. It is urgent that as a political force of our people they see from what point it is most effective to use that force on behalf of our poor—whether isolated and impotent in a government dominated by a repressive military or as one more force incorporated into a broad-based design for a popular government, whose foundation would not be the present armed forces, constantly more corrupt, but the agreement of the majority of our people."[8]

The next day a bomb placed by the far right destroyed the church's radio transmitter. The nation was shocked, as were people far away. A message of support came from a meeting of Latin American bishops in Brazil. Even the junta sent a message deploring the attack. Letters and donations for rebuilding the station flooded the chancery offices. A cab driver who had stopped for a red light recognized the archbishop in the car alongside and handed him five colóns ($2), crying, "For the radio!"

On Sunday, February 24, many people brought tape recorders to church to take the sermon back with them to their communities. And a Costa Rican short-wave radio station, Radionoticias del Continente, recorded it to broadcast immediately afterward to all Central America.[9]

It was the first Sunday of Lent, and the gospel was of Christ's temptations in the desert. "This Sunday speaks to us of a victory, the victory of Christ over the enemy of God's plan of salvation," Romero said. The devil challenged Christ to turn stones into bread, "but bread is not made only from stones. The bread that must nourish all has to be the just distribution of property. It has to be when the rich give up what they have in order to share with the poor. It has to be a society arranged according to the heart and the justice of God. This is the redemption that I bring, says Christ."[10]

The devil tempted Christ to power over all kingdoms and nations of the earth in exchange for an act of idolatry. "What a tremendous and timely lesson for our days! Why do men fight in El Salvador? For power." In his plan of salvation, God rejects the idols of power and wealth. "Woe to the powerful when they do not take into account the power of God, the only powerful one—when they try to subjugate people to their power by torturing, by killing, by massacring! What terrible idolatry is being offered to the god of power, the god of money! So many victims, so much blood, for which God, the true God, the author of human life, will charge a high price from these idolaters of power!"[11]

And just as Christ rejects the temptation to provide merely material salvation and to seize power, he also rejects the temptation to receive glory and adulation by diving from the pinnacle of the temple. "It's not necessary to perform grandiose actions. A triumphalistic religion or political life is not necessary, and it does much harm. . . . This is God's design: the simple life, the ordinary life—but giving it a meaning of love, of freedom. How beautiful our country would be if we all lived this design of God, each one busy in his or her job, without pretensions of dominating anyone, simply earning and eating in justice the bread that each one's family needs!"[12]

Romero went on to speak of the Holy Spirit as the force that impels God's plan of salvation, and of faith as the way in which people share in the victory of God's plan. He noted events of the week: his third anniversary as archbishop, messages of support he had received, communities he had visited in the archdiocese, a priest to be ordained on the following Saturday, and once again a list of murders, machine gun attacks, and bombs—one of them set off in the library of the Central American University.

Toward the end of the sermon Romero directed a lengthy call to conversion to the oligarchy:

> If they don't want to listen to me, let them at least listen to the voice of Pope John Paul II, who this very week, at the beginning of Lent, exhorted the Catholics of the world to give up superfluous wealth in order to help the needy as a sign of Lenten penance. . . . The pope said that the church's concern is not only that there be a fairer sharing of wealth, but that this sharing be because people have an attitude of wanting to share not only possessions but life itself with those who are disadvantaged in our society. This is beautiful. Social justice is not just a law that mandates sharing. Seen in a Christian manner, it is an internal attitude like that of Christ, who, being rich, became poor so as to be able to share his love with the poor. I hope that this call of the church will not further harden the hearts of the oligarchs but will

move them to conversion. Let them share what they are and have. Let them not keep on silencing with violence the voice of those of us who offer this invitation. Let them not keep on killing those of us who are trying to achieve a more just sharing of the power and wealth of our country. I speak in the first person, because this week I received notice that I am on the list of those who are to be eliminated next week. But let it be known that no one can any longer kill the voice of justice.[13]

Unless they were well substantiated, Romero did not take threats seriously, much less bother to mention them in his homilies. That he mentioned this one in so dramatic a fashion showed that he regarded it as indeed serious. On the day before the homily, Romero noted in his diary that the nuncio to Costa Rica had warned him again that his life was in danger. Before that, the foreign minister of Nicaragua, Miguel D'Escoto, had written him to offer Nicaragua as a haven. Romero replied that he could not leave his people and accepted with them "the risks of the moment."[14]

During the last week of February, the first full week of Lent, Archbishop Romero made his annual retreat with six priests of the vicariate of Chalatenango at the Passionist Sisters' retreat house in Planes de Renderos, on the hills above San Salvador. They had planned to go to the pine-wooded place in the mountains of Guatemala that he had visited in early December, but the four highest officials of the archdiocese had urged him not to leave the country. "Your presence here among us is more necessary than ever. The good of the country and of the church and your personal security demand it," they wrote in a memorandum.[15]

Romero's elderly confessor, Secundo Azcue, visited him at the retreat house. "I dare to consider this last retreat of his as his prayer in the garden," he later wrote. "Archbishop Romero foresaw his very probable and imminent death. He felt terror at it as Jesus did in the garden. But he did not leave his post and his duty, ready to drink the chalice that the Father might give him to drink."[16]

In the notes that he made during the retreat, Romero wrote that he expressed to Father Azcue his fear that he was neglecting his own spirituality, taking less care than before in making his confessions and in following the daily order of prayer that he had followed since his seminary days. "By way of guiding me, he observed that there might be a tendency toward scrupulousness in regard to the confessions and that the principal matter was my interior dispositions." And in regard to his spiritual exercises, his confessor told him, it was good to have a plan for his spiritual life, "but without becoming a slave to it, because in this too the principal matter should be life and spirit as the soul of all my activity."

Romero also expressed fear of death. "I find it hard to accept a violent death, which in these circumstances is very possible. The nuncio to Costa

Rica even warned me of imminent dangers I would face this week. Father gave me strength by telling me that my disposition should be to give my life for God, whatever might be the end of my life. The circumstances yet unknown will be lived through with God's grace. God assisted the martyrs and, if it is necessary, I will feel him very close when I offer him my last breath. More important than the moment of death is giving him all of life and living for him."

Romero also spoke with both Father Azcue and his fellow retreatants about another serious matter, his difficulties with his fellow bishops. He noted that he found very helpful for his guidance this consideration: "If they criticize my performance as a pastor, what alternative do they propose? It confirmed for me that the one thing that matters is the radicalness of the gospel, which not all can understand. One can give way in some accidental aspects, but one cannot yield in radically following the gospel. This radicalness must always bring about contradictions and even painful divisions."

The discussions with his fellow priests during the retreat were frank. The other retreatants noted that he was not accessible enough, let himself be overwhelmed with problems, was irascible, inconsistent in the way he received others, causing fear in those who did not know him. He could give sharp answers that humiliated others. All this they attributed not to character defect but to his not sharing with others the burden of the heavy problems that he had to bear. Romero noted that he thought it was also due to lack of organization in his life, his spiritual life in particular. "I'll therefore give priority to my spiritual life, being careful to live in contact with God. My principal concern will be to become more identified with Jesus each day, accepting his gospel more radically. Toward this interior knowledge and following of Jesus I will direct my devotion to the Blessed Virgin and my specific moments of prayer: meditation, mass, breviary, rosary, reading, examination of conscience, spiritual retreat. I will also organize my weekly day of rest, even though it be a half day, and in the company of priests. . . . I must also correct my excessive haste in making decisions, which I afterward change."

He was still dealing with the same basic problems of perfectionism, rigidity, timidity, and overwork that he had written about in his retreat notes in 1966, 1970, and 1972. But now his writing revealed a much greater serenity and acceptance of himself, a greater maturity and inner freedom.

He noted various ways he might show his love and concern for his priests, as well as for the seminarians and for the nuns who worked in the diocese, through greater contact with them, and some general ways of better organizing the government of the archdiocese.

The climax of the retreat was a meditation on the reign of God and the following of Christ. Romero copied in his notebook the prayer of offering that St. Ignatius Loyola proposes to the retreatant engaged in that meditation, a prayer that Romero had prayed many times before in retreats. He added:

> Thus do I express my consecration to the heart of Jesus, who was ever a source of inspiration and joy in my life. Thus also I place under his loving providence all my life and I accept with faith in him my death, however hard it be. I do not want to express an intention to him, such as that my death be for my country's peace or our church's flourishing. Christ's heart will know how to direct it to the purpose he wishes. For me to be happy and confident, it is sufficient to know with assurance that in him is my life and my death, that in spite of my sins I have placed my trust in him and I will not be confounded, and others will continue with greater wisdom and holiness the works of the church and the nation.

The week during which Romero made his retreat was bloody, especially in the countryside. In his homily the following Sunday, he commented: "These military operations, besides being inhuman, are unconstitutional. Without any logical grounds, on the basis of rumors and without accounting for their actions, the security forces take over for three days or longer various populated areas, establishing occupying armies and occupied zones where they abolish, as though under a state of siege, the most fundamental rights of the Salvadoran peasant. With what right can they later complain of the occupation of farms by other forces?"[17]

During the week the Coordinating Commission published a platform for a new government to be established after the overthrow of the existing one.[18] Among other reforms, the security forces would be abolished and a civilian police force established. A new army would be formed during the revolutionary process, incorporating the decent elements of the old army; human rights would be respected, past crimes investigated and punished, and economic and social reforms instituted.

In his Sunday homily Romero called it "a further step in the process of unification" of the democratic sectors and people in general. "I hope," he said, "that the different political groups and organizations will react responsibly to this invitation, declaring their viewpoints and working together to create a popular majority alliance that will be the legitimate expression of the people's will." He had made a similar appeal, he recalled, following the pronouncement of October 15. "Now as then, I do not say they should join this process in an uncritical way but should give their critical, constructive contribution to make viable a democratic solution for the country. It is a declaration that we can understand one another and that the people can find their way and should not wait for it to be imposed by force. It is not for the church to identify itself with a program. The church does not have the technical competence to opine from the perspective of the social sciences on how in practice to make viable this program. Its mission is to encourage those processes that tend toward unity and that seek greater justice and respect the most fundamental human rights. The church also claims, at this moment in the process, the power to intervene from the standpoint of its own competence as defender of Christian and human values."[19]

On Saturday, March 1, Romero ordained a priest in the Sacred Heart basilica and rejoiced at the presence of the many priests who concelebrated the mass with him and the many seminarians that the archdiocese now had. So numerous were those applying that many had to be turned away.[20]

For weeks the cathedral had been occupied by protest groups, and Romero tended to be more indulgent with the occupations now that the groups had so little opportunity to protest peacefully. All of his last Sunday homilies were preached in the basilica. It was there that he received a peace prize from Swedish Ecumenical Action on March 9. The organization's secretary-general had come for the occasion, and the Swedish ambassador was present. Present also were the bodies of Roberto Castellanos, an official of the Nationalist Democratic Union, and his young Danish wife, who had both been arrested and then left dead on a roadside.

"The unexpected presence of these two beloved dead," Romero said, ". . . with their esteemed families, is at this moment, for a preacher of peace, a very powerful spur. The voice of distant lands and, for that reason, of impartial, disinterested judgments, helps us to understand what often among us here is purposely not understood. The voice of eternity in the presence of these dead here in these two coffins is also a word of stimulus from an eschatological, eternal perspective, telling us that the Christian way is the true way to peace."[21]

Romero preached on personal conversion in the light of Luke 13:1–9, which contains the words "Unless you repent, you will all perish." He then asked, "What does it mean today in El Salvador to be converted to the Lord by the ways of Christ?" He went on to review events of the week "so that each one of us and all of us as a community in meditation may say whether we are walking as God's people or are withdrawing like those who disobeyed the Lord."[22] He read a list even longer than usual of murders perpetrated by the security forces and terrorists of the right and added:

> We do not overlook the sins of the left also. But they are not in proportion to the amount of repressive violence. The actions of the political-military groups [of the left] do not explain the repression. This week their victims have been three policemen in Ilobasco and three or four farm guards or local commanders—no more than ten in all, which is the same proportion of 1.5 a day as in the preceding two months. There were also some other actions like the attack on the Guardia Nacional barracks and other harassments. But the seventy killings by the security forces and the so-called paramilitary forces had almost nothing to do with repelling these subversive at-

tacks. They are part, rather, of a general program of annihilation of those of the left, who by themselves would not commit violence or further it were it not for the social injustice that they want to do away with.[23]

The week had also seen the proclamation of the awaited land reform and the nationalization of the banks. They both were reforms that went against the power of the oligarchy, as Romero observed. But they also raised the question of how they fit into the government's general program, which by now evidently included as an essential element the bloody repression of those who had different ideas for the country's future.

"The government should understand that although these reforms are necessary and desirable for the public, that public has not been taken directly into account. The land reform is presented all at once as a politico-military action of the armed forces and, what is more serious, it could lead to a systematic militarization of the whole country through the militarized haciendas."

The nationalization of the banks, Romero said, was a harder blow to the oligarchy than the land reform. He continued:

It shows that the junta's program is not in itself oligarchic, although it may still be capitalist and pro-imperialist. Its possible difficulties lie in two things. First, it is part of a more general program, behind which are the Americans, and that program includes massive repression. And that would not be good. Second, it runs the risk of being managed so as not to favor the general populace. Both possibilities put us on our guard. Events will show if they are only possible or are real. If the repressive aspect is avoided and the land reform goes as far as the nationalization of the financial system, perhaps—this would be the ideal—a coming together of the left's program and the government's program could be thought of. We know that involved in the program of the left are not only the known organized groups, but intellectually very capable people, and this must be taken into account. The measure of this possible coming together is the end of the repression. While the repression continues, no force of the people will trust working with the government.[24]

Romero concluded the homily by reading Héctor Dada's letter of resignation from the junta. Days before, Dada had finally despaired of working with the military and had stepped down. He and Romero were friends, and Dada was a regular participant in the weekly working breakfasts. Not only the junta, but the Christian Democratic party, was coming apart. To replace Dada, José Napoleón Duarte, the party's head who had held himself in reserve, would now enter the junta. On March 10 Dada and five other leading members of the party resigned from it. Of the party's leadership, the principal ones remaining were Duarte and Morales Ehrlich, both on the junta.

At 5:00 P.M. on Sunday, March 9, Romero said a mass in the Sacred Heart basilica for Mario Zamora, a Christian Democratic leader who had been brutally murdered by a rightist death squad a week before. Many Christian Democratic members attended the mass. The next morning a workman found a suitcase with seventy-two sticks of dynamite that had failed to go off, enough to destroy the basilica and the whole block. "Instead of feeling fear, let us feel more confidence," Romero told the people the next Sunday. "God takes care of us. Nothing bad can happen to one who trusts in God."[25]

By March 16 the two refugee centers that Romero had set up—one at the parish church of San José de la Montaña, next to the seminary and archdiocesan offices, and the other in the Domus Mariae retreat house, in the Mejicanos district—were housing 189 refugees from the countryside. Fifty-six were children under ten years of age. By their own accounts, the refugees had to abandon their homes and fields when members of the Guardia Nacional and ORDEN invaded their hamlets, burning houses and crops, and killing parents before the eyes of their children.[26] The next week, two more refugee centers were opened.[27]

About forty guardsmen raided the rectory of the parish of Zacamil in the outskirts of San Salvador at 1:00 A.M. on March 12. The priests, Belgians, had discontinued sleeping in the house before that, and only material damages were inflicted. On March 9 military forces fired on a protest group occupying the church of El Rosario. Bombs damaged the priests' cooperative, the weekly newspaper *El Independiente,* the Human Rights Commission offices, and the locale of the mothers of disappeared persons, all in the week of March 9. And the killings continued.[28] It was the same week that the leaders of the Christian Democratic party resigned from the party because of the "worsened repression, which increasingly is applied against the popular organizations and the people in general."[29]

On March 16 Romero preached on reconciliation in one of his longest homilies, an hour and three-quarters. "How much we need here in El Salvador to meditate a little on this parable of the prodigal son," he said. "The denouncements of the left against the right and the hatred of the right for the left appear irreconcilable, and those in the middle say, wherever the violence comes from, be tough on them both. And thus we live in groups, polarized, and perhaps even those of the same group don't love each other, because there can be no love at all where people take sides to the point of hating others. We need to burst these dikes, we need to feel that there is a Father who loves us all and awaits us all. We need to learn to pray the Our Father and tell him: Forgive us as we forgive."[30]

He concluded the homily with a series of appeals. To the oligarchy: "You are principal protagonists in this hour of change. On you depends in great part the end of the violence. . . . If you realize that you are possessing the land that belongs to all Salvadorans, be reconciled with God and with human beings, yielding with pleasure what will be for the peace of the people and the peace of your own consciences.''

To the government: "I see two sectors: those who have good will but cannot do what they want, and those stubborn and powerful ones who are responsible for the repression. To the first I say: Make your power felt or confess that you cannot command, and unmask those who are doing the country great harm under your shelter. And to those who are in power and do not want to cooperate with reform and instead are hindering it by the repression that they foment, I say: Do not be obstructionists—in so historic a moment for the nation you are performing a sad role of betrayal.''

To the Coordinating Commission: "You are a hope if you continue to mature by opening up and dialoging.''

To the guerrilla groups: "Someone criticized me as if I wanted to lump together in one sector the popular forces and the guerrilla groups. The difference is always very clear in my mind. To the latter, and to those who advocate violent solutions, I appeal to understand that nothing violent can be lasting. There are still prospects, even human ones, for reasonable solutions. And above all there is God's word, which has cried to us today: reconciliation! God wills it—let us be reconciled, and we shall make of El Salvador a land of brothers and sisters, all children of one Father who awaits us all with outstretched arms.''[31]

The day before he spoke, military operations in rural areas left another toll of dead: in a hamlet called La Laguna, a husband and wife and their children of thirteen and seven years, besides eleven other campesinos; in another, called Plan de Ocotes, four campesinos, including two children; in the hamlet of El Rosario, three other campesinos. The next day, Sunday, four members of ORDEN killed two campesinos and the little son of one of them in Arcatao; a military force killed another campesino in a hamlet of Jutiapa.[32] The same day, after the basilica mass, Romero celebrated the third anniversary of Rutilio Grande's death in Aguilares, but attendance was small and he noticed the atmosphere of fear.[33]

On Monday, March 17, the Coordinating Commission had called a general strike. Bombs went off in various places in the capital and the rest of the country. Military forces besieged the national university from early morning and bursts of machine gun fire were heard all day. In a hacienda called Colima, eighteen persons died, at least fifteen of them campesinos, in what the government called a skirmish. All told, at least sixty died in the day's events.

On Tuesday four bodies of campesinos were found, and on Wednesday three more after a military assault. That evening military forces raided two union halls in San Salvador, in one of which members were holding a wake for a member killed after being arrested. Two more died in the attack. The press reported nine campesinos dead in what the armed forces called an encounter. The repression continued for the rest of the week.[34]

On Friday, March 21, members of FAPU who were occupying the cathedral appealed to the archdiocese to help them bury seventeen bodies that they had in the cathedral. They wanted to bury them there because they were afraid of violence if they went to the cemetery. Romero appealed to the minister of defense, who got the Red Cross and the health ministry involved in the case. At that point FAPU and the BPR, which was also involved in the occupation, disagreed on whether to go to the cemetery or bury the bodies in the cathedral.

Next, the head of the national police called the archbishop to say that the occupiers of the cathedral had captured a policeman. Romero sent a delegate to the cathedral, who was told they did not have a captive. But the policeman had been there, had been beaten and tortured, and Romero's delegates found him later in the military hospital. Romero told the story in his Sunday homily. "We do not at all approve of anything so cruel," he said. "The person takes precedence over all our ways of thought and must be respected." Meanwhile, the BPR and FAPU had agreed to disagree, and the BPR had taken its bodies to the cemetery while FAPU had buried its in the cathedral.[35] Romero's support for the organizations' right to exist and to pursue their aims still left him in an uneasy relationship with them, and the Coordinating Commission was not enough to eliminate the differences and rivalries among them.

On Sunday, March 23, Romero was still using the basilica instead of the cathedral—though he had said a mass in the cathedral on March 10 for nine victims of the repression, even while it was under occupation.[36] He disapproved of the occupations of churches, but he was flexible in practice.

YSAX was back on the air at last, and Romero's homily went out to the nation. Radionoticias del Continente continued broadcasting his homilies by short wave—even though its station in Costa Rica had suffered a bomb attack. For the many who might be hearing him for the first time, he repeated once more why he spoke of politics and temporal matters when he commented on the word of God:

> I have been trying during these Sundays of Lent to uncover in divine revelation, in the word read here at mass, God's program to save peoples and individuals. Today, when history offers our people various proposals, we can say with assurance: the program that better reflects God's program will prevail. And this is the church's mission. And so, in the light of God's word revealing God's plan for the happiness of peoples, we have the duty of also pointing out the realities, of seeing how God's plan is reflected among us or despised among us. Let no one take it ill that in the light of God's words read in our mass we illuminate social, political, and economic realities. If we did not, this would not be our own Christianity. It is thus that Christ willed to become incarnate, so that the light that he brings from the Father

may become the life of people and of nations.

I know that many are scandalized at what I say and charge that it forsakes the preaching of the gospel to meddle in politics. I do not accept that accusation. No, I strive that we may not just have on paper and study in theory all that Vatican Council II and the meetings at Medellín and Puebla have tried to further in us, but that we may live it and interpret it in this conflict-ridden reality, preaching the gospel as it should be preached for our people. I ask the Lord during the week, while I gather the people's cries and the sorrow stemming from so much crime, the ignominy of so much violence, to give me the fitting word to console, to denounce, to call to repentance. And though I continue to be a voice that cries in the desert, I know that the church is making the effort to fulfill its mission.[37]

Romero preached on liberation, the true liberation proclaimed by the church, based on the dignity of the human being, promoted by God in the history of peoples, achieving its "true and definitive dimension" in its transcendence. "We run the great risk of wanting to get out of pressing situations with quick solutions and we forget that quick solutions can patch things up without being real solutions. A genuine solution must fit into God's definitive program. Whatever solution we decide on for better land distribution, for better management of money in El Salvador, for a political arrangement suited to the common good of Salvadorans, will have to be sought always in the context of definitive liberation."[38] That meant recognizing God's initiative in liberating, as seen in the Bible. It meant recognizing sin as the root of the evils from which people must be freed. It meant great faith in Jesus Christ. "There can be quick liberations, but only people of faith are going to bring about definitive, solid liberations."[39]

He recounted at length the violence of the past week and concluded the homily, which had lasted an hour and three-quarters: "It would be interesting at this point, but I do not want to take more of your time, to make an analysis of these months of a new government that was meant to get us out of these horrible conditions. If what is intended is to decapitate the people's organizing efforts and impede the political development that the people want, a different program cannot move forward. Without roots in the people, no government can avail, much less so when it wants to impose its program through bloodshed and suffering."

The people applauded, and he went on: "I would like to appeal in a special way to the army's enlisted men, and in particular to the ranks of the Guardia Nacional and the police—those in the barracks. Brothers: you are part of our own people. You kill your own campesino brothers and sisters. And before an order to kill that a man may give, God's law must prevail that says: Thou shalt not kill! No soldier is obliged to obey an order against the law of God. No one has to fulfill an immoral law. It is time to take back your consciences and to obey your consciences rather than the orders of sin. The church, defender of the rights of God, of the law of God, of human dignity, of the person, cannot remain silent before such abomination. We want the government to understand seriously that reforms are worth nothing if they are stained with so much blood. In the name of God, and in the name of this suffering people, whose laments rise to heaven each day more tumultuous, I beg you, I beseech you, I order you in the name of God: Stop the repression!"

Applause interrupted the appeal five times, and prolonged applause, almost a half-minute, followed at the end. Emotion strengthened and charged his voice, which had sounded tired a moment before, as he reached the climactic sentences "Thou shalt not kill!" and "Stop the repression!" He ended the homily: "The church preaches its liberation just as we have studied it today in the Holy Bible—a liberation that includes, above all, respect for the dignity of the person, the salvation of the people's common good, and transcendence, which looks before all to God, and from God alone derives its hope and its force."[40]

After the mass Romero stood on the steps of the basilica greeting people, listening to them. Some offered him little children to take in his arms. Others touched him and blessed themselves. Finally he was able to get back inside and unvest. Someone gave him a cup of tea for his throat, which had sounded tired at times during the long homily. A long press conference with foreign journalists awaited him. (In recent weeks this had become usual after the Sunday mass.) Afterward, there was another meeting for a while in private.

The mass had begun at 8:00 A.M. and it was after 1:00 P.M. when he arrived at the Barrazas' house with Salvador. He felt satisfied but tired, and he took off his shoes and put up his feet to watch a puppet show on television with the family. This was his favorite place to relax, especially for Sunday dinner. Salvador asked him what he would like to drink. He usually had a Campari, but when he wanted to unwind it was Scotch on the rocks. He took the Scotch this time. The children drew near and he played and teased with them, throwing drops of water and a pillow or two. Little Virginia, his godchild, mischievously pulled a gray hair from his head.

At dinner he would usually keep watching the puppets on television, but today he did not want to. He was silent and took off his glasses, which was unusual. At table he was unusually quiet; he gave Eugenia a silent look as though he wanted to tell her something, and tears came to his eyes. The family wondered what was wrong. Then he began to talk about his best friends, recounting their virtues. He lay down to rest after dinner.

At half-past three he left with Salvador and Eugenia for a hamlet called Calle Real. On the way he listened to the marimba cassette he had bought in Guatemala.

They arrived, with his usual punctuality, at four o'clock sharp. He had a mass and confirmation there, and once more Barraza watched that transformation in his bearing as he approached the church and donned his episcopal attire. After the mass he said goodbye to all the people at the church door and accepted gifts people had brought: fruit, eggs, a chicken and a rooster, money for the seminary and the radio station. Tired once again, he was quiet on the way back to the Barraza home.

He watched a sad story on television about an old clown. "It's true," he said. "When one gets old, he's not good for anything." But back at the hospital at half-past eight, he recovered his good spirits. He gave the Sisters the chicken and rooster he had received, and talked and joked with them. The sisters served some wine to celebrate the return of YSAX to the air. At ten o'clock he looked over his agenda for the next day with Barraza and Sister Teresa, who acted as a part-time secretary for him at the hospital, before he went to bed.

On Mondays Barraza liked to take Romero to the country or to the shore for a rest, but lately the archbishop had been too busy. This Monday, March 24, he worked in his office in the morning. At eleven o'clock he was ready to leave with a priest of Opus Dei for a picnic and study session at the seashore with a group of priests. He returned home at half-past three in order to go to a doctor's appointment at four o'clock; he had a slight ear infection. Barraza picked him up at the doctor's office.

"How good that you came," said Romero. He used the formal verb form instead of the familiar form that he usually employed in speaking to Barraza. It showed he was in a serious frame of mind.

"You're overtired," said Barraza.

"We have time for you to take me to Santa Tecla," said Romero. He wanted to go to confession but still be back at the hospital at half-past five. On the way to Santa Tecla, he talked about having a platform installed in the basilica for next Sunday's Palm Sunday ceremonies. Barraza agreed to see that it was done.

Romero found Father Azcue at the old Jesuit house in Santa Tecla, where he had made his thirty-day retreat a quarter century before. "I want to feel clean in the Lord's presence," he told the confessor.

The confession was brief, and they prepared to leave, but someone produced lemonade, and he stood drinking it in the entryway. An old friend appeared, Raúl Romero from San Miguel, and they joked for a minute. He and Barraza hurried back to the hospital, speaking again of the platform for the basilica. Barraza left him at the hospital at half-past five.

An announcement had been published in the newspapers for the 6:00 P.M. mass. Some of Romero's friends were unhappy that it had stated that the archbishop would say the mass. The threats to his life were serious. One or two persons even wanted him to let someone else say the mass. Lately he had been sleeping in his old room behind the chapel altar across from the sacristy, and he had confessed to an occasional sleepless night in his house, fearing a bomb or a kidnapping. During his retreat in February, he had remarked that a bullet could pass through the thin wall of his retreat-house room.[41] One night at the Sisters' country house on Planes de Renderos a car and voices had awakened him and he spent a few fearful minutes wondering if he should run into the woods. And on March 21 he had named additional canons to the cathedral chapter so that there would be a quorum to elect a temporary successor in case of his death.[42]

The 6:00 P.M. mass was for the anniversary of the death of the mother of a friend, Jorge Pinto, whose weekly newspaper, *El Independiente,* had been bombed less than two weeks before. It would be a simple mass, for her family and relatives mostly. Sisters, nurses, and patients from the little hospital would also be there.

He read the first lesson, 1 Corinthians 15:20–28: "Christ is indeed raised from the dead, the first fruits of those who have fallen asleep.... Christ must reign until God has put all enemies under his feet, and the last of the enemies is death ... so that God may be all in all."

He led the people in Psalm 23: "The Lord is my shepherd.... Though I walk in the valley of the shadow, I fear no evil. You are at my side with your rod and staff to give me courage.... And I will dwell in the Lord's house for years to come."

The gospel reading was John 12:23–26: "The hour has come for the Son of Man to be glorified.... Unless the grain of wheat falls to the earth and dies, it remains only a grain. But if it dies, it bears much fruit...."

The homily took only ten minutes. Romero spoke of Sarita's simple dedication to building the kingdom of God, the encouragement she gave to her children. "You just heard in Christ's gospel that one must not love oneself so much as to avoid getting involved in the risks of life that history demands of us, and that those who try to fend off the danger will lose their lives. But whoever out of love for Christ give themselves to the service of others will live, like the grain of wheat that dies, but only apparently. If it did not die, it would remain alone.... Only in undoing itself does it produce the harvest."

He read a passage from Vatican II: "... The expectation of a new earth must not weaken but rather stimulate our concern for cultivating this one. For here grows the body of a new human family, a body which even now is able to give some kind of foreshadowing of the new age.... That kingdom is already present in mystery. When the Lord returns, it will be brought into full flower."[43]

He exhorted all to follow Doña Sarita's example, each one undertaking the task in his or her own way, with hope, with faith, with love for God. "This holy mass, this eucharist, is an act of faith. With Christian faith we know that at this moment the wheaten host is changed into the body of the Lord, who offered himself for the world's redemption, and in this chalice the wine is transformed into the blood that was the price of salvation. May this body immolated and this blood sacrificed for humans nourish us also, so that we may give our body and blood to suffering and to pain—like Christ, not for self, but to teach justice and peace to our people. So, let us join together intimately in faith and hope at this moment of prayer for Doña Sarita and ourselves."

At that moment a shot rang out.[44]

Archbishop Romero was standing behind the altar, facing the people. He slumped to the floor behind the altar, at the foot of the large crucifix. The congregants were stunned for a moment; some crouched in the pews. Several nuns and other people ran to him, and turned him onto his back. A photographer present for the mass began to take pictures. Romero was unconscious, gasping, blood pouring from his mouth and nose. The bullet had entered his left breast and lodged in his back. Fragments of the bullet scattered through his chest, causing heavy internal bleeding.

Blood was turning the violet vestment and white alb red as the people carried him from the chapel to a small truck outside. Down the drive, down the street, down the hill it went, five minutes, to the Policlínica hospital. In the emergency room, he lay on a table, still gasping, strangling on his own blood, still unconscious, as the nun on emergency-room duty probed for a vein in his arm to start a transfusion. The veins had collapsed from lack of blood. In a few minutes he stopped gasping and was dead.[45]

The next morning, Tuesday, March 25, Romero's body was taken to the Sacred Heart basilica, where clergy and people celebrated a mass. Many more waited outside the packed church. On Wednesday several thousand[46] people accompanied him in silent procession to his cathedral, now vacated by the BPR and scrubbed clean after the occupation. Guardsmen tried to arrest three youths as the procession left the basilica, but the crowd and a number of foreign journalists protested, and they let the youths go. Crowds of people filed past the body in the cathedral for the rest of the week, from early morning until late at night.[47]

Foreign governments condemned the assassination. The church's schools and institutions closed for three days of mourning. Notices of mourning and sympathy filled the newspapers, not only from Catholic institutions but from those of the government, and even from the junta, which decreed three days of national mourning. The Coordinating Commission decreed eight days of mourning and four of general strike. The oligarchy's business associations also joined the chorus of lamentation, but their radio and television stations continued their programs as though nothing had happened. Meanwhile, journalists from abroad streamed into the country.[48]

The day after Romero's death the Salvadoran bishops' conference published a statement, whose style suggested the authorship of Bishop Rivera. "Many hundreds of deaths, including those of six priests," they said, had preceded the archbishop's "in a context of violence that reaches the limits of madness." From the time he became archbishop, Romero "tirelessly proclaimed the message of salvation and the inalienable dignity of the human being made to the image of God, and he denounced with inexorable vigor institutionalized injustice and abuses against human rights. This gained him the esteem of those near and far, but it also aroused the animosity of those who were vexed by the force of his evangelical word and his witness. For being faithful to the truth, he fell like the great prophets 'between the sanctuary and the altar' " (Matt. 23:35). The bishops condemned violence "whether to hinder or to further the reforms the country needs," and they hoped that the archbishop's death just before Holy Week might lead "to the conversion and reconciliation of the family of El Salvador, a conversion that must favor the worthy yearning to live together as a nation in greater justice and brotherhood."[49]

The bishops planned to concelebrate a mass with the nuncio in the cathedral on Thursday, March 27, but canceled it on short notice. Bishop Revelo told the press that they thought the circumstances would be "untimely," and then explained that they decided there would be too many concelebrated masses, since there would be another at the funeral on Sunday, at which they would all be present.[50]

Hostile remarks from bystanders, however, had greeted Bishop Aparicio on Tuesday in the basilica when he came to view Romero's body. During the week a group of priests, nuns, and grass-roots ecclesial community members began a fast in the cathedral and hung a large banner over the entrance proclaiming that Aparicio, Revelo, Alvarez, Freddy Delgado, the junta, and the United States ambassador should stay away. Monsignor Urioste, as acting head of the archdiocese, sent a trusted seminarian to demand that the banner be taken down. But the fasters refused, and in those hectic, busy, and tense days further efforts to remove it were unsuccessful.[51] It remained as a sign of the divisions of the Salvadoran church; of the Salvadoran bishops, only Rivera came to the funeral mass.

The pope sent Cardinal Ernesto Corripio of Mexico to represent him at the funeral, which took place on Palm Sunday. The nuncio was there, as were bishops from Costa Rica, Guatemala, Panama, Peru, the United States, Ecuador, France, Brazil, Ireland, Spain, Mexico, and England. Along with them, the foreign minister of Nicaragua's revolutionary government, Father Miguel D'Escoto, was a concelebrant, as was Gustavo Gutiérrez, the Peruvian liberation theologian. Protestants from the United States National Council of Churches and the World Council of Churches came. Almost three hundred priests from El Salvador and many other nations concelebrated with the pope's delegate.

The altar was set up before the front door of the cathedral, as had been done the year before for the funeral of the martyrs of El Despertar. The crowd, thousands[52] from all parts of the country, gathered in front of the steps. The police and security forces were out of sight, and Boy Scouts and representatives of the popular organizations kept order. All went smoothly at first.

The mass was already under way when a large delegation from the Coordinating Commission marched into the crowded plaza and sent some of its members to place a wreath at the coffin before the altar at the cathedral steps. The group waited quietly on the edge of the crowd while the mass went on. Corripio was preaching his homily when suddenly a bomb exploded near the Coordinating Commission's delegation at the further corner of the National Palace, which faces the plaza at right angles to the façade of the cathedral. Immediately shooting began from the same area, and the crowd began to flee.

Most of the people fled into the streets on the other side of the square, but many stormed the doors of the cathedral to enter. An iron fence kept the crowd from the front steps, where the coffin and altar were. Hurriedly the coffin was moved inside, partly, it seems, because some had the idea in the confusion that the extreme right was coming to steal the body. This could be the source of the government's later assertion that the leftists tried to steal it. The gate of the fence was locked to keep the crowd back during the mass, and before it could be opened some people were climbing the fence and others were being trampled. Most of the day's forty dead died under the feet of others. In the cathedral thousands were soon packed so tightly they could hardly breathe.[53] They remained almost two hours until they were sure that the shooting was over.

Inside the cathedral, while shots and explosions echoed outside, Corripio and a few others hastily buried the body in the tomb prepared in the east transept. Like Romero's last mass in the hospital chapel, this one was not to be finished.

That afternoon the government broadcast a rambling statement that blamed the Coordinating Commission for the violence, saying its delegation had set off bombs and fired on the crowd, had tried to steal the archbishop's body, and had held the "distinguished visitors" in the cathedral "under the pretext of protecting them from danger if they went outside, because of patrols by the public forces."[54] In the evening twenty-four of the foreign visitors managed to get together at the seminary to discuss the day's events. They issued a statement, signed by eight bishops and sixteen others, denying the government's version. Witnesses, they said, had seen shooting from the second floor of the National Palace, and some had said the bomb came from there. The Coordinating Commission's delegation had brought a wreath to the coffin and had then waited quietly, until the bomb went off. The leftists had not pressured anyone to stay in the cathedral.[55]

The epitaph on Romero's tomb states simply his episcopal motto: "*Sentir con la Iglesia*" — "To Be of One Mind and Heart with the Church." It is the motto he chose when he became a bishop, and it sums up his life. "He was married to the church," said Dr. Rodolfo Semsch.[56] His tomb bears testimony to that commitment.

José Calderón Salazar, Guatemala correspondent of the Mexican newspaper *Excelsior,* reported the following words spoken to him over the telephone by Archbishop Romero about two weeks before his death:

I have often been threatened with death. I must tell you, as a Christian, I do not believe in death without resurrection. If I am killed, I shall arise in the Salvadoran people. I say so without boasting, with the greatest humility.

As a shepherd, I am obliged by divine mandate to give my life for those I love—for all Salvadorans, even for those who may be going to kill me. If the threats are carried out, from this moment I offer my blood to God for the redemption and for the resurrection of El Salvador.

Martyrdom is a grace of God that I do not believe I deserve. But if God accepts the sacrifice of my life, let my blood be a seed of freedom and the sign that hope will soon be reality. Let my death, if it is accepted by God, be for my people's liberation and as a witness of hope in the future.

You may say, if they succeed in killing me, that I pardon and bless those who do it. Would, indeed, that they might be convinced that they will waste their time. A bishop will die, but God's church, which is the people, will never perish.[57]

⊰{ Appendix }⊱

Romero's Killers

Romero was shot at about 6:30 P.M. on March 24, 1980, as he concluded the homily of the mass for Jorge Pinto's mother. As the shot reverberated and Romero fell to the floor, shock and confusion struck those present. No one in the chapel saw the assassin, since the shot came through the open door at the rear. In the moments after the shot, the people were concerned about their own safety and about attending to Romero, who lay on the floor bleeding, and the assassin quickly got away. In the confusion, some associated the flash of the news photographer's camera with the shot and grabbed the photographer, who had to explain himself later at the archdiocesan offices.

The day after the murder, Colonel García, the defense minister, suggested to the United States ambassador, Robert White, that a Cuban exile sharpshooter had killed Romero, and White repeated the story to the press. Rightists said the left had killed him to create a martyr. Others conjectured that extreme rightists had murdered the archbishop in hope of provoking an uprising and massacring the participants, as in 1932.[1] The courts assigned the case to an investigative judge, as the Salvadoran judicial system provides.[2]

In his book *El Grito del Más Pequeño,* Jorge Pinto, who had attended the mass for his mother, says that his friend Napoleón Martínez arrived late at the mass and saw several police patrol cars covering the escape of three men from the chapel. Martínez, said Pinto, had heard shots "a second before" and he felt a chill when the men looked at him, although he was as yet unaware of what had just happened at the chapel.[3]

Martínez's wife, however, told a somewhat different story in a declaration that she made to the archdiocese after her husband's 1981 disappearance. She said that Martínez arrived late and saw a man outside the chapel fire a shot into the air as if to frighten him. The man then ran to a red car. Martínez entered the chapel and found that Romero had been shot. About a week later some men entered the jewelry store owned by Martínez and roughed him up, after asking him if he knew who had killed Romero. They also found the blood-stained shirt Martínez had worn that night; apparently, he had helped carry Romero from the chapel. Then, on May 28, someone shot Martínez's wife, wounding her five times, and while she was in the hospital, unknown persons came searching for her, causing her to change hospitals and the name she was registered under. Finally, in April or May 1981, Martínez and one of his employees were kidnapped; the employee was thrown out of a car alive, but Martínez was not seen again.[4]

Pinto also relates that a nanny was tending children outside the chapel while their mother was at the mass. The nanny saw a small red car that she recognized as the car that daily brought policemen to guard the house of a neighbor. She now saw three policemen in plainclothes (it is not clear if Pinto means they were the same policemen who guarded the house each day) and one of them "fired his little rifle."

Also according to Pinto, each day for two weeks before the shooting a man who lived near the Divine Providence Hospital observed across from his house a police jeep with the hood raised, and a man appeared to be repairing the jeep. A small red car would come from the direction of the hospital and pick up the man each day. On the evening of March 24 three men came in the red car, "one of them quite young, with light complexion and curly hair, with a little rifle in his hand." The car stopped and proceeded toward the hospital with only two men. The neighbor heard shots, and the red car returned quickly. It left with only its driver, and the others went off in the jeep, each vehicle in a different direction.

On the basis of what Martínez had told him immediately after the murder about seeing patrol cars outside the chapel where Romero was shot, Pinto declared to foreign journalists at the Policlínica just after Romero's death that the police had killed him. Later, two detectives investigating the murder called on Pinto at his office. They were, he says, extremely nervous. He repeated to them his opinion that the police had committed the murder, but he refused to name any witnesses lest they too become victims. "I think if you want to investigate you should look around you," he said, "and when you find the assassin, you should guard your lives, because you too are candidates for the grave."[5]

Three days after Romero's murder, two men entered the home of Atilio Ramírez Amaya, the judge assigned to investigate the case by the Salvadoran judicial system, and shot at him, wounding a servant. According to a newspaper report, Ramírez repelled them with a shotgun, and they drove away in a white Peugeot which had been parked outside the house, where other men were waiting.[6]

Ramírez left the country a few days later for a convention in Venezuela,[7] and he did not return. On April 20, *El Independiente,* the little weekly newspaper owned and edited by Jorge Pinto, published a news report saying Ramírez had declared in Venezuela that a hired assassin had killed the archbishop under orders from Major Roberto D'Aubuisson and General José Alberto Medrano, former military officers. Medrano was the founder of ORDEN. D'Aubuisson had been an intelligence officer for the Guardia Nacional until the first junta, when he left the military. Medrano's name would not reoccur in reports on the possible murderers;[8] D'Aubuisson's would.

In February, D'Aubuisson had achieved notoriety by appearing on television several times to accuse various persons of subversion, among them Romero and the Christian Democratic leader Mario Zamora. Shortly afterward, armed men entered Zamora's home and murdered him, and at the mass that Romero celebrated for him a week later with a crowd of Christian Democrats a suitcase loaded with explosives was left but failed to go off (see chap. X). Whether or not Ramírez had actually accused D'Aubuisson,[9] D'Aubuisson's television performance invited suspicion.

Early in May, D'Aubuissson was one of two dozen men arrested and charged with plotting to overthrow the government of the military-Christian Democratic junta. One of the group, Captain Alvaro Rafael Saravia, had a notebook filled with records of payments made for weapons, ammunition, and other expenses. Among the entries were expenditures for items like a telescopic sight, car, and driver that could have been for the Romero assassination. The United States embassy received a copy of the notebook, and Ambassador Robert White later informed the State Department that D'Aubuisson was the brain behind the archbishop's murder. White had asked three "knowledgeable Salvadorans" to read Saravia's notebook, and all three concluded that D'Aubuisson was responsible for the Romero murder.[10] In congressional testimony in February 1984, White said that six wealthy landowners living in Miami "organize, fund, and direct death squads through their agent, Major Roberto D'Aubuisson."[11] White's statement was based on information that a source he regarded as totally reliable had given to the embassy a few months after Romero's murder.[12]

During the 1980's, various journalists investigating the death squads and their connections with the armed forces and leaders of the oligarchy reported that D'Aubuisson was a leading figure in right-wing violence in El Salvador, and some of them said that D'Aubuisson had ordered Romero's assassination. Journalists' informants named two different men as the gunman—Edgar Pérez Linares, a National Police detective,[13] and Walter Antonio Alvarez, a former Guardia Nacional member.[14] D'Aubuisson consistently denied being involved in Romero's murder or any death squad violence. In one interview, however, he admitted that when he was a Guardia Nacional intelligence officer, "we began to act incorrectly and not take them [those they picked up for interrogation] to the judge, but make them 'disappear' instead, so the same chain [of having them set free after leftists threatened the judges] wouldn't continue."[15] Although the journalists' investigations have presented considerable evidence linking D'Aubuisson, Saravia, and other prominent members of the Nationalist Republican Alliance (ARENA) to clandestine murder squads,[16] the Salvadoran legal system has ignored this evidence.

D'Aubuisson and others founded ARENA in September 1980, and D'Aubuisson remained prominent in Salvadoran politics through the

1980's, even becoming president of the National Assembly in 1982. Opposition from the United States administration, anxious to maintain the support of the United States Congress for the Salvadoran government's war against the left, kept D'Aubuisson out of the presidency.

The judge who took on the task of investigating Romero's murder after Judge Ramírez did not investigate the attack on his predecessor, saying that it was not pertinent to the Romero case.[17] The investigation proceeded in fits and starts and with little apparent enthusiasm. Few witnesses of the murder dared to speak to the National Police detectives making the investigation. The license plates on the white Peugeot used by those who attacked Ramírez proved to belong to a white Toyota, but the police could not track down the registered owner.[18] The National Police suspended the investigation in May 1980, and the office of the attorney general received it.

The attorney general's investigators did not get going until November 1982, when they summoned witnesses of the attack on Ramírez and tried to track down the owner of the white Toyota. Efforts to locate him and the injured housekeeper were fruitless, and by early 1984 the judge canceled the summons for the domestic. He also canceled summonses for Napoleón Martínez, now disappeared, for Jorge Pinto, who had fled the country after the army destroyed his newspaper plant in January 1981,[19] and for a Divine Providence Hospital worker who had quit his job and could not be found. But the judge ordered renewed efforts to summon Napoleón González, editor of *La Crónica del Pueblo,* who had been present at the assassination and who had also had to flee the country, and he ordered the appearance of the policemen who had begun the investigation. Only one of the policemen made a declaration, however, saying that he went to the chapel on March 24 with three others, that they spoke with some nuns who said that Romero fell back bleeding, and that they never went to the Policlínica, because it was full of people.

Early in 1984, summonses were issued for four of the nuns and one of the workers from the Divine Providence Hospital and for the rector of the cathedral; but by late 1984 the attorney general's office had obtained none of their declarations, and the file reveals no informal conversations with any of them. The office concluded that it had no idea who the authors of the crime were, and it shelved the investigation.

In June 1985, some of the attorney general's people wrote to the judge asking that he allow them to follow up on the Ramírez case and that he summon the nuns and other witnesses. They also wanted to verify that Pinto and González were not in the country. The judge signed orders for the check on Pinto and González, and he ordered a report on all those working at the Divine Providence Hospital at the time of the murder, but he did not summon the witnesses.

At this point in the case, a sensational videotape was broadcast in El

Salvador in which a man named Adalberto Salazar Collier declared that he was a leftist guerrilla and that he had taken part in the Romero murder. Fearing for his life after the video was shown, Salazar turned himself over to the Guardia Nacional, saying that he had been in jail from 1979 to 1981 and had been paid to make the video confession. A check on the jail records showed he was indeed there at the time of the murder. In his story he also named the persons who had induced him to make the confession, some of them military officers. The attorney general's investigators wanted to check on the persons named, but the judge refused the request, asking that the investigators explain their objectives in requesting the information. The issue was never followed up.

Meanwhile, the attorney general's office had no success in obtaining a copy of the video itself; none of the television stations had a copy or could say who had brought it to them to broadcast. However, noted Robert Weiner, a lawyer investigating the Romero case for the human rights organization Americas Watch, Salazar had said the Guardia Nacional had shown the video to him, and Weiner wondered why the Guardia had a copy. At one point, he noted, the judge suggested that since the video was presented to the stations on behalf of ARENA, the investigators might check with them. The judge did not, however, summon any ARENA members. ARENA had become the principal opposition party to the Christian Democrats, who were now governing the country with the support of the United States government and the permission of the armed forces.

Monsignor Urioste and Archbishop Rivera, who had succeeded Romero, gave declarations in 1985, and in late 1985 and early 1986 some of the nuns from the Divine Providence Hospital also did so.[20]

In June 1987 Roberto Girón Flores, a Christian Democrat, took office as attorney general, replacing José Francisco Guerrero, and said he would make a special effort to clear up the Romero case. Guerrero and D'Aubuisson immediately declared they had information that would throw light on the case. Girón summoned them to make statements, and Guerrero complied; but D'Aubuisson refused, pleading his immunity as a member of the National Assembly.[21]

A major break in the case came in late 1987 with the declaration of Amado Antonio Garay, who said he had been Alvaro Saravia's chauffeur. On the day of Romero's murder, he said, Saravia made him drive a young bearded man to the Divine Providence Hospital in a red four-door Volkswagen. The man had Garay stop directly in front of the chapel, where Garay saw a priest saying mass inside. The passenger had Garay bend over and pretend to be working on the car's gearshift. As Garay did so, he was startled by a gunshot from the rear seat. Turning around, he saw that the passenger was holding "a kind of rifle" pointed toward the chapel, and he smelled gun smoke. He looked toward the chapel and saw people moving and heard shouts. The gunman told him to keep calm and drive away slowly.

Garay said he then returned the man to the house where he had got him and where he had left Saravia. The gunman told Saravia, "Mission accomplished." Saravia took the gunman inside the house to listen to the news. Later, Saravia had Garay drive him in a different car to another house, not Saravia's own, where the two spent the night, along with two men that Garay knew, one of whom was a bodyguard of Saravia and D'Aubuisson. The next day, Garay learned of Romero's death on the radio and realized that the man he had driven had killed the archbishop.

Garay said that three days after the shooting he drove Saravia to see D'Aubuisson, whom Saravia told, "We did what was planned — killed Archbishop Arnulfo Romero." D'Aubuisson complained that Saravia had acted too soon. "We did it as you ordered," said Saravia. After this, Garay became fearful for his and his family's safety, and he left El Salvador about two months after the murder. About four months later his wife joined him abroad, after being threatened by men who wanted to know her husband's whereabouts.[22]

Saravia's notebook, found in 1980, listed payments to "Amado" on March 16, 19, 20, and 25. The payment on the 25th, the day after the murder, was for taxi fare for "leaving the vehicles."

Garay made a declaration before the Commission for the Investigation of Criminal Offenses on November 19, 1987, and made a second statement, under oath, on November 20 before the Fourth Criminal Court of San Salvador. The next day the judge of the Fourth Criminal Court took Garay on a reconstruction of the events to have him point out the places mentioned in his deposition, including the chapel of the Divine Providence Hospital.[23] On November 23, President José Napoleón Duarte revealed that Garay, who had been living out of the country and keeping quiet out of fear, had been found and had accused D'Aubuisson. Duarte claimed that he himself had now fulfilled the promise he made at the beginning of his presidency to solve the Romero murder case.[24]

At this moment a congressional election campaign was under way, and the return of leftist politicians to the country and the murder of the president of the Salvadoran Human Rights Commission were embarrassing the Christian Democratic government. It was not the first time the Romero case had been used to score political points. During the 1984 presidential campaign Duarte had suggested that D'Aubuisson was involved in the Romero murder. In 1985, D'Aubuisson for his part had shown on television the supposed confession of the purported guerrilla commander, Adalberto Salazar. And in 1987, when the archdiocese demanded that Romero's killers be excluded from a proposed amnesty, D'Aubuisson took it on himself to introduce the provision as his own in the National Assembly.[25]

After Duarte made public Garay's accusation of D'Aubuisson, ARENA counterattacked by publishing the pages of Jorge Pinto's book that dealt with the Romero murder, including Pinto's accusation of police involvement. ARENA also accused Duarte of making up "false and contradictory evidence" to discredit D'Aubuisson and to "protect the guilty ones who were under his [Duarte's] orders."[26] D'Aubuisson declared that Colonel Reynaldo López Nuila, National Police chief at the time of the assassination and Duarte's vice-minister for public security, should be investigated.[27]

According to a *Washington Post* report,[28] Garay passed several lie detector tests on his testimony and also identified the marksman who shot Romero as Héctor Antonio Regalado, a dentist and the head of security at the National Assembly when D'Aubuisson was president of it. Girón, the Christian Democratic attorney general, proceeded to try to extradite Saravia from the United States, and Saravia was arrested in Florida. The United States federal court granted the extradition request on September 27, 1988, finding probable cause to believe that Romero's death was accomplished by a premeditated plan to assassinate him and that Saravia was "a knowing, active participant in the execution of that plan."[29]

But rightists controlled the Salvadoran Supreme Court, and ARENA had won control of the National Assembly earlier that year. In December 1988, the Supreme Court ruled that Garay's testimony was not credible, because too much time had passed after the events, and that the attorney general had no power to seek extradition. It invalidated the extradition demand. The next day, the ARENA deputies who dominated the National Assembly removed Girón from office for "incompetence and immorality." The case collapsed, and the United States government had to release Saravia.[30] In March 1989, the Christian Democrats, discredited by governmental corruption and their failure to end the civil war or relieve the country's dire economic situation, lost the presidency to the ARENA candidate, Alfredo Cristiani, and ARENA's control of the government was complete.

●

Since Romero's death, the murders of tens of thousands of Salvadorans have been left unpunished like his. In death Romero is one with the oppressed and persecuted, and that oneness is recognized by the continual visits to his tomb by El Salvador's people. "This is communion in love," he said after the murder of Rafael Palacios. "It would be sad, if in a country where murder is being committed so horribly, we were not to find priests also among the victims. They are the testimony of a church incarnated in the problems of its people."[31]

Notes

I. The New Pilot (February–May 1977)

1. Report of the Latin America Bureau, "Violence and Fraud in El Salvador," London, July 1977, p. 21, citing Jesuit statement, Guatemala City, Feb. 1977.

2. Letters of Willibrord Denaux and Bernard Survil published in *Orientación*, Mar. 27, 1977. The letters also describe their expulsions.

3. Latin America Bureau, "Violence and Fraud," pp. 20–21; Rodolfo Cardenal, *Historia de una Esperanza: Vida de Rutilio Grande* (San Salvador: UCA Editores, 1985), pp. 543–548.

4. *Orientación,* San Salvador, Jan. 16, 1977.

5. Latin America Bureau, "Violence and Fraud," pp. 1–7; Cardenal, *Historia,* pp. 509–510.

6. Minutes of CEDES, the bishops' conference of El Salvador, July 10–13, 1978; Cardenal, *Historia,* pp. 434–438; Mario Lungo, *La Lucha de las Masas en El Salvador* (San Salvador: UCA Editores, 1987), p. 64.

7. Enrique Dussel, *De Medellín a Puebla, Una Década de Sangre y Esperanza (1968–1979)* (Mexico City: Centro de Estudios Ecuménicos, 1980), p. 391; José Luis Ortega, S.J., press conference at Puebla, Mexico, Feb. 24, 1977, in *Mons. Oscar A. Romero, Su Muerte y Reacciones* (San Salvador: Publicaciones Pastorales del Arzobispado, 1982), p. 586; Cardenal, *Historia,* p. 538.

8. ANEP, in an ad published in *El Mundo,* San Salvador, Dec. 8, 1976.

9. Frente Feminino Salvadoreño, in an ad in *El Diario de Hoy,* Dec. 8, 1976.

10. ANEP, *El Mundo,* Dec. 8, 1976.

11. Asociación Salvadoreña Agropecuaria, in an ad in *El Diario de Hoy,* Dec. 9, 1976; and Frente Feminino, *El Mundo,* Dec. 8, 1976.

12. Asociación Salvadoreña Agropecuaria, *El Diario de Hoy,* Dec. 9, 1976.

13. Ibid.

14. Jesús Delgado, *Oscar A. Romero: Biografía* (Madrid: Ediciones Paulinas, 1986), pp. 69–70. Delgado, a Salvadoran priest, worked in the archdiocese before, during, and after the Romero years and frequently advised and assisted Romero.

15. Latin America Bureau, "Violence and Fraud," pp. 29–30; *Latin America Political Report,* vol. XI, no. 9 (Mar. 4, 1977), p. 65.

16. Address at mass for Archbishop Romero in San Salvador, Mar. 25, 1980, published in *Orientación,* Apr. 13, 1980.

17. Latin America Bureau, "Violence and Fraud," pp. 29–31; Rivera, address in *Orientación,* Apr. 13, 1980.

18. Address in *Orientación,* April 13, 1980.

19. Latin America Bureau, "Violence and Fraud," p. 31.

20. Arzobispado de San Salvador, bulletin no. 1, Mar. 1, 1977, in *Orientación,* Mar. 27, 1977, and *ECA,* Mar. 1977, p. 254.

21. Bulletin no. 2, Mar. 7, 1977, in *Orientación,* Mar. 27, 1977, and *ECA,* Mar. 1977, pp. 254–255.

22. Minutes of CEDES, Mar. 5, 1977; text of statement also in *ECA,* Mar. 1977, pp. 251–253.

23. Rivera, address in *Orientación,* Apr. 13, 1980.

24. Bulletin no. 2, Mar. 7, 1977; Delgado, *Oscar A. Romero,* p. 73.

25. Delgado, *Oscar A. Romero,* p. 70.

26. G. L., "Monseñor Oscar A. Romero, Nuevo Arzobispo de San Salvador, Crónica de Seis Semanas," *ECA,* Mar. 1977, pp. 207–208.

27. "Informe de la reuniín del clero de la arquidiócesis de San Salvador con los señores obispos," Mar. 10, 1977 (private document).

28. G. L., "Monseñor," p. 208; Cardenal, *Historia,* p. 561.

29. Address in *Orientación,* Apr. 13, 1980.

30. Rodolfo Cardenal, S.J., *Rutilio Grande, Mártir de la Evangelización Rural en El Salvador* (San Salvador: UCA Editores, 1978), p. 80.

31. Cardenal, *Historia,* pp. 573–574, relates that three small children whom Grande had picked up on the way were riding in the rear seat of the jeep and were not hurt. The murderers surrounded Grande's overturned jeep, and the children ran into the cane fields, hearing another shot as they ran away.

32. Oscar A. Romero, "Informe del Arzobispo de San Salvador a la Secretaría de Estado de Su Santidad sobre el Asesinato del P. Rutilio Grande, S.J., y Otros Sucesos," Rome, Mar. 29, 1977 (private report). According to Cardenal, *Historia,* p. 576, Molina called Romero at 7:00 P.M., shortly after the murder, "when only a few persons knew what had happened."

33. Letter of Romero to Molina, Mar. 14, 1977.

34. Unpublished diary of the Jesuit provincial; Cardenal, *Historia,* pp. 575–577.

35. Address in *Orientación,* Apr. 13, 1980.

36. In an interview with the author.

37. Text in "Voz y Pensamiento de Monseñor Oscar A. Romero, Arzobispo de San Salvador," pamphlet, Secretariado Social Interdiocesano, San Salvador, 1977. Also in *Orientación,* Apr. 3, 1977.

38. Cardenal, *Historia,* p. 576.

39. Letter of Romero to Molina, Mar. 14, 1977.

40. Letter of Molina to Romero, Mar. 14, 1977.

41. Bulletin no. 14, in *ECA,* Apr.–May 1977, pp. 337–339. Cardenal, *Historia,* pp. 573–574 and 595–596, identifies the suspect as Benito Estrada and gives a fairly complete account of the Grande murder. He also notes, on p. 596, that on Mar. 21, 1985, Col. Roberto E. Santibáñez declared in a press conference in Washington, D.C., that one assassin was Juan Garay Flores, a member of a group of officers that had trained at the International Police Academy in Washington with Major Roberto D'Aubuisson and Santibáñez himself.

42. Minutes of CEDES, Mar. 15, 1977.

43. Unpublished dossier prepared for Vatican authorities, section 4, "Reacción de la Iglesia ante la Persecución."

44. Ibid.

45. Ibid.

46. Ibid.

47. Ibid.

48. Ibid.

49. Ibid.

50. Ibid.

51. Bulletin no. 6, Mar. 15, 1977, in *ECA,* Mar. 1977, pp. 256–257.

52. A priest of the archdiocesan offices told the author he and others delivered the circular to parishes the same day. The mistake in the wording of the circular seems to be an effect of the feverish activity in the offices during those days.

53. Dossier, section 4.

54. Ibid.; see also Cardenal, *Historia,* pp. 590–591.

55. The account of the interview with the nuncio is from the dossier; see also Cardenal, *Historia,* pp. 587–588.

56. Dossier, section 4; Cardenal, *Historia,* pp. 585–587.

57. The accounts of the interview with the secretary and of the canonists' meeting are from the dossier, section 4; see also Cardenal, *Historia,* pp. 588–590.

58. G. L., "Monseñor," p. 208.

59. Letter of Gerada to Romero, Mar. 19, 1977.

60. In a letter of Mar. 21 to the bishops printed in *Orientación,* Mar. 27, 1977, the vicars of the archdiocese reported that 100,000 persons attended the mass. The letter thanked Romero for his "firm pastoral stance in these moments of increased sorrow in our church." It also thanked Bishop Barrera and the clergy of Santa Ana and the clergy of the rest of the country for their solidarity, pointedly not including the other two bishops.

61. G. L., "Monseñor," p. 208.

62. Cardenal, *Historia,* pp. 591–592.

63. Letter of Romero to the nuncio, Mar. 21, 1977.

64. Dossier, section 4; Cardenal, *Historia,* pp. 592–593.

65. *La Prensa Gráfica,* Feb. 10, 1977; Delgado, *Oscar A. Romero,* p. 21, citing an essay by Romero in *Chaparrastique,* Sept. 29, 1962.

66. Romero's letter to Baggio, May 21, 1978.

67. Letter to Gerada, Mar. 30, 1977.

68. Delgado, *Oscar A. Romero,* pp. 69–70.

69. Letter to Baggio, Mar. 30, 1977.

70. Letter to Baggio, Sept. 9, 1977.

71. The account of Romero's trip to Rome is based on interviews with his two traveling companions, besides the written sources cited.

72. For example, *Diario Latino,* Mar. 22, 1977, featured two-inch headlines on its first page proclaiming: "Leftist Orientation in Schools Reported." The story was about a group of parents complaining about material based on the Medellín conference given to their daughters as part of the church's reaction to the March 12 murders.

73. Declaration of March 25, 1977.

74. Bulletin no. 8, Mar. 31, 1977, in *ECA,* Apr.–May 1977, pp. 331–332.

75. "Iglesia de la Pascua." The text of the letter is in *Orientación,* Apr. 17, 1977. Translations of all four of Romero's pastoral letters can be found in *Voice of the Voiceless* (Maryknoll, N.Y.: Orbis, 1985).

76. Document on Youth, no. 15.

77. Introduction, no. 4.

78. Poverty, no. 2.

79. Pastoral Constitution on the Church in the Modern World, no. 11.

80. "Evangelization in the Modern World," apostolic exhortation *Evangelii Nuntiandi,* Dec. 8, 1975, no. 34.

81. Romero cites Cardinal Eduardo Pironio's *Escritos Pastorales* (n.p., n.d.), p. 211.

82. An English version was published by the United States Catholic Conference (Washington, D.C., 1976).

83. Bulletin no. 9, Apr. 21, 1977, in *ECA,* Apr.–May 1977, pp. 332–334.

84. *La Prensa Gráfica,* Apr. 21, 1977.

85. Bulletin no. 9.

86. *La Prensa Gráfica* and *El Diario de Hoy,* Apr. 25, 1977.

87. Bulletin no. 10, Apr. 23, and bulletin no. 11, Apr. 26, 1977, in *ECA,* Apr.–May 1977, pp. 334–335.

88. Text in *ECA,* Apr.–May 1977, pp. 327–330.

89. Bulletin no. 11 and no. 12.

90. Bulletin no. 13, May 5, 1977, in *ECA,* Apr.–May 1977, pp. 335–337.

91. Ibid.

92. Ibid.

93. Ibid.

94. This account of the episode is from a May 7, 1977, statement of the Salvadoran Jesuits; an interview with the Jesuit provincial; an unpublished account of the case drawn up by the Jesuits' Central American province; and Romero's letter to Molina of May 6, 1977.

95. Letter to Molina, May 6, 1977.

96. Homily published in *Orientación,* May 15, 1977, and in "Voz y Pensamiento de Monseñor Oscar A. Romero," pp. 9–21.

97. *El Mundo* and *La Prensa Gráfica,* May 11, 1977.

98. Delgado, *Oscar A. Romero,* p. 90, says that a hostile murmur greeted Romero as he entered the church.

99. "Voz y Pensamiento," pp. 23–28, and *ECA,* Apr.–May 1977, pp. 342–343.

100. Bulletin no. 15, May 11, 1977, in *ECA,* Apr.–May 1977, p. 339.

101. *El Diario de Hoy,* May 13, 1977.

102. Text in *ECA,* Apr.–May 1977, pp. 343–345, and in *La Voz de los Sin Voz: La Palabra Viva de Monseñor Romero,* edited, with introductions and commentaries, by R. Cardenal, I. Martín-Baró, and J. Sobrino (San Salvador: UCA Editores, 1980), pp. 201–205.

103. Minutes of CEDES, May 13, 1977.

104. Minutes of CEDES, May 17, 1977; text of message in *ECA,* Apr.–May 1977, pp. 340–341.

105. Latin America Bureau, "Violence and Fraud," pp. 17–18, citing unpublished eye-witness accounts and *El Diario de Hoy,* May 20, 1977; Ortega, press conference in *Mons. Romero, Su Muerte y Reacciones,* pp. 584–585; Cardenal, *Historia,* pp. 596–598.

106. Bulletin no. 16, May 20, 1977, in *ECA,* Apr.–May 1977, pp. 339–340.

107. Bulletin no. 16; Cardenal, *Historia,* p. 597.

108. Letter to Molina, May 23, 1977. The author saw the bullet-riddled tabernacle a year later and spoke with parishioners.

109. Bulletin no. 16.

110. Letter of May 23, 1977.

111. Unpublished homily.

II. From Carpenter to Bishop (1917–1976)

1. Birth record in Ciudad Barrios, reproduced in J. Jiménez and M. Navarrete, "Reseña Biográfica: Monseñor Romero" (San Salvador, 1980), p. 6. The record

notes that he was legitimate and Ladino, that is, of mixed race.

2. Record in parish church, Ciudad Barrios.

3. Author's interview.

4. Jesús Delgado, *Oscar A. Romero: Biografía* (Madrid: Ediciones Paulinas, 1986), p. 9.

5. Jiménez and Navarrete, "Reseña," p. 2, and author's interviews in Ciudad Barrios.

6. Author's interviews.

7. Delgado, *Oscar A. Romero,* p. 12.

8. Ibid., pp. 11–12.

9. Interviews with Salvador Barraza and family.

10. Interviews in Ciudad Barrios.

11. Delgado, *Oscar A. Romero,* p. 13.

12. Interviews in Ciudad Barrios.

13. Rodolfo Barón Castro, *La Población de El Salvador,* second edition (San Salvador: UCA Editores, 1978), p. 545. The adjacent rural area had a population of 22,780.

14. *Chaparrastique,* Sept. 15, 1962, quoted by Delgado, *Oscar A. Romero,* p. 16.

15. Quoted by Delgado, *Oscar A. Romero,* p. 17.

16. Records of San José de la Montaña seminary.

17. Delgado, *Oscar A. Romero,* p. 11, says that Romero was seventeen when his father died. The references to east and west in the quoted passage, however, suggest that he was in San Salvador, not San Miguel, at the time, since San Miguel is southeast of Ciudad Barrios and San Salvador is west of it. This would make Romero nineteen or twenty at his father's death.

18. This is a diary that Romero recorded on cassettes from Mar. 31, 1978, to his death, with some interruptions; it was a record of his activity as archbishop, with some personal observations also. An earlier diary on small sheets of paper in a filing box was written while he was in Rome as a seminarian from 1937 to 1943. Both of these are referred to as his diary, since they are easily distinguished. They are different from the notes on his retreats and turning points in his life that he kept in three notebooks from 1966 until his death; these are referred to as his retreat notes or spiritual notes. Romero preserved still other notes from his seminary days and from institutes or courses he attended as a bishop, but these contain few of his own thoughts.

19. Author's correspondence with Father Alfonso Alfonzo Vaz.

20. Testimony of Salvador Barraza.

21. From the diary that Romero kept intermittently during his years in Rome.

22. Delgado, *Oscar A. Romero,* pp. 22–23.

23. Letter to the author.

24. Letter to the author.

25. *Chaparrastique,* Sept. 29, 1962, quoted by Delgado, *Oscar A. Romero,* p. 21.

26. Letter to the author from John R. Crocker, S.J., registrar of the Pontifical Gregorian University.

27. Letter to the author from Fernando Londoño, S.J., Rector of the Latin American College.

28. Delgado, *Oscar A. Romero,* p. 22.

29. Letter from Crocker; *Informazioni PUG,* occasional newsletter of the Pontifical Gregorian University, Nov. 13, 1981, in an obituary note on Romero.

30. Feb. 4, 1943.

31. Romero left the Latin American College on Aug. 16, according to the college records, as Londoño wrote to the author.

32. Delgado, *Oscar A. Romero,* pp. 25–27.

33. Details of Romero's years as a priest in the San Miguel diocese are from interviews with family and friends, besides other sources indicated.

34. Jiménez and Navarrete, "Reseña," p. 11.

35. Interviews with the Romero family.

36. Delgado, *Oscar A. Romero,* pp. 28–29.

37. Ibid., p. 29.

38. Ibid., p. 30.

39. Segundo Azcue, S.J., who became his confessor when he was archbishop, first met him at this time and recounted this information in a memoir published in *Noticias de la Provincia Centroamericana,* Apr. 1980 (privately circulated) and in *Orientación,* May 11, 1980.

40. Delgado, *Oscar A. Romero,* pp. 30–31.

41. Delgado, *Oscar A. Romero,* pp. 32–37, interprets Romero's appointment as a way of easing him out of San Miguel while still recognizing and making good use of his notable abilities. The new bishop was Lawrence Graziano, an American Franciscan, who told the author in a 1981 telephone interview that he had no personal conflict with Romero.

42. Romero's spiritual notes.

43. Interviews with Jesuits.

44. Minutes of Central American Bishops' Secretariat.

45. Barón Castro, *La Población,* p. 501.

46. Statement by Chávez in *Unitas* (San Salvador), July–Sept. 1969, p. 14.

47. Author's interview with Archbishop Chávez.

48. Romero's retreat notes.

49. The description of the ordination is from the tape recording of Romero's interview on radio station YSAX, June 22, 1977.

50. Delgado, *Oscar A. Romero,* p. 44.

51. Author's interview.

52. Interview with Rivera.

53. Interview with Rosa.

54. Romero's retreat notes bear out that he made at least two retreats preached by Opus Dei priests. The record of his retreats may not be complete.

55. Letter to Paul VI, July 12, 1975.

56. Delgado, *Oscar A. Romero,* p. 50.

57. Ana Cristina Cepeda, Rose Marie Galindo, Emilio Baltodano, Rodolfo Cardenal, and Armando Oliva, "*Orientación* y *Justicia y Paz,* Reformismo y Radicalismo en la Prensa de la Iglesia Salvadoreña," *ECA,* Oct. 1973, p. 712. The authors say that Romero fired Simán for his aggressive anticommunism. However, Delgado, *Oscar A. Romero,* pp. 51–52, says that Simán had popularized the paper too much for Romero, who wanted it to concentrate on straightforward exposition and defense of church teaching.

58. Statement of June 25, 1973; interview with Bishop Rivera in *El Diario de Hoy,* June 28, 1973.

59. *El Mundo* and *La Prensa Gráfica,* June 25, 1973.

60. The account of the 1973 Externado controversy is based on interviews with

Jesuits involved, especially with the principal at the time, Juan Roberto Zarruk, on a perusal of the San Salvador newspapers of the time, and on records in Jesuit archives.

61. Delgado, *Oscar A. Romero,* pp. 55–56.

62. Ana Cristina Cepeda et al., "Orientación," *ECA,* Oct. 1973, pp. 705–727, and Jan.–Feb. 1974, pp. 51–80.

63. Ibid., Jan.–Feb. 1974, p. 75.

64. Ibid., p. 79.

65. Author's interview.

66. Romero's diary, entries of May 24 and June 8, 1978.

67. Author's interview with Semsch. A cultured and gentlemanly man, Dr. Semsch survived Romero less than a year. In January 1981 unidentified gunmen killed him at his office, along with his son.

68. Author's interview.

69. Author's interview with Jaime Martínez, S.J.

70. Minutes of Central American Bishops' Secretariat.

71. Minutes of CEDES, May 28, 1968.

72. Minutes of CEDES, Jan. 14, 1971.

73. Author's interview with the former provincial.

74. Author's interview with Amando López, S.J.

75. Minutes of CEDES, Feb. 5, 1973.

76. Minutes of CEDES, Apr. 9–11, 1973.

77. Ibid.

78. Minutes of CEDES Apr. 9–11, 1973, and May 30, 1973.

79. Interview with Rivera.

80. Quoted by Delgado, *Oscar A. Romero,* p. 59.

81. Delgado, *Oscar A. Romero,* p. 60.

82. *Noticias Aliadas* (Lima), Dec. 31, 1974; National Catholic News Service, Dec. 26, 1974; Religious News Service, Jan. 3, 1975.

83. *Noticias Aliadas,* June 12, 19, and 26, 1975; National Catholic News Service, June 19, 1975.

84. *Noticias Aliadas,* July 10, 1975; National Catholic News Service, July 10, 1975.

85. Vatican II, Pastoral Constitution on the Church in the Modern World (*Gaudium et Spes*), no. 69.

86. Testimony of a priest present in Santiago de María at the time.

87. Juan Hernández-Pico, César Jerez, Ignacio Ellacuría, Emilio Baltodano, and Román Mayorga, *El Salvador: Año Político 1971–1972* (San Salvador: Publicaciones de la Universidad Centroamericana José Simeón Cañas, 1973). The book contains a section critical of the actions and statements of the bishops and of some priests during the events preceding and following the fraudulent election.

88. Delgado, *Oscar A. Romero,* pp. 61–62.

89. Testimony of a priest who worked for him in Santiago de María and in San Salvador.

90. Interview with the Passionist.

91. Ibid.

92. The account of the Los Naranjos affair is taken from Delgado, *Oscar A. Romero,* pp. 63–66.

93. *Evangelii Nuntiandi,* nos. 30–39.

94. August 15, 1976.

95. *Cristología desde América Latina* (Mexico City: CRT, 1976); published in English as *Christology at the Crossroads* (Maryknoll, N.Y.: Orbis Books, 1978).

96. Author's interview.

III. The People's Voice (June–July 1977)

1. Interview with Romero, January 1979.

2. Text of homily in *La Voz de los Sin Voz: La Palabra Viva de Monseñor Romero*, edited, with introductions and commentaries, by R. Cardenal, I. Martín-Baró, and J. Sobrino (San Salvador: UCA Editores, 1980), pp. 207–212; also in *ECA*, June 1977, pp. 431–433.

3. The account of the mass is from *Orientación*, June 26, 1977, from the tape recording of the homily, and from interviews with witnesses.

4. San Salvador, June 1977; also in *ECA*, June 1977, pp. 434–450.

5. Author's interview with the provincial.

6. *La Prensa Gráfica* and *El Mundo*.

7. *Orientación*, June 5, 1977.

8. Memorandum in Romero's handwriting.

9. Letter of priests' senate to Cardinal Jean Villot, July 18, 1977.

10. Ibid.

11. *Orientación*, July 17, 1977.

12. July 9, 1977.

13. Juan Hernández-Pico et al., *El Salvador: Año Político 1971–1972* (San Salvador: Publicaciones de la Universidad Centroamericana José Simeón Cañas, 1973), p. 159.

14. *Orientación*, July 17, 1977.

15. G. L., "La Presencia de Monseñor Romero el Primero de Julio," *ECA*, July 1977, p. 496.

16. Minutes of CEDES, July 11–13, 1977.

17. The letter is dated July 29, 1977, and is marked "very confidential" in Romero's hand. However, Romero referred in a letter to Baggio of Dec. 12, 1977, to his "confidential letter" sent from Costa Rica on Aug. 1, and he again referred to the Aug. 1 date for the letter when he wrote to Baggio on May 21, 1978. His passport shows that he left El Salvador on July 28 and returned on August 2, and he pre-recorded his homily of July 31 with the explanation that he would be in Costa Rica for a meeting of Central American bishops on that Sunday. There may have been two drafts of the letter, or he may have simply trusted his memory as to the date of the letter when he referred to it later.

18. Letter of Mar. 25, 1977, published in *Orientación*, Apr. 24, 1977.

19. Unpublished homily.

20. The quotations used here are from *Orientación*, July 31, 1977. Hundreds of similar letters have been preserved.

IV. The Body of Christ in History (August–December 1977)

1. Document on Justice, no. 5.

2. Archbishop Romero left an account of the interview, how it came about, and its aftermath in a document of Sept. 9, 1977. The memorandum prepared for President Romero is dated Aug. 10.

3. "Man in the News: General Carlos Humberto Romero," *Latin America Political Report,* July 1, 1977, p. 195; Latin America Bureau, "El Salvador Bajo el General Romero" (London, 1977), p. 8.

4. *La Prensa Gráfica* and *El Diario de Hoy,* July 4, 1977.

5. Unpublished homily.

6. *ECA,* July 1977, p. 527.

7. Archbishop's account of Sept. 9, 1977.

8. Ibid.

9. Memorandum of Aug. 10, 1977.

10. Account of Sept. 9, 1977.

11. Letter from Archbishop Romero to President Romero, Sept. 13, 1977.

12. Account of Sept. 9, 1977.

13. Jesuit record of the meeting.

14. Notes in Romero's hand.

15. Urioste's record of the discussion; Romero's diary; memo of Llach to Archbishop Romero, June 27, 1978; letter of Llach to Romero of same date, telling him to "reconvene" the bilateral commission. Interviews with participants in the efforts at dialog supplemented the written sources used in this section.

16. *Orientación,* Aug. 28, 1977.

17. Interviews with hospital Sisters.

18. *Orientación,* Sept. 4, 1977.

19. *Orientación,* Sept. 11, 1977.

20. Minutes of the priests' senate.

21. Transcript of Revelo's remarks and Vatican Radio's commentary telephoned from Rome to San Salvador, Oct. 6, 1977.

22. Jesús Delgado, *Oscar A. Romero: Biografía* (Madrid: Ediciones Paulinas, 1986), p. 72, says that as soon as Romero was named archbishop he went to see Revelo to ask him to be his auxiliary. According to this account, Revelo consented only reluctantly, and Romero then wrote immediately to Rome asking for Revelo's immediate appointment, which arrived in April. "But by then," says Delgado, "some things had happened that changed the attitude of the clergy of San Salvador toward Archbishop Romero and, in a very different way, the attitude of Bishop Revelo." Delgado does not say what then happened to Revelo's appointment. It is difficult to harmonize this account, however, with Romero's letter to Revelo just quoted, which seems to suppose that Revelo had requested his transfer to San Salvador.

23. To Bishop Aparicio, Nov. 10, 1977.

24. *Mons. Oscar A. Romero: Su Pensamiento,* vol. III (San Salvador: Publicaciones Pastorales del Arzobispado, 1980), p. 7.

25. Ibid., p. 119.

26. Revelo's letter to Romero, Jan. 16, 1978.

27. Tape recording of the ceremony.

28. *Orientación,* Mar. 5, 1978.

29. *Orientación,* Nov. 13, 1977.

30. Minutes of CEDES, Dec. 15, 1977.

31. *Orientación,* Nov. 13, 1977, says Ventura was taken to the police station in Anamorós. However, a priest working in the area says he was taken to San Francisco Gotera.

32. Minutes of CEDES, Dec. 15, 1977.

33. Archdiocesan bulletins no. 29, Nov. 11, 1977, and no. 30, Nov. 14, 1977.

34. According to *El Mundo* and *El Diario de Hoy* of Nov. 15, 1977, an otherwise unheard-of group calling itself the Revolutionary Workers Organization of the People's Armed Forces took responsibility for the action.

35. *Orientación*, Nov. 20, 1977.

36. Romero's homily of Nov. 20, published in *Orientación*, Nov. 27, 1977.

37. Delgado, *Oscar A. Romero,* p. 109.

38. *Orientación*, Nov. 27, 1977.

39. Letter of Romero to the Congregation for the Clergy, Feb. 3, 1978.

40. Decree of July 30, 1976.

41. *El Mundo,* Nov. 24, 1977.

42. *La Prensa Gráfica,* Nov. 28, 1977.

43. *El Mundo,* Nov. 30, 1977. They also tried canonical action to pressure Quinteros to submit, but Romero observed in a letter of Aug. 27, 1979, to the Congregation for the Clergy, "The situation is still exactly the same."

44. Romero's homily is in *Mons. Oscar A. Romero: Su Pensamiento,* vol. III, pp. 79–85. It alludes to the situation but does not mention Quinteros by name.

45. From a seminarian who was present at both funerals.

46. *La Opinión,* no. 11, Dec. 1977.

47. *La Opinión,* no. 9, Nov. 1977.

48. "Comentarios a la Ley de Defensa y Garantía del Orden Público," *ECA,* Dec. 1977, p. 912.

49. *Mons. Oscar A. Romero: Su Pensamiento,* vol. III, pp. 2–4.

50. The International Commission of Jurists sent an investigator, Donald T. Fox, a New York lawyer, to El Salvador in July 1978. His report was released by the American Association for the International Commission of Jurists, Inc., 777 United Nations Plaza, New York, N.Y. 10017.

51. Homily of Mar. 4, 1979, in *Mons. Oscar A. Romero: Su Pensamiento,* vol. VI (San Salvador: Publicaciones Pastorales del Arzobispado, 1981), p. 186.

52. Homily in *Mons. Oscar A. Romero: Su Pensamiento,* vol. III, pp. 13–18.

53. Letter of Nov. 25, 1977.

54. Letters of Nov. 28, 1977.

55. Letter of Nov. 28, 1977.

56. Nov. 20, 1977. Romero probably referred to the Spanish-language edition.

V. Pastoral Fortitude (January–June 1978)

1. Statement of Jan. 12, 1978, in *Orientación*, Jan. 22, 1978.

2. Letter of Timothy S. Healy, S.J., president of Georgetown, to the author.

3. Letter of Healy to the author, and *Orientación*, Feb. 19, 1978. The address published in *Orientación*, Feb. 19, 1978, and in *La Voz de los Sin Voz: La Palabra Viva de Monseñor Romero,* edited, with introductions and commentaries by R. Cardenal et al. (San Salvador: UCA Editores, 1980), pp. 175–180. An English translation is in *Voice of the Voiceless* (Maryknoll, N.Y.: Orbis, 1985), pp. 162–167.

4. Tape recording of the address.

5. Interview with one of the Jesuits.

6. Letters of Carter to Archbishop Romero, Feb. 23 and Mar. 16, 1978; letters of Archbishop Romero to Carter, Mar. 7 and Apr. 1, 1978; letter of Carter to the author; interview with the Jesuit provincial; provincial's notes on Carter's phone call.

7. *Mons. Oscar A. Romero: Su Pensamiento,* Vol. IV (San Salvador: Publicaciones Pastorales del Arzobispado, 1981), p. 78.

8. "Los Sucesos de San Pedro Perulapán," *ECA*, Apr. 1978, pp. 223–247.

9. Memo of seminary staff to Romero, Apr. 18, 1978.

10. Romero's diary.

11. Letter of Mar. 7, 1978.

12. Minutes of CEDES, Mar. 15, 1978.

13. Letter of Romero to Cardinal Baggio, May 21, 1978.

14. Minutes of CEDES, Apr. 3, 1978.

15. Letter of Apr. 26, 1978.

16. Minutes of CEDES, July 11–13, Sept. 16, and Dec. 15, 1977.

17. Rough copy of letter prepared by Romero for Aparicio, dated May 22, 1978.

18. Memo of Jan. 10, 1978.

19. Minutes of CEDES, July 11–13, 1977.

20. Nuncio's letter to the president of CEDES, Jan. 12, 1978.

21. Minutes of CEDES, Jan. 16–18, 1978.

22. Gerada's letter to Romero, Apr. 4, 1978.

23. The letter is dated June 5, 1978.

24. Urioste's memorandum of the interview.

25. *ECA*, May 1978, p. 330.

26. Ibid.; *Mons. Oscar A. Romero: Su Pensamiento,* Vol. IV, pp. 192–193.

27. Text in *ECA*, May 1978, pp. 330–332; in *Mons. Oscar A. Romero: Su Pensamiento,* Vol. IV, pp. 243–248; and in *La Voz de los Sin Voz,* pp. 405–410.

28. Tape recording of the homily.

29. Letter of Baggio to Romero, May 16, 1978. Romero noted in his diary that he received it on May 24.

30. Minutes of CEDES, Apr. 17, 1978.

31. Romero's diary mentions Father Azcue and Dr. Semsch.

32. With a covering letter to Baggio dated June 2, 1978.

33. Letter of Romero to Pironio, June 8, 1978.

34. Romero filled several notebooks with his notes on this and similar gatherings.

35. Memorandum of June 24, 1978.

36. A 1988 interview with Revelo by María Elena Matheus y Carlos Ernesto Mendoza, "Iglesia y Política: Historias Prohibidas," *Análisis* (San Salvador), Aug.–Sept. 1988 (Vol. I, No. 8), p. 58, quotes Revelo as saying that he was told by Baggio in October 1977 that he was being named auxiliary to Romero in order to be a "different voice" from the archbishop and that he asked not to be named auxiliary under those terms.

37. Pastoral Constitution on the Church in the Modern World (*Gaudium et Spes*), no. 1.

38. Manuscript "Por qué fui a Roma" in Romero's files.

39. Urioste's memorandum of the interview, and two letters of Llach to Archbishop Romero, June 27, 1978.

VI. The Church and the Organizations (July–December 1978)

1. Minutes of CEDES, Apr. 17, 1978; Romero's diary.

2. Letter of Romero to John Paul II, Nov. 7, 1978.

3. Ibid.

4. Minutes of CEDES, Aug. 16, 1978.

5. Minutes of CEDES, July 10–13, 1978.

6. Minutes of CEDES, Aug. 16, 1978.

7. Text in *ECA,* Sept. 1978, pp. 776–778.

8. However, Romero's diary shows that the group did not always meet.

9. The account of the writing of the pastoral letter is based on interviews with various persons who collaborated on it, besides the other sources cited.

10. An English translation was published by the Catholic Institute for International Relations, London, 1980. Translations of all four of Romero's pastoral letters are now also found in *Voice of the Voiceless* (Maryknoll, N.Y.: Orbis, 1985).

11. Pastoral Constitution on the Church in the Modern World (*Gaudium et Spes*), no. 11.

12. Ibid., no. 42.

13. Paul VI, apostolic exhortation *Evangelii Nuntiandi,* no. 37.

14. Peace, no. 16.

15. August 23, 1968, cited in Medellín, Peace, no. 17.

16. Peace, no. 15.

17. Encyclical "On the Development of Peoples" (*Populorum Progressio*), no. 31.

18. Peace, no. 19.

19. The letter here quotes from "Lo Stato Democratico e la Violenza," *l'Osservatore Romano,* July 23, 1978.

20. Sept. 4, 1978.

21. *Orientación*, Nov. 12 and 19, 1978.

22. Nov. 23, 1978.

23. Guillermo Manuel Ungo, "Los Derechos Humanos, Condición Necesaria para la Paz y Convivencia Social en El Salvador," *ECA,* July–Aug. 1979, pp. 492–496.

24. The text of the instruction is in *Orientación*, Dec. 17, 24, and 31, 1978, and Jan. 7, 1979.

25. Romero's diary.

VII. The Church, the People, and the Government (January–May 1979)

1. *Mons. Oscar A. Romero: Su Pensamiento,* Vol. VI (San Salvador: Publicaciones Pastorales del Arzobispado, 1981), p. 130.

2. The author was in San Salvador at this time, spoke with Archbishop Romero, read the local newspapers, participated in the funeral mass, and visited the neighborhood of El Despertar three days after the events, when the retreat house was still closed off by guardsmen. Documentary sources used for this account are the tape recording of Romero's homily on Jan. 21, 1979; archdiocesan bulletins no. 55 (Jan. 20, 1979) and no. 56 (Jan. 21, 1979); *El Mundo,* Jan. 22, 1979; and "Terror en El Salvador," *ECA,* Jan.–Feb. 1979, pp. 85–92, which contains statements of the archdiocese, the government, the clergy, the Human Rights Commission of El Salvador, and the Conference of Religious of El Salvador.

3. *Mons. Oscar A. Romero: Su Pensamiento,* Vol. VI, p. 129.

4. Ibid., pp. 131–132.

5. Ibid., p. 133, and tape recording of the homily.

6. *Mons. Oscar A. Romero: Su Pensamiento,* Vol. VI, p. 135.

7. Ibid., pp. 136–137.

8. Statement of Feb. 1, 1979, published in *Orientación*, Feb. 4, 1979.

9. Religious News Service, Jan. 25, 1979, and notes of the author, who was among the journalists at the Puebla conference and observed Romero and occasionally spoke with him during this time.

10. An American priest, Frederic Kelly, S.J., observed this detail and spoke briefly with Romero after he left the cathedral. The account of the press conference is from the author's notes and his report written the next day and from a partial transcript in *Mons. Romero: Su Muerte y Reacciones* (San Salvador: Publicaciones Pastorales del Arzobispado, 1982), pp. 581–591.

11. Romero's diary.

12. Letter dated Feb. 10, 1979.

13. Report by José J. Castellanos in *El Heraldo de México,* Feb. 7, 1979; *El Mundo* and *La Prensa Gráfica,* Feb. 3, 1979; senate's letter of Feb. 7, 1979.

14. Text in Romero's files.

15. Besides the sources cited, the account of the Puebla conference and of Romero's activities there are based on Romero's diary, on interviews with priests who accompanied Romero, and on the author's own observation.

16. *Mons. Oscar A. Romero: Su Pensamiento,* Vol. VI, p. 151.

17. Ibid., p. 153.

18. Ibid., pp. 154–155.

19. Ibid., pp. 157–159.

20. Ibid., pp. 319–320.

21. Homily of May 13, 1979; *Mons. Oscar A. Romero: Su Pensamiento,* Vol. VI, p. 328.

22. Romero's diary.

23. Ibid.

24. Statistics from the 1979 *Annuario Pontificio.*

25. Romero's diary.

26. Eugenio C. Anaya, h., "Crónica del Mes, Mayo," *ECA,* June 1979, p. 450.

27. Ibid.

28. Ibid., pp. 450–451.

29. Ibid., p. 451.

30. Homily of May, 13, 1979, in *Mons. Oscar A. Romero: Su Pensamiento,* Vol. VI, pp. 328–329.

31. Ibid., p. 339.

32. Ibid., pp. 339–340.

33. Ibid., p. 341.

34. H. O., "La Iglesia y los Acontecimientos de Mayo en El Salvador," *ECA,* June 1979, pp. 436–437.

35. *Mons. Oscar A. Romero: Su Pensamiento,* Vol. VI, p. 355.

36. Ibid., p. 356.

37. Ibid., p. 357.

38. Ibid., pp. 368–369.

39. Ibid., pp. 369–370.

40. Letter of Freddy Delgado to Romero, May 23, 1979.

41. *Mons. Oscar A. Romero: Su Pensamiento,* Vol. VI, p. 371.

42. Ibid., p. 383.

VIII. The Church in the Nation's Crisis (June–October 1979)

1. Eugenio C. Anaya, h., "Crónica del Mes, Junio–Julio," *ECA,* July–Aug. 1979, pp. 711–714.

2. Jesús Delgado, *Oscar A. Romero: Biografía* (Madrid: Paulinas, 1986), p. 131.

3. *Mons. Oscar A. Romero: Su Pensamiento,* Vol. VII (San Salvador: Publicaciones Pastorales del Arzobispado, 1988), pp. 9–12.

4. Ibid., pp. 27–28.

5. Ibid., pp. 35–37.

6. Anaya, "Crónica del Mes, Junio–Julio," p. 711.

7. The document mentions the occupations of the French and Costa Rican embassies on May 4, but not the May 8 massacre. Archbishop Rivera says it was sent to the nunciature. The document has now been published, in *Análisis* (San Salvador), Aug.-Sept. 1988 (Vol. I, No. 8), pp. 127–133. The same issue, pp. 53–60, carries an interview with Bishop Revelo (see chap. V, note 36, above) in which he declares that Romero was manipulated for three years by a small group of priests.

8. Romero's diary.

9. Ibid.

10. Ibid.

11. Eugenio C. Anaya, h., "Crónica del Mes, Agosto," *ECA,* Sept. 1979, p. 825; Romero's homily of Aug. 5, 1979, in *Mons. Oscar A. Romero: Su Pensamiento,* Vol. VII, pp. 131–132.

12. Statement of Aug. 10, 1979, published in *Orientación,* Aug. 12, 1979, and in "Noticias y Comentarios" (mimeographed bulletin), Secretaría de Comunicación Social, Arzobispado de San Salvador, Aug. 15, 1979.

13. Statement of Aug. 10, 1979, published in *Orientación,* Aug. 19, 1979, and in "Noticias y Comentarios," Aug. 15, 1979. Although Aparicio's statement and that of the other bishops are both dated Aug. 10, the latter seem to have prepared and published theirs in his absence and he to have hastily issued his on returning to the country the same day. Romero read them both in his homily of Aug. 12.

14. Romero's diary; homilies of Aug. 5 and 12, 1979, in *Mons. Oscar A. Romero: Su Pensamiento,* Vol. VII, pp. 132 and 155–156.

15. "Noticias y Comentarios," Aug. 15, 1979.

16. Letter to CEDES.

17. Romero's diary.

18. *La Prensa Gráfica,* Sept. 13, 1979.

19. Broadcast of Sept. 13, 1979, in *El Salvador: Entre el Terror y la Esperanza* (San Salvador: UCA Editores, 1982), pp. 478–480.

20. *Mons. Oscar A. Romero: Su Pensamiento,* Vol. VII, pp. 267–269.

21. *La Prensa Gráfica,* Sept. 19, 1979.

22. Romero's diary and the minutes of the senate meeting.

23. Broadcast of Sept. 18, 1979, in *El Salvador: Entre el Terror y la Esperanza,* p. 489.

24. *Mons. Oscar A. Romero: Su Pensamiento,* pp. 99–100.

25. Ibid., pp. 101–102.

26. Ibid., p. 103.

27. Ibid., pp. 104–105.

28. Homily of Aug. 13, 1978, in James R. Brockman, S.J., ed. and trans., *The Violence of Love: The Pastoral Wisdom of Archbishop Oscar Romero* (San Francisco: Harper & Row, 1988), pp. 94–95.

29. Homily of May 20, 1979, in *Mons. Oscar A. Romero: Su Pensamiento,* Vol. VI (San Salvador: Publicaciones Pastorales del Arzobispado, 1981), p. 349.

30. *Mons. Oscar A. Romero: Su Pensamiento,* Vol. VII, p. 147. Translations of all

four of Romero's pastoral letters can be found in *Voice of the Voiceless* (Maryknoll, N.Y.: Orbis, 1985).

31. Ibid.

32. Ibid., p. 148, referring to Puebla, nos. 31–39.

33. Puebla, no. 44.

34. Pastoral letter, no. 15.

35. Puebla, no. 42.

36. No. 19.

37. *Mons. Oscar A. Romero: Su Pensamiento,* Vol. VII, p. 149.

38. Pastoral letter, no. 20.

39. *Mons. Oscar A. Romero: Su Pensamiento,* Vol. VII, p. 149.

40. Pastoral letter, no. 23.

41. *Mons. Oscar A. Romero: Su Pensamiento,* Vol. VII, p. 149.

42. Pastoral letter, no. 24; Puebla, Message to the Peoples of Latin America, no. 3.

43. Pastoral letter, no. 69.

44. Ibid., no. 71.

45. Ibid., no. 72.

46. Ibid., no. 73.

47. "On the Development of Peoples" (*Populorum Progressio*), no. 31; Medellín, Peace, no. 19; pastoral letter, no. 74.

48. Pastoral letter, no. 75.

49. Ibid., no. 76.

50. Medellín, Peace, no. 15, quoting Paul VI's speech of Aug. 23, 1968, in Bogotá.

51. Pastoral letter, no. 78.

52. Apostolic letter of Pope Paul VI, May 14, 1971.

53. No. 79.

54. Puebla, no. 92.

55. Pastoral letter, no. 81; homily of Aug. 6, 1979, in *Mons. Oscar A. Romero: Su Pensamiento,* Vol. VII, p. 152.

56. *Mons. Oscar A. Romero: Su Pensamiento,* Vol. VII, p. 153.

57. Pastoral letter, no. 86.

58. Puebla, no. 1160.

59. Ibid., no. 1161.

60. Ibid., no. 1162.

61. Ibid., no. 1163, quoting John Paul II speaking to workers in Monterrey, Mexico, Jan. 31, 1979.

62. Pastoral letter, no. 87.

63. *Mons. Oscar A. Romero: Su Pensamiento,* Vol. VII, p. 153.

64. No. 89.

65. Puebla, no. 457.

66. Pastoral letter, no. 89.

67. Ibid., no. 90.

68. Ibid., no. 91.

69. *Mons. Oscar A. Romero: Su Pensamiento,* Vol. VII, pp. 153–154.

70. Pastoral letter, no. 92.

71. Ibid., no. 93.

72. Ibid., no. 94.

73. Ibid., no. 94.

74. Interview with Fabián Amaya.

75. In his diary on July 20 and in his homily at the July 20 mass Romero referred to guardsmen and police officers surrounding the cathedral.

76. *Mons. Oscar A. Romero: Su Pensamiento,* Vol. VII, pp. 112–113.

77. Homily of Aug. 19, 1979, in *Mons. Oscar A. Romero: Su Pensamiento,* Vol. VII, p. 186.

78. Romero's diary, and homily of Aug. 26, 1979, in *Mons. Oscar A. Romero: Su Pensamiento,* Vol. VII, pp. 208–209.

79. Commentary of YSAX, Aug. 17, 1979, in *El Salvador: Entre el Terror y la Esperanza,* pp. 408–410.

80. Homily of Aug. 19, 1979, in *Mons. Oscar A. Romero: Su Pensamiento,* Vol. VII, p. 189.

81. E. C. A. G., "Crónica del Mes (Agosto del 1979)," ECA, Sept. 1979, pp. 826–827.

82. *Mons. Oscar A. Romero: Su Pensamiento,* Vol. VII, pp. 211–214.

83. Ibid., pp. 227–228; the letter, dated Sept. 3, was also published in *Orientación,* Sept. 9, 1979.

84. *Mons. Oscar A. Romero: Su Pensamiento,* Vol. VII, p. 269; the letter is dated Sept. 12, 1979.

85. Ibid., p. 248.

86. Delgado, *Oscar A. Romero,* p. 151.

87. *Mons. Oscar A. Romero: Su Pensamiento,* Vol. VII, p. 333.

88. Homily of Oct. 14, 1979, *Mons. Oscar A. Romero: Su Pensamiento,* Vol. VII, p. 350.

89. Ibid., p. 354.

IX. October 15 and After (October 1979–January 1980)

1. Account from Romero's diary. Text of statement also in *ECA,* Oct.–Nov. 1979, pp. 1019–1020.

2. Romero's diary.

3. Eugenio C. Anaya, h., "Crónica del Mes, Sept.–Oct.," *ECA,* Oct.–Nov. 1979, p. 1005.

4. Homily of Oct. 21, 1979, leaflet, p. 24.

5. Ibid., pp. 12–16.

6. Ibid., pp. 16–22.

7. Ibid., pp. 22–24.

8. Eugenio C. Anaya, h., "Crónica del Mes, Sept.–Oct.," p. 1007.

9. Homily of Oct. 28, 1979, leaflet, p. 32.

10. Ibid., pp. 33–34.

11. Homily of Nov. 4, 1979, leaflet, pp. 21–22.

12. Homily of Nov. 25, 1979, leaflet, pp. 35–36.

13. Ibid., p. 42.

14. Minutes of CEDES, Nov. 19, 1979.

15. Transcript of the tape recording of the session.

16. Minutes of CEDES, Nov. 19, 1979.

17. *El Salvador: Entre el Terror y la Esperanza* (San Salvador: UCA Editores, 1982), p. 659.

18. Minutes of CEDES, Dec. 2, 1979.

19. Letter of December 3, 1979.

20. Minutes of CEDES, Dec. 5, 1979.

21. Letter of Mar. 13, 1980.

22. Homily of Dec. 9, 1979, leaflet, p. 19, and manuscript account of Salvador Barraza. A lightly edited form of Barraza's account is in *Mons. Oscar Arnulfo Romero: Su Muerte y Reacciones* (San Salvador: Publicaciones Pastorales del Arzobispado, 1982).

23. Homily of Dec. 9, 1979, pp. 29–34.

24. Romero's diary, Oct. 20, 1979.

25. Eugenio C. Anaya, h., "Crónica del Mes, Nov.–Dec.," *ECA,* Dec. 1979, p. 1089.

26. Homily of Dec. 16, 1979, leaflet, pp. 32–43.

27. Romero's diary and the minutes of the priests' senate.

28. Romero's diary; homily of Dec. 23, 1979, leaflet, pp. 24–26.

29. Anaya, "Crónica del Mes, Nov.–Dec.," p. 1089.

30. Text in *ECA,* Jan.–Feb. 1980, pp. 117–119.

31. Homily of Jan. 6, 1980, leaflet, p. 27.

32. Eugenio C. Anaya, h., "Crónica del Mes, Enero," *ECA,* Jan.–Feb. 1980, p. 101.

33. Homily of Jan. 6, 1980, pp. 30–31.

34. Anaya, "Crónica del Mes, Enero," pp. 101–102.

35. Homily of Jan. 6, 1980, pp. 31–32.

36. Letter to the author.

37. Romero's diary.

38. Romero's homily of Jan. 6, 1980, pp. 21–22. Other details of this episode are from Romero's diary.

39. Letter to the author.

40. Anaya, "Crónica del Mes, Enero," pp. 101–104.

41. Homily of Jan. 20, 1980, in *La Voz de los Sin Voz: La Palabra Viva de Monseñor Romero,* edited, with introductions and commentaries, by R. Cardenal et al. (San Salvador: UCA Editores, 1980), p. 238. The term "social mortgage" was used by John Paul II in his address inaugurating the Puebla conference, III, 4.

42. Homily of Jan. 13, 1980, leaflet, pp. 38–39.

43. Homily of Jan. 20, 1980, *La Voz de los Sin Voz*, p. 239.

44. Homily of Jan. 13, 1980, leaflet, p. 35.

45. Homily of Jan. 20, 1980, *La Voz de los Sin Voz*, pp. 241–242.

46. Ibid., pp. 244–245.

47. Romero's diary.

48. Anaya, "Crónica del Mes, Enero," pp. 104–105.

49. The account of the Jan. 22 events is from Francisco Andrés Escobar, "En la Línea de la Muerte," *ECA,* Jan.–Feb. 1980, pp. 21–35, and from Romero's homily of Jan. 27, 1980, leaflet, pp. 18–20.

50. Homily of Jan. 27, 1980, leaflet, pp. 20–22.

51. Homily of Jan. 20, 1980, *La Voz de los Sin Voz*, p. 236.

52. Romero's diary; telephone interview with Romero in Rome, published in *Orientación,* Feb. 3, 1980. The interview is also in *¡Cese la Represión!* (Madrid: Editorial Popular, S.A., 1980), p. 106.

53. Homily of Feb. 10, 1980, leaflet, p. 15. The accounts of the conversation with the pope given in the telephone interview, Romero's diary, and the Feb. 10 homily

are slightly different but substantially the same. Romero was speaking in each case from his memory of the conversation.

54. Interview in *Orientación,* Feb. 3, 1980.

55. Jesús Delgado, *Oscar A. Romero: Biografía* (Madrid: Paulinas, 1986), pp. 164–165, feels that the October coup d'état vindicated Romero in the eyes of church authorities and brought about his warm reception in Rome.

56. *Orientación,* Feb. 17, 1980.

57. Text of the discourse in *La Voz de los Sin Voz,* pp. 181–193. An English version is in *Voice of the Voiceless,* (Maryknoll, N.Y.: Orbis, 1985), pp. 177–187.

X. The Final Weeks (February–March 1980)

1. *Voice of the Voiceless* (Maryknoll, N.Y.: Orbis, 1985), pp. 188–189.

2. Homily of Mar. 16, 1980, leaflet, p. 19.

3. Romero's diary.

4. *La Voz de los Sin Voz: La Palabra Viva de Monseñor Romero,* edited, with introductions and commentaries, by R. Cardenal et al. (San Salvador: UCA Editores, 1980), pp. 258–259.

5. Ibid., pp. 252–254.

6. Ibid., pp. 256–257; Medellín, The Church's Poverty, no. 4c.

7. *La Voz de los Sin Voz,* p. 262.

8. Ibid., p. 264.

9. Homily of Feb. 24, 1980, leaflet, pp. 1–4.

10. Ibid., leaflet, pp. 5–6.

11. Ibid., p. 6.

12. Ibid., p. 7.

13. Ibid., p. 15.

14. D'Escoto's letter of Feb. 15, 1980, and Romero's letter of Feb. 27, 1980.

15. Feb. 23, 1980.

16. Account in *Noticias de la Provincia Centroamericana,* Apr. 1980 (privately circulated) and in *Orientación,* May 11, 1980.

17. Homily of Mar. 2, 1980, leaflet, p. 13.

18. Text in *ECA,* Mar.–Apr. 1980, pp. 343–345.

19. Homily of Mar. 2, 1980, leaflet, pp. 14–15.

20. Ibid., pp. 10–11.

21. Homily of Mar. 9, 1980, leaflet, p. 1.

22. Ibid., pp. 8–9.

23. Ibid., p. 13.

24. Ibid., p. 15.

25. Homily of Mar. 16, 1980, leaflet, pp. 13–14.

26. Ibid., p. 11.

27. Homily of Mar. 23, 1980, *La Voz de los Sin Voz,* p. 285.

28. Homily of Mar. 16, 1980, leaflet, pp. 12–17.

29. Text in *ECA,* Mar.–Apr. 1980, pp. 378–379.

30. Homily of Mar. 16, 1980, leaflet, p. 7.

31. Ibid., pp. 19–20.

32. Homily of March 23, 1980, *La Voz de los Sin Voz,* p. 286.

33. Ibid., p. 281.

34. Ibid., pp. 286–291.

35. Ibid., pp. 284–285.

36. Romero's diary.

37. Tape recording of the homily; *La Voz de los Sin Voz*, p. 271.

38. Tape recording of the homily; *La Voz de los Sin Voz*, p. 278.

39. Tape recording of the homily; *La Voz de los Sin Voz*, p. 280.

40. Tape recording of the homily; *La Voz de los Sin Voz*, pp. 291–292.

41. Interview with Fabián Amaya.

42. Ibid.

43. Pastoral Constitution on the Church in the Modern World (*Gaudium et Spes*), no. 39, from *The Documents of Vatican II*, Walter M. Abbott, S.J., and Msgr. Joseph Gallagher, eds. (New York: America Press, 1966), pp. 237–238.

44. The tape recording of the mass shows that only one second elapsed between the end of the homily and the shot. Romero may have intended to say more, but his final words seem to be the end of his planned homily; he often concluded his homilies with an invitation to share in the eucharist. His final words about the eucharist may be the reason for false reports that he was shot during the offertory or while elevating the host.

45. The account of Romero's last two days and death is based on interviews with witnesses, on the tape recording of the final mass, on Jesús Delgado, *Oscar A. Romero: Biografía* (Madrid: Paulinas, 1986), pp. 195–205, on the account of Salvador Barraza, and on *Orientación*, Mar. 30 and Sept. 21, 1980. Jorge Pinto has left his memory of Romero's assassination in *El Grito del Más Pequeño* (Mexico City: Editorial Comete and Licenciada Victoria Eugenia Montes, n.d.), pp. 276–284.

46. *El Mondo*, Mar. 26, 1980, reported 15,000; *El Independiente*, Mar. 27, 1980, reported more than 10,000. These and other news reports are reprinted in *Mons. Oscar Arnulfo Romero: Su Muerte y Reacciones* (San Salvador: Publicaciones Pastorales del Arzobispado, 1982), which also contains the texts of numerous condemnations of the assassination.

47. Eugenio C. Anaya, h., "Crónica del Mes, Marzo," *ECA*, Mar.-Apr. 1980, pp. 332–333.

48. Ibid.

49. *Orientación*, Mar. 30, 1980; reprinted in *Mons. Oscar Arnulfo Romero: Su Muerte y Reacciones*, pp. 55–56.

50. El Mundo, Mar. 28, 1980; also reprinted in *Mons. Oscar Arnulfo Romero: Su Muerte y Reacciones*, p. 57.

51. Author's interviews with the seminarian and with Urioste.

52. National Catholic News Service, in a dispatch of Mar. 31, 1980, said that organizers estimated the crowd at 200,000 and the government estimated it at 30,000. The dispatch said that almost 30 bishops, 300 priests, and 500 nuns were present.

53. Witnesses told the author that they saw the body of a girl about eight years old with a bullet hole in the forehead. Christopher Dickey, in the *Washington Post*, Apr. 1, 1980, reported "less than ten dead of gunshot wounds" among more than 30 dead. NC News Service, Apr. 1, 1980, reported "more than 40 dead and 250 injured, according to hospital and Red Cross sources."

54. Text in *El Diario de Hoy*, Mar. 31, 1980; reprinted also in *Mons. Oscar Arnulfo Romero: Su Muerte y Reacciones*, pp. 266–267. The government maintained that the security forces were confined to barracks at the time, but a friend of Romero told the author he had seen uniformed forces on the street when coming to the funeral. The foreign church people's statement after the funeral declared, "We saw or were

able to verify the security forces' presence from early morning hours in the streets of San Salvador and in the approaches to the city."

55. The statement was widely disseminated and published. While witnesses' accounts of the funeral vary, it seems clear that a bomb exploded at the southwest corner of the plaza, near the National Palace, followed by one or more others and by immediate sniper fire from at least one building, returned by armed persons in the plaza. News photographs seem to show the crowd fleeing from the National Palace and leftists shooting toward it. The shooting and explosions continued for a considerable time, perhaps an hour or more, while thousands packed the cathedral. Among witnesses interviewed, two priests assured the author they saw shooting from a second-floor window of the palace. Published testimony of witnesses include those of Dermot Keogh, *Romero: El Salvador's Martyr* (Dublin: Dominican Publications, 1981), pp. 106–122; Joseph B. Treaster, *New York Times,* Mar. 31 and Apr. 1, 1980; Christopher Dickey, *Washington Post,* Mar. 31 and Apr. 1, 1980; Archbishop John Quinn, NC News Service, Apr. 7; Simon E. Smith, S.J., *National Jesuit News,* May 1980; James L. Connor, S.J., "El Salvador's Agony and U.S. Policies," *America,* Apr. 26, 1980, pp. 360–363; Eugenio C. Anaya, h., "Crónica del Mes, Marzo," *ECA,* Mar.–Apr. 1980, pp. 332–333; Juan Vives Suriá, *El Diario de Caracas,* Apr. 8, 1980; Jorge Lara-Braud, " 'El Pueblo Unido Jamás Será Vencido,' " *Christianity and Crisis,* May 12, 1980, pp. 114, 148–150; Ignacio Martín-Baró, S.J., "Oscar Romero: Voice of the Downtrodden," in *Voice of the Voiceless* (Maryknoll, N.Y.: Orbis, 1985), pp. 18–19, and "El Liderazgo de Monseñor Romero: Un Análisis Psico-Social," *ECA,* Mar. 1981, pp. 171–172. *Mons. Oscar Arnulfo Romero: Su Muerte y Reacciones,* pp. 225–323, contains various other accounts, including those of government and church authorities and of the popular organizations.

56. Author's interview.

57. *Orientación,* Apr. 13, 1980.

Appendix: Romero's Killers

1. An Associated Press dispatch of March 25 in *La Prensa Gráfica,* Mar. 26, 1980, reprinted in *Mons. Oscar A. Romero: Su Muerte y Reacciones* (San Salvador: Publicaciones Pastorales del Arzobispado, 1982), pp. 184–185. Robert White informed the author in a letter that the false story about the Cuban was given him by García.

2. *La Prensa Gráfica,* Mar. 27, 1980, reprinted in *Mons. Oscar A. Romero: Su Muerte y Reacciones,* pp. 186–187.

3. Jorge Pinto, *El Grito del Más Pequeño* (Mexico City: Editorial Comete and Licenciada Victoria Eugenia Montes, n.d.), pp. 282–283.

4. Robert O. Weiner, a lawyer investigating the case for Americas Watch, in a report to the archdiocesan human rights office, Tutela Legal, in September 1987.

5. Pinto, *El Grito,* pp. 281–284.

6. *Diario Latino,* Mar. 29, 1980, reprinted in *Mons. Oscar A. Romero: Su Muerte y Reacciones,* pp. 189–190.

7. *El Mundo,* Apr. 2, 1980, reprinted in *Mons. Oscar A. Romero: Su Muerte y Reacciones,* pp. 190–191.

8. Unknown persons murdered Medrano in 1985.

9. In the case file Weiner found a memo that said Ramírez's son denied to the detectives investigating the murder that his father had accused D'Aubuisson.

10. Letter of White to the author.

11. Douglas Farah, *Washington Post,* Aug. 29, 1988.

12. White's letter to the author.

13. Douglas Farah, *Washington Post,* Aug. 29, 1988, and Douglas Farah and Tom Gibb, *Mother Jones,* Jan. 1989, p. 14.

14. Craig Pyes, "Who Killed Archbishop Romero?" *The Nation,* Oct. 13, 1984, p. 353.

15. Craig Pyes and Laurie Becklund, of the *Albuquerque Journal* and *Los Angeles Times,* respectively, Dec. 18, 1983. Their reports, based on many interviews, including some with military and civilians involved in death squad activity, ran in the *Journal,* Dec. 18–22, and in the *Times,* Dec. 18–19, 1983.

16. Articles of Pyes, Becklund, Farah, and Gibb cited above, as well as Farah, *Washington Post,* Aug. 28, 1988; Dennis Volman, *Christian Science Monitor,* May 8, 1984; Allan Nairn, "Behind the Death Squads," *The Progressive,* May 1984; Stephen Kinzer, *New York Times,* Mar. 3, 1984; Christopher Dickey, "Behind the Death Squads," *The New Republic,* Dec. 26, 1983.

17. Author's interview with Weiner.

18. Robert Weiner remarked in his report to Tutela Legal in 1987 that no one seemed to have tried very hard to track the owner; the first summons to the owner that he found was dated 1983.

19. Pinto, *El Grito,* pp. 336–342.

20. Weiner's report summarizes the judicial investigation up to September 1987.

21. Anon., "Crónica del Mes, Mayo–Junio," *ECA,* May–June 1987, p. 365.

22. Garay's sworn declaration to the Fourth Criminal Court of San Salvador, *ECA,* Nov.–Dec. 1987, pp. 938–940; decision of Linnea Johnson, United States Magistrate, United States District Court, Southern District of Florida, "Certification of Extraditability and Order of Commitment, Case No. 87–3598–CIV–EX-TRADITION–JOHNSON, in re: Extradition of Alvaro Rafael Saravia, September 27, 1988," which summarizes Garay's declarations to the Salvadoran court and the attorney general's office.

23. Johnson's decision.

24. William Branigin, *Washington Post,* Nov. 24, 1987.

25. Clifford Krauss and Robert Weiner, *Atlanta Constitution,* Mar. 24, 1988, reviewed how politics dominated the case from the beginning. They said Duarte's premature publicity impaired the case by frightening away potential witnesses.

26. ARENA manifesto, undated, *ECA,* Nov.–Dec. 1987, pp. 941–943.

27. *Carta a las Iglesias,* San Salvador, No. 152, Nov. 16–30, 1987, p. 3.

28. Douglas Farah, *Washington Post,* Dec. 28, 1988.

29. Johnson's decision.

30. Farah, *Washington Post,* Dec. 28, 1988; *Facts on File,* Vol. 48, No. 2510, Dec. 31, 1988, p. 993; Lindsey Gruson, *New York Times,* Jan. 7, 1989.

31. *Mons. Oscar A. Romero: Su Pensamiento,* Vol. VII (San Salvador: Publicaciones Pastorales del Arzobispado, 1988), pp. 35–37.

Index

Primary Sources Available in English

For works by Archbishop Romero, see James R. Brockman, ed. and trans., *The Violence of Love: The Pastoral Wisdom of Archbishop Oscar Romero* (San Francisco: Harper & Row, 1988), and *Voice of the Voiceless: The Four Pastoral Letters and Other Statements*, trans. Michael J. Walsh (Maryknoll, N.Y.: Orbis, 1985), which also contains introductory essays by Jon Sobrino and Ignacio Martín-Baró.

For English translations of the Medellín and Puebla documents see, respectively, Louis M. Colonnese, ed., *The Church in the Present-Day Transformation of Latin America in the Light of the Council*, Vol. II, *Conclusions* (Washington, D.C.: United States Catholic Conference, 1970), and John Eagleson and Philip Scharper, eds., *Puebla and Beyond: Documentation and Commentary* (Maryknoll, N.Y.: Orbis, 1979).

About the Author

James R. Brockman, S.J., met Archbishop Romero in 1978 and 1979, and went to El Salvador shortly after Romero's assassination to research his life. In addition to *Romero: A Life*, he has compiled and translated several collections of Romero's writings, including *The Church Is All of You: Thoughts of Archbishop Oscar Romero* and *The Violence of Love: The Pastoral Wisdom of Archbishop Oscar Romero*. From 1961 through 1973, he traveled extensively in Latin America, spending extended periods in Peru, Colombia, Nicaragua, and El Salvador; from 1974 to 1980, he served as associate editor of the review *America*. His numerous articles (English and Spanish) have appeared in *Christian Century, Third World Quarterly; Spirituality Today; Mensaje* (Chile); and *Acción* (Paraguay). A native of Cincinnati, Father Brockman now resides in Chicago.